Euro
City Breaks

It's only 60 years since the end of the Second World War but the transformation of Europe in that time is nothing short of staggering. The continent that tore itself apart, then built a physical and ideological barrier through its heart before knocking it all down, may not yet be ready to embrace Churchill's vision of a 'United States of Europe' but 25 of its nations are now members of a single trading market and 12 have so far signed up to a single currency. Such startling political developments have, inevitably, had a major impact on European travel. Passport and customs checks are a thing of the past at most borders, there's no need to change currency every time you leave home and air fares have been dropping faster than the temperature on a winter's night in St Petersburg. It is now possible to fly from London to Naples for less than the cost of a pizza, see the best of the city and fly back in time for Sunday dinner. You can gaze in awe at Picasso's *Guernica* in Madrid one weekend and climb to the top of Norman Foster's Reichstag in Berlin the next; spend a night at the opera in Verona one week, and a night on the tiles in Tallinn the next. Rome or Riga? Valencia or Venice? Belfast or Bologna? Each has its own appeal, whether it's museums and galleries stuffed with priceless treasures, delicious food, cheap booze or stunning architecture. There's so much choice it's hard to make one. So read on...

The guide

→

Footprint's *European City Breaks* is the perfect guide for those who want to get away but don't know where to let off steam, propose to their lover, hide, or simply wallow indulgently in a bit of luxury. The 40 cities listed in this book are all worth at least a weekend of anyone's time. We have taken the strain out of choosing where to sleep, where to eat and what to see by selecting the very top hotels and restaurants, divided into three price categories – expensive, mid-range and cheap – the best bars and clubs and the pick of the sights. From the Acropolis in Athens to Bilbao's Guggenheim Museum, we've highlighted the best of Europe's heritage, old and new, artistic and technological. Throughout the guide you'll find handy star ratings in the introduction to each city which give an immediate idea of the city's strong and weak points (see also page 6). There's a festivals calendar on page 8, so you can decide whether to head for, or avoid, a place at a specific time of year, and some of the best festivals are described in more detail under the relevant city. We've also included a surprise 'guest city': New York. Not European – but a city that Europeans love to visit. Wherever you end up going, *European City Breaks* is there to point you in the right direction. Go on – give yourself a break.

Contents

Star cities

Where to go

We've given every city in the book scores out of 5 (1 = lowest, 5 = highest) in eight categories: Arts and culture, Eating, Nightlife, Outdoors, Romance, Shopping, Sightseeing and Value for money so you can see their weak and their strong points. These scores are shown in the introduction to each city and should help you choose the right destination for your city break. The highest scoring cities in each category are listed below.

⊕ Arts and culture

Cities that have an outstanding reputation for all-round cultural excellence, with vibrant art, literature, theatre and music scenes.

Berlin ⟫p45
Florence ⟫p101
London ⟫p130
Madrid ⟫p149

New York ⟫p172
Paris ⟫p182
Rome ⟫p212
Venice ⟫p257

⊙ Eating

Cities that have a thriving culinary scene and a number of world-class restaurants.

Antwerp ⟫p19
Bologna ⟫p57
Brussels ⟫p63
London ⟫p130

Lyon ⟫p143
New York ⟫p172
Paris ⟫p182

SoHo, New York

🌙 Nightlife

The ultimate places to party after dark.

♥ Romance

The best places to propose or to enjoy a spontaneous romantic weekend with your lover.

◉ Sightseeing

The places to go for world famous sights: museums, monuments, castles, towers, ferris wheels, etc

Spanish Steps, Rome

▲ Outdoors

Cities that incorporate plenty of green space or provide easy access to nearby wilderness areas.

◎ Shopping

Cities with outstanding and varied retail therapy opportunities.

€ Value for money

The best places to go if you are on a tight budget.

Festivals

January
New Year's Day Concert *Vienna*
Paris Grand Parade *1st*
Three Kings Day Parade *New York, 6th*
Fête des Rois (Festival of Kings) *Paris, first Sun after Epiphany (6th)*
Burns Night *Edinburgh and Glasgow, 25th*
Celtic Connections (music) *Glasgow, last 2 weeks*

February
Carnival *widespread but especially in Venice, Verona, Bilbao, Lisbon, Seville and Sitges near Barcelona, throughout Feb*
Chinese New Year *especially in Amsterdam, London and New York, date varies*
Berlin International Film Festival *date varies*

March
St Patrick's Day *Dublin and New York, 17th*
Las Fallas Fire Festival *Valencia, 15-19th ➤p255*
Spring Music Festival *Budapest, mid Mar-early Apr*

April
Settimana per la Cultura *Naples, Easter*
Semana Santa (Holy week) *Seville, Easter ➤p233*
Feria d'Abril (April Fair) *Seville, date varies ➤p233*
Scoppio del Carro *Florence, Easter Sun*
London Marathon *late Apr*
Printemps Baroque du Sablon (chamber music) *Brussels, late Apr*
Koninginnedag (Queen's Day) *Amsterdam, 30th*

May
Maggio Musicale Fiorentino *Florence, late Apr-late Jun*
Fiestas de San Isidro *Madrid, 2nd week*
Prague Spring International Music Festival *mid May-early Jun*
Reykjavík Arts Festival *mid May-early Jun*
Chelsea Flower Show *London, end May*
Whitsun Carnival *Copenhagen, end May*
Vogalonga (rowing competition) *Venice, end May*
Early Summer Festival *Bologna, May-Jun*
Wiener Festwochen *Vienna, May-Jun*
Vienna Opera Festival *May-Jun*

June
Summer Dance Festival *Berlin, early Jun*
Stars of the White Nights Festival (music, opera and ballet) *St Petersburg, end May-mid Jul*
Karneval der Kulturen (Carnival of Cultures) *Berlin, Pentecost weekend*
Amsterdam Roots Festival (music) *late Jun*
Festa del Naviglio (summer fête) *Milan, first Sun*

Great Irish Houses Music Festival *Dublin, mid Jun*
Dublin Writers Festival *mid-Jun*
Festos dos Santos Populares *Lisbon, 12th, and throughout Jun*
Prague Fringe Festival *end May-early Jun*
Riga Opera Festival *mid-Jun*
Festival of the Sea *Reykjavík, 1st Fri for 4 days*
Bloomsday Festival (James Joyce) *Dublin, 16th*
Fête de la Musique *Paris, 21st*
Sankt Hans Aften (St John's Eve) *Copenhagen, 23rd*
Roskilde Music Festival *Copenhagen, late Jun*
Calcio Storico (costumed football) *Florence, late Jun*
Christopher Street Day *Berlin, late Jun* ➽*p51*
Traffic Torino Free Festival (music) *Turin, end Jun-early Jul*
Istanbul Festival of Arts and Culture *Jun-Jul*
International Istanbul Music Festival *Jun-Jul*
Glasgow Jazz Festival *mid Jun*
Arena di Verona Opera Season *Jun-Aug*
Zomer van Antwerpen (arts) *Antwerp, Jun-Aug*
Fourvière Arts Nights *Lyon, Jun-Aug*
Summer Festival (arts) *Barcelona, Jun-Aug*
Estate Romana (music) *Rome, Jun-Sep*
Hellenic Festival (arts) *Athens, Jun-Sep* ➽*p28*

July
Tour de France *ends Paris*
Neopolis Music Festival *Naples, dates vary*
Stockholm Jazz Festival *dates vary*
Beer Festival *Tallinn, early Jul*
Bastille Day *Paris, 14th*
Copenhagen Jazz Festival *first Fri for 10 days*
Festa del Redentore (Feast of the Redeember) *Venice, 3rd Sat*
ImPulsTanz Dance Festival *Vienna, Jul-Aug*

La Tomatina

Ljubljana Summer Festival (cultural events) *Jul-Aug*

August
Edinburgh Festivals *end Jul-early Sep* ➽*p99*
Sziget Music Festival *near Budapest, mid-Aug*
Aste Nagusia (Basque festival) *Bilbao, late Aug*
La Tomatina *Buñol, near Valencia, last Wed*
Notting Hill Carnival *London, last Sun*
Venice Film Festival *Aug-Sep*

September
La Regata di Venezia *Venice, 1st Sun*
Flower Festival *Amsterdam, 4th*
Festes de la Merce (street party) *Barcelona, 24th*
Oktoberfest (beer festival) *Munich, mid Sep-Oct* ➽*p165*
Reykjavík Film and Jazz festivals *Sep-Oct*
Autumn Festival *Prague, Sep-Oct*
Dublin Fringe Festival *Sep-Oct*

October
Budapest Autumn Music Festival *late Oct*
Salon du Chocolat *Paris, late Oct*

November
Festival of La Salute (All Saints Day) *Venice, 21st*
Macy's Thanksgiving Day Parade *New York, last Wed*

December
Christmas markets *especially Vienna, Munich, Berlin, Copenhagen, Prague, Antwerp and Stockholm*
Tivoli Gardens (Christmas festival) *Copenhagen, mid Nov-end Dec*
New Year's Eve *Especially in Athens, Berlin, Dublin, Edinburgh, London, Paris, Prague, Stockhom and Venice, 31st*

Amsterdam

Amsterdam shouldn't really exist. Sounds dramatic, but it's true. Bedraggled and damp, the city was dragged out of marshy bogs, dried out and carved into the place we know today. It was an unconventional start, and one which seems to have set the tone for things to come. Today, Amsterdam is Europe's most eccentric city. Here, locals shun the car and choose instead to career around on bicycles. Prostitution is both legal and very public and this is the only city in the world where you can stroll into a coffeeshop, peruse a cannabis menu and smoke a joint. And the Dutch became the first country to introduce marriage between gay couples.

Alongside these eccentricities are, conversely, some of Europe's greatest traditional sights. The Rijksmuseum and Van Gogh Museum have amongst the finest art collections in the world, while smaller museums such as the Anne Frank House or Rembrandthuis provide a real insight to the city's past.

Amsterdam's eccentricities also attract criticism. Rumours of a crack-down on coffeeshops – called for by Justice Minister Donner – are unlikely to come to much. But the murder in 2004 of film-maker Theo Van Gogh by an Islamic extremist has caused much soul-searching about Amsterdam's live-and-let-live attitude. Nevertheless, a healthy dose of Dutch pragmatism means problems are always approached sensibly – be they soggy marshes, soft drugs or sex – making this liberal oddball as engaging as ever.

Arts & culture
★★★★

Eating
★★★

Nightlife
★★★★

Outdoors
★★

Romance
★★★

Shopping
★★★

Sightseeing
★★★★

Value for money
★★★

Overall score
★★★✦

At a glance

Amsterdam's old centre is hemmed in by the IJ River and Centraal Station to the north, and spreads south in a web of medieval streets and canals. The main arteries are Damrak and Ronkin, busy thoroughfares which split the centre into the **Nieuwe Zijde** (New Side) to the west of the Dam, and the **Oude Zijde** (Old Side) to the east. The Red Light District lies just to the east of Damrak (the Old Side), a surprisingly pretty but predictably seedy grid of streets. Beyond here are the **Nieuwmarkt** and **Plantage** districts, home to Amsterdam's biggest flea market and Rembrandt's house. To the north are the **Eastern Islands**, extensively renovated docklands holding some impressively adventurous architecture. West of Damrak, Nieuwe Zijde is Amsterdam's main shopping area and leads to the **Grachtengordel**, the four major canals

In Amsterdam, the water is the mistress and the land the vassal

Felix Marti-Ibanez

that ring the old centre. South of the Grachtengordel is the **Museum Quarter**, full of grand old buildings – most famously the enormous, neo-Gothic Rijksmuseum overlooking the grassy Museumplein.

★ *Don't leave town without experiencing Gezelligheid – roughly translated as a cosy or relaxing time – in a brown café.*

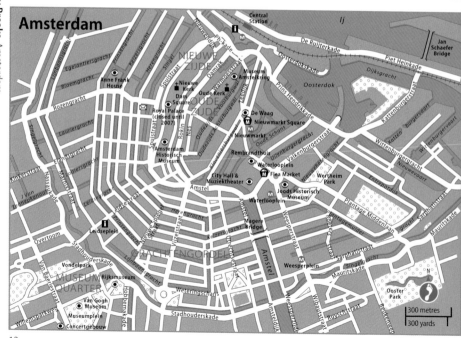

24 hours in the city

Sip a coffee at *Café Luxemberg* before heading south to the Museumsplein. Pop into the **Rijksmuseum** and ogle Rembrandt's *Nightwatch*, one of the highlights still on view while the museum undergoes renovation. A few steps along Museumplein brings you to the **Van Gogh Museum**, which warrants a good few hours. After a perk up at *Het Blauwe Theehuis*, a popular tea house by Vondelpark, wander north along the canals of the Grachtengordel to **Anne Frank's House**. Lunch at one of the pavement cafés on Nieuwmarkt and then either head south for a snoop around the **flea market** on Waterlooplein, or east to gawp at the painted ladies of the **Red Light District**. (Don't miss the attic chapel in the Museum Amstelkring while you're there.) Have an early evening drink in *Café Sluyswacht*, on Jodenbreestraat and then cross town for contemporary Dutch cuisine

Café de Waard, Leidseplein

in the history-soaked interior of *d'Vijff Vlieghen*. Finish off on the 11th floor of the former central post office, Oosterdokskade 3-5, now housing the very hip *Club 11* and watch the city twinkling below you.

⊖ Travel essentials

Getting there Schiphol Airport lies 15 km southwest of the city centre. The train station is directly below Schiphol Plaza, the main concourse, and trains run every 15 mins 0445-2400, and every hour thereafter (€3.40 for a single), taking 15 mins to reach Centraal Station. Various buses run to the centre, including the 370 which stops in the Museum Quarter. A taxi to the centre takes around 20 mins and should cost about €35. **Schiphol Travel Taxi**, T0900-8876, is a good-value shared minibus.

Centraal Station, Amsterdam's main station, is right in the centre of town at the end of Damrak. Trains are run by **Nederlandse Spoorwegen** (NS), T0900-9296, www.ns.nl, with regular international connections.

Getting around Most of the city's main sights are within easy walking distance from each other. However,

the public transport system is excellent; trams are the most useful way of getting about but there is also a good system of buses and a small metro (best for outlying districts). All public transport is run by the **GVB**, www.gvb.nl, which has an information and main ticket office opposite Centraal Station. Tickets can also be bought from machines by tram stops, newsagents and on trams and buses. Buying strip tickets (*Strippenkaart*) is much cheaper than buying tickets on trams or buses. The strips must be validated when you board. The number of strips that need to be stamped depends on how many zones you cross (central Amsterdam is all Zone 1). Note that for a trip in zone 1, you must stamp 2 strips; to travel through 2 zones, stamp 3 strips, and so on. Once stamped, a ticket is valid for 1 hr. A *Strippenkaart* with 15 strips costs €6.50. Alternatively travel passes, valid on the whole

network, cost €6.30, €10 or €13 for 24, 48 and 72 hrs. **Taxis** have ranks around the city; but are pricey.

Tourist information The main office is opposite Centraal Station, T0900-4004040, www.amsterdamtourist.nl, daily 0900-1700. There's another inside the station, Mon-Sat 0800-2000, Sun 0900-1700; and the another on the corner of Leidseplein and Leidsestraat, Sun-Thu 0915-1700, Fri-Sat 0915-1900. The **I Amsterdam Card** offers unlimited travel on public transport, a free canal boat trip, and extensive discounts on museums. Tickets cost €33, €43 or €53 for 1, 2, or 3 days. Available from the tourist and GVB information offices.

A number of companies offer various canal tours, but most useful is the **Museum Boat**, T020-5301090, www.lovers.nl, a hop-on hop-off service which stops at all major museums (€14.25).

👁 Sights

Dam Square
ⓘ *Tram 4, 9, 14, 16, 24 or 25.*

Known simply as "the Dam", this broad, tourist- and pigeon-filled square lies at the core of Amsterdam's medieval centre. It was in fact the original dam which crossed the Amstel – and gave the city its name. The **Royal Palace** ⓘ *T020-6204060*, originally the town hall, was built between 1648 and 1665 in an imposing Dutch Classicist style. It switched to the royal residence when Louis Bonapart kicked out the mayor in 1808 during the French occupation. Now used for state functions, guided tours are available, but the palace is closed until Sep 2007 for renovations. Next door is the **Nieuwe Kerk**, dating from 1408. In the centre of the square is the city's War Memorial, a rather stark obelisk and a popular meeting place.

Red Light District
ⓘ *Tram 4, 9, 14, 16, 24 or 25.*

Amsterdam's infamous Red Light District covers the area to the east of Damrak,

Red Light District

and yes, it is just as seedy as you'd expect. Prostitutes pose in windows, groups of beery lads barter with pimps, and touts try to entice passers by with promises of live sex shows. But the area is also such a tourist attraction that it rarely feels threatening (at least not during the day). You'll be sharing the pavement with giggling couples popping into sex shops and family groups strolling nonchalantly past the window brothels. The area also has some of the city's most attractive old houses. Stroll along Warmoesstraat to take in the elegant façades, interspersed with sex shops and red-lit windows, and along any of the little streets branching off between Oudezijds Voorburgwal and Ousezijds Achterburgwal canals.

Two important sights in the area are, ironically, religious. Just east of Warmoesstraat is **De Oude Kerk** ⓘ *Mon-Sat 1100-1700, Sun 1300-1700*, Amsterdam's oldest church, an attractive Gothic structure with a beautiful tower, dating from the 14th century. A few steps north is the **Museum Amstelkring** ⓘ *T020-6246604, www.museumamstelkring.nl, Mon-Sat 1000-1700, Sun 1300-1700, €7*,

an ordinary townhouse with an extraordinary attic, containing the city's only surviving clandestine church. It dates from the reformation, when public Catholic worship was outlawed.

Nieuwmarkt Square
ⓘ *Metro Nieuwmarkt.*

Once a major market square for inhabitants from the nearby Jewish quarter – all but wiped out during the Nazi occupation – this broad square is today flanked with cafés and shops, leading to the city's "Chinatown" in Zeedijk, just to the north. The square is towered over by **De Waag**, a 15th-century fortress-like structure, once a city gate. During the week there's a small fruit and veg market and an antique market every Sunday in summer.

Waterlooplein
ⓘ *Tram 4, 9 or 14. Metro Waterlooplein.*

Amsterdam's oldest **flea market** ⓘ *Mon-Sat 0900-1700*, is a labyrinthine sprawl of stalls, stuffed with second-hand clothes, old vinyl records, tie-die imports and leather jackets. The square is lorded over by the 1986 City Hall and

Dam Square

Nieuwmarkt Square

Up in smoke

Thank heavens for Bob Marley. Without Bob and the Rastafarian flag – green, gold and red stripes – tourists would have a tough time spotting a coffeeshop in Amsterdam. That's coffeeshop, not coffeehouse. The difference, of course, is that the former is permitted to sell cannabis, although it's illegal to advertise this fact. Hence all the Rasta paraphernalia, a sure-fire way to tell tourists that they've come to the right (or wrong) place, depending on their views. Amsterdam remains the only city in the world with such a liberal view on soft drugs, attracting a fare percentage of drug tourists, much to the annoyance of many locals. The law is very clear on what it will tolerate: an individual can possess 30 g and can buy up to 5 g of cannabis at a time from a licensed purveyor – any use of hard drugs (heroin, cocaine and ecstasy) is strictly illegal. Coffeeshops aren't permitted to sell alcohol and there's an age limit of 18. Recent rumblings about limiting tourists' access to coffeeshops are unfounded, and for now, at least, it seems this unique side of Amsterdam is here to stay.

Muziektheater, designed by Willem Holzbauer and known locally as the Stopera (a combination of 'Stad', and 'Opera'). Although the complex was hugely controversial when it was built, the theatre now has an excellent reputation. Free concerts are held here at least once a week.

Rembrandthuis

ⓘ T020-5200400, www.rembrandt
huis.nl. Mon-Sat 1000-1700, Sun 1100-
1700, €7.50. Metro to Nieuwmarkt,
Hoogstraat exit. Tram 9 or 14.

Rembrandthuis

This graceful house was Rembrandt's home from 1639 and 1658. He lived in the elegant rooms on the ground floor and worked in the large studio upstairs during his most successful period. Today the rooms are stocked with original fittings and period furniture. Also on display is a superb collection of his etchings – over 260 pieces. 2006 is the fourth centenary of Rembrandt's birth, so expect special events and exhibitions.

Nieuwe Zijde (New Side)

ⓘ Tram 1, 2, 13 or 17.

The New Side of the medieval centre was actually settled earlier than the Oude Zijde, and today covers the area west of the Dam. It's a mixed area of uninspiring shopping and pretty side-streets, leading to the Grachtengordel. Worth a look is the **Amsterdam Historisch Museum** ⓘ www.ahm.nl, Mon-Fri 1000-1700, Sat-Sun 1100-1700, €6, housed in the old city orphanage. There are some interesting paintings and the building itself, with its two courtyards and winding corridors, is fascinating.

Anne Frank House

ⓘ T020-5567100, www.annefrank.org. Mar-Aug 0900-2100; Sep-Feb 0900-1900, closed Yom Kippur, €7.50. Tram 13 or 17. Bus 21, 170, 171 or 172 to Westermarkt.

The gripping, heartbreaking story of Anne Frank is one of the most enduring accounts of life in hiding during WWII. At 263 Prinsengracht is the unassuming house where the Frank family hid with friends for two years during the Nazi occupation of Amsterdam. The museum provides a harrowing glimpse

Anne Frank House

of the claustrophobic lives led behind blacked-out windows, and the diary itself, sitting alone in a glass case, is startlingly poignant. The only survivor of the Frank family was Anne's father Otto, who returned to the house, published the diary, and helped open the museum in 1960. The entrance is now in a modern building next door.

Rijksmuseum

ⓘ T020-6747000, www.rijksmuseum.nl. Daily 0900-1800. €9. Tram 2 or 5 to Hobbemastraat, 12 to Concertgebouw, or 6, 7 or 10 to Spiegelgracht.

Amsterdam's enormous flagship museum is undergoing extensive renovation until 2008, although parts of the museum remain open. The museum itself, designed by Pierre Cuypers, is a striking neo-Gothic riot of towers, turrets and stained-glass windows dominating the Museum Quarter. Inside, the collection is split into various sections, most famous of which is the extraordinary Dutch Golden Age collection of paintings. Other sections include sculpture, decorative arts, prints and photographs, but be warned that many of these are

Van Gogh Museum

currently closed. The museum's prize piece, Rembrandt's *Nightwatch*, is however still on show, and it's worth a visit for this alone. The painting was originally called The Militia Company of Captain Frans Banning Cocq, but became known as the Nightwatch when the picture darkened with grime over the years - its since been cleaned to reveal its true daytime setting.

Van Gogh Museum

ⓘ T020-5705200, www.vangogh museum.nl. Sat-Thu 1000-1800, Fri 1000-2200. €10; €13.50 for special exhibitions. Tram 2, 3, 5 or 12 to between Paulus Potterstraat and Van Baerlestraat.

One of Amsterdam's finest museums holds the world's largest Vincent Van Gogh collection, over 200 pieces bequeathed by his art collector brother, Theo. The modern building is split into five periods, starting with Van Gogh's dark Dutch works, and evolving, via Paris and Arles in the south of France, into his extraordinarily lively and colourful palette for which he is known. Strikingly, Van Gogh's career was little longer than a decade, but this

marvellous collection does much to highlight how rich and productive those ten years were. Highlights include *The Potato Eaters*, *Bedroom in Arles* and *Wheatfield with Crows*. Also in the museum are the artist's sketches, as well as works by his contemporaries, including close friend Paul Gauguin – Van Gogh famously cut off his ear after an argument with his artist friend.

Joods Historisch Museum

ⓘ T020-5310310, www.jhm.nl. Daily 1100-1700, closed Yom Kippur. €6.50. Metro Waterlooplein. Tram 9 or 14.

The Jewish History Museum is housed in a beautiful series of four synagogues dating from the 17th century, lined by walkways. Although the museum first opened in 1930, it was closed and ransacked during the Second World War and it was not until the 1980s that it was restored and re-opened. It now houses a thorough collection depicting the history of Jewish life in the Netherlands, highlighting the enormous contribution Jews made to the development of Amsterdam.

Joods Historisch Museum

Rijksmuseum

● Sleeping

Amsterdam's status as a hip city break destination means its vast number of beds don't often come cheap; moreover, most places get booked up, particularly in late spring (tulip season) and summer, so it's always essential to book ahead. Avoid the hotel touts, who hang around Centraal Station.

€€€ Amstel Inter-Continental, Professor Tulpplein 1, T020-6226060, www.amsterdam.intercontinental.com. The city's grande dame towers on the bank of the Amstel, and attracts an impressive list of rock stars and royalty. It's a classically large, elegant hotel, with posh rooms complete with Dutch wallpaper and huge beds. The restaurant is highly acclaimed and boasts 2 Michelin stars.

€€€ The Dylan, Keizersgracht 384, T020-5302010, www.dylan amsterdam.com. Style guru Anouchka Hempel designed this small hotel, which recently underwent a change in management (and name – this used to be *Blakes*). Rooms are individually themed, all centred on a courtyard, and there is an excellent fusion restaurant downstairs.

€€€ Hotel 717, Prinsengracht 717, T020-4270717, www.717hotel.nl. This hotel feels like a mix between a glossy magazine shoot and the home of a rich art-collector friend. Each of the 8 rooms are impeccably designed, crammed with artwork, beautiful fabrics, pale colours and an eclectic mix of antiques. Good canal-side location, too.

€€ Ambassade, Herengracht 341, T020-5550222, www.ambassade-hotel.nl. 10 17th-century canal-side houses make up this hotel in a lovely spot on Herengracht. This is one for

bookworms – regulars include John Le Carré, Umberto Eco, and Salman Rushdie (check out the signed copies in the library). Rooms are traditional and plush; those in the eaves are the most appealing.

€€ Canal House Hotel, Keizersgracht 148, T020-6225182, www.canal house.nl. Crammed with antiques, this 26-room hotel tries to maintain an early 1800s atmosphere in its lovely 17th century shell. That means no televisions, but plenty of lofty ceilings, solid furniture and homely quilts. There's an elegant breakfast room, small bar and the location on the Keizersgracht Canal is peaceful.

€€ Seven Bridges, Reguliersgracht 31, T020-6231329. The owners don't believe in flashing their wares on the internet, which gives an idea of the old-fashioned welcome you'll get here. It's quiet and rooms overlook the canal (and the famous Seven Bridges) or a small garden. Breakfast is served in your room. Book several months in advance.

€ Amistad Hotel, Kerkstraat 42, T020-6248074, www.amistad.nl. Run by husband-and-husband team Johan and Joost, the Amistad is one of the most popular gay hotels in town. Simple, colourful rooms come with or without en suite bathrooms, and have wooden floors and bright artwork.

€ Winston, Warmoesstraat 129, T020-6231380, www.winston.nl. This kooky, noisy "art hotel" has individually designed rooms. They are small (most with bathroom) but are decorated with anything from bright primary colours, to fish motifs, to x-rays – check the website. Good location on the edge of the Red Light District, bar and nightclub with a party atmosphere, and decent breakfasts are included in the price.

● Eating

Traditional Dutch fare isn't the lightest of cuisines – expect hearty meat-and-potato dishes, thick pancakes oozing all sorts of fillings, and hefty *broodjes* (sandwiches) stacked with meat, cheeses or fish. Having said that, chefs across the city are also wallowing in an orgy of fusion cuisine, which often puts French or Asian slants on Dutch dishes. Holland's colonial heritage also means lots of Indonesian flavours, and the city's multicultural population ensures plenty of Chinese, Thai, Italian and Japanese restaurants to choose from. Prices, although steeper since the introduction of the Euro, remain reasonable.

Breakfast

† **De Bakkerswinkel**, Warmoesstraat 69, T020-4898000. Breakfast and lunch only. Closed Mon. Bustling, airy deli/café serving excellent brunches, sandwiches, and fat slices of quiche.

† **Winkel**, Noordermarkt 43, T020-6230223. Breakfast and lunch only. Big breakfasts and legendary apple cake at this lively café. Be prepared to queue on Mon and Sat (market days).

Lunch

†† **Haesje Claes**, Spuistraat 273-275, T020-6249998. Old-style Dutch comfort eating in this popular wood-panelled restaurant. *Stampot* is a speciality, a filling stew of potatoes mashed with cabbage and served with sausage – perfect on a rainy afternoon. Good fish dishes if you fancy something lighter.

† **Café Luxembourg**, Spui 24, T020-6206264. Elegant café with a long marble bar and equally long menu, including favourites like split-pea soup,

kroketten (croquettes) and salmon burgers. Newspapers and a slow pace in the mornings; more frenetic at lunch and dinner.

¶ Pannekoekhuis Upstairs, Grimburgwal 2, T020-6265603. Students flock to this tiny pancake house dolling out good-value servings of filled sweet and savoury pancakes. Service can be slow.

Dinner

¶¶¶ Blauw aan de Wal, Achterburgwal 99, T020-3302257. This is a real find, hidden away down an alley in the heart of the Red Light District. Chic Mediterranean cuisine is the order of the day, with old wood floors, bare brick walls and a pretty courtyard making it all rather romantic.

¶¶¶ Christophe, Leliegracht 46, T020-6250807. Dinner only. Classic Michelin-starred restaurant in a quiet canal-side location. The atmosphere is discreet and elegant (jackets are required) and the food is a sumptuous feast of French-inspired contemporary cooking. Reservations essential.

¶¶ Brasserie Harkema, Nes 67, T020-4282222. Lunch and dinner daily. This hot new kid on the block is a weird fusion of traditional French-style brasserie and ultra-modern industrial styling. Locals love it, though, and the food is fast and good.

¶¶ d'Vijff Vlieghen, Spuistraat 294-302, T020-5304060. Dinner only. You won't have 'The Five Flies' to yourself, but the food is worth braving the tour groups. The menu is top-notch Dutch, served in a gorgeous string of 17th-century houses filled with antiques and Delft tiles. Look out for the Rembrandt etchings on the walls.

¶¶ Kantjil en de Tijger, Spuistraat 291-293, T020-6200994. Refreshingly

free of the usual "oriental" decor, this large, chic space specializes in *rijsttafel* – go there hungry, as you'll be getting up to 20 dishes. The spicy coconut prawns are good, too.

¶ Café Bern, Nieuwmarkt 9, T020-6220034. Dinner only. Typically laid-back brown café, specializing in cheese fondues (an unofficial national dish, hijacked from Switzerland) which punters wash down with a shot of strong stuff.

66 99 These friendly pubs, found all over the old centre and along the canals, are a great place to meet locals and try Dutch beer.

🌓 Nightlife

Day by Day is a useful monthly English language listings guide produced by the tourist office, covering everything from live music and events to exhibitions and museums.

Bars and coffeeshops

Don't be put off by the term *bruine cafés* (brown cafés) – these ubiquitous café-bars are the cosy mainstay of Amsterdam's nightlife. They're actually called that because smoke has stained the walls with nicotine over the years. Lovely. Nevertheless, these friendly pubs, found all over the old centre and along the canals, are a great place to meet locals and try Dutch beer. To try something altogether more exotic, you'll have to head to a coffeeshop, again found all over the centre of

town – and usually identified by the leaf motif or Rasta flag in the window. These generally have menus selling different types of cannabis, but note that you can't smoke (anything other than cigarettes) in ordinary bars. Also be warned to take it easy – particularly with hash cakes and cookies which can pack a powerful punch.

For a chilled out bar scene, often with DJs and dancing late into the night, try out some of the newer lounge bars; many are found around Nieuwezijds Voorburgwal, as well as the more traditional nightlife spots around Rembrandtplein and Leidseplein.

Amsterdam has a huge gay and lesbian scene – many call it the gay capital of Europe – with countless gay-friendly hotels, bars and clubs, mostly focused on the area around Reguliersdwarsstraat.

Clubs and live music

The club scene isn't as cutting-edge as you might hope, although there are some good places worth popping into in the centre – **Winston**, on Warmoesstraat is hip at the moment, and **Melkweg**, on Lijnbaansgracht, is a long-running favourite, functioning as a full-on arts centre, and therefore a good place to catch live music, too.

Classical music and theatre

The city's finest venue for opera is the **Muziektheater**, more popularly known as the Stopera, on Waterlooplein, T020-6255455, www.stopera.nl. The grand old **Concertgebouw**, T020-6718345, www.concertgebouw.nl, is the venue for classical music and one of the most visited concert halls in the world.

If Brussels is Belgium's biggest hitter, Antwerp is certainly a heavyweight contender. This waterfront metropolis has huge horizons: Europe's second largest port and a world centre for the diamond trade, it has reinvented itself as a modern city without forgetting its 16th-century heyday. Despite war damage, there are constant reminders of Antwerp's medieval and Renaissance past, from the impossibly delicate cathedral spire to the magnificent Rubens canvases in churches and museums. A spectacular stint as Europe's Cultural Capital in 1993 helped revive the disused quays of the Zuid – now a haven for barflies and gastronauts – and the gritty northern Eilandje. With its heritage of creative energy Antwerp has become one of Europe's fashion hubs and its myriad restaurants set impossibly high standards.

Antwerp

Arts & culture
★★★★

Eating
★★★★★

Nightlife
★★★★

Outdoors
★★

Romance
★★

Shopping
★★★★

Sightseeing
★★

Value for money
★★★

Overall score
★★★★✦

● Sights

Around Grote Markt

Antwerp's grandest square is lined with guildhouses topped with scrolling gables and golden statuary. The central fountain depicts Brabo, a Roman soldier who, according to legend, chopped off the hand of a giant who imposed tolls on ships. Some say this is how the city gained its name – "hand werpen", or hand-throwing – though this is given short shrift by pedantic etymologists. Whatever the truth, it's a suitably dramatic monument, with water gushing from the tyrant's severed hand.

South of the square, the **Cathedral of Our Lady** ⓘ *Handschoenmarkt. Mon-Fri 1000-1700, Sat 1000-1500, Sun 1300-1600. Carillon concerts Jun-mid Sep Mon 2100, Fri 1130,* is among the most graceful pieces of medieval architecture in northern Europe. Its slender spire was supposed to have a twin, but the money ran out; the stump sits rather

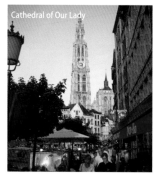

Cathedral of Our Lady

forlornly next to the finished article. Inside, Rubens' cherub-rich *Descent from the Cross* is the main attraction.

About 200 m east of Grote Markt, **Hendrik Conscienceplein** is the city's most charming square. Built by the Jesuits, it was dubbed 'Little Rome'. It's dominated by the exuberantly baroque **Carolus Borromeus Church** ⓘ *Mon-Sat 1000-1230, 1400-1700, Sun services only,* which has an uplifting cream and gold interior. Almost inevitably, Rubens had a hand in the design.

Rubenshuis

ⓘ *Wapper 9-11, T03-201 1555, www.museum.antwerpen.be. Tue-Sun 1000-1700. €6.*

Although little remains as it was, this is the place to learn about Rubens and his times. When the artist-cum-diplomat built this Italianate mansion, it was the talk of the town. Roam from room to room (the audio commentary is a must) and admire the atelier before stepping into the garden, familiar from many of his paintings. It's easy to imagine the master strolling here with intellectuals and politicians, showing off a rare tulip or potato plant from the New World.

Fine Arts Museum

ⓘ *Leopold de Waelplaats, T03-238 7809, www.museum.antwerpen.be/kmska. Tue-Sun 1000-1700. €6.*

The city's showpiece museum is an imposing neoclassical affair in the Zuid, with a well-judged collection of (mostly)

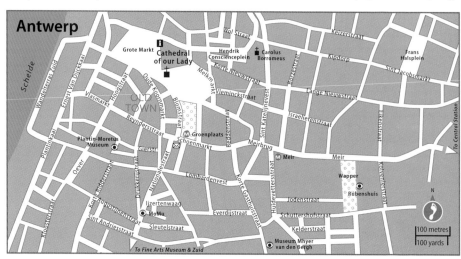

Antwerp

Schelde · Wandelterras Zuid · Ernest Van Dijckkaal · Vlasmarkt · Hoogstraat · Oude Koornmarkt · Blomstraat · Reyndersstraat · Gierstraat · Nationalestraat · Plantin-Moretus Museum · Oever · Kloosterstraat · Sint Andriesstraat · Korte Ridderstraat · Sint Augustijnenstraat · IJzerenwaag · MoMu · Sleutelstraat · Everdijstraat · Lombardenvest · Grote Markt · Cathedral of our Lady · Wol Straat · Hendrik Conscienceplein · Carolus Borromeus · Korte Nieuwstraat · Melkmarkt · Vleminckxstraat · Braderstraat · Sint Katelijnevest · Meirbrug · Groenplaats · Schoenmarkt · Korte Gasthuisstraat · Huidevettersstraat · Meir · Wapper · Rubenshuis · Jodenstraat · Schuttershofstraat · Kelderstraat · Israelietenstraat · Lange Nieuwstraat · Borzestraat · Keizerstraat · Kipdorp · Sint Jacobsmarkt · Frans Halsplein · Elkenstraat · Kolveniersstraat · To Central Station · Museum Mhyer van den Bergh · To Fine Arts Museum & Zuid · OLD TOWN · 100 metres · 100 yards · N

Excursion: Ghent

If you're looking for Bruges without the tourists, take a 40-minute train ride to medieval Ghent. Laced with dreamy waterways, it's a university city, more youthful and alive than "Bruges-la-morte", but more reflective and less showy than Antwerp. You can easily explore the centre on foot – just as well, as Ghent has the highest concentration of listed monuments in the country. It has an equally impressive concentration of pubs, ranging from 'brown' taverns to sleek 1970s-style bars and cluttered bohemian hang-outs. It's suited to structureless rambling, but there are a few must-sees: **Jan Van Eyck's** *Lamb of God* ⓘ *Sint Baafsplein, T09-269 2045, Mon-Sat 0930-1630, Sun from 1300, €3*, a gloriously luminous altarpiece in St Bavo's Cathedral; the spooky **Gravensteen Castle** ⓘ *Sint-Veerleplein, T09-225 9306, Apr-Sep 0900-1800, Oct-Mar 0900-1700, €6*, built in 1180 and endlessly rebuilt; **Graslei** and **Korenlei**, rows of glittering guildhouses on either side of the Lys; and **Smak** ⓘ *Citadelpark, T09-221 1703, www.smak.be, Tue-Sun 1000-1800, €5*. Belgium's hardest-hitting contemporary art museum.

Flemish art from the city's glory days and the 20th century. Upstairs are huge canvases by Rubens and his students, Van Dyck and Jordaens, as well as exquisite works by Van Eyck, Memling and Quentin Metsys. Downstairs, you can enter the disturbing world of James Ensor, whose mask-wearing grotesques and skeletons still shock, then return to normality with Rik Wouters's tender portraits of his wife.

Plantin-Moreus Museum

ⓘ *Vrijdagmarkt 22, T03-221 1450. Tue-Sun 1000-1700 (last entry at 1600). €4.*

A sumptuous Renaissance mansion and one-time printing press, the former home of the humanist Christopher Plantin is the only museum on Unesco's World Heritage list. Plantin's most famous work was a five-language Bible, a world first. Amid the beams, books, proofreading desks and working 16th-century presses, are the family quarters, hung with exquisite portraits by Rubens. In summer, the inner courtyard is filled with the scent of lavender and roses.

Museum Mayer van den Bergh

ⓘ *Lange Gasthuisstraat 19, T03-232 0103. Tue-Sun 1000-1700. €4.*

Also available

Antwerp & Ghent

Footprint

Price: **£6.99**
ISBN: 1 904777 75 9
www.footprintbooks.com

This dazzling array of paintings, statuary, tapestries and medieval missals was assembled by a 19th- century collector. Amid the many marvels are two unmissables: Breughel's *Mad Meg*, a nightmarish allegory on the theme of folly, and his delightful *Twelve Proverbs*, a witty slant on popular peasant sayings.

MoMu

ⓘ *Nationalestraat 28, T03-470 2770, www.momu.be. Tue-Sun 1000-1800, Thu until 2100. €5.*

Home to some of the fashion world's brightest talents – Van Noten, Demeulemeester, Margiela and many more – Antwerp does expensive clothes shops well. You can find out what makes the designers tick by visiting the light-filled Modenatie building, which houses the the world- famous Fashion Academy and this fascinating fashion museum with temporary exhibitions.

⊖ Travel essentials

Getting there Eurostar, www.eurostar.com, runs trains from London Waterloo to Brussels Gare du Midi, from where it's a 40-min train ride to Antwerp's Central Station. Returns start at £59. From the airport, there's a shuttle bus to town, while a taxi costs about €22.

Getting around The city is compact and easily walkable; there's also a good bus, tram and metro network, operated by De Lijn, www.delijn.be. Day pass €3. Bike-mad Antwerpenaars take full advantage of the city's cycle lanes; for rental, try **De Windroos**, Steenplein, T03-480 9388.

Tourist information Grote Markt, T03-232 0103, www.visit antwerpen.be. Provides free city maps and a host of useful brochures.

⊜ Sleeping

€€€ De Witte Lelie, Keizerstraat 16-18, T03-226 1966, www.dewittelelie.be. Antwerp's best boutique hotel: 10 ultra-stylish rooms in 3 adjacent 17th-century town houses on a quiet street, within easy walking distance of the old centre. Parking and patio garden.
€€ Hotel t' Sandt, Zand 13-19, T03-232 9390, www.hotel-sandt.be. An elegant establishment with an alluring aura of discreet luxury. The breakfast room has the feel of a French country house, with pastel-painted antiques aplenty.
€€ Julien, Korte Nieuwstraat 24, T03-229 0600, www.hoteljulien.com. On the eastern edge of the Old Town, this designer hotel is sleek, stylized and exceedingly friendly. Pinky-green lights glow in the hallway; breakfast is served on trendy ceramics and the rooms are calm and comfortable,

with cut-above touches such as truly thick curtains.
€ Postiljon, Blauwmoezelstraat 6, T03-231 7575. In the shadow of the cathedral, this old inn is now a cheap, cheerful family-run affair. Some rooms have bathrooms. Great location, if you don't mind the sound of morning bells.
€ Scheldezicht, Sint-Jansvliet 10-12, T032-316602, www.hotelschelde zicht.be. A pretty and old-fashioned family-run hotel which doesn't stand on ceremony. The only real flourish is the extravagant spiral staircase – but it's comfortable, and reasonably priced.

⊙ Eating

₸₸₸ Gin Fish, Haarstraat 9, T03-231 3207. Tue-Sat, 1800-2230. Seafood supremo Didier Garnich whips up his dishes in an open kitchen surrounded by a handful of customers on bar stools. There's no menu, and everyone gets the same delicious 4-course meal, with fabulously fresh fish very much to the fore. It's almost too efficient, but it's nothing if not memorable.
₸₸₸ Kommilfoo, Vlaamse Kaai 17, T03-237 3000. Closed Sat lunch-Mon. This prizewinning restaurant in the Zuid has a superb 4-course Chef's Fantasy menu for €68, including wine. Expect red-onion soup with Westmalle beer, millefeuille of langoustines with parmesan or cod with cauliflower purée and fennel.
₸₸ Le Zoute Zoen, Zirkstraat 15-17, T03-226 9220. Closed Mon. A charming bistro with wax-caked candelabras, a mosaic floor and shelves cluttered with curios. The food is Belgo-French with an Italian twist, and in a city that caters mainly to carnivores, vegetarian-friendly.

₸ Bar 2, Vrijdagmarkt 19, T03-227 5436. Wed, Thu, Sat from 1000, Fri from 0800, Sun 1200-2300. A trendy, unfussy *eetcafé* that serves wok dishes, salads and excellent sandwiches, on a square that, come Fri morning, buzzes with an open-air auction.
₸ Bassin, Tavernierkaai 1, T03-225 3637. Mon-Fri 1200-2300, Sat 1800-2300, Sun 1200-2200. At this cheerful, riverside brasserie, north of the centre, classic Flemish cuisine is prepared "grandma's way". Try superb *stoofvlees* (beef stewed in beer), home-made prawn croquettes, cod gratinée and *stoemp* (mash) with sausages.
₸ De Bloemkool, Groendalstraat 20, T03-227 3742. Mon-Tue and Sun 1130-1730, Wed 1130-1630, Fri-Sat 1130-2130. In the heart of the shopping district, this is an ideal spot for ladies and gents who lunch. There's a small terrace and a pleasant glass-roofed area at the back. The spag bol is splendid and the superior salads come with individual pots of proper dressing.

⊙ Nightlife

Finding a good bar in Antwerp is like falling off a log – and after a few Belgian brews, you may well do precisely that. The densest concentrations of drinking dens are in the Old Town and the Zuid. In town, try **De Muze**, Melkmarkt 15, for smoky jazz vibes; or **Witzli-Poetzli**, Blauwmoezelstraat 4, for scruffy boho charm. In the Zuid, **Mogador**, Graaf van Egmontstraat 57, attracts a classy pre-club crowd; **The Heming Way**, Waalse Kaai 19, serves cocktails to a cool Cuban soundtrack; and the shabby-chic **Bar Tabac**, Waalse Kaai 43, is the thinking man's choice for a late-night session.

If your last visit to Athens was before 2004, you're in for a surprise: Athens has been spruced up, refined and beautified, bringing it into the 21st century with gusto. Ancient monuments have been restored, neoclassical façades repainted, billboards and neon lighting torn down, the metro extended, tramlines added, pedestrian zones paved and trees planted. But in a city where countless layers of history sit concrete-upon-brick-upon-stone, you'll still find a curious juxtaposition of Western European, Balkan and Middle Eastern cultures, all of which are reflected in the food, the music and the architecture. This is also the city that, back in its ancient heyday, invented hedonism and you'll not be disappointed on that score now – Athens nightlife is beautiful, extravagant and inexhaustible.

Arts & culture
★★★

Eating
★★★

Nightlife
★★★★★

Outdoors
★

Romance
★★

Shopping
★★

Sightseeing
★★★★

Value for money
★★

Overall score
★★✦

At a glance

Take the **Acropolis** as your main point of reference. If you are on a short-stay, you'll probably be based in **Plaka**, Athens' oldest residential neighbourhood skirting the Acropolis' northern and eastern slopes. The northern limit of Plaka is marked by **Ermou** (the main shopping street) running east-west from **Syntagma** (home to the Greek Parliament) to **Monastiraki**, best known for its Sunday morning flea market and its metro station then proceeds to smart residential **Thissio** and Gazi. On the far side of Ermou lies **Psirri**, and northeast of Syntagma, the rocky mound of **Mount Lycabettus** rises above the posh area of **Kolonaki**. Gazi and Psirri deserve a special mention: both former-industrial zones, they have recently been transformed into night-time districts filled with trendy bars, restaurants, clubs and art galleries. Another welcome addition to Athens is the new **Archaeological Promenade**, a 4 km paved, lamp-lit walkway that now links the city's ancient sites.

Athens embodies the pre-eminent quality of the antique world, Art.

Benjamin Disraeli

Starting from the new Acropolis metro station, Dionissiou Areopagitou curves around the south side of the Acropolis to join Apostolou Pavlou, which then runs alongside the Ancient Agora to bring you to Thissio. From here Adrianou runs east to Plaka, while Ermou runs west past **Kerameikos** (ancient Athens' cemetery) towards Gazi.

★ *Don't leave town without grabbing a souvlaki takeaway.*

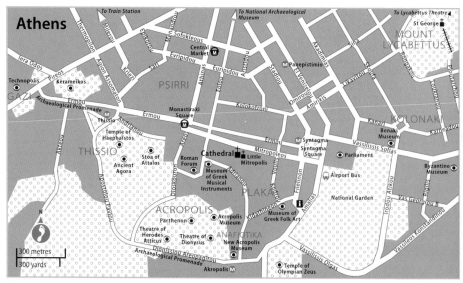

◉ Sights

Acropolis

ⓘ *Acropolis Hill, Plaka, T210-3210219, www.culture.gr. Daily 0800-1900 (summer), 0830-1500 (winter). €12 (this ticket also gives free entry to the Ancient Agora, Roman Forum, Theatre of Dionysus, Kerameikos and the Temple of Olympian Zeus and is valid for 4 days). Metro Acropolis or Monastiraki.*

Most stunning at night, when it rises above the modern city bathed in golden floodlighting, the Acropolis is a rocky mound crowned by three ancient temples, symbolizing the birth of Athens and indeed of Western civilization. Today it receives some three million visitors per year, and it's also the biggest selling point for hotel rooms and restaurant terraces claiming to glimpse its magic.

The largest and most revered temple is the fifth century BC **Parthenon**, built entirely from marble. Supported by 46 Doric columns, it was originally intended as a sanctuary for Athena and housed a giant gold and ivory statue of

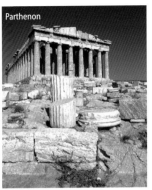
Parthenon

the goddess. The controversial "Elgin Marbles" (Greeks prefer to call them the Parthenon Marbles), were a series of bas-reliefs that once formed the internal frieze. In 1816 Lord Elgin, British Ambassador to Athens, which was under Ottoman occupation at time, sold them to the British Museum in London, where they remain to this day.

Close by, you can also visit the **Acropolis Museum** which houses many treasures, including five caryatids (columns designed to represent maidens) which once supported another

temple on the site, the **Erechtheion** (a temple dedicated to Athena and Poseidon who are said to have fought for the patronage of Athens on this spot). Other museum offerings are stone carvings found on the site, including the Calf Bearer (a statue of a young man carrying a sacrificial calf on his shoulders, dating from 570 BC) and the Peplos Kore and the Almond-Eyed Kore (statues of maidens which would have been votive offerings to Athena, 550-500 BC).

Work is now underway on the **New Acropolis Museum**, opposite the Acropolis metro station in Plaka. An all-glass structure designed by Swiss architect Bernard Tschumi, it will eventually take over from the existing museum. It is scheduled to open in 2007.

Plaka

ⓘ *Metro Acropolis or Monastiraki.*

Built into the hillside below the Acropolis, Plaka is Athens' oldest residential quarter. Touristy but undeniably charming, it's made up of cobbled alleys lined with pastel-coloured neoclassical mansions dating

---

◉ Travel essentials

Getting there Athens International Airport (Eleftherios Venizelos), T210-3530000, is 27 km northeast of the city. There are several frequent express bus services (€2.90 for same-day unlimited travel on all the city's public transport), journey time about 40 mins. Alternatively, take the train (every 30 mins, 0550-2250, €6). A taxi will cost you about €25.

Getting around Most of the main attractions lie within walking distance of one another in the city centre, parts of which are paved and pedestrian-only.

Buses are cheap, frequent but often crowded (single ticket €0.45). There are 3 metro lines (single ticket €0.70), the main nodal points being Monastiraki, Syntagma and Omonia. On the blue line, some, but not all, trains run all the way from Monastiraki to the airport. The green line is especially useful for reaching the port to Piraeus. Athens' taxis are among the cheapest in Europe, and Athenian taxi drivers among the most erratic. Taxis are no luxury – everyone takes them and it is quite normal to share a ride with other

passengers going in a similar direction. There are 2 new tramlines connecting Syntagma in the city centre to the coast, and are ideal for reaching beaches in the Glyfada area. Single ticket €0.60.

Tourist information Greek National Tourism Organisation (GNTO) walk-in visitors' centre, Amalias 26 (close to Syntagma), T210-3310716, Mon-Fri 0900-1900; Sat-Sun 1000-1600. GNTO airport office, T210-3530448, Mon-Fri 0800-1900, Sat-Sun 1000-1600. GNTO Head Office, Tsocha 2, Ambelokipi, T210-8707000, www.gnto.gr.

from the late 19th century (the period immediately after liberation from the Ottoman Turks, when Greece was trying to re-establish its cultural identity). The only really old buildings remaining here are Byzantine churches. Particularly notable is the 12th-century **Little Mitropolis** ⓘ *daily 0700-1300,* standing next to the far less attractive 19th-century **Cathedral**, and the residential area **Anafiotika**. Besides the countless souvenir shops and tavernas, look out for the museums of **Greek Musical Instruments** ⓘ *Diogenous 1-3, Tue and Thu-Sun 1000-1400, Wed 1200-1800, free,* and **Greek Folk Art** ⓘ *Kidathineon 17, Tue-Sun 1000-1400, €2,* a cluster of whitewashed Cycladic-style houses built by settlers from the island of Anafi.

Ancient Agora

ⓘ *Adrianou 24, Monastiraki, T210-3310963, www.culture.gr. Daily 0800-1900 (summer), 0800-1500 (winter). €4. Metro Monastiraki.*

A romantic wilderness of coarse grazing land and olive trees, strewn with fallen columns and crowned by an ancient temple, during Athens' Golden Age this was its main marketplace, as well as the

Temple of Haephaistos, Ancient Agora

city's political, administrative and cultural heart. It was here that Socrates and St Paul made their public speeches, and where democracy was born, though today you need some imagination to interpret it as such.

The buildings that remain recognizably intact are the remarkably well-preserved fifth century BC **Temple of Haephaistos**, and the **Stoa of Attalos**, a two-storey structure from the second century BC, which originally functioned as a trading centre but today houses the **Agora Museum**, displaying ancient finds from the site.

Central Market

ⓘ *Sofokleous and Evripidou. Mon-Sat 0900-1500. Metro Monastiraki or Omonia.*

Modern day Athenians shop within the halls of the vast covered market, an iron and glass structure erected in 1870. A veritable feast for the eyes, here you will find stalls trading in seasonal Mediterranean fruit and vegetables, dried figs, nuts, olives and spices. In the seafood section you'll see glittering silver-scaled fish and copious quantities

of octopus and squid displayed upon mounds of freshly-ground ice, while the meat section (definitely not for the squeamish) is populated by bloodsplattered butchers hacking at carcasses on sections of tree trunks that improvise as chopping boards.

National Archaeological Museum

ⓘ *Patission 44, Omonia, T210-8217717, www.culture.gr. Daily 0800-1900 (summer), Mon 1030-1700, Tue-Sun 0830-1500 (winter). €6. Metro Victoria.*

With possibly the world's finest collection of ancient Greek art, this one is a must-see. Reopened in 2004, after lengthy closure for renovation, the light, airy, marble-floored exhibition spaces show off elegant classical sculpture to maximum effect. Its vast so don't try to see everything, but be sure to also catch the subtly-coloured, 16th-century BC **Thira Frescoes**, found buried below lava following a volcanic explosion on the island Santorini, and the **Mycenaen Collection**, a horde of gold jewellery and weaponry dating from between the 16th and 11th centuries BC.

Plaka

Central Market

Benaki Museum

ⓘ *Vassilissis Sofias and Koumbari 1, Kolonaki, T210-3671000, www.benaki.gr. Mon, Wed, Fri, Sat 0900-1700, Thu 0900-2400, Sun 0900-1500. €6 (free Thu). Metro Syntagma.*

Antonios Benakis (1873-1954) was a Greek from Alexandria, Egypt, and an avid art collector. Before he died, he gave this neoclassical house and his entire collection to the Greek state. A journey through the history of Greek art from 3000 BC up to the 20th century, exhibits include sculpture, ceramics, jewellery, paintings, furniture and costumes, all laid out in chronological order. Top attractions is a horde of second century BC golden filigree jewellery inlaid with precious stones known as the **Thessaly Treasure**, two early paintings by **El Greco**, and the reconstruction of two wooden-panelled living rooms from a mid-18th century, Ottoman-inspired house in Northern Greece.

Byzantine Museum

ⓘ *Vassilissis Sofias 22, Kolonaki, T210-7232178, www.culture.gr. Tue-Sun 0830-1500. €4. Metro Evangelismos.*

National Archaeological Museum

Byzantine Museum

Hidden below the courtyard of an Italianate villa, this new, open-plan, split-level, underground exhibition space opened in 2004. Pieces are displayed in chronological order, following the development of the Byzantine Empire from the advent of Christianity (when many pagan symbols were absorbed by the creed) right up to the fall of Constantinople in 1453. The exhibition starts with stone carvings, sculpture and mosaics taken from early basilicas. It then continues with icons depicting sultry-eyed saints against golden backgrounds, frescoes illustrating biblical events, and minutely-detailed silver and gold jewellery and ecclesiastical artefacts.

Mount Lycabettus

ⓘ *Metro Evangelismos.*

Athens' highest vantage point at 295 m, Lycabettus affords panoramic views, so you can see the lot: the city, the mountains and the sea, all in one go. A network of footpaths lead up through pinewoods and sub-tropical vegetation to the summit – if the hike is too steep, take a taxi or catch the funicular ⓘ *from Ploutarchou Street in Kolonaki, every 30 mins, 0900-0300,* for a 2-minute whiz through a cliff side tunnel. The peak is capped by the tiny, white **Church of St George**, and a series of terraces hosting the *Orizontes* restaurant and a café. Carved into the rocks on the north-facing slope, the open-air **Lycabettus Theatre** stages summer concerts. Recent performers include Moby, the Prodigy and Patti Smith.

Technopolis

ⓘ *Pireos 100, Gazi, T210-3460981. Hours variable depending on exhibitions in course. Free. Metro Thissio.*

Technopolis (Art City) occupies the former City Gasworks. A multi-purpose arts complex, the disused gas tanks and brick outbuildings have been converted to provide a series of spaces for exhibitions, concerts (Tindersticks and Tricky have played here) and theatre, while the towering brick chimneys are lit red at night and remain the symbol of new art in an urban environment. There's also a small **Maria Callas Museum** ⓘ *Pireos 100, Mon-Fri 0900-2100, free.*

Mount Lycabettus

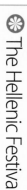

Each summer, from June to the end of September, the Hellenic Festival stages open-air theatre, opera, classical music and dance at the ancient Odeon of Herodes Atticus, plus rock concerts at the hilltop Lycabettus Theatre. A stunning venue, the second-century Odeon is carved into the rocks of the southern slope of the Acropolis. The building was commissioned by the Roman consul, Herodes Atticus, in memory of his wife Regilla. The 28-m high façade serves as a backdrop to the stage, and the semicircular theatre space, with a radius of 38 m, can seat an audience of 5000. The modern festival dates back to 1955, and legendary figures that have graced its stage include Maria Callas, Margot Fonteyn and Rudolph Nureyev. More recently, summer 2005 saw performances by Placido Domingo, Dario Fo, the Duke Ellington Orchestra and the Bolshoi Theatre. Performances begin at 2100 (June to August) and 2030 (September). Advance booking begins three weeks prior to each performance (see www.hellenicfestival.gr for the latest programme).

Tickets are available from: **Hellenic Festival Box Office** ⓘ *39 Panepistimiou (in the arcade), T210-9282900. Mon-Fri 0830-1600 and Sat 0900-1430.* **Odeon of Herodes Atticus** ⓘ *Dionysiou Areopagitou, T210-9282900. Daily 0900-1400 and 1800-2100. Telephone reservations by credit card, T210-9282900. Mon-Thu 0830-2000 and Sat 0900-1430.*

⊜ Sleeping

For romance, opt for Plaka. Syntagma is where you'll find grand expensive hotels, the Greek Parliament, and lots of traffic. Kolonaki is for image-conscious shopaholics and socialites, but fun if you can take the pace. Avoid Syngrou, its functional and impersonal, and aimed primarily at business travellers.

€€€ **Electra Palace**, Nikodimou 18, Plaka, T210-3370000, www.electra hotels.gr. The EP's yellow- and-white neoclassical façade, complete with wrought-iron balconies, was added during renovation for the Olympics. It's now Plaka's most stylish hotel. Some rooms have an Acropolis view. There's a spa and fitness centre, plus plans for an outdoor rooftop pool.

€€€ **Fresh**, Sophocleous 26 and Klisthenous, Psirri, T210-5248511, www.freshhotel.gr. This hotel opened in 2004 and immediately featured in *Wallpaper* magazine. Close to the gritty Central Market, the look is minimalist, with fresh flowers, lounge music, and vivid orange, green and pink details adding to the fun. There's a summer rooftop bar with a pool and sundeck, and nouvelle Greek cuisine.

€€€ **St George Lycabettus**, Kleomenous 2, Kolonaki, T210-7290711, www.sglycabettus.gr. On the rocky, pine-scented slopes of Mt Lycabettus, bordering chic Kolonaki, this white 1970s building offers 158 plush modern rooms, most with balconies and Acropolis views. There's a funky bar-restaurant and the top-floor Grand Balcon has stunning views. There's also a roof garden with pool.

€€ **Central Hotel**, Apolonos 21, Plaka, T210-3234357, www.centralhotel.gr. On the edge of Plaka, this hotel was fully renovated in 2003. The rooms are light and airy with minimalist Italian furniture in pale- coloured wood, and puffy white duvets. There's a roof terrace with Acropolis views and a jacuzzi, plus a ground-floor restaurant.

€€ **Hotel Plaka**, Kapnikareas 7, Plaka, T210-3222096, www.plakahotel.gr. Smart and discreet, this hotels lies in a side street between Monastiraki and Syntagma metro stations. The 67 rooms have pine floors, minimalist furniture and primary-coloured fabrics. There's a roof garden with a bar on summer evenings, so you can watch the sun set over the Acropolis.

€ **Marble House**, An Zinni 35, Koukaki, T210-9228294 and 9234058, www.marblehouse.gr. This small family-run hotel lies in a peaceful residential area, just a 10-min walk from Plaka and the Acropolis. The 16 rooms are clean and simple, with mini-bars and ceiling fans.

€ **Student and Travellers' Inn**, Kidathineon 16, Plaka, T210-3244808, www.studenttravellersinn.com. Just off Plaka's prettiest square, this upscale youth hostel offers singles, doubles and quadruples, plus dorms. All the rooms are spotless and have wooden floors, a sink and mirror, and some have bathrooms. Young, friendly English-speakers run the reception. There's internet access and an internal courtyard garden with a big screen TV.

Eating

Plaka is fine for lunch but to really tap into Athenian nightlife, dine in Psirri or Gazi, where funky new eateries breathe life into standard Greek taverna fare and stay open well beyond midnight.

Breakfast

Gallery Café, Adrianou 33, Monastiraki, T210-3249080. Overlooking the Ancient Agora, this café has a lounge atmosphere with exposed stonework, sofas and coffee tables, cool music and modern art on the walls.

Tristato, Dedalou 34 and Geronda, Plaka, T210-3244472. In a pedestrian side street just off Platia Filomousou, this old-fashioned café is a great place for morning coffee or an afternoon pot of herbal tea.

Lunch

O Platanos, Diogenous 4, Plaka, T210-3220666. One of the oldest and best-hidden tavernas in Plaka, O Platanos dates back to 1932. Homely meat-and-vegetable casseroles such as lamb with aubergine, and veal with spinach, are served at tables on a bougainvillea-covered terrace in the shade of an old plane tree, after which restaurant is named.

To Kouti, Adrianou 23, Monastiraki, T210-3213229. Playful salads, meat and seafood dishes, seasoned with spices and aromatic herbs, are guaranteed to make your taste buds sing. Great for dinner, or lunch after a trip to Monastiraki's Sun flea market.

Dinner

Orizontes, Mt Lycabettus, Kolonaki, T210-7227065. The high point of Athens, 295m above sea level, is the place to eat if you have only one night in town, plus the money to foot the bill. Perched atop Mt Lycabettus there are stunning views across the city and the menu features refined, fusion cuisine, by TV-celebrity chef Yannis Geldis. Reservations recommended.

Mamacas, Persefonis 41, Gazi, T210-3464984. In trendy Gazi, Mamacas has a Mykonos-inspired, whitewashed-

> 66 99 **Ask Athenians what they think their city does better than any other European capital and they will probably tell you about the nightlife.**

wood dining room, plus outdoor tables backed by the silhouette of the disused gasworks. The menu features Greek taverna classics with a twist, and there's a seductive wine bar annex.

Zeideron, Taki 10-12, Psirri, T210-3215368. The perfect place to start a night out in Psirri, Zeideron serves colourful, modern taverna fare. In summer, take a table on the busy pedestrian street; in winter there's a romantic old-fashioned dining room downstairs, and a light and airy glass conservatory up top.

Nightlife

Ask Athenians what they think their city does better than any other European capital and they will probably tell you about the nightlife. All year round Psirri and Gazi are rocking. In Psirri, **Soul**, Evripidou 65, is a glamorous but fun cocktail bar in a red-walled courtyard garden with sofas and finger food, while nearby **Psirra**, Miaouli 19, pulls the grungy intellectual crowd, who drink *rakomelo* (hot raki with honey and cinnamon) at street side tables. In upmarket Kolonaki, **Balthazar**, Tsoha 27, is a see-and-be-seen bar-restaurant in a beautifully-lit walled garden, rivalled in terms of sophistication only by **Mommy**, Delphon 4, off Skoufa 62, a bar-restaurant with 1970s revival decor and a hip 30-something clientele. In Plaka, **Kidathineon**, Platia Filomousou, is a romantic, old-fashioned café overlooking a leafy square, perfect for a nightcap. The best clubs are in Gazi: **Nipiagogio**, Kleanthous 8, occupies a former kindergarten, with drinks and dancing till the last customers leave at 0600. By the sea in Voula, **Destijl** is a large dance club with a restaurant and palm-lined beach, open all year.

In summer, many of the big clubs in the centre are closed as they move out to the coastal strip from Kalamaki to Varkiza. They have surprise new beach locations each year, but names to look out for include **Privilege**, **Venue** and **Envy**. Some double as swanky bathing establishments during the day, with waterside music and cocktails around sunset, and the party mood setting in after midnight.

Barcelona

Barcelona dips its toes in the Mediterranean, lolls back against the Pyrenees and basks in year-round sunshine. The skyline is indelibly marked by the visionary architect Antoni Gaudí, whose delirious buildings – resembling dragons, cliffs or gingerbread houses – seem to have magically erupted across the city. And at the heart of Barcelona lie the ancient passages, gargoyles and ghostly spires of the old Gothic city, apparently untouched by modernity. Add fantastic and varied nightlife, discerning cuisine, a nose for the latest and best in fashion and design, and a population bent on having a good time and it's not surprising that, in the last decade, Barcelona has become the most popular city in Europe.

But beneath the glamorous exterior lies a city that had to work hard to get attention. Not so long ago, Gaudí's *La Pedrera* was a grime-coated bingo hall and parts of the city were too dangerous to visit. The 1992 Olympics stopped the rot and, with breathtaking energy, Barcelona reinvented itself, sloughing off the dirt and sleaze to emerge as the most seductive city on the Mediterranean. Forget flamenco, sangría and other stock Spanish clichés, Barcelona is the proud capital of the ancient kingdom of Catalunya, with a distinct language and its own customs and traditions. These are staunchly preserved and exuberantly celebrated, with fire-spitting dragons, demons and giants.

Arts & culture
★★★★

Eating
★★★★

Nightlife
★★★★★

Outdoors
★★★

Romance
★★★

Shopping
★★★★★

Sightseeing
★★★★

Value for money
★★

Overall score
★★★★

At a glance

Finding your way around the Catalan capital isn't difficult. The Old City (Ciutat Vella) is at its heart, divided by the **Ramblas**, the city's famous tree-lined promenade, which meanders from Plaça de Catalunya down to the port. To the east of the Ramblas is the shadowy, medieval maze of the **Barri Gòtic** – the Gothic Quarter – with the flamboyant cathedral at its centre. This has been the heart of the city since Roman times and still buzzes day and night. East of the Barri Gòtic is **La Ribera**, another medieval district, which has become the coolest neighbourhood in a

Barcelona, the great enchantress

Joan Maragall, Ode to Barcelona

city famed for its addiction to fashion. Packed with über-chic boutiques, designer stores and the trendiest restaurants, bars and clubs, it rubs shoulders with Sant Pere, still a charmingly old-fashioned neighbourhood, but rapidly rising in the style stakes. West of the

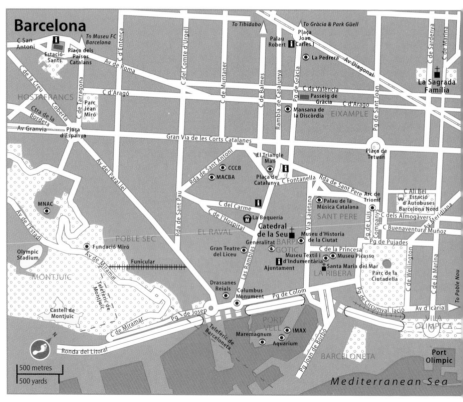

European City Breaks Barcelona

Ramblas, **El Raval** spreads south to the raffish old theatre district of Paral.lel. Once a notorious red-light district, the Raval was given a massive clean-up and the glossy Museum of Contemporary Art in the 1990s and now has hip galleries, vintage stores and bohemian bars.

When the city burst out of its medieval walls in the 19th century, the rich commissioned new mansions in the airy grid of the **Eixample** (meaning 'extension' in Catalan). Gaudí and his Modernista colleagues had a ball, leaving a spectacular legacy which now comprises one of the greatest concentrations of art nouveau architecture in the world. Beyond the Eixample district is **Gràcia**, once independent from the city and still with a relaxed vibe of its own. On the outskirts is **Park Güell**, Gaudí's fairytale extravaganza with magical views over the city.

To the west of the centre, overlooking the sea, is **Montjuïc Hill**. The Olympics left their mark here with a string of excellent sporting facilities. Close by is the **Fundació Miró**, dedicated to the Catalan master with a huge number of photo opportunities. At the bottom of the hill is MNAC.

The regenerated waterfront stretches northeast from the Columbus monument at the foot of the Ramblas. **Port Vell**'s warehouses hold restaurants, museums and an entertainment complex, while the glitzy **Port Olímpic** is hugely popular, crammed with bars and seafood restaurants and flanked by sandy beaches. Beyond it lies the site of the Universal Forum of Cultures 2004, a sleek business and entertainment complex built on reclaimed land. In contrast, the traditional dock-workers' neighbourhood of **Barceloneta** is more atmospheric, with tiny tapas bars tucked away in its depths. The city's outskirts are home to parks, funfairs and museums: the best views can be had from **Tibidabo**, Barcelona's funfair mountain and highest peak, reached by a rickety tram and funicular.

★ *Don't leave town without having cocktails at a xiringuito (snack bar) right on the beach.*

24 hours in the city

Get a feel for the city by strolling down the **Ramblas**, with a stop at **La Boquería** market on the way to take in the sights, sounds and smells. Alternatively, have a coffee at **Café de l'Òpera** and watch the world go by. Then dive into the chaotic maze of the **Barri Gòtic**, where you'll find the Gothic cathedral (take the lift to the roof for fantastic views) and plenty of great shops, bars and restaurants. If you prefer something a bit edgier, head across the Ramblas to **El Raval**, which is home to the excellent Museum of Contemporary Art (**MACBA**), and lots of vintage clothes stores and galleries. Have lunch on the terrace at **Plaça dels Àngels** and afterwards explore the elegant **Passeig de Gràcia**, home to the city's most emblematic Modernista buildings, including Gaudí's **Casa Batlló** and **La Pedrera**. An equally valid alternative would be to visit the extraordinary **Sagrada Família**. In the late afternoon head to the seafront for a stroll and a dip. In the evening, check out the fashionable bars and clubs of **La Ribera**, or take in a game at the legendary **Nou Camp** stadium – if you can get tickets.

◉ Sights

Las Ramblas
ⓘ *Metro Plaça de Catalunya/Liceu*

The best introduction to Barcelona is a stroll down Las Ramblas, the mile-long promenade that meanders down from Plaça de Catalunya to the port. It may look like one street but it is made up of five separate *ramblas*, each with its own name and characteristics. Together they present an oddly appealing mixture of the picturesque and the tacky: street entertainers, fast-food outlets, crumbling theatres, whimsical Modernista mansions and pretty turn-of-the-century kiosks overflowing with flowers and songbirds. It's at its best early in the morning and on Sunday afternoons.

Halfway down is **La Boquería**, the city's irresistible market, with its

Mercat de la Boqueria

wrought-iron roof and Modernista sign. Inside are piles of gleaming fruit, vegetables, fish and other local specialities, plus a liberal sprinkling of tiny bars for coffee or cava. Nearer the port is the city's 19th-century opera house, the **Gran Teatre del Liceu**.

Barri Gòtic
ⓘ *Metro Liceu*

The Barri Gòtic has been the hub of the city for more than 2000 years. It's one of the best-preserved Gothic quarters in Europe, a dizzy maze of palaces, squares and churches piled on top of an original Roman settlement. The area is grubby, noisy, chaotic and packed with shops, bars and clubs. The streets are just as crowded at midnight as they are at midday.

Exploring the narrow alleyways, it's impossible to miss the **Catedral de la Seu** (Plaça Nova) with its dramatic spires and neo-Gothic façade. The cathedral dates back to the 13th century and the magnificent interior is suitably dim and hushed. A lift behind the altar swoops to the top for a bird's-eye view of huddled rooftops.

Close by, the imposing medieval

◉ Travel essentials

Getting there Barcelona International Airport is 12 km south of the city (flights T93-298 38 38, www.aena.es). International airlines use terminals A and B. The **airport train** (€2.85) runs to Plaça de Catalunya and Estació-Sants every 30 mins, 0613-2340. A1 **Aerobús** (€3.60) runs to Plaça de Catalunya, via Estació-Sants and Plaça d'Espanya, every 12 mins, 0600-2400. **Taxis** are available from outside the terminals and cost €25 to the centre, or more after 2200 and at weekends (supplements for luggage). **Estació-Sants** (metro Sants) is the main train station. Many trains also stop at **Passeig de Gràcia**. For timetables and prices: T902-240 202, www.renfe.es.

Getting around The Old City and Eixample, north of Plaça de Catalunya, are easy to walk around. Some sights, like the Sagrada Família and Park Güell,

require a short bus or metro ride; others, like Montjuïc and Tibidabo, are reached by cable car or funicular.

Public transport is cheap and efficient; the main hub is Plaça de Catalunya. 6 **metro** lines run Mon-Thu 0500-2300, Fri-Sat 0500- 0200, Sun 0600-2400. **Buses** run Mon-Sat 0600-2230 (less frequently Sun), and nightbuses (N) 2230-0400. Gràcia and Tibidabo are served by **FGC** train, (T93-205 15 15, www.fgc.net). A single bus or metro ticket costs €1.15; a T-Dia (€4.80) allows unlimited journeys on the network 1 day; a T-10 (€6.30) allows 10 trips and can be shared. For maps and information, visit the TMB office under Plaça Universitat (T93-443 08 59, www.tmb.net). There's a **taxi** stand on Plaça de Catalunya, opposite the main tourist office, or call **Barnataxi**, T93-357

77 55 or **Fono-Taxi**, T93-300 11 00.

Tourist information The main office is at Plaça de Catalunya, T90-630 12 82, daily 0900-2100. It books accommodation and tours and sells discount cards and street maps. It also offers walking tours with various themes; prices range from €8.50-10.50. There are branches at Plaça Sant Jaume, Estació-Sants and the airport. Also check out www.barcelonaturisme. com and www.bcn.es. The **Barcelona Card** (€17 for 1 day, €30 for 5 days) gives unlimited travel by public transport plus discounts at shops, restaurants and major museums. The **Montjuïc Card** (€20) includes 1-day's admission to all museums, public transport (including cable car), bike hire and other discounts. The hop-on/hop-off **Bus Turístic** (1 day €17, 2 days €21) tours the sights every 20 mins.

façades of the **Generalitat** (Catalan Parliament) and the **Ajuntament** (City Council) square up to each other across the Plaça Sant Jaume. From here, shadowy passages, scattered with Roman ruins and ancient churches, lead to lovely squares like the Plaça Sant Just, the Plaça Felip Neri, and the Plaça del Pi.

Museu d'Història de la Ciutat

ⓘ *Plaça del Rei s/n, T93-315 11 11, www.museuhistoria.bcn.es. Oct-May Tue-Sat 1000-1400, 1600-2000, Sun 1000-1500; Jun-Sep Tue-Sat 1000-2000, Sun 1000-1500. €4 (includes entry to Museu-Monestir de Pedralbes, Museu-Casa Verdaguer and the Interpretation Centre for the Park Güell). Metro Jaume I.*

This fascinating museum reveals the history of the city layer by layer. A glass lift glides down to the subterranean excavations of Roman Barcino, revealing 2000-year-old watchtowers, baths, temples, homes and businesses, discovered less than a century ago. Towards the site of the cathedral, the Roman ruins become interspersed with the remnants of

Mirador del Rei Martí

MACBA

fifth-century Visigothic churches. Stairs lead up to the medieval Royal Palace and the Golden Age of the city's history. The echoing Saló de Tinell, built in 1359, is a masterpiece of Catalan Gothic, and the Mirador del Rei Martí watchtower offers fabulous views across the Old City.

MACBA

ⓘ *Plaça dels Àngels, El Raval, T93-412 08 10, www.macba.es. 25 Sep-24 Jun Mon, Wed-Fri 1100-1930, Sat 1000-2000, Sun 1000-1500; 25 Jun-24 Sep Mon, Wed-Fri 1000-2000; Jul-Aug Thu until 2400, Sun 1000-1500. €4-7.50 (depending on whether you want entrance to 1 floor, 2 floors or the whole museum). Free on Wed and from 2000 on Thu (Jul-Aug). Metro Universitat.*

Richard Meiers' huge, glassy home for MACBA was built in 1995 as a symbol of the city's urban renewal. The collection is loosely structured around three periods; the 1940s and 1950s are represented by members of the Dau al Set, a loose collection of writers and artists influenced by the surrealists and

Joan Miró. Work from the 1960s and 1970s shows the impact of popular and consumer culture on art, while the 1980s and early 1990s are marked by a return to painting and traditional forms, plus good photographic pieces. Excellent temporary exhibitions focus on the latest digital and multimedia works. MACBA has a great bookshop and a café-bar in the spacious square that it shares with the **CCCB** (Centre of Contemporary Culture).

Passeig de Gràcia

ⓘ *Metro Passeig de Gràcia*

At the heart of the Eixample is this glossy boulevard of chic boutiques, neoclassical office buildings and Modernista mansions. The most famous stretch is the **Mansana de la Discòrdia** ('block of discord') between Carrer Consell de Cent and Carrer d'Aragó, where three Modernista masterpieces nudge up against each other: **Casa Lleó i Morera**, transformed by Domènech i Montaner in 1902; **Casa Amatller**, designed by Puig i Cadafalch as a polychrome fairytale castle; and **Casa Batlló**

Casa Batlló

ⓘ T93-216 03 06, www.casabatllo.es, daily 0900-2000, €10, by Antoni Gaudí. Covered with shimmering *trencadis* (broken tiles) and culminating in a scaly roof, it gleams like an undersea dragon. The interior is soft and undulating, like whipped ice cream.

La Pedrera
ⓘ C Provença 261-265, T902-400 973, www.caixacatalunya.es. Daily 1000-2000, last admission 1930. €8, free admission to temporary exhibitions. Metro Diagonal.

Casa Milà, better known as La Pedrera (the 'stone quarry'), rises like a cream cliff draped with wrought-iron balconies. There's a recreation of a 1911 apartment on the first floor, with many original fittings. The attic houses **L'Espai Gaudí**, a museum of the architect's life and work in the city, but the climax of a visit is the sinuous rooftop terrace, studded with chimneys, air vents and stairwells disguised as extraordinary bulbous crosses and plump *trencadí*-covered towers. You can enjoy a drink and live music on the rooftop on summer weekends.

La Pedrera rooftop

La Sagrada Familia

La Sagrada Família
ⓘ C Mallorca 401, Eixample, T93-08 04 14, www.sagradafamilia.org. Oct-Mar daily 0900-1800; Apr-Sep daily 0900-2000. €8. Metro Sagrada Família.

Gaudí's unfinished masterpiece, the Expiatory Temple of the Holy Family, is the most emblematic and controversial monument in Barcelona. The towers measure almost 100 m and the central spire, when finished, will soar 180 m into the sky. The temple is set for completion in 2026, the anniversary of Gaudí's death.

Gaudí designed three façades for the temple but only the Nativity façade was completed by the time of his death in 1926. The *Passion* façade on the other side of the church is grim and lifeless in comparison. Inside, work has begun on the construction of four huge columns to support the enormous domed roof.

There's a lift up the towers (€2); brave visitors can climb even higher, before descending via the vertiginous spiral staircase. Underneath, the crypt contains Gaudí's tomb and an interactive museum.

Best of the rest

Santa María del Mar ⓘ *Plaça de Santa María del Mar, La Ribera. Metro Jaume I.* This lovely 14th-century church is one of the purest examples of Catalan Gothic.

Museu Picasso ⓘ *C Montcada 15-23, La Ribera. www.museu picasso.bcn.es. Closed Sun-Mon. €6. Metro Jaume I.* Very popular collection dominated by early works created in Barcelona.

Museu Tèxtil i d'Indumentària ⓘ *C Montcada 12-14, www.museutextil.bcn.es. Closed Mon. €3.50. Metro Jaume I.* Fashion from the 16th century to the present day, housed in converted Gothic palaces, with a delightful café.

CCCB ⓘ *C Montalegre 5, El Raval. Closed Mon. €6. Metro Universitat.* Hosts eclectic exhibitions on aspects of contemporary culture not covered by MACBA.

Drassanes Reials ⓘ *Av Drassanes s/n, www.diba.es/maritim. Daily. €6. Metro Drassanes.* Vast medieval shipyards contain an excellent maritime museum.

Museu FC Barcelona ⓘ *Nou Camp, www.fcbarcelona.com. €9.90. Metro Collblanc.* Football paraphernalia plus a guided tour of the legendary stadium (€6 without tour).

Tibidabo ⓘ *Mar-Sep only. FGC to Av Tibidabo, then tram Blau, then funicular.* The mountain has a great old-fashioned funfair at its summit and breathtaking views across the city.

Modernisme

The great rediscovery and celebration of Catalunya's cultural identity known as the *Renaixença* (Renaissance) began in the 1850s. Architecture, literature, painting, sculpture, furniture, craft and design were galvanized by the new spirit of cultural and political optimism. This arts movement came to be known as *Modernisme* and was partly influenced by the international art nouveau and Jugenstil movements. When the medieval city walls were torn down in 1854, Ildefons Cerdà's airy grid-shaped extension (Eixample in Catalan) was constructed, giving the most influential architects of the day the chance to display their originality and virtuosity. Three names stand out: Antoni Gaudí i Cornet, Lluis Domènech i Montaner and Josep Puig i Cadafalch. You can choose your favourite in the Mansana de la Discòrdia (see page 35). The list of Modernista monuments in Barcelona is breathtakingly long, highlights include Gaudí's Casa Batlló, La Pedrera, Park Güell and the Sagrada Família; Montaner's Palau de la Música Catalana; and Puig i Cadafalch's Casa Amatller.

MNAC

ⓘ *Palau Nacional, Montjuïc , T93-622 03 60, www.mnac.es. Tue-Sat 1000-1900, Sun 1000-1430. €8, prices for temporary exhibitions vary. Metro Espanya.*

Housed in the dour Palau Nacional on Montjuïc is a magnificent collection of the best of Catalan art. The highlight is the array of spellbinding Romanesque murals gathered from Catalan churches and displayed on reconstructed church interiors. The Gothic collection reflects Catalunya's

glory years from the 13th to the 15th centuries, with rooms devoted to the three outstanding painters of the time: Bernat Martorell, Lluís Dalmau and Jaume Huguet. Tacked on at the end is a small collection of works from the 15th to the 18th centuries, including a couple of pieces by Zurbarán, Goya and El Greco. At the end of 2004, the Museu d'Art Modern joined the rest of MNAC's collection in a new gallery.

Fundació Miró

ⓘ *Parc de Montjuïc s/n, T93-443 94 70, www.bcn.fjmiro.es. Oct-Jun Tue-Sat 1000-1900, until 2130 on Thu, Sun 1000-1430. €7.20, temporary exhibitions €3.20. Metro Espanya or funicular from Paral.lel.*

The fabulous Fundació Miró is set in a white, light-drenched building by Josep Lluís Sert on Montjuïc. It contains the most important and comprehensive gathering of Miró's works in the world, from his early experiments with Cubism and Fauvism through to his later paintings, which are increasingly gestural and impulsive. There are spectacular

sculptures from the 1960s and 1970s; some are displayed on the rooftop sculpture terrace.

Park Güell

ⓘ *C Olot 7, T93-130 488. Nov-Feb daily 1000-1800; Mar and Oct 1000-1900; Apr and Sep 1000-2000; May-Aug 1000-2100. Free. Metro Lesseps, then a (signposted) 10-min walk, or bus 24.*

Whimsical Park Güell is perhaps the most delightful of Gaudí's visionary creations. Two fairytale pavilions

MNAC

Parc Güell

European City Breaks Barcelona

guard the entrance (one houses an exhibition, T93-285 68 99, Mon-Fri 1100-1500, €2), from where stairs sweep up past the famous multi-coloured salamander which has become one of Barcelona's best-known and best-loved symbols. The steps culminate in the **Sala Hipóstila**, also known as the Hall of a Hundred Columns because of the thick Doric columns which support its undulating roof. Gaudí's talented collaborator, the architect and mosaicist Josep Maria Jujol, was given free reign to colour the vaulted ceiling with elaborate whimsy; look carefully and you'll see the designs are made of smashed china, ceramic dolls' heads, wine glasses and old bottles. Above the hall is the main square with its snaking bench, thickly encrusted with *trencadís*, like the scales of a monstrous dragon. Surrounding it are porticoes and viaducts, made from unworked stone, which hug the slopes of the hillside for more than 3 km.

Just off the main esplanade is the **Casa Museu Gaudí** (T93-219 38 11, €4), housed in the small Torre Rosa, Gaudí's home for the last years of his life.

Playa Barceloneta

Frank Gehry's fish

Seafront

ⓘ *Metro Barceloneta/Ciutadella-Vila Olímpica*

Barcelona's seafront was the main focus of Olympic redevelopment in the early 1990s. A boardwalk runs from the foot of the Ramblas to the glittering **Port Vell** (Old Port) development which includes a marina, restaurants, shopping centre, IMAX and the impressive **Aquàrium** (€13). To the northeast is the old fishermen's neighbourhood of **Barceloneta**, a district of narrow streets and traditional seafood bars. From here the **Telèferic** (€9) begins its vertiginous journey over the harbour to Montjuïc. Beyond Barceloneta stretch the city's beaches, not especially lovely, but always packed in summer. They edge past the brash, glistening marina and leisure complex at the **Port Olímpic**, marked by Frank Gehry's shimmering copper fish. Further out is the quiet old workers' district, **Poble Nou**, site of the 2004 **Universal Forum of Cultures.**

Sleeping

Barcelona is one of the most popular weekend destinations in Europe and, although the number of beds has increased dramatically, you should always book as early as possible and never just turn up and hope to find somewhere to stay. Book through an agent or check out online deals at www.barcelonahotels.com and www.barcelona-on-line.com.

Most of the cheaper places are in the Old City (Barri Gòtic, La Ribera and El Raval); these are also the noisiest places to stay. The smartest (and quietest) places are generally concentrated in the Eixample. Hotels are ranked with one to five stars; *pensiones* have fewer facilities and are ranked with one to three stars. Note that a modest hotel may be known as a *'hostal'*; this is not the same as a 'hostel', which will have dormitory accommodation.

€€€ **Arts Barcelona**, C Marina 19-21, Vila Olímpica, T93-221 10 00, www.ritzcarlton.com. Metro Ciutadella-Vila Olímpica. One of the city's most glamorous hotels, the **Arts** occupies one of the enormous glassy towers at the entrance to the Port Olímpic. It was inaugurated in 1992 and offers 33 floors of unbridled luxury, including indoor and outdoor pools, a fine restaurant, a piano bar overlooking the hotel gardens and the sea, a sauna, a gym and a beauty centre.

€€€-€€ **Prestige**, Passeig de Gràcia 62, Eixample, T93-272 41 80, www.prestigepaseodegracia.com. Metro Passeig de Gràcia. An ultra-stylish hotel in a perfect location. The building dates from the 1930s, but the interior is the epitome of chic, minimalist design. High-quality fittings include Bang and Olufsen TVs and music systems, a free minibar and crisp white furnishings. Facilities include 24-hr room service, a gym and beauty centre, an oriental garden and a futuristic library full of the latest glossy coffee-table books.

€€ **Actual**, C Rosselló 238, Eixample, T93-552 05 50, www.hotelactual.com. Metro Diagonal. On the same block as La Pedrera, *Actual* is decorated in the slickest minimalist style, with plenty of white marble and dark wood. The rooms are small but impeccably furnished with crisp white fabrics and ultra-modern bathrooms. It also offers triple rooms, perfect for families. There are often special offers on its website.

€€ **Banys Orientals**, C Argentería 37, La Ribera, T93-269 84 90, www.hotelbanysorientals.com. Metro Jaume I. A chic boutique-style hotel close to the Museu Picasso. Rooms are a little small, but are furnished with sleek modern fabrics.

€€-€ **Hostal Palacios**, Rambla de Catalunya 27, Eixample, T93-301 30 79, www.hostalpalacios.com. Metro Passeig de Gràcia. A lovely *hostal* with just a handful of rooms in a restored Modernista building. You'll find original floor tiles, carved wooden doors and a comfortable lounge with internet access and a piano. Bedrooms retain Modernista mouldings, while bathrooms are modern and pristine.

€ **Gat Raval**, C Joaquín Costa 44, El Raval, T93-481 66 70, www.gat accommodation.com. Metro Universitat. A hip *hostal* painted in black, white and lime green on one of the Raval's funkiest streets. The modern rooms are bright, clean and well equipped.

€ **Peninsular**, C de Sant Pau 34-36, El Raval, T93-302 31 38. Metro Liceu. One of the best-value options is set in an old convent. There's a charming interior patio crammed with trailing plants and Modernista detailing. The rooms are plain and basic but perfectly comfortable.

Eating

Catalan dishes are simple and rely on fresh local ingredients. Meat and fish are often grilled or cooked slowly in the oven (*al horno*). There are some delicious vegetable dishes, like *escalivada*, a salad of roasted aubergine, peppers and onions. Rice dishes are also popular. Wash it all down with Catalan wine, sparkling cava or local Estrella beer.

Breakfast is usually a milky coffee (*café amb llet/café con leche*) and a pastry. Lunch is taken seriously and eaten at around 1400, when many restaurants offer a fixed-price 2-course menu including a drink. Tapas are not as much of a tradition here as in other parts of Spain, but there are plenty of old-fashioned bars near the harbour that offer fresh seafood tapas. Dinner is rarely eaten before 2100 and tends to be lighter than the midday meal.

Breakfast

El Café de l'Òpera, Las Ramblas 74. Metro Liceu. Opposite the Liceu Opera House, this is the perfect café for people-watching. Original Modernista fittings and an old-world ambience.

La Pallaresa, C Petritxol 11, Barri Gòtic. Metro Liceu. This is where to get your *chocolate con churros* (thick hot chocolate with fried dough strips) in the morning – locals swear it's the best *xocolatería* in the city.

Lunch

¶¶¶ L'Olivé, C Balmes 47, Eixample, T93-452 19 90. Metro Hospital Clínic. A popular, lively restaurant serving traditional Catalan dishes, using the freshest market produce. Try *rap amb all cremat* (monkfish with roast garlic).

¶¶ Sal, Passeig Marítim s/n, Barceloneta, T93-224 07 07. With a fantastic beachside location, this trendy restaurant and bar serves excellent contemporary Mediterranean fare. The grilled sardines are fabulous, and they do a great paella at lunchtimes if you book in advance.

¶ Bar Pinotxo, Mercat de la Boquería 66-67, Las Ramblas, closed Sun. Metro Liceu. The best-loved counter bar in the market, serving excellent, freshly prepared food; don't miss the tortilla with artichokes.

¶ Pla dels Àngels, C Ferlandina 23, El Raval, T93-329 40 47. Metro Universitat. This large, popular restaurant opposite MACBA has bright, modern decor and a summer terrace. It serves extremely well-priced salads, meats and pastas, plus excellent wine.

Dinner

¶¶¶ Beltxenea, C Mallorca 275, Eixample, T93-215 30 24. Closed Sun. Metro Diagonal. A grand restaurant with a romantic terrace overlooking an immaculately manicured garden. The cuisine is as magnificent as the surroundings, featuring Basque classics like *merluza koskera a la vasca* (hake cheeks simmered with clams and parsley). A real treat.

¶ Cal Pep, Plaça Olles 8, La Ribera. Metro Barceloneta. A classic: there's a smart, brick-lined restaurant at the back, but it's more entertaining to stand at the bar as Pep grills fish and steaks and holds court at the same time. The house cava is excellent.

¶ Lacharale, c/d'Ataülf 5, Barri Gòtic, T93-310 69 43. Tucked away down a tiny street behind the Ayuntamiento (City Hall), this is hard to find but well worth the effort. The menu is short and simple. Try the delicious salads, grilled prawns in garlic or the tasty stir-fries.

❝❞ This style-obsessed city has a staggering number of ultra-hip bars and clubs playing the latest dance music

◉ Nightlife

To find out what's on, check the listings guide *Guía del Ocio*, *B-Guided* magazine or look out for flyers. Up-to-date information is also provided at www.bcn.es.

Bars and clubs

Barcelona is a popular stop on the international DJ circuit, with cutting-edge clubs (*discotecas*) playing the very latest tunes. Some of the best clubs can be found on **Calle Nou de Francesc** in the Barri Gòtic and along the painfully hip **Passeig del Born** in La Ribera. There are also several excellent bars in the Ciutat Vella, where you can enjoy a mellow *copa* on a candlelit terrace. **El Raval** has a concentration of funky bohemian clubs as well as louche bars where you can sip absinthe in timeless surroundings. Bigger clubs, catering for the frenetic summer party crowd, can be found on **Montjuïc** and around the Port Olímpic, while gay clubs are clustered in the so-called '*Gaixample*', east of Passeig del Gràcia.

Contemporary music

There are plenty of live music venue. Popular clubs like **Jamboree** (Plaça Reial 17, Barri Gòtic) and **Luz de Gas** (Muntaner 246, Gràcia) offer a real mixed bag of musical styles. Check out the **Harlem Jazz Club** (Comtessa de Sobradiel 8, Barri Gòtic) for a taste of the city's excellent jazz scene. Latin and African music is also popular.

For lovers of electronica, the **Sónar** (www.sonar.es) summer festival of multimedia music and art is fantastic. The **BAM** festival in Sep is another great time to catch some alternative sounds.

Classical music and theatre

Enjoy a night at the opera at the beautiful **Gran Teatre de Liceu** (p34) or a rousing performance by the Orfeó Català in the stunning Modernista surroundings of the **Palau de la Música**, C Sant Francesc de Paula 2, Sant Pere, T93-295 72 00, www.palaumusica.org. **Ciutat del Teatre**, Plaça Margarida Xirgu, Montjuïc, T93-227 39 00, www.diba.es/iteatre, metro Espanya, encompasses several drama and dance performance spaces and a theatre museum. Performing arts fill the city in Jun and Jul for the renowned **Festival de Barcelona Grec** (www.barcelonafestival.com).

Belfast burgeons in a way that would have been the stuff of science fiction not too long ago. From a place of deserted, burnt-out and frightening streets to a busy metropolis and hub of culture and hedonism, the city has undergone a transformation in the last decade that beggars belief. The dour Victorian edifices which once loomed over the city are now chic, post modern hotels, trendy bars and temples to consumerism. The murals, which once screamed out the pain and sectarianism of the city's underclass, are now beautifully-maintained works of aesthetic/political significance that feature as stops on visitors' itineraries. No one is more surprised at this turnaround than the people of Belfast themselves. They stand back and wonder as the budget airlines put their city on the tourist map rather than the political one.

Arts & culture
★★

Eating
★★★★

Nightlife
★★★

Outdoors
★★

Romance
★

Shopping
★

Sightseeing
★★

Value for money
★★★★

Overall score
★★✦

⊙ Sights

City centre

Belfast's central streets are a series of wide boulevards lined with grand Victorian buildings. At its heart is **Donegall Square** and in particular the **City Hall** ⓘ *T028-9027 0456, tours Jun-Sep Mon-Fri 1100, 1400, 1500, Sat 1430; Oct-May Mon-Fri 1100, 1430, Sat 1430, free,* a working administrative building and a pompous Victorian testament to what money can build. Completed in 1906, the Portland stone edifice, designed by Brumwell Thomas and covering 1½ acres, is topped by a copper dome 173 ft high.

Northeast of City Hall and close to the river is another cluster of late 19th-century constructions, most notably the now beautifully restored and stabilized **Albert Clocktower**. Built in 1865-9, it leaned a little more with

Crown Liquor Saloon

every year that passed and as early as 1879 had to have several bits chopped off to prevent them bringing the whole thing down.

Close by, on Great Victoria Street, is the beautiful **Crown Liquor Saloon**, a great institution, which looks like an over-the-top 1990s theme pub but is in fact the genuine Victorian article. It was built for Patrick Flanagan, a publican, in

1839 and later encased in the glorious exterior tiles you see today. (See Nightlife below.) Opposite it is the **Grand Opera House** ⓘ *box office T028-9024 1919,* designed by British theatre architect Frank Matcham and opened in 1895 as a popular variety hall. The theatre is mostly restoration work nowadays after two IRA bombs reduced it to rubble in 1991 and 1993. The best way to see it is when it is in operation. Inside is lurid red velvet, elephant head brackets and a fake renaissance painted ceiling, circa 1991.

Laganside

Entirely recreated from the derelict ruins of the city's once huge shipbuilding and shipping industries Laganside is a model of urban regeneration. Pretty riverside walks take you along the multimillion pound developments of the area, through well-designed plazas and dynamic street art. Stretched across the river is the weir making the upstream

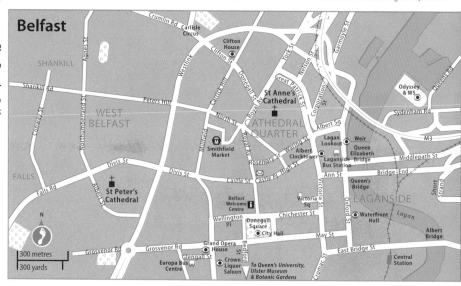

Belfast map

banks, which once looked over festering mud twice a day, a pleasant place to live and work. Part of the weir is the **Lagan Lookout** ⓘ *1 Donegall Quay, T028-9031 5444, Apr-Sep Mon- Fri 1100-1700, Sat 1200-1700, Sun 1400-1700; Oct- Mar Tue-Fri 1100-1530, Sat 1300-1630, Sun 1400-1630, £1.50*, a tiny museum charting the history of the river and the building of the weir. Walking out across the weir to look at the river and the two great cranes Samson and Goliath gives an idea of what this area must once have been. Crowning the new development is the arts venue **Waterfront Hall** ⓘ *Lanyon Pl, T028-9033 4455*, and close by is the **Odyssey Complex** with the interactive **W5** ⓘ *2 Queen's Quay, T028-9046 7700, www.w5online.co.uk, daily Mon-Fri 1000-1800, Sat and Sun 1200-1800, last admission 1700, £5.50*, a science and engineering centre aimed at families and schools. There are also lots of restaurants, cinemas and clubs in the complex.

Cathedral Quarter

Still in development, the Cathedral Quarter is taking on its own distinctive feel. The area is attracting good new restaurants, clubs, galleries and other

St Anne's Cathedral

Ulster Museum

small businesses. People took big risks with their venture capital when they moved into the empty streets and are now seeing their foresight pay off. At the centre sits the Anglican **St Anne's Cathedral** in a modern little park, one of the few churches in the city open to the public daily. To the north, **Clifton House** ⓘ *Carlisle Circus, T028-9033 4201, www.cliftonbelfast. org.uk*, was built in 1774 as a poor house. It is still in service today as sheltered housing for the elderly. An exhibition of the building's history can be viewed by appointment.

Golden Mile and Queen's University

The traditional centre of tourism in the city, the area around the Queen's University, has always been home to the liveliest nightlife thanks to its huge population of students. This is the area where most visitors stay and eat. The **Ulster Museum** ⓘ *Mon-Fri, 1000-1700, Sat 1300-1700, Sun, 1400-1700, free, exhibitions change regularly*, offers a thoughtful afternoon and the **Botanic Gardens** ⓘ *Apr-Sep Mon-Fri 1000-1700, Sat, Sun, bank holidays, 1400-1600;*

Oct-Mar Mon-Fri 1000-1600, closed 1300-1400, free, a quiet retreat. The **university** ⓘ *University Rd, T028-9033 5252*, itself hosts many events and, while it isn't Trinity College, Dublin, offers an hour's stroll around the grounds.

West Belfast

West Belfast was a working-class area which developed around the linen industry – an area where sectarian violence created two entirely separate communities as far back as the late 19th century: the Catholic Falls and the Protestant Shankill. When the Troubles started in 1969, West Belfast, separated from the city centre by the Westlink motorway, became a battleground. The **Falls Road**, **Crumlin Road**, **Divis Street**, the **Shankill** are names that ring of riot, burning, assassination and mayhem. However, now a nervous peace dominates the small council estates and Victorian terraces of the area. This is the place no visitor should leave the city without visiting. Bus tours and black taxi tours make the visit easy but it is possible to walk the length of the Falls Road and the Shankill Road and visit all the things to see.

European City Breaks Belfast

⊕ Travel essentials

Getting there **Belfast International Airport**, at Aldergrove, T028-9448 4848, www.belfastairport.com, is 19 miles (30 km) west of the city. From outside the airport, **Airbus 300**, T028-9033 3000, www.translink.co.uk, runs to the Europa and Laganside bus stations every 30 mins, hourly on Sun. Cost is around £6 for a single, £9 return. Taxis go from beside the bus stop and cost around £24. **Belfast City Airport**, T028-9093 9093, www.belfastcityairport.com, is 3 miles (5 km) northeast of the city. A direct bus service travels from the airport to the

Europa Bus Centre every 40 mins 0600-2150 Mon-Sat, hourly on Sun. **Citybus** 21 runs from Sydenham, near the airport, to City Hall. Sydenham Halt rail station is nearby and will connect with Central Station. Taxis from City airport cost around £7.

Getting around The city centre is easily manageable on foot unless you want to explore West Belfast, in which case you might prefer to take a tour of the area in a black cab. There are taxi stands outside the Europa bus station, and in Donegall Sq, Smithfield market

and North St. The Smithfield market taxis travel into Catholic West Belfast, taking several passengers at a time for about £1 per passenger, while the North St taxis travel to Protestant West Belfast. The Donegall Sq and Europa bus station taxis have a starting price of £1.50 and do not wait to load up with passengers first. **West Belfast Taxi Tours**, 5-7 Conway St, T028-9031 5777.

Tourist information Belfast Welcome Centre, 47 Donegall Pl, T028-9024 6609, www.gotobelfast.com.

⊕ Sleeping

€€€ **Belfast Hilton**, 4 Lanyon Pl, T028-9027 7000, www.hilton.co.uk/belfast. If you can possibly afford it – stay here. It is a masterpiece of modernity in a sea of pompous Victoriana. Discounts at weekends and serves a good breakfast.

€€€ **Ten Square**, 10 Donegall Sq East, T028-9024 1001, www.tensquare.co.uk. Very classy hotel in beautiful old bank buildings beside City Hall. Deep colours and lots of attention to detail.

€€ **Malmaison Belfast**, 34-38 Victoria St, T028-9022 0200, www.malmaison-belfast.com. Sexy black, cream and burgundy decor in beautiful old warehouse buildings. Broadband, cable TV and DVD players.

€€ **Crescent Townhouse**, 13 Lower Cres, T028-9032 3349, www.crescent townhouse.com. A small hotel with large, attractively appointed rooms set in the centre of the Golden Mile.

€€-€ **Benedicts of Belfast**, 7-21 Bradbury Pl, Shaftesbury Sq, T028-9059 1999, www.benedictshotel.co.uk. Vaguely Gothic decor in this central hotel with big rooms that represents excellent value for money.

⊕ Eating

⫴ **Restaurant Michael Deane's**, 38 Howard St, T028-9056 0000. The place to be seen in Belfast. Reservations well in advance. Great for a special occasion.

⫴ **Roscoff Brasserie**, 7-11 Linenhall St, T028-9031 1150. TV chef Paul Rankin's newest effort. French brasserie cuisine, white tablecloths, sophisticated and efficient atmosphere, masterly food.

⫴ **The Errigle Inn**, 312-320 Ormeau Rd, T028-9064 1410. A labyrinth of bars whose Tom McGurran bar can claim a Michelin star for its ludicrously underpriced gastropub-style food.

⫴ **Tedford's**, 5 Donegall Quay, T028-9043 4000. An established fish restaurant close to the Waterfront, with Asian overtones in what was once an old ship's chandler shop.

⫴ **Irene and Nan's**, 12 Brunswick St, T028-9023 9123. A very trendy café/bar at night but during the day and early evening offers some great food. Try the early evening 2- or 3-course set menus which barely get up into double figures plus laughably inexpensive wine list.

⊕ Nightlife

Belfast has excellent pubs, especially in some of the little 'entries' (alleyways) which line the main thoroughfares of the centre. Some are all etched glass and mahogany panels, folksy and ancient; the **Crown Liquor Saloon**, 46 Great Victoria St, T028-9024 9476, being the most famous example. Many of them offer live music: **Maddens**, Berry St, T028-9024 4114 and **White's Tavern**, Winecellar Entry, T028-9024 3080. The last few years have seen a burgeoning of ultra-cool, minimalist, steel and glass style bars where cash-rich, time-poor Belfast white collar workers eat, drink and chill out. These are predominantly in the city centre and the Cathedral Quarter but there are neat places outside the centre especially in the Lisburn Road and around the university.

Most of the city's clubs are above pubs in the **Golden Mile**. They go in and out of fashion and get regular makeovers. The **Cathedral Quarter** is also a place to keep an eye on. The best place to look for what is on and where is in the free *The Big List*.

The capital of Germany since 1999, Berlin is a city reborn – a phoenix risen from the flames of Second World War destruction and Cold War division. Arguably the hippest European capital, it attracts some of the most progressive fashionistas, artists and musicians from all over the world. The city may have needed a long period in rehab but it is now confident enough to woo British architects, Italian designers and Polish restorers to its burgeoning multinational community. These days Babylonian mosaics, French bakeries and Norman Foster creations are comfortably integrated into the buildings of Schinkel and the operas of Wagner. Anything goes in Berlin, from illegal parties held in derelict cellars underneath the city to open air music on the banks of the Spree.

Berlin

Arts & culture
★★★★★

Eating
★★★

Nightlife
★★★★★

Outdoors
★★

Romance
★★

Shopping
★★★

Sightseeing
★★★★

Value for money
★★★

Overall score
★★★★⯪

45

At a glance

Mitte, former bohemian hub of East Berlin, is now the heart of the reunified capital and, along with its more conservative West Berlin neighbour, **Tiergarten**, is the focus of most visitors' attention. Here, the **Brandenburg Gate** and the **Reichstag** stand amid a rash of new government buildings and sprawling acres of woodland, grass and lakes, making it clear that Berlin is, once again, the capital of Germany. **Friedrichstrasse** is the main artery dividing the eastern and western halves of the city. About 15 minutes walk east lies **Museum Island**, where you will find the city's most important museums, while **Potsdamer Platz**, south of the Brandenburg Gate, shows off Berlin's ultra-modern colours. Northeast of Mitte, **Prenzlauerberg** has become *the* hip place to live and play since the Wall came down. **Friedrichshain**, east of Mitte, is less attractive but still on the up. **Kreuzberg**, south of Mitte in what was West Berlin, has a large Turkish

I am so homesick for the Kurfürstendamm, for Berlin's tempo, verve and ballyhoo.

Hildegard Knef (German singer and actress)

community and, like its more chi chi neighbour **Schöneberg** to the west, is still a centre for the gay community. To the west of Tiergarten, **Charlottenburg**, once a showcase of capitalism, now has to compete with Mitte and Prenzlauerberg.

★ *Don't leave town without a trip up the Television Tower in Alexander Platz: go just before sunset to see the best of Berlin by day and by night.*

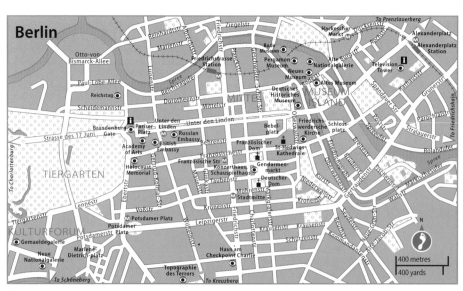

24 hours in the city

Reichstag

Visit the **Reichstag** first thing (it's open 0800-2400) and climb up to the cupola for the views. Then head for the **Adlon Hotel** for coffee, pausing to reflect at the **Brandenburg Gate**. Afterwards, head east along Unter den Linden as far as Bebelplatz (where the 1933 book burnings took place) and cross the road to spend an hour or two in the newly restored **Deutsches Historisches Museum**. Cross the river on to Museum Island and visit the outstanding **Pergamon Museum**, before having a late lunch. (Try the tasty snacks from the riverside sausage stands.) Walk through the Lustgarten, across the Schlossplatz and then cross the river again, continuing west to the **Gendarmenmarkt**, where there may be an afternoon concert in one of the cathedrals. On nearby **Friedrichstrasse**, with its stylish shops, is the museum commemorating **Checkpoint Charlie**. From here, following the fragment of the Wall west, it is possible to reach the futuristic-looking **Potsdamer Platz** for a spot of dinner. Later, take a tour of the über-chic bars and cafés around **Mitte**.

⊖ Travel essentials

Berlin has 2 main airports and the website www.berlin-airport.de covers both. **Tegel (Berlin International) Airport** is 8 km northwest of the centre. Buses No X9 (20 mins to Zoo) and No 109 (30 mins to Zoo) pass most of the hotels. No 128 is better for those heading north or east. All pass many U-Bahn stations en route but the U-Bahn itself does not serve Tegel. The TXL express bus goes to Mitte. A 1-way ticket costs €2.10. Taxis are plentiful and will cost about €20 to Zoo Station or €30 to Mitte. A tip of 5-10% is normal. **Schönefeld (Berlin-Brandenburg) Airport** currently has rather tortuous links to the city. A shuttle bus links the terminal with the S-Bahn station Schönefeld on the main line to the east. Trains into town take about 40 mins. Some 8 bus routes link the airport with southern and eastern Berlin. The No 171 goes to Rudow (U7), from where you can connect with the underground. There are also 2 night buses and a nighttime S-Bahn service on this route. A taxi to Friedrichstrasse costs €40. From 2007 there will be an express train to the city centre.

Getting around The city is divided into 3 travel zones: A, B, and C. You are only likely to visit zone C if going to Potsdam. A single ticket valid for any number of journeys within 2 hrs costs €2.10. Day passes for zones A and B combined cost €6.10. Tickets and passes are available at the Tegel Airport office, at the BVG enquiry centre outside Zoo Station (www.bvg.de) and from machines on all station platforms. **Buses** run day and night throughout the city, with timetables shown at every bus stop. **Bus 100** is a favourite route and links most of the major sights in the centre. **Taxis** are plentiful. There are ranks at most U-Bahn and S-Bahn stations in the suburbs or they can be hailed in the city centre. Prices start at around €2, with a charge of around €1 per km. The extensive and speedy urban rail system consists of **U-Bahn** (underground) and **S-Bahn** (overground) services, with stations throughout the city. The S-Bahn goes as far as Potsdam in the west and Schönefeld Airport in the southeast. Both services operate at night.

Tourist information Berlin Tourist Information, T030-250025, www.berlin-tourist-information.de, has offices in the Europa-Center at Budapesterstr 45, 1 Nov-31 Mar Mon-Sat 1000-1900, Sun 1000-1800; at the Brandenburg Gate, 1 Nov-31 Mar, daily 1000-1800; and at the Television Tower at Alexanderplatz, 1 Nov-31 Mar, daily 1000-1800. All offices have extended opening hours from 1 Apr-31 Oct. **New Berlin Tours**, www.newberlintours.com, offers excellent free tours of the city.

⊚ Sights

Brandenburg Gate
ⓘ *S-Bahn Unter den Linden.*

Built in 1791, Berlin's most famous icon has witnessed the highs and lows of German history. Left isolated by the construction of the Berlin Wall in 1961, the gate became the emblematic backdrop to that epoch-altering event on 9 November 1989 when the border was opened and young people from both sides of the city rushed forward to scale the defining symbol of the Cold War.

On the east side of the gate, **Pariser Platz** has been transformed from a concrete wilderness into an elegant diplomatic and financial centre and regained its pre-war status as one of the city's most prestigious addresses. The French embassy has been rebuilt on the north side, while, opposite, is the newly reopened **Academy of Arts** ⓘ *Pariser Platz 4, www.adk.de.* This Günther Behnisch building houses the private archives of cultural greats such as Bertolt Brecht and Günter Grass, as well as promoting German arts through

Pariser Platz

Holocaust Memorial

exhibitions and performances. Next to the Academy is the unmissable **DZ bank building**, designed by Frank Gehry. Inside is an enormous sculpture whose twists and turns provide a startling, incongruous contrast with the bank's façade.

South of Pariser Platz, 150 m from the Brandenburg Gate, is the **Memorial to the murdered Jews** ⓘ *Wilhelmstr 22, 23, information centre Tue-Sun 1000-2000 (last entrance 1915).* Completed in May 2005, this 'forest of stelae', represents the gravestones of Jews murdered under the Nazi regime. It initially provoked much controversy due to its bleak design and the exclusion of graves for non-Jewish victims. However, the memorial, designed by Peter Eisenman, now elicits a positive response from most Berliners.

Reichstag
ⓘ *Ebertstr. Daily 0800-2400 (last entry 2200). Free. S-Bahn Unter den Linden.*

The imposing late-19th century Reichstag building has been restored to its former glory and is once again at the heart of German political life, as well as

being open to the public. The undoubted highlight is Norman Foster's outlandish glass dome. The views from the top are not to be missed, though the long queues certainly are (get there early or visit at night to avoid them). The Reichstag is one of many government buildings along the Spree and backs onto **Tiergarten Park**. This area has seen more redevelopment than most but, despite pressure from developers, the park's wide open spaces, lakes and woods have not been compromised. North of Tiergarten is **Hamburg Station-Museum for the Present** ⓘ *Invalidenstr 50, www.smb.spk-berlin.de, Tue-Fri, Sun 1000-1800, Sat 1100-2000, Sun 1100-1800, €8, S-Bahn Lehrter Bahnhof.* Trains stopped running here in the 19th century, replaced in the late 1980s by a series of challenging art, including works by Joseph Beuys.

Potsdamer Platz
ⓘ *S-Bahn Potsdamer Platz.*

Once as desolate as Pariser Platz due to its proximity to the Wall, **Potsdamer Platz**, at the southeastern corner of Tiergarten park, is now almost a town in

Potsdamer Platz

ts own right; a new Manhattan of skyscrapers, cinemas, embassies and museums. Just to the west lies the **Kulturforum**, which encompasses not only the **Berlin Philharmonie** but also one of the world's most prestigious art collections at the **Gemäldegallerie** ⓘ *www.smb.spk-berlin.de, Tue, Wed, Fri-Sun 1000-1800, Thu 1000-2200 , €8,* and international and German paintings from the 20th century at the **Neue Nationalgalerie** ⓘ *www.smb.spk-berlin.de, Tue, Wed, Fri 1000-1800, Thu 1000-2200, Sat, Sun 1100-1800, €8.*

Unter den Linden

ⓘ *S-Bahn Unter den Linden.*

Unter den Linden ('Beneath the Lime Trees') runs eastwards from the Brandenburg Gate and Pariser Platz, the trees in the centre now making a congenial pedestrian precinct between the two wide traffic lanes on either side. On the south side stands the **Russian Embassy**, an excellent example of social realism but now a tad incongruous in a Berlin eager to forget its links with the former USSR. At the eastern end of Unter den Linden is the revamped **Deutsches Historisches**

Unter den Linden

Gendarmenmarkt

Museum ⓘ *www.dhm.de, daily 1000-1800, €2, U Bahn Französischestr.* Completed in 2004/2005 and housed over three floors, the museum will open its permanent exhibition in 2006. In the meantime there are usually three temporary exhibitions held in the wing designed by I M Pei.

Gendarmenmarkt

ⓘ *U-Bahn Stadtmitte*

If there is still a tendency to judge Germany by the worst periods of its history, a stop in **Gendarmenmarkt** will show the country at its most liberal. It became the centre of a French community around 1700 when Prussia gave refuge to 6000 Huguenots. On the north side, the **Französischer Dom** ('French Cathedral'), now home to the **Huguenot Museum** ⓘ *1200-1700 Tue-Sat, 1100-1700 Sun, €2,* dates from this time, as does the similarly proportioned **Deutscher Dom** ⓘ *1000-2000 Tue, 1000-1800 Wed-Sun,* on the south side. The **Konzerthaus** or Schauspielhaus in the centre of the square was one of the earliest

buildings designed by the prolific architect, Karl Friedrich Schinkel (1781-1841).

Museum Island

ⓘ *Bode Museum, Neues Museum, Altes Museum, Pergamon Museum, Alte Nationalgalerie, www.smb.spk-berlin.de. Tue-Sun 1000-1800, Thu till 2200, €6 but free the first Sun in the month. S-Bahn Hackescher Markt.*

Museum Island is an extraordinary collection of first-rate galleries in the middle of the Spree. The **Altes Museum**, designed by Schinkel and considered his finest work, exhibits classical works, concentrating on ancient Greece but going back to the Etruscans as well. The **Pergamon Museum** houses one of the world's great archaeological collections, with entire complexes on display that are dramatically lit at night. The second century BC Pergamon Altar and the Babylonian Street are the stars of the show. The **Alte Nationalgalerie** is a collection of 250 paintings brought together by the banker Joachim Wagener. Now most of Berlin's 19th-century art is displayed here.

Pergamon Museum

Alexanderplatz

ⓘ *S/U-Bahn Alexanderplatz.*

East of the museums, 'Alex' has, in an architectural sense, stood still for over 30 years, a time-warped legacy of old East Berlin. In the early 1970s, the best that the town could offer was here on a vast pedestrian precinct. The 365 m **Television Tower** ⓘ *www.berliner fernsehturm.de, Mar-Oct 0900-2400; Nov-Feb 1000-2400, €7.50,* completed the image of a modern town centre. The **Weltzeituhr** (World Clock) has always been a convenient meeting point, although when it was built in 1969, it was seen by some East Berliners as a cruel reminder of all the places they could not visit.

Charlottenberg

ⓘ *S/U-Bahn Zoologischer Garten, U-Bahn Richard-Wagner Platz or Sophie-Charlotte Platz.*

Charlottenburg has lost much of its cachet since reunification but still boasts many of the institutions that made West Berlin famous. First among these is the iconic **Gedächtniskirche** (Memorial Church) ⓘ *Breitscheidplatz, daily*

Alexanderplatz

Price: £4.99
ISBN: 1 903471 57 5
www.footprintbooks.com

0900-1900 for the church, Mon-Sat 1000-1600 for the exhibition, built shortly after the death of Kaiser Wilhelm in 1888 and largely destroyed by an air-raid in 1943. Lavish **Schloss Charlottenburg** (Charlottenburg Palace) ⓘ *Tue-Sun 1000-1700, €7,* is a one-stop shop for two centuries of German architecture from 1700 to 1900. It was built as a summer residence for Queen Charlotte (1669-1705) by her husband Friedrich I (1657-1713) and was expanded into its present baroque and rococo form in 1701 when Friedrich crowned himself King of Prussia. On a similarly massive scale was the recent renovation work carried out (at a cost of €242 million) on Hitler's **Olympiastadion**, a few kilometres northwest, in readiness for the 2006 World Cup Finals.

Kreuzberg

ⓘ *U-Bahn Hallesches Tor, Koch Str, Kottbusser Tor.*

Once a haven of alternative living, before everyone moved to Prenzlauerberg, Kreuzberg is now home to a large Turkish community, as well as some of the city's most moving and disturbing

◉ Best of the rest

The Story of Berlin ⓘ *Kurfürsten-damm 207, www.story-of-berlin.de. Daily 1000- 2000 last admission at 1800. €9.30.* Brings the city's eventful past to life. Don't miss the tour of the nuclear shelter, a completely sealed off underground town.
Molecule Man Sculpture ⓘ *Treptower Park, by the banks of the Spree, S-Bahn Treptower Park.* Arresting 100 ft aluminium sculpture designed in 1997 for the Allianz Corporation.
East Side Gallery ⓘ *Running along Mühlenstr to Warschauerstr, www.eastsidegallery.com. U-Bahn Warschauer Str.* One of the last remaining stretches of the Wall is decorated with street art to form arguably one of the most historical galleries in Germany.
Sans Souci ⓘ *Tue-Sun 0900-1700, €8, S-Bahn Potsdamer Hauptbahnhof, then bus 695.* Frederick the Great's summer pleasure palace.

sights. Nazi crimes are detailed at the open-air **Topographie des Terrors** ⓘ *Niederkirchnerstr, www.topo graphie.de, daily 1000-1800, free,* while the **Haus am Checkpoint Charlie** ⓘ *Friedrichstr 43-45, www.mauer-museum.com, daily 0900-2200, €7,* documents East Berliners' desperate attempts to cross the border. The powerful, innovative **Jüdisches Museum** ⓘ *Lindenstr 9-14, www.jm berlin.de, Mon 1000-2200, Tue-Sun 1000-2000, €5,* presents 2000 years of German-Jewish history, including a harrowing section on the Holocaust.

Berlin's big gay pride

Berlin has welcomed the gay scene since the 'roaring twenties' when Marlene Dietrich and Christopher Isherwood lived and entertained around **Nollendorfplatz** in **Schöneberg**. Hitler's rise to power in 1933 and his deportation of gay people to the camps put a stop to this (outside Nollendorfplatz U-Bahn station there is a plaque to commemorate the victims). However, now with an openly gay mayor of Berlin, the gay and lesbian scene is more vibrant than ever. Some areas are more gay than others, but around the centre it's all quite mixed, with lots of bars and clubs catering to a gay and straight crowd. **Kreuzberg** has a very liberal feel to it, whereas Nollendorfplatz is more hardcore. **Friedrichshain** and **Prenzlauerberg** are the new kids on the on the block and, as a result, have quite an experimental feel to them. **Christopher Street Day**, www.csd-berlin.de, which takes place every July, is the most flamboyant festival in Berlin. Loud and outrageous, this gay and lesbian parade was named after the New York Stonewall riots of 1969 and is not one for the fainthearted.

● Sleeping

Berlin has a good selection of accommodation. Its more upmarket hotels are often large, modern affairs at the forefront of contemporary design. There are also many traditional pensions, particularly on and around the Kurfürstendamm in Tiergarten and Charlottenburg. Mitte and Prenzlauerberg have some first rate arty and individual hotels.

€€€ **Adlon**, Unter den Linden 77, T030-22610, www.hotel-adlon.de. Beside the Brandenburg Gate, the Adlon is not discreet but that doesn't seem to deter a regular turnover of celebrities. They follow in hallowed footsteps: Albert Einstein, Charlie Chaplin and Theodore Roosevelt all stayed here. The current building is a replica of the original: opulent and showy but also impressively stylish.

€€€ **Grand Hyatt**, Marlene-Dietrich-Platz, T030-2553 1234, www.berlin.grand.hyatt.com. S/U-Bahn Potsdamer Platz, U-Bahn Mendelssohn-Bartholdy-Park. A superb combination of Oriental and Bauhaus deluxe minimalism, the angular lines of Potsdamer Platz itself are continued into the interior of this top class hotel. More useful and personal design minutiae are everywhere and on Sun you don't have to check out until 1800.

€€ **Hotel Art Nouveau**, Leibnizstr. 59, Charlottenburg, T030-3277 440, www.hotelartnouveau.de. U-Bahn Adenauerplatz. A friendly and helpful fourth floor hotel in a restored art nouveau building with contemporary touches. There's a buffet breakfast and an 'honesty bar'.

€€ **Ku'Damm 101**, Kurfürstendamm 101, Charlottenburg, T030-5200 550, www.kudamm101.com. U-Bahn Adenauerplatz. This bold hotel opened in January 2003 and makes a good out-of-centre base. Its minimalist take on vaguely '50s and '70s themes involves curves: lots of them. Even the buffet breakfast (on the 7th floor with spectacular views) is visually striking.

€ **Circus Hostels**, Rosa-Luxemburg-Str 39-41 and Weinbergsweg 1a, T030-2839 1433, www.circus-berlin.de. U-Bahn Rosa-Luxemburg-Platz and Rosenthaler Platz. Very popular hostel, for a good reason. Much smarter and cleaner than most backpacker hostels and both in perfect locations.

€ **mitArt Pension**, Friedrichstr 127, T030-2839 0430. U-Bahn Oranienburger Tor. Still primarily a gallery, this friendly and memorably stylish hotel exhibits works of art suspended from the ceiling. Service is personal, breakfast is copious and delicious and the rooms are homely.

🍴 Eating

In no other German city can you eat as well, or as internationally, as in Berlin. There are now many great restaurants and, though often pricey, they are on the whole very good value for money. As well as international cuisine, there are lots of traditional German restaurants serving generous portions of heavy but extremely tasty food.

Breakfast

🍴 **Anna Blume**, Kollwitzstr 83, corner of Sredzkistr, T030- 4404 8749. U-Bahn Senefelderplatz. Daily 0800-0200. A restaurant/café/florist that smells divine. Try the breakfast served in 3 tiers (€12 for 2).

Lunch

🍴🍴 **Borchardt**, Französische Str 47, T030-2038 7110. U-Bahn Französische Str. Daily 1130-0100 Kitchen closes at 2400. Restaurant serving international cuisine and favoured by politicians and journalists. The interior is 18th-century and the mosaics and period-style floors make this Gerndarmenmarkt institution well worth a visit. The food is also first rate.

🍴🍴 **Restauration 1900**, Husemannstr 1, T030-442 2494, www.restauration-1900.de. U-Bahn Eberswalder Str, Senefelder Platz. Daily from 0930 (summer) 1100-2400 (winter). A local hang-out on Kollwitz Platz. Dishes include traditional German cuisine, such as pork knuckle and braised oxtail, but generally it has an global feel. At weekends a delicious and quite substantial brunch is served.

🍴 **Monsieur Vuong**, Alte Schönhauser Str 46, T030-872643. U-Bahn Rosa

Luxemburg Platz. Mon-Sat 1200-2400, Sun 1400-0200. Attracts both prominent Berliner media types and a regular young street crowd. At €6.50 for the Indochinese menu it's no wonder why.

> ❝❞ **The further east you go the more shabby-chic the bars tend to be; the further west the smarter and more elegant they become.**

Dinner

🍴🍴🍴 **Schwarzenraben**, Neue Schönhauser Str, 13, T030-2839 1698, www.schwarzenraben.de. S-Bahn Hackescher Markt, U-Bahn Weinmeisterstr. Daily 1000-2400. This former soup kitchen is now a fashionable bar and restaurant serving superb Italian food. There is a champagne bar downstairs where the elegant clientele while away a few self-indulgent hours.

🍴 **Yosoy**, Rosenthaler Str, 37, T030-2839 1213. S-Bahn Hackescher Markt, U-Bahn Weinmeisterstr. Daily from 1100. The feeling that you're in a North African souk is all pervasive when visiting this late-night haunt, where delicious tapas are served on tiled counters. A pleasant alternative to the super-smart Mitte bars.

🍴 **Schulter Junge**, corner Lychener Str and Danziger Str. U-Bahn Eberswalder Str. This restaurant is more like a real German *kneipe* or pub. The food is typically German, delicious and plentiful. Try *schnitzel* and *eierpfann-kuchen* (pancakes) with apple sauce.

🌙 Nightlife

Berlin offers some of the best nightlife in Europe: laid-back, accessible and cutting edge at the same time. The further east you go the more shabby-chic the bars tend to be; the further west the smarter and more elegant they become. You'll never be pushed for somewhere to go. Mitte has more than its fair share of suitable watering holes, with the area around **Oranierburger Str** being particularly popular with tourists. For something a bit more authentically Berlin, **Prenzlauerberg** is the place to go. From U-Bahn Rosenthaler Platz, head up Weinbergsweg into **Kastanienallee** where you'll find many hip bars and restaurants. Bars usually open at 2200 and then close when the last guest leaves.

The club scene attracts top performers, be it LTJ Bukem at **Club Casino** or Bob Dylan at the **Columbia Halle**. Berlin is also host to secret **Geheimtip parties**, part of the east-side nightlife. If you are lucky you might discover the location for favourites, such as the **Mittwochclub**, every Wed.

Berlin's classical music scene is world-renowned. The **Berlin Philharmonic Orchestra** is based at the Berliner Philharmonie Herbert-von-Karajan-Str 1, T030-2548 8132, www.berliner-philharmoniker.de, daily 0900-1800. Equally prestigious is the exquisitely restored **Staatsoper**, Unter den Linden 7, T030-2035 4555, www.staatsoper-berlin.org, where opera and ballet are performed. Unsold tickets are available for €10 before a performance.

Bilbao

In an amazingly short time, and without losing sight of its roots, the dirty industrial city of Bilbao – a name that once conjured images of rusted pig-iron – has transformed itself with huge success into an exciting, buzzy, cultural hub. The Guggenheim Museum is the undoubted flagship of this triumphant progress, a sinuous fantasy of a building. It inspires because of what it is, but also because the city had the vision to put it there. While the museum has led the turnaround, much of what is enjoyable about Bilbao already existed. Bustling bar-life, harmonious architecture, a superb eating culture and a sense of pride in being a working city. The exciting new developments, with constant improvement and beautification being carried out, can only add to those qualities.

Arts & culture
★★★

Eating
★★★★

Nightlife
★★★

Outdoors
★★★★

Romance
★★

Shopping
★

Sightseeing
★★

Value for money
★★★★

Overall score
★★★

Sights

Casco Viejo (Old Town)

Tucked into a bend in the river, Bilbao's Casco Viejo (Old Town) has something of the medina about it and evokes a cramped medieval past. Designer clothing stores occupy the ground floors where families once huddled behind the city walls, and an array of memorable bars serve up fine Spanish wine and a cavalcade of elaborate bartop snacks, from delicious *tortilla* from a generations-old family recipe, to gourmet post-modern creations that wouldn't look out of place in the Guggenheim. Most Bilbaínos live and work elsewhere in the city and the true soul of the Casco emerges from early evening, when people descend on it like bees returning to the hive, strolling the streets, listening to buskers, debating the quality of the

Casco Viejo

pintxos (snacks) in the myriad bars, and sipping drinks in the setting sun.

The parallel **Siete Calles** (Seven Streets) form the oldest part of town (**Somera** is particularly interesting), the slender spire of the graceful Gothic **Catedral de Santiago** rising from the tightly packed maze. On the waterfront

here is the **Mercado de la Ribera**, a lovely art-deco market building with over 400 stalls on three floors of fruit, vegetables, meat and fish. **Plaza Nueva**, described by Unamuno as "my cold and uniform Plaza Nueva", will appeal to lovers of symmetry. Its courtly, neoclassical arches conceal an excellent selection of restaurants and bars, serving some of the best *pintxos* in town. On Sundays there's a flea market here. On Plaza Miguel de Unamuno is **Museo Vasco** ⓘ *T944-155423, Tue-Sat 1100-1700, Sun 1100-1400, €3 (free on Thu),* housing an interesting, if higgledy-piggledy series of Basque artefacts found over the centuries. Atop a steep hill above the Casco Viejo is Bilbao's most important church, the **Basilica de Begoña** ⓘ *Metro Casco Viejo, or take the lift from C Esperanza, at street level, bear right, then turn right up C Virgen de Begoña,* home of Vizcaya's patron the Virgin of Begoña.

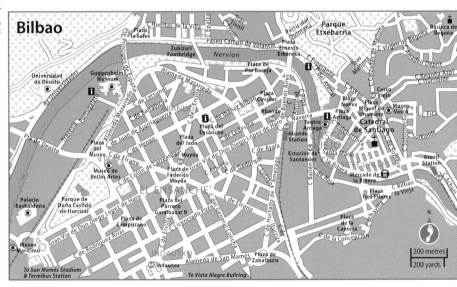

Guggenheim Museum

ⓘ *Abandoibarra Etorbidea 2, T944-359000, www.guggenheim-bilbao.es. Tue-Sun 1000-2000, Jul-Aug also Mon. €10, combined ticket with Museo de Bellas Artes €11.*

The riverbank is the obvious beneficiary of Bilbao's leap into the 21st century: Calatrava's eerily skeletal **Zubizuri footbridge** and Gehry's exuberant, shimmering Guggenheim Museum bring art and architecture together, making the Nervión river the city's axis once more. If you only take one stroll in Bilbao, make it an evening paseo from the Casco Viejo along the river to the Guggenheim, sitting like some unearthly vehicle that's just landed. It's mostly filled with temporary exhibits from the Permanent Collection of the Guggenheim Foundation.

Other riverbank sights

Further downstream the bizarre **Palacio Euskalduna**, opened in 1998 on the site of the last Bilbao shipyard, is now a major venue for concerts, particularly classical. Below it is the

Zubizuri Bridge

Bilbao

Also available

Price: £6.99
ISBN: 1 904777 79 1
www.footprintbooks.com

new **Museo Marítimo** ⓘ *Tue-Fri 1000-1400, 1600-1800, Sat-Sun 1000-1400, 1600- 2000, €7,* a salty treat that includes a number of different boats as part of its exterior exhibition.

On the right bank across the river from here is the university barrio of **Deusto**. Frequented by students, artists and agitators, the cafés and bars hum with political discussion.

El Ensanche

El Ensanche, the new town, has an elegant European feel to it. In 1876 the area across the river from the Casco Viejo was drawn up into segments. The wealth of the city is evident here, with stately banks and classy shops lining its avenues. It's divided into *barrios*; the studenty **Indautxu** is to the south, while besuited **Abando** is nearer the river. Here you'll find the recently facelifted **Museo de Bellas Artes** ⓘ *Plaza del Museo 2, T944-396060, Tue-Sat 1000-2000, Sun 1000-1400, €4.50,* more traditional than the nearby Guggenheim, as well as Bilbao's two gladiatorial arenas: **Vista Alegre** bullring and **San Mamés stadium**, home of Athletic Bilbao.

◉ Best of the rest

Getxo 20 km from the centre, Bilbao's coastal suburb has pretty old lanes and good beaches.
Museo de la Paz ⓘ *Plaza Foru 1, T946-270213. Tue-Sat 1000-1400, 1600-1900, Sun 1000-1400, no lunchtime closing Jul-Aug. €4.* Moving but positive museum in the excellent town of Gernika, Basque spiritual capital brutally bombed during the Civil War.
Lekeitio A pretty Basque fishing port with a picturesque harbour and good eating.
Mundaka A little surf village desperately seeking its lost wave, but very relaxing for a night.
Vitoria Less than an hour south is the stately Basque capital, whose **Artium** ⓘ *C Francia 24, T945-209020, www.artium.org, Tue-Sun 1100-2000, Fri-Sat -2030, €4.50,* is its own temple to the avant-garde.
Puente Vizcaya An impressive bridge at Areeta metro which zips cars and passengers to and fro via a hanging 'gondola'.

◉ Sleeping

€€ Gran Domine, Alameda Mazarredo 61, T944-253300, www.granhotel dominebilbao.com. Metro Moyúa, tram stops outside. Inspiringly designed modern hotel opposite the Guggenheim with a façade of tilted glass panels and a delightful interior.
€€ Indautxu, Pl Bombero Etxariz, T944-211198. Sister to the *Gran Domine* and has bags more character than most business-level establishments.
€€ Petit Palace Arana, C Bidebarrieta 2, T944-156411, www.hthoteles.com. With an

Travel essentials

Getting there Bilbao International Airport, T944- 869663/4 is a beautiful Santiago Calatrava-designed building 10 km northeast of the city. Buses to the centre (Plaza Moyúa and bus station) take 20-30 mins and cost €1.15, running every half-hour or so. A taxi will cost about €20.

Getting around Bilbao is reasonably walkable (the Guggenheim is an easy 20-min stroll along the river from the old town) but for further-flung parts such as the beach or the bus station, the new, fast and efficient **metro** is an excellent service. A single fare costs €1.15, a day pass is €3.

The newly re-established **tram** network is very handy, particularly for reaching the Guggenheim from the old town. There's just one line so far, which runs from Atxuri station along the river, skirting the Casco Viejo (stopping behind the Teatro Arriaga, then continues on the other side of the Nervión, stopping at the Guggenheim and the bus station among other places. A single fare costs €1; there are machines at the tram stops. It runs every 10-15 mins.

Buses are really only useful for getting out of Bilbao. The station (Termibus) is near the football stadium (metro San Mamés, tram stops outside). San Sebastián (1 hr 20 mins, €8) and Vitoria (55 mins, €4.80), are served from here, but several Basque towns are served from the stop next to Abando station on C Hurtado Amezaga.

Tourist information Temporarily moved to the Teatro Arriaga on the edge of the old town, Pl Arriaga s/n, T944-795760, bit@ayto.bilbao.net, Mon-Sat 0930-1400, 1600-1930, Sun 0930-1400. And in the new town at Pl Ensanche 11, Mon-Fri 0900-1400, 1600-1930. There is also a smaller office by the Guggenheim Museum at Abandoibarra Etorbidea 2, Tue-Fri 1100-1430, 1530-1800, Sat 1100-1500, 1600-1900, Sun 1100-1400, Jul-Aug Mon-Sat 1000-1500, 1600-1900, Sun 1000-1500 and an office at the airport. See the city's website, www.bilbao.net, for more information.

---

unbeatable location at the mouth of the Casco Viejo warren, this beautiful building has been very sensitively converted into a smart modern hotel with great facilities.

€ **Hostal Begoña**, C Amistad 2, T944-230134, www.hostalbegona.com. A welcoming modern hotel packed with flair and comfort.

€ **Hotel Sirimiri**, Pl de la Encarnación 3, T944-330759, www.hotelsirimiri.com. A gem of a hotel with a genial owner, gym, sauna and free parking.

€ **Iturrienea Ostatua**, C Santa María, T944-161500. Beautiful *pensión* lined in stone, wood, and idiosyncratic objects. Delicious breakfasts.

Eating

Pintxos

Casco Viejo is the best place to head for *pintxos* and evening drinks. The best areas are the Plaza Nueva and around the Siete Calles. In El Ensanche there's another concentration of bars on Av Licenciado Poza and the smaller C García Rivero off it and the narrow C Ledesma, a street back from Gran Vía, is also a popular place to head after work. Don't miss:

€ **Café-Bar Bilbao**, Pl Nueva 6, T944-151671. A sparky place with top service and a selection of some of the best *pintxos* to be had around the old town, all carefully labelled and irresistible. Try them with a *txakolí*, a slightly fizzy local wine.

Restaurants

There are some good restaurants in the Casco Viejo, but also plenty of options scattered through the Ensanche and Deusto.

¶¶¶ **Guria**, Gran Vía 66, El Ensanche, T944-415780. Metro San Mamés. One of Bilbao's top restaurants, its stock-in-trade is *bacalao*. *Menús* €41-62, otherwise, €60 per head minimum. There's also a cheaper bistro menu and a mighty selection of brandies.

¶¶ **Victor**, Pl Nueva 2, Casco Viejo, T944-151678. An elegant but relaxed place to try Bilbao's signature dish, *bacalao al pil-pil*.

¶¶ **Kasko**, C Santa María, T944-160311. With funky decor inspired by the fish and high-class new Basque food, sometimes accompanied by a pianist. One of Casco Viejo's best.

¶¶ **Serantes and Serantes II**, C Licenciado Poza 16, Alameda Urquijo 51, El Ensanche, T944-102066. Metro Indautxu. Not as pricey as their high reputation would suggest, very fresh fish dishes around the €20 mark. The daily special is usually excellent, or tackle some expensive but delicious *cigalas*, the 4WD of the prawn world.

¶ **Saibigain**, C Barrenkale Barrena 16, Casco Viejo, T944-150123. Down-to-earth, traditional Basque place with hanging hams and a good lunch for €8.50. It's worth the wait to grab a table upstairs, a less frenetic place to sit down and eat than in the bar.

With streets like embroidered cloth, threaded with the arches of continuous colonnades, the heart of Bologna is a giant cloister. Under processions of classical columns and in the shadows cast between the half-moons of its winding alleys, the city reveals her secrets to the unhurried visitor prepared to be led astray. Above and behind its chiaroscuro porticoes, Bologna is a rose-red city of bombastic churches and vainglorious palaces, a litter of monuments and masterpieces that are lasting testaments to the architectural flattery bestowed by both papal and civic forces. They both vied for control of the city, producing a legacy of political dissent which in the 20th century saw the city labelled red for ideological rather than aesthetic reasons.

Arts & culture
★★★

Eating
★★★★★

Nightlife
★★★

Outdoors
★★

Romance
★★★★

Shopping
★★★★

Sightseeing
★★★

Value for money
★★★

Overall score
★★★★⌡

At a glance

The heart of Bologna is its Roman core, **piazza Maggiore**, at the confluence of the city's two main roads, via Ugo Bassi and via Rizzoli. The **Centro Storico** (Old Centre) is defined by a perimeter road which follows the line of the old city walls. East of piazza Maggiore is the bustling **Quadrilatero**. To the northeast runs via Rizzoli and beyond the **due torri** (two towers) is **via Zamboni**, the heart of studentland. West along via delle Belle Arti is **La Pinacoteca**. South along the main drag, via dell'Indipendenza, is the city's **cathedral**. Southeast from piazza Maggiore is the **Santo Stefano** complex. Connected to the city by a colonnade of

Bologna is the Italy that works

Charles Richards, The New Italians

666 arches, the sanctuary of the **Madonna di San Luca** sits atop one of the Apennine foothills.

★ *Don't leave town without trying some freshly made tortellini.*

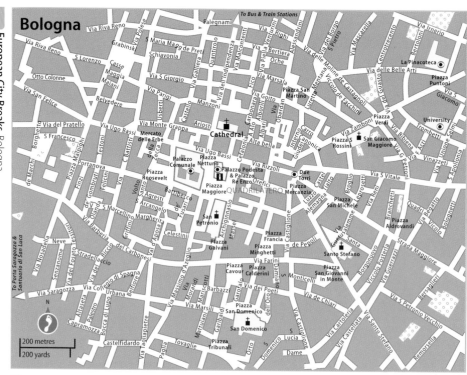

⊙ Sights

Piazza Maggiore

This grandiose square is the backdrop to a human theatre of poseurs and street artists. Standing in the middle of the entirely pedestrianized piazza you feel you could be in the central courtyard of a great castle, enclosed and protected by towers. The forbidding, late-Gothic weight of the **Basilica di San Petronio** ⓘ *T051-225442, 0730-1300, 1430-1830 (winter), -1930 (summer), free,* dominates the square. As the façade and half-arches down the western exterior tell, this ambitious project was never fully realized. Funded by public money, the basilica, which is a civic temple not a cathedral, was conceived as a monument of opposition to the papacy in Rome and was originally intended to be larger than St Peter's (but the papacy, fearful of this ambition, diverted money elsewhere).

Palazzo Comunale

The first stone was laid in 1390 and the current state only achieved several centuries later.

On the west side, the tall, thick and crenellated mass of the **Palazzo Comunale** ⓘ *piazza Maggiore 6, T051-201111, Tue-Sat 0930- 1830, Sun 1000-1830, closed Mon, entry to galleries €4,* is the city's town hall. Built in 1287, it is more like a small city within a city and is notable, other than for its sheer

grandiosity, for it's clocktower, built in 1773. Inside are some interesting rooms: especially the **Sala Farnese**, home of the city's public art collection, including paintings and frescoes by masters of the Bolognese school and works by Tintoretto; and the **Museo Morandi**, the largest collection of paintings by Giorgio Morandi, Bologna's most famous contemporary artist.

The castle-like construction in the centre of piazza Maggiore in fact combines two buildings, the **Palazzo Podesta** and the **Palazzo Re Enzo**. Before becoming the governor's residence, the Palazzo Podesta was originally designed in the early 13th century to house the city's law court. Built in 1244 as an extra wing of the Palazzo del Podesta, the Palazzo Re Enzo takes its name from the man who was its prisoner for 22 years (the young king of Sardinia and illegitimate son of Frederick the Great). The building became known as Enzo's *dorata prigione* (golden prison) on account of its luxuriousness.

⊜ Travel essentials

Getting there Marconi International Airport, T051- 6479615 (0630-2330), www.bologna-airport.it, is 6 km northwest of the city centre. Taxis (€12-15) depart from a rank outside Terminal A, or a bus (€4) runs every 15 mins (0540-2320) and takes about 20 mins. **Forlì Airport**, T0543-474990, www.forli-airport.it, has a direct bus service (€10) to Bologna's bus station (on piazza XX Settembre next to the train station). It takes around 1 hr 15 mins. A train connects Bologna with Forlì town. For the return, the direct buses from Bologna to Forlì airport depart once a day to coincide with necessary check-in times.

Getting around Central Bologna is easily covered on foot. It takes under an hour to walk across the Centro Storico to the other. Alternatively you could hire an honest, old-fashioned, sit-up-and-beg type bicycle. If you do want to rest your feet, the centre and suburbs are covered by an efficient network of orange buses run by the ATC, **Trasporti Pubblici Bologna**, T051-290290, www.atc.bo.it. Information on services can be found in the train and coach station in piazza XX Settembre as well as at their city office on via Marconi. Tickets costs €1 and last for an hour from the time you validate it in the machine upon boarding. You can use it for as many journeys as

you wish. The City Pass is valid for up to 7 journeys across multiple days (€6.50). Tickets can be bought at *tabacchi* (tobacconists), bars and newspaper kiosks, or on the bus in a machine that accepts €1 coins only.

Tourist information Bologna Turismo, under Palazzo Podesta, piazza Maggiore, T051-246541, www.bolognaturismo.info. Daily 0900-2000. Provides more free maps and leaflets than you could possibly need. A **Bologna dei Musei Card** (1- or 3-day pass costing €6 or €8) allows unlimited access to Bologna's museums.

European City Breaks Bologna

Piazza Nettuno

Alongside the Palazzo Comunale in neighbouring piazza Nettuno is Bologna's former stock exchange and only art-deco building the **Biblioteca Multimediale Sala Borsa** ⓘ *T051-204400, daily 0900-2400*. It's now the pride of Bologna's contemporary urban development plans and has a multimedia exhibition hall and library containing all sorts of documentation on contemporary culture and Bologna's history. Outside on piazza Nettuno is **Fontana del Nettuno**, Bologna's bronze statue of the Roman God of the Sea, completed between 1563 and 1566, which has become a symbol of the city and a favourite backdrop for posing visitors. Also outside the Sala Borsa is a memorial to the victims of the massacre by the local puppet fascist rump at the end of the Second World War.

Il Quadrilatero

The Quadrilatero is the name given to the grid of narrow streets hidden behind the east of piazza Maggiore. These streets were home to the small

Via Ranocchi in the Quadrilatero

businessmen of medieval Bologna and each street still bears the name of the powerful associations of artisans and merchants it was known for: *orefici* (jewellers), *clavature* (locksmiths), *pescherie* (fishmongers), *drapperie* (textile merchants). By day these are still among Bologna's liveliest market streets. By night they become the stage for Bologna's beautiful youth as they strut in and out of the many bars that have become some of the city's trendiest early evening nightspots.

Due Torri

Northeast of piazza Maggiore, down via Rizzoli are the *due torri* (two towers) that have become the city's icon. These 12th-century skyscrapers served as watchtowers to warn against an attack on the city and have wonderful views of the surrounding countryside from the top. At a height of nearly 98 m, **La Torre degli Asinelli** is the taller of the two. Built almost simultaneously, the leaning **Torre Garisenda** (*closed to the public*), was originally much higher than its current 47.5 m.

Chiesa di San Giacomo

ⓘ *T051-225970. Daily 0645-1300, 1600-1800.*

Continue down via Rizzoli to reach the anarchic and bohemian atmosphere of **via Zamboni** and the heart of student land. Along this street are the main faculty buildings and museums of Europe's oldest university with a dense concentration of bars and cafés under its porticoes. Here at piazza Rossini is **Chiesa di San Giacomo Maggiore**, one of Bologna's most elegant and significant churches, with the hidden treasure in its Renaissance interior of a cycle of scenes by Lorenzo Costa, Francia and Aspertini.

La Pinoteca

ⓘ *via delle Belle Arti 56, T051-4209411/4211984, www.pinacotecabologna.it. Tue-Sun 0900-1900, closed Mon. €4.*

Returning west along via delle Belle Arti you will find the Pinacoteca, with its large collection of masterpieces by the Bolognese masters, including Tibaldi, Reni, the Carracci brothers, Guercino and some late Titian. The gallery was founded by Napoleon.

Fontana del Nettuno

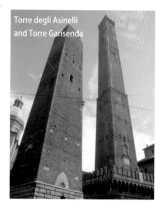
Torre degli Asinelli and Torre Garisenda

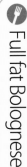

Full fat Bolognese

Bologna is to food what Milan is to fashion. The city strains with restaurants in the same way that your belt might after you have spent a few days helplessly gorging yourself on the typically abundant and delicious food. Although famous for its cuisine, Italy is a land full of deeply felt regional identities, where food is an expression this identity. It is not unusual to hear Italians from different areas claiming theirs to be the home of the best food in Italy. Rich, substantial and varied, *la cucina bolognese* has a better claim than most, something of which the Bolognesi will lose no opportunity to remind you. But, whatever your view, suffice it to say that food here is taken (and eaten) seriously and copiously; in a city with street names such as vicolo Baciadame (Lady-kisser Lane) and via Fregatette (Tit-rubbing Street), food is enjoyed with gastro-erotic pleasure. And as the city's nickname *la grassa* (the fat) suggests, you are unlikely to go home anything other than totally sated, and certainly no thinner.

Chiesa Santo Stefano

ⓘ T051-223256, www.abbaziasanto stefano.it. Daily 0900-1200, 1530-1830.

The three arteries of via Santo Stefano, via Castiglione and Strada Maggiore, which lead southeast from piazza Maggiore, are the most tranquil and picturesque part of town. You can stroll up and down endless arcades enjoying the shifting perspectives of palatial buildings as they are framed by each arch. The beauty of this area is nowhere more evident than in the triangular piazza Santo Stefano, site of the intricate complex of churches and maze of cloisters and chapels of the Chiesa Santo Stefano, one of the great architectural and artistic wonders of the city. Along with the Basilica di San Petronio and the Due Torri, this church is one of the must-sees of Bologna. At its peak it was a Russian doll of seven interlinked churches within churches.

Chiesa di San Domenico

ⓘ T051-6400411. Daily 0700-1300, 1530-1930.

Nearby, occupying the entire southern side of the eponymous piazza is the church of San Domenico. Begun in 1221 to commemorate the life of Domingo de Guzman, the founder of the Dominican Order, this church contains one of the masterpieces of Bolognese heritage, the Fabergé-esque *arca* or canopy to Nicola Pisano's tomb of the saint in the right-hand nave, designed and carved by Niccolo de Bari.

Santuario di San Luca

ⓘ T051-6142339. Mon-Sat 0700-1230 and 1430-1900. Sun 1230-1430. Free.

Stretching for 3.6 km and encompassing 666 arches and 15 chapels en route, the construction of the portico which leads devotees of San Luca up the colle della Guardia from the Saragozza gate (without getting sunburnt), is the longest continuous arcade in the world. Follow the porticoes all the way from Porta Saragozza, in the southwest of the Centro Storico, up the hill to San Luca. The views from the top are spectacular.

Sleeping

As a conference centre Bologna has plenty of accommodation aimed at the business market and in recent years something of the hip hotel revolution has rubbed off on some of the top end addresses.

€€€ **Corona d'Oro**, via Oberdan 12, T051-7457611, www.bolognart hotels.it. Just north of via Rizzoli. Recently refurbished the 14th-century palazzo of the Azzoguidi family has been a hotel since the early 1800s. Antique charm with elegant Venetian-style belle époque veranda and rooms with frescoes and wood-panelling. Breakfast room but no restaurant.

€€€ **Novecento**, piazza Galileo 4, T051-7547311, www.bolognart hotels.it. A true boutique hotel with angular contemporary decor in Viennese secession style. A peaceful, luxurious and uniquely hip address.

€€ **Orologio**, via IV Novembre 10, T051-7547411, www.bolognart hotels.it. On a pedestrianized street with fine views over the palazzo comunale. The eponymous clock is on the façade (it doesn't strike at night). Traditional if slightly retro luxury.

€ **Paradise**, via Cattani 7, T051-231792, www.hotelparadisebologna.it. Off via dell' Independanza, this friendly and pretty hotel has 18 rooms, the top ones with good views and architectural character. Following a refit, all are brightly decorated. Monica and Marisa will make you feel at home.

€ **Porta San Mamolo**, via del Falcone 6/8, T051-583056, www.hotel-portasanmamolo.it. Between via Paglietta and via Miramonte Ruini. A small romantic hotel in a formerly seedy district of the historic centre.

Eating

ŸŸŸ **Antica Osteria Romagnola**, via Rialto 13, T051-263699. Closed Mon and Tue at lunch. Comfortingly anonymous from the outside, Antonio's restaurant is rustic, welcoming and always noisy, with dark wood panels, musical instruments and mirrors on the walls. Superb local and regional cuisine tailor-made to your taste.

ŸŸŸ **Drogheria della Rosa**, via Cartoleria 10, T051-222529. Closed Sun. This cosy restaurant run by the ebullient Emanuele Addone used to be a food store and still has original features. Superior dishes from all over Emilia-Romagna are served in an intimate atmosphere with an exceptional wine list.

ŸŸ **Annamaria**, via delle Belle Arti 17, T051-266894. Closed Mon and Tue lunch. In the lively university district, this famous and hospitable restaurant is often frequented by actors – famous or otherwise. The menu is rooted in Bolognese tradition with fresh pasta and sauces centre stage.

ŸŸ **Da Fabio**, via del Cestello 2, T051-220481. Dinner only, closed Sun. Wonderful and plentiful regional dishes in this cosy, intimate and unprepossessing little restaurant with personal service.

ŸŸ **Meloncello**, via Saragozza 240, T051-6143947. Closed Mon evening and Tue. Superbly positioned in the corner of the city leading out through Porta Saragozza. Intimate and a little bit musty, it's like the extension of a family home. Essential to book ahead during the festival of San Luca in May.

Ÿ **Dell'Orsa**, via Mentana 1, T051-231576. Daily until 0100. Popular student lunch hangout serving simple

regional dishes all day. Great crostini and a broad range of beers.

Ÿ **Serghei**, via Piella 12, T051-233533. Closed Sat eve and Sun. Started as a salon for card players who wanted a snack, this small trattoria has lost nothing of its origins. It serves wholesome and abundant Bolognese dishes – perfect for famished students.

Nightlife

Bologna has had a kicking nightlife ever since the city became a university centre and the drinking traditions of Bologna's down-at-heel osterie go back almost a 1000 years. Clubs attract international DJ names while the gay scene fuels a lot of the creativity behind Bologna's many hybrid art-dance spaces. Activity centres around 2 or 3 areas: kick off with **Rosa Rose** in the Quadrilatero, or **Café de Paris** in piazza Minghetti. Then move on to the concentration of bars in either the university district, around via del Pratello, or for something smoother, **SushiCafe** or **Farmagia** around piazza Malpighi.

Shopping

Bologna is good for everything from books and fashion labels to antiques and bric-a-brac. For clothes, head for **via M d'Azeglio**, **via Farini** and catwalk-like **Galleria Cavour arcade** off Farini. Gourmets will have eyes bigger than their wallets and suitcases in the market streets of the **Quadrilatero**. For something more unusual and ethnic try the Momo-esque café-club-antiques shop, **Inde le Palais**, home to Bologna's local commercial radio.

With Brussels, it's rarely a case of love at first sight, but this is a city that soon gets under your skin. Despite its grey image, the 'capital' of Europe is not short of showpiece buildings or stunning works of art – and its shabby, slightly frayed feel could be regarded as all part of its charm. The EU presence lends the city an upbeat, cosmopolitan atmosphere, while the Dutch-speaking minority adds a cultural cutting edge… and all the city's communities unite in their appreciation of the finer things in life. The cooking really is superlative, even in the humblest corner café; the beer is out of this world, and the local penchant for self-deprecating humour gives the nightlife an earthy, unpretentious vibe. Oh, and the frîtes are mighty fine, too.

Brussels

Arts & culture
★★★★

Eating
★★★★★

Nightlife
★★★

Outdoors
★

Romance
★★

Shopping
★★

Sightseeing
★★★

Value for money
★★★

Overall score
★★★

At a glance

The core of Brussels is the plectrum-shaped **Pentagone**, home to the Upper and Lower Towns. At the Lower Town's heart is the **Grand'Place**, an awe-inspiringly opulent square graced with gilt-strewn guildhouses and a Gothic town hall. Around it bustle bars and restaurants in a warren of medieval streets known as the **Ilôt Sacré** ('Sacred Isle'). The **Upper Town**, otherwise known as the Royal Quarter, is almost oppressively monumental, its wide boulevards, mansions and palaces still lofty and inaccessible. The view back across town makes the uphill trudge worthwhile, however, and the Fine and Modern Arts Museums are essential viewing. Down rue de la Régence, under the shadow of the preposterously grandiose Palais de Justice, is the chic **Sablon** district, its main square lined with elegant houses, smart cafés and swish antiques shops. For something a little earthier, head into the **Marolles**, a traditional working-class area with a fabulous flea market. East of the Pentagone is the **European Quarter**, where quiet squares of stunning art nouveau architecture nestle amid the concrete colossi that house the EU institutions. To the south lie **St Gilles** and **Ixelles**, two characterful communes, laced with leafy squares, belle époque buildings, ethnic eateries and cosy cafés.

> Let me tell you what I think: Brussels is the most, most, most city in the world.
>
> *William Cliff*

★ *Don't leave town without a comedy Manneken Pis corkscrew: it's the perfect souvenir for laddish friends back home.*

⊖ Travel essentials

Getting there From London, the easiest route to Brussels is by rail, a 2 hr 30 min trip from Waterloo to Gare du Midi (zuid station) with **Eurostar** (www.euro star.com); returns from £59. The city has 2 airports. **Brussels International** is served by several airlines from destinations throughout Europe. From the airport, there are 4 trains an hour to the city's 3 stations; the 20-min ride costs €2.60. A taxi costs €30 each way. **Ryanair** flies from Glasgow Prestwick, Dublin and Shannon to **Brussels South** (Charleroi), a 1-hr bus ride from the capital.

Getting around The Pentagone is easily negotiable on foot; for journeys further afield, there's an excellent tram, bus and metro network, run by **Société des Transports Intercommunaux Bruxellois (STIB/MIVB)**, online at www.stib.irisnet.be. A day pass for all forms of transport costs €3.80. Cycling in the city centre is not recommended (given the tramlines, cobbles and traffic-clogged boulevards). You get free public transport with the **Brussels Card**, available at the Gare du Midi, the main tourist office and from hotels and museums. It is valid for 3 days, and it offers free access to 30 museums in the city, a free city map and guide and 25% discounts in shops, restaurants and bars across the city (cost €30).

Tourist information The main **Brussels International** tourist office is located in the Town Hall, on the Grand'Place, T02-513 8940, www.brusselsinternational.be. Open Mon-Sat 0900-1800; Sun 0900-1800 in summer, 1000-1400 in winter, closed Sun Jan-Easter. It sells the Brussels Card (see Getting around, above), maps and guides. There's also a room-finding service for visitors who arrive in the city without a hotel reservation.

Note that most museums are closed Mon; some are also closed at lunchtime on other days.

24 hours in the city

The die-hard Bruxellois breakfasts on beer, but a coffee on a **Grand'Place** terrace may have more appeal. Once you've drunk it all in, amble through the Ilôt Sacré, visiting the **Galeries St Hubert**, one of the world's first covered shopping arcades, and, if you can't beat the urge, paying homage to the **Manneken Pis**. Head up the Mont des Arts to the Upper Town, stopping at the art nouveau Old England building to visit the marvellous **Musical Instruments Museum**: the top-floor café is a good spot for lunch with a view. See the Bruegels and Magrittes at the **Fine and Modern Arts Museums**, then stroll down to the Sablon for a spot of window-shopping, or, if you're an architecture buff, take a tram to **St Gilles** and visit the house of Victor Horta, the master architect of art nouveau. In the evening, head to the streets around tranquil **Place Ste Catherine** for fine fish and moules-frites in any of a dozen wonderful places – or splurge at **Comme**

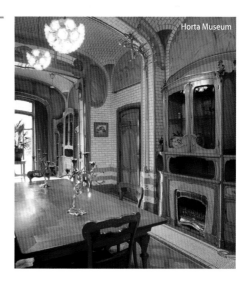

Horta Museum

Chez Soi, a veritable temple of gastronomy – before hunkering down for some serious beer appreciation in the bountiful bars of the Old Town.

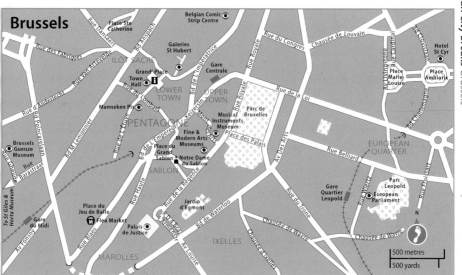

◉ Sights

Grand'Place

On this jaw-droppingly gorgeous square, it's hard to know where to stare first – at the exquisite gothic **Town Hall**, with its curlicued masonry and soaring spire, or the glorious baroque **guildhouses**, honey- coloured and dripping with gilt and leaded glass. Jean Cocteau called the square "the greatest theatre in the world", and its story is nothing if not dramatic: Louis XIV's artillery razed the square in 1695, but the doughty burghers rebuilt it in just four years. Each house belonged to a guild, and identifying the trade from the golden statues atop each building is all part of the fun. Victor Hugo lived at **Nos 26-27, 'The Pigeon'**, during his exile from France; Marx brooded over the Communist Manifesto at the workers' café in **No 9, 'The Swan'**, now a swanky restaurant. The best terrace is at **Nos 1-2, 'Le Roy d'Espagne'**, formerly the bakers' guild. Drinks are not cheap, but the views are priceless.

Grand'Place

Galeries St Hubert

Ilôt Sacré

The jumble of medieval streets around the Grand'Place has long been anything but sacred. Their names attest to intense mercantile activity – Butchers' Street, Herring Street, Spur-Makers' Street – and they remain a blur of shops, restaurants, bars and clubs. The eateries around rue des Bouchers, with vast seafood displays outside, are expert in relieving unwary tourists of their cash and are best avoided. (If that sounds bad, night-time visitors in the 19th century were considered lucky to leave with their lives!) That said, there are other great places to eat and drink, and the atmosphere can be positively Bruegelian. The **Galeries St Hubert**, one of the world's first covered shopping arcades, is an oasis of calm amid the surrounding hubbub; a cool, airy glass structure from 1847, it houses a theatre, a cinema and several cafés and restaurants.

Belgian Comic Strip Centre
ⓘ *Rue des Sables 20, T02-219 1980.*
Tue-Sun 1000-1800. €6.20.

Tintin fans are in for a treat here; but there's more to *bande dessinée* than the intrepid boy reporter. While this marvellous museum, converted from a Horta-designed art nouveau department store, gives Hergé ample coverage, it's a great place to catch up on Belgium's other memorable comic- book creations. And, more ignominiously, the origins of the Smurfs. Parents be warned: they take the 'ninth art' seriously in Belgium, and the top-floor displays show just how grown-up the genre can be.

Manneken Pis
ⓘ *Rue de l'Etuve*

Symbol of Bruxellois irreverence, anti-war icon or shamelessly tacky photo opportunity? Here's your chance to decide, if you can force your way through the camcorder-wielding crowd that surrounds Brussels's smallest tourist attraction. Mystery surrounds his origins, but the pint-size piddler's current incarnation is a copy of a statue fashioned by Jérôme Duquesnoy in 1619 and smashed into smithereens two centuries later. He's often decked

Belgian Comic Strip Centre

Excursion: Bruges

Romantic, mysterious, lost in time: all typical epithets for Bruges, with its sleepy canals, old stone bridges, circling swans and pinkish Gothic spires. Unfortunately: "jam-packed with tourists" is another, as this dreamy medieval city, a 50-minute train ride from Brussels, pulls in the crowds. Thankfully, it's at its most alluring amid a little off-season fog. Start at the city's heart, the **Markt**, admiring the soaring belfry and the elaborate 13th-century Halle (Cloth Hall), an eloquent illustration of how wealthy this Hansa city was before its river silted up in the 15th century. From here, stroll to the **Burg**, for the dazzling gothic town hall, the romanesque Basilica of the Holy Blood and the surprisingly harmonious addition of Toyo Ito's sleek, ultra-modern pavilion, built for the city's

stint as European Capital of Culture in 2002. Don't miss the 13th-century **Church of Our Lady**, with the tallest brick spire in the world, or the **Gruuthuse**, owned by one of the 15th century's wealthiest families. The **Begijnhof**, a complex of pretty 13th-century white-washed houses, is especially lovely when splashed with daffodils in spring; and courting couples will find it hard to resist the **Minnewater** ('Lake of Love'). Art-lovers must make time for two superb museums: the Flemish Primitives and Mannerists are the main attractions at the **Groeningemuseum** (Dijver 12) and the **Memling Museum** (Mariastraat 38).

Manneken Pis

out in costumes donated by visiting dignitaries, from the Elector of Bavaria, in 1698, to Elvis.

Fine and Modern Arts Museums

ⓘ *Rue de la Régence 3/Place Royale 1-2, T02-508 3211, www.fine-arts-museum.be. Tue-Sun 1000-1700. €5*

These twin museums comprise the country's finest collection. The Fine is a conventional 19th-century gallery with a superb survey of works by the artists once grouped together as the 'Flemish Primitives': Van der Weyden, Memling, Bouts and, most important, Pieter Bruegel the Elder. It's also replete with vast Rubens canvases and superbly observed smaller works. The Modern is an unusual subterranean spiral with the world's largest collection of works by the master Surrealist René Magritte; there's also a good sample of

20th-century greats – Picasso, Matisse, Bacon, Dalí – and Belgian masters: Paul Delvaux, James Ensor, Leon Spilliaert and Constant Permeke.

Fine and Modern Art Museums

Musical Instruments Museum

ⓘ *Rue Montagne de la Cour 2, T02-545 0130, www.mim.fgov.be. Tue-Fri 0930-1700, Sat-Sun 1000-1700. €5 (includes headphone hire).*

No prizes for guessing what's on show here – but the setting is a real surprise. The frills and flourishes of the ornate Old England building, a delightful art nouveau department store in glass and black iron, are an apt counterpoint to the exquisite craftsmanship of the exhibits. The painted pianos from pre-revolutionary France are a highlight, as are the weird and wonderful folk instruments. The top-floor restaurant has some of the best views in town.

Place du Grand Sablon

The Grand'Place may be the city's grandest square but the Sablon has a little more, well, class. Although the baroque houses lack their counterparts' flamboyance, they're still drop-dead gorgeous. The antiques shops at street level are reassuringly expensive, the cafés and restaurants smart and perfect

Musical Instruments Museum

Flea market

for observing how Brussels' other half lives. There's a wonderful Gothic church, **Notre Dame du Sablon**, at the square's southeastern side.

Place du Jeu de Balle

If you find the Sablon too stuffy, head downhill to the grittier, more ramshackle Marolles, a traditionally working-class district in the shadow of the preposterously overblown Palais de Justice. It sprawls around rues Blaes and Haute (on which Bruegel lived, at no 132), but its heart is the daily **flea market** on place du Jeu de Balle (0600-1400). Amid the mountains of tat, there are some serious bargains, especially for early birds.

Horta Museum

ⓘ *Rue Américaine 23-25, T02-543 0490, www.hortamuseum.be. Tue-Sun 1400-1730. €5. Tram 81 or 92.*

Victor Horta was, perhaps, the greatest exponent of art nouveau, and the house he built for himself in St Gilles is an exquisite reminder of his philosophy and craftsmanship. Horta believed in

total design, right down to the doorknobs – he even advised clients' wives on what to wear – but he never let the style's unmistakable swirls and curls get out of control. The exterior is relatively modest but, inside, the house is a symphony of burnished wood, stained glass, delicate wrought iron and immensely covetable antiques.

European Quarter

Home to the Commission, the Council of Europe and the European Parliament, as well as countless NGOs, lobby groups, media organizations and multinationals, this district east of the Old Town is like an entirely separate city, one where English is the lingua franca, but where you'll hear dozens of languages on every street. Visit between Monday and Friday, as the area's deserted at weekends and the relentlessly functional post-war office blocks can deaden the soul. Amid the glass, steel and concrete boxes, however, are two lovely squares, **place Ambiorix** and **place Marie-Louise**. The Hôtel St-Cyr, at 11 place Ambiorix, is so ridiculously ornate, it's beyond parody.

European Quarter

Beer necessities

Brewing is one of Belgium's grandest traditions, and the appreciation of a really good beer, poured reverently into its special glass, is one of the high points of any visit to Brussels. Even if you don't consider yourself an ale aficionado, you'll savour a trip to the **Brussels Gueuze Museum** ⓘ *Cantillon brewery, rue Gheude 56, T02-521 4928, www.cantillon.be; Mon-Fri 0830-1700, Sat 1000-1700, closed Sun; €3.50,* the capital's last bastion of traditional lambic production. The basis for the fabled fruit beers, lambic is the only brew to ferment spontaneously, without yeast: the roof is left open to allow spores from the local atmosphere to infuse the liquid. Learn more on the brewery tour, marvelling at the musty ambience, the huge copper vats and the unbridled enthusiasm of the owner. Then it's tasting time: the kriek (cherry) and framboise (raspberry) beers are sharper, fruitier and more refreshing than the sweetened stuff on sale in most cafés, but the real deal is the gueuze, a complex blend of lambics that has a sharp, sour, almost vinegary taste. If you don't like it on the first try, you can buy 75cl bottles to enjoy at home and/or inflict on your nearest and dearest.

⬤ Sleeping

Although there are plenty of characterful establishments, the hotel trade in Brussels depends primarily on business – great news for short-breakers, as rates plummet at the weekend. Expect reductions of at least 30% and often considerably more. Summer prices are also extremely keen. The Old Town has a good concentration of hotels; there are also good options in the European Quarter and Ixelles. Try www.bookings.be for late deals; for B&Bs, visit www.bnb-brussels.be or www.bedandbreakfastbelgium.com.

€€€ Amigo, rue de l'Amigo 1-3, T02-547 4747, www.hotelamigo.com. Part of Rocco Forte's exclusive portfolio, this is an immensely stylish establishment near the Grand'Place. Once a prison (the poet Paul Verlaine was incarcerated here after shooting his lover, Rimbaud), it's now a liberating mix of ancient and modern, with lush tapestries and Flemish masters complemented by top-quality contemporary fabrics and fittings.

€€€ Le Dixseptième, rue de la Madeleine 25, T02-517 1717, www.ledixseptieme.be. Don't be fooled by the discreet façade – this was once the Spanish ambassador's residence. Now it's really spoiling us with a superbly restored 17th-century interior, relaxed service and 24 dreamily luxurious, classically kitted-out rooms.

€€ Saint-Michel, Grand'Place 11, T02-511 0956. The unique selling point is the address: this is the only hotel on the Grand'Place, to the left of the Town Hall. Some of the rooms have gobsmacking views. Don't bother unless you can get one, though.

€€ Welcome, rue du Peuplier 5, T02-219 9546, www.hotelwelcome.com. Amid the fish restaurants of Place Ste Catherine is this wonderful little hotel with 15 world-themed rooms. The Congo is all leopard-print fabrics; the Japan, sleek, stark and serene. It's too well done to be kitsch, and the owners have charm to spare.

€€-€ Noga, rue du Béguinage 38, T02-218 6763, www.nogahotel.com. There's a nautical theme in this quiet place on a side street near Place Ste Catherine. The rooms are bright, boldly coloured and extremely comfortable, and the clincher is what the website calls "Noga's little extras": bike hire, a piano in the lounge, a snooker room. It's also great value.

€ Galia, place du Jeu de Balle 15-16, T02-502 4243, www.hotelgalia.com. Clean, simple rooms in a modern building at the heart of the Marolles, and handy for flea market fiends.

⊘ Eating

Even the self-deprecating Bruxellois can't help being proud of their city's culinary prowess, and with good reason: it's almost impossible to have a bad meal here, unless you're foolish enough to succumb to the wiles of the waiters on rue des Bouchers. Brasseries and cafés usually have an all-day menu, with staples such as spaghetti bolognaise, omelettes and a range of croques. Portions are enormous, so go easy on the starters.

Breakfast

🍴 **Het Warm Water**, rue des Renards 25, T02-513 9159, www.hetwarm water.be. Sun-Tue 0800-1900, Thu-Sat 0800-2100, closed Wed. For brekkie, brunch and Belgian specialities, with a side order of authentic Marollien atmosphere, you can't beat this place off place du Jeu de Balle. Earthy, homely cuisine – Brussels soup, pottekees cheese and endive omelette – as well as croissants and muesli. Brunch on Sun (1100-1500) is a riotous affair.

Lunch

🍴🍴 **Le Paon Royal**, rue du Vieux Marché aux Grains 6, T02-513 08 68, www.lepaonroyal.com. Tue-Sat 1130-2130. Lunchtime special €8. The Royal Peacock is the quintessence of Brussels bonhomie. Off Place Ste Catherine, it's a homely place with a country-pub feel serving shrimp croquettes, veal cooked in cherry beer and eels in a pungent green sauce. Excellent beer too.

🍴 **Au Bain-Marie**, rue Breydel 46, T02-280 4888. Mon-Fri 1200-1500. If you really must eat healthily, you'll find it hard to better this light, airy restaurant at the heart of the European Quarter, with a meat-free mod Med menu. There's a cosmopolitan crowd from the nearby Commission building, so you can brush up on your languages while munching your bruschetta.

Dinner

🍴🍴🍴 **Comme Chez Soi**, place Rouppe 23, T02-512 2921. Closed Sun and Mon. Booking (well ahead) essential. Pierre Wynants has maintained 3 Michelin stars for something approaching an eternity, and his art nouveau-style restaurant is one of northern Europe's finest. Provençal poussin with crayfish béarnaise, or sole

fillets with shrimps and Riesling mousseline, should whet the appetite. It's not cheap, but there are set menus, and the waiters offer seconds.

🍴 **Bij Den Boer**, quai aux Briques 60, T02-512 6122. Mon-Sat 1200-1430, 1800-2230. There are posher and trendier places to eat fish in the Ste Catherine area but this resolutely old-fashioned restaurant has rugged charm aplenty. It's a sea of burnished

66 99 Even the self-deprecating Bruxellois can't help being proud of their city's culinary prowess, and with good reason...

wood and check tablecloths, with specials chalked up on the mirrors. House specialities include fish soup, mussels five ways, North Sea bouillabaisse and poached skate wing: it's all sea-fresh, simply prepared and sensational. The 4-course menu is great value at €25.

🍴 **La Roue d'Or**, rue des Chapeliers 26, T02-514 2554. Daily 1200-0030. Although its striking decor tips a (bowler) hat to Magritte and the Surrealist movement, the polished wood and mirrors give the game away: the Golden Wheel is basically a brasserie, and a jolly good one at that. Just off the Grand'Place, it offers a mix of French (cassoulet, andouillette AAAAA) and Belgian dishes (sausage and *stoemp*, creamy fish or chicken *waterzooi*), handling both cuisines with aplomb. The double-fried chips are to die for.

⦿ Nightlife

With so many great beers to try, it's a good job Brussels is rammed with marvellous bars. Inexplicably, the expat crowd stick to the European Quarter's Irish joints; leave them to it and focus on the Old Town. Place St Géry's terraces are a magnet for the beautiful people, but rue du Marché au Charbon has more edge, with salsa at **Cartagena** (No 70), the boho **Au Soleil** (No 86) and the LHB haven, **Belgica** (No 32), among its many charms.

The intersection of rue Dansaert and rue des Chartreux is another good crawling point: on the former, **L'Archiduc** (No 6) is a seriously cool art-deco jazz bar with a liner-style interior and suitably smoky sounds; on the latter, **Le Greenwich** (No 7) is a classic old café where chess players congregate; and on nearby rue Orts, the **Beurs Café**, attached to a Flemish cultural centre, is a super-cool post-industrial space.

Beyond the Old Town, chaussée de Charleroi (tram 91 or 92) is lounge central. Try **Les Salons de l'Atalaïde** (no 89), **Le Living Room** (no 50) and **Kolya** (no 102). Off the main drag are two great conversions: **Knopff**, rue St Bernard 1, a cooler-than-thou bar-restaurant in the titular Symbolist painter's former atelier; and the hugely romantic wine bar **Amadeus**, 13 rue Veydt, in Rodin's studio.

Finally, beer buffs should head straight for **Chez Moeder Lambic**, 68 rue de Savoie; pré-Métro Horta, a loveably scruffy St Gilles institution that stocks every Belgian brew you can think of. It's open till (at least) 0300 most nights.

Since Hungary's EU accession in 2004, some investment has flowed into Budapest but prosperity is yet to reach the doors of ordinary Hungarians. Still, the city bears the imprint of its communist years pretty lightly and shares much of the imposing grandeur of its Hapsburg neighbour, Vienna, although it is more derelict – and more charming for it. The two cities Buda and Pest, joined administratively in the 19th century, are still kept apart by the grey sweep of the Danube. Above its waters lie belle époque buildings and the weathered stone of neoclassical and baroque mansions. The home of Liszt and Bartók has a rich musical heritage, as well as an underground arts and bar scene, not to mention beautiful mosaic Turkish baths where you can steam yourself back to life after a night on the town.

Budapest

Arts & culture
★★★★★

Eating
★

Nightlife
★★★★

Outdoors
★★

Romance
★★★★

Shopping
★

Sightseeing
★★★

Value for money
★★★★

Overall score
★★★

At a glance

Buda's Castle Hill rises just over 180 m on the west side of the Danube to offer brilliant views of both the neighbouring hilltop, **Gellért**, to the south, and the low-level sprawl of **Pest** across the river to the east. Pest incorporates two thirds of the city and is more dynamic and grimy than its west bank rival. The Chain Bridge links Castle Hill with **Belváros** on the east bank. This is where the medieval city grew up. It is bordered by a semicircular series of roads (József Attila ut, Károly körút, Múzeum körút and Vámház körút), which together are dubbed the '**Little Boulevard**'. Cutting straight through the inner city, parallel to the Danube, is the shopping street-cum-tourist zone, **Váci út**; to its northeast is **Deák Ferenc tér**, the starting point for the city's most important and grandiose thoroughfare, **Andrássy út**, which runs northeast for over 2 km to the city park, **Városliget**, and **Heroes Square** (Hösök Tere). The '**Great Boulevard**' is a broader arc

...beneath the noisy boom of Budapest there was that presence of a wistful and melancholy tone...

John Lukacs

that apes the semicircle of the Little Boulevard, running from Margit Hid (Margaret Bridge) at the toe-tip of Margit Island in the north, crossing Andrássy út at Oktogon, then looping back to the river at Petőfi Híd to the south of the city.

★ *Don't leave town without subjecting yourself to the elevator shaft at the House of Terror.*

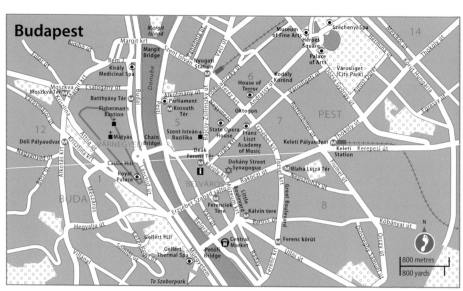

24 hours in the city

Central Market

For an early morning view of Budapest's World Heritage status head for Buda's Castle District. Enter through the northern **Vienna Gate** (Bécsi kapu tér) and stroll past the ceramic roof of the **National Archives**, before exploring the cobblestone sidestreets and ducking west for a leafy walk along the ramparts. Have a late breakfast at **Ruszwurm**, then head on towards Holy Trinity Square to see the **Mátyás Church** and the **Fishermen's Bastion**. Walk or take the funicular down the hill to the river and then take a tram south to the **Gellért** thermal spa for a swim and a pummel. After a snack lunch at the **Central Market** in Pest, head north, up Váci út, to reach **Szent István Bazilika**, and then stroll along Andrássy út to the **House of Terror**. You can recover from the horrors of the 20th century by contemplating the achievements of the Spanish masters at the **Museum of Fine Arts** on Heroes Square. Head back to the river for an early evening **cruise** before enjoying a recital at the **Opera**

House or the **Liszt Academy**. Supper could be something modishly Hungarian at **Vörös és Fehér**, followed by table football and a nightcap at one of the trendy kerts. If that sounds too down-at-heel, try one of the bars on Liszt Ferenc Square or the A38 boat on the river between Petőfi and Lágymányosi bridges in Buda.

⊖ Travel essentials

Getting there Ferihegy International Airport is 23 km southeast of the city, T01-296 9696. There are 2 terminals: Terminal 1 serves the burgeoning low-cost airlines, while Terminal 2 serves most other airlines, including Hungarian airline, Malev. A handy airport minibus, T01-296 8555, runs to any address in the city (HUF 2100 one way, HUF 3600 return); it's cheaper than a taxi but you must book your return journey 24 hrs in advance. **Direct trains**, T(+36)1-461 5500. www.elvira.hu, link Budapest with 16 European cities, including Vienna, every 3 hrs (2½ hrs); Berlin (12 hrs), Paris (16 hrs), Zagreb and Ljubliana (6 hrs).

Getting around Walking around Budapest is a pleasure but the public transport network of **buses**, **trams**, **trolleybuses**, plus 3 **metro** lines, is excellent, cheap and runs until 2300. You can buy single journey tickets or booklets at newsagents, stations and stops. These must be validated once on board; you face a HUF 2000 on-the-spot fine if you travel without a ticket. The tourist office's **Budapest Card** gives you access to unlimited public transport in the city for 48 hrs (HUF 4700) or 72 hrs (HUF 5900) as well as discounts on sights, activities and thermal baths. Despite traffic congestion, **cycling** is an increasingly popular way of getting round the city. Bikes can be rented from many of the city's hotels and hostels, and from **Velo-Touring**, T01-319 0571, www.velo-touring.hu. Budapest **taxis**

have yellow number plates and run on a meter; drivers will expect a 10% tip on top of the fare. Booking by phone is very quick and is cheaper than hailing a cab on the street: try **Budataxi**, T01-233 3333; **Budapest Taxi**, T01-433 3333, **Rádió Taxi**, T01-377 7777; **Fo Taxi** T01-222 2222, or **City Taxi** T01-211 1111.

Tourist information Budapest's **Tourinform** office is at Deák tér/Sütő utca 2, T01-438 8080, www.budapest info.hu, daily 0800-2000. **Budatours**, T01-374 7070, www.budatours.hu, run a 2-hr city tour, HUF 4300, starting from outside Metro station M1, Bajcsy-Zsilinkszky út at Andrassy út 2.

Exchange rate Hungarian Forint (HUF). £1 = HUF 370.34. €1 = HUF 253.35.

◉ Sights

Várhegy and Király Palota (Castle Hill and Royal Palace)

A fortress was first built on Buda's unmistakable World Heritage hilltop following the Mongol invasion of 1241, which almost razed the settlements of low-lying Obuda and Pest. The Royal Palace occupies the southern slopes of the hill and commands regal views over the quays and boats of Pest but, although the site was successfully defended over the centuries, its buildings proved to be less resilient: the palace was destroyed first in battle with the Turks in the 17th century and, again, during the German retreat from the Second World War, and each time it was rebuilt in the architectural vernacular of the day. Today, its stately neoclassical buildings and stone parapets house a rash of cultural institutes: the **Hungarian National Gallery** ⓘ *T01-4397325, www.mng.hu, Tue-Sun 1000-1800, free;* the **Budapest History Museum** ⓘ *T01-225 7809, www.btm.hu, Wed-Mon 1000-1800, HUF 800;* the **National Széchényi Library** ⓘ *T01-224 3700,*

Royal Palace

Fishermen's Bastion

www.oszk.hu, Tue-Fri 0900-2100, Sat 0800-2000; and the **Ludwig Museum** ⓘ *T01-555 3444, www.ludwig museum.hu, Tue, Fri, Sun 1000-1800, Wed 1200-1800, Thu 1200-2000, Sat 1000-2000, HUF 1000.* Look out for the bronze sculpture of King Mátyás at the hunt, looking every inch like Errol Flynn.

Mátyás Templom, Fishermen's Bastion and Várnegyed

ⓘ *Szentháromság tér, District 1, T01-355 3657. Daily 0600-2000. HUF 270-550.*

The two-thirds of Buda that wasn't taken up with palace buildings was left to the civilians. At the centre of this area is **Holy Trinity Square** (Szentháromság tér) and the lovely **Mátyás Church**, painted with Asian and Turkish-influenced geometric heraldic motifs. The church has had to wear a number of religious hats down the ages: it was shared between Catholics and Protestants and became a Mosque during the Turkish occupation of 1541. The Gothic body of the church was built in the 13th century, the tower in the 15th. A facelift, timed to coincide with the 1896 millennium celebration,

gave it back its eye-popping frescoes, medieval-style tiles and stained glass. The whole project was overseen by Frigyes Schulek, who also designed the neo-Romanesque trim to the church, known as the **Fishermen's Bastion**.

North of the square, in **Várnegyed**, are the squat merchants', noblemen's and courtiers' residences, painted umber, olive, yellow, ochre and cream. Heavy doors open on to courtyards, with wells and plane trees, and shallow stone reliefs decorate the façades. Parts of the area are medieval but much was rebuilt in the baroque and Louis XVI styles when the Turks left after the 1686 siege.

Parliament

ⓘ *Kossuth Lajos tér, District 5, T01-317 9800. Visits by guided tour only (tickets from the gate), daily 1000, 1200, 1400, 1800.*

The puffed-up Parliament building on the Pest embankment doesn't let the side down. It is a splendid piece of pomp, modelled on the Palace of Westminster, and it's as impressive inside as out: full of frescoes and sculptures, deep red carpets, stained-glass windows, hundred-bulb chandeliers, four-tonne

Parliament

monolithic granite colonnades and the crown, sceptre, orb and sword of the Hungarian coronation.

Szent István Bazilika (St Stephen's Basilica)

ⓘ *Szent István tér, District 5, T01-317 2859. Summer 0900-1700; winter 1000-1600.*

Budapest's largest church, completed in 1905, is a fat neoclassical building perfumed with the myrrh of its votive candles and dominated by marble (15 different types), mosaics and paintings. If Matyas Church is Budapest's fussy Westminster Abbey, then St Stephen's is the city's St Paul's. It is named after the founder of the Hungarian state, Catholic King Szent István, whose mummified arm is kept on the left side of the chapel, and who sits carved from Italian marble on the high altar. Go up to the dome for amazing rooftop views of the **Postal Savings Bank**, designed by Ödön Lechner. What appears, at street level, to be an unremarkable white building, reveals itself from above to be a perfect aesthetic expression of the building's function: the bank's roof is embroidered with bees, the honey-gathering symbols of saving.

Postal Savings Bank

Opera House

Magyar Állami Operaház (State Opera House)

ⓘ *Andrássy út 22, District 6, T01-331 2550. Tours at 1500 and 1600, HUF 2200.*

Hungary punches well above its weight in terms of musical virtuosity, and the Hungarian State Opera House is an appropriate physical representation of the country's acoustic refinement. The sphinx-flanked entrance gives onto a Fabergé-egg of an interior. Built in 1884 in neo-Renaissance style to Miklós Ybl's design, the architecture is best enjoyed during a ballet or opera performance; tickets are decidedly affordable by London standards (HUF 300-6300).

Andrássy út

This UNESCO-protected boulevard runs for 2.5 km, like a grandiose spoke, from inner-city Pest at Szent István's to the Hösök Tere and City Park in the northeast. It was built in the late 19th century at the time of the administrative union of Buda, Óbuda and Pest, after the Austro-Hungarian Compromise. Its buildings are almost absurdly beautiful and can be divided loosely into three sections: closest to the Danube are four-storey residential blocks, then two-storey mansions give way to palaces and gardens the further out you get. Modelled on the Champs-Elysées and designed by Ybl, it is one of the world's finest urban landscapes. Look out particularly for the **Postal Museum** ⓘ *T01-269 6838, Tue-Sun 1000-1800, HUF 100*, which is notable for its architecture rather than its exhibits, and **Kodály Körönd**, a series of mansion blocks with amazing frescoed façades.

Terror Háza (House of Terror)

ⓘ *Andrássy út 60, District 6, T01-374 2600, www.houseofterror.hu. Tue-Fri 1000-1800, Sat-Sun 1000-1930, closed Mon. HUF 1200.*

Brace yourself: this is sightseeing as harrowing 20th-century history lesson. Number 60 Andrássy út was, from 1939 to 1944, the House of Loyalty, party HQ of the Hungarian Nazi Arrow Cross Party. Between 1945 and '56 it went on to become the head of the Soviet terror organizations ÁVO and ÁVH. Both were remarkable for institutionalized brutality and the torture of subjects. The emphasis

House of Terror

Buda bathtime

Residents on the Buda side of the city have water pressure sloshing from their taps with the force of a hardly-harnessed Niagara: Budapest lies on top of somewhere between 80 and 120 active springs and wells from which 70 million litres of water burst forth daily. The medicinal properties of the city's springs were recognized during the Turkish occupation and, by 1500, the Turks had bequeathed their Hungarian subjects some beautiful Ottoman baths, featuring high domes with shafts of light searing through the steam and tile mosaics lining the 18°C plunge pools. Today, the baths remain a brilliant way to atone for a night on the Buda or Pest tiles, despite the off-putting appearance of most bathhouse staff. Baths tend to be single sex, although swimming pools are usually mixed. Specific treatments for rheumatism, physiotherapy and inhalation are available, but on weekends from April to September, most people head outside to lounge around and sunbathe with the papers, stirring only to complete extremely lackadaisacal laps of the swimming pool. The best baths in town are: **Gellért**, Kelenhegyi Út 4-6, T01-466 6166, Mon-Sat 0600-1900, Sat-Sun 0600-1700, HUF 2400-2900, which is full of art nouveau furnishings, mosaics and stained-glass windows; the neo-baroque **Széchenyi Spa**, Állatkerti Út 11, District 14, T01-363 3210, May-Sep 0600-1900, Oct-Apr 0600-1700, HUF 1300-2200, which has much-photographed chess boards in its pool, and the gay favourite, **Király Medicinal**, Fő utca 82-84, T01-201 4392, Mon, Wed, Fri 0700-1800 for women, Tue, Thu, Sat 0900-2000 for men, HUF 1000.

here is on experience over mere exhibition. Nagging music and newsreel footage make this document of the crimes of the successive terror regimes so vivid as to turn your stomach. Documentary footage contrasts the order and iconography of the Nazi regime with the relative scrappiness of Soviet rule but the museum has also been criticized for describing the atrocities of the latter in detail, while providing only relatively cursory treatment of the Nazi genocide.

Szépművészeti Múzeum (Museum of Fine Arts)

ⓘ Dózsa György út 41, Heroes Sq, District 4, T01-469 7100, www.szepmuveszeti.hu. Tue-Sun 1000-1730.

This imitation of a Greek temple at the City Park end of Andrássy út houses an excellent collection of Spanish masters including seven El Grecos and five Goyas. Its walls carry bleary oil paintings of lachrymose saints, acts of martyrdom, beheadings and sermons. Outside, the **Millennium Monument** marks the 1000th anniversary of the Magyar Conquest, with archangel Gabriel on top of a column and the seven tribal chieftains beneath him. Across Heroes Square, the inevitable showcase for political gatherings and shows of Communist and Soviet might, sits the **Palace of Arts**. Behind the square is the **City Park**, location of the **Széchenyi baths** and the winter ice-skating rink.

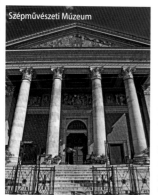

Szépművészeti Múzeum

Széchenyi baths

Sleeping

Budapest has its share of un-imaginative Soviet-style business hotels but there are some treats too. The city also has a strong homestay tradition, as well as serviced apartments, which are available for both long-term rental and short lets.

€€€ Art'Otel, Bem Rakpart 16-19, T01-487 9487, www.artotels.com. On the Buda side of the Danube, overlooking Parliament, this hotel is spruce, slick and more minimalist than the Gresham. The 148 rooms in 4 baroque townhouses have floor-to-ceiling windows and snappy service.

€€€ Four Seasons Hotel Gresham Palace, Chain Bridge, Roosevelt tér 5-6, T01-268 6000 www.fourseasons.com/budapest. The art nouveau/secessionist Gresham Palace was built to accommodate wealthy British aristocrats. These days rooms have huge fluffy pillows, giant bathrooms and the best views in Pest. There's also an infinity pool, gym, spa and a flawlessly polished service ethic.

€€ Danubius Hotel Gellért, Szent Gellért tér 1, T01-889 5500, www.danubiushotels.com/gellert. The grand dame among Budapest's hotels. Its carpets can be dank and it reeks of the Soviet era but the views across the Liberty Bridge are splendid, and it has character in spades. Rates include admission to the excellent on-site Gellért Thermal Baths.

€€ Hotel Pest, Paulay Ede u. 31, District 6, T01-343 1198, www.hotelpest.hu. An 18th-century apartment building just a stone's throw from the Opera House is now an elegant, 3-star hotel with 25 immaculate rooms overlooking a ivy-clad courtyard.

€€ Residence Izabella, Izabella út/Andrássy út, T01-475 5900, www.mamaison.com/budapest/izabella. This residential apartment in a 19th-century building has been exactingly refurbished. Suites have 1-3 bedrooms, plus kitchen, lounge and dining room. Room service, breakfast, laundry, concierge, AV system, sauna, pool room and home theatre are all available.

€ Kalmar Bed & Breakfast, Kelenhegyi út 7-9, T01-430 0831. Something of a time warp, Kalmar is a 1900 mansion turned idiosyncratic pension sitting in its own garden on the southeast slope of Gellért hill, a few hundred yards back from the Danube. It's a family-run concern, with large, clean rooms. There are double rooms, suites, plus a top-floor apartment that can sleep 4; all have antique furniture, high ceilings, large windows and TVs.

Eating

The country that gave us goulash hasn't earned a place at the top table of global edible culture. Hungarians know their way round a knuckle of ham, sure enough, but stout, artery-thickening cuisine is the norm; most dishes tend to come soused in thick creamy sauces. That said, you can get lucky. There is a lively metropolitan restaurant scene at the top end, serving fish fresh from Lake Balaton, and the countryside seems to produce so much fruit that the Hungarians have no option but to use it in spiced soups – a cool cinnamon-spiked peach broth is not uncommon in late summer. Cakes are a strong suit, as are *lángos*, a pizza-like dough that's fried, then smeared with sour cream and garlic.

Best of the rest

Gellérthegy (Gellért Hill)
ⓘ District 6. Citadel built by the Austrians as a symbol of supremacy after the 1848 revolution.

Chain Bridge The oldest bridge to span the Danube (1849). The engineer of Hammersmith Bridge, William Tierney Clark designed it; Scotsman Adam Clark built it.

Dohány Street Synagogue
ⓘ Dohány utca 2, Mon-Thu 1000-1700 (winter -1500) Fri, Sun, 1000-1400, HUF 400-1000. Central Europe's largest Jewish community gave rise to its largest synagogue. The 'Holocaust tree' in the synagogue garden has metal branches and dog-collar leaves bearing the names of Jewish lives lost.

Liszt Ferenc Zeneakadémia (Franz Liszt Academy of Music)
ⓘ Liszt Ferenc tér 8, District 6, T01-462 4600. Amazing art nouveau building and one of the city's main concert halls.

Margitsziget (Margaret Island). The lungs of the city, a favourite destination for romantics and joggers.

Szoborpark (Statue Park)
ⓘ 1000-sunset, Balatoni út/Szabadkai utca, District 22, www.szoborpark.hu. HUF 600. Buses leave daily at 1100 from Deák tér. 'Disneyland of Communism' displaying the tonne-weight statues that once lined the city's streets: Marx, Engels, Lenin, Hungarian labour movement heroes, plus the hammer and sickle.

Vörös és Fehér, Andrássy út 41, District 6, T01-413 1545. Daily 1200-2400. Modish bar just opposite the Opera House that's part-owned by the Budapest Wine Society. The cellar is excellent but there's also a good Magyar/international menu: saddles of venison, paprika catfish, filet mignon, beef consommé and goulash.

Café Kör, Sas utca 17, Szent István Bazilika, T01-311 0053. Mon-Sat 1000-2200, closed Sun. A modest bistro on the heels of the Basilika that, in a glut of high-price showy restaurants, still attracts locals as much as passing sightseers. Flavours are Hungarian (goulash and goose liver, aubergine cream, cottage cheese dumplings with hot forest fruit sauce) with some lighter European notes. Booking is strongly recommended. Also serves breakfast.

Gerbeaud, Vörösmarty tér 7, Deák Ferenc tér, District 5, T01-429 9000. A 150-year-old institution hanging with chandeliers. The café's signature dessert is a cake with nuts, jam and apricot, covered in chocolate. Once part of the weekend ritual of the middle classes, it is now firmly etched on the tourist's itinerary.

Café Gusto, Frankel Leó utca, District 2, T01-316 3970. Closed Sun. One of the tiniest cafés in Budapest that in its relatively short lifespan (14 years) has become a real local institution. Although its only just acquired a gas cooker (so now you can get lasagne along with beef *carpaccio*), Gusto has a loyal fanbase among the city's intelligentsia. On match days, a TV is slapped on a centre table.

Ruszwurm Cukrászda, Szentháromság utca 7, Várhegy, District 1, T01-375 5284. A glory clock hangs behind the old-world cherrywood counter at this perfect Biedermeier relic.

Gilt chandeliers, velvet banquettes, 19th-century ornaments and china-ware – this is the place for strudels, gingerbread and salt cakes.

Central Market Hall, Fővám Krt 1-3, District 4. Pile 'em high is the philosophy at the cheap food counters ranged around the top of the grand Market Hall built in 1890. Mounds of cabbage, stews of butter beans, stringy pickles and plenty of choice for sordid looking sausages. Sophisticated it ain't.

Nightlife

Bars and clubs

There are the chi-chi metropolitan sit-outs at **Liszt Ferenc Square**, or slightly seedier coffee shops along **Raday utca** and, in summer, there are chic and dressy clubs on **Margit Island**. The cool **A38** boat, moored on the Buda side between Petőfi and Lágymányosi bridges, T01-464 3946, T01-464 3940, www.a38.hu, is a cutting-edge concert venue housed in a Ukrainian stone carrier ship.

66 99 Ten out of ten for hipness goes to the late-night speakeasies known as kerts...

Ten out of 10 for hipness, though, goes to the **kerts**, Budapest-style late-night speakeasies that set up in the disused courtyards of the city's derelict housing squares. Unpopular with sleep-deprived neighbours, they squat in uninhabitable dwellings until local opposition forces the fridge, chairs, tables and, invariably, table football tables, to move a few doors down to

the next condemned and neglected ghost house. Understandably shy of publicity, they seldom have street signs or set addresses, so ask a local to direct you through the medieval district or look out for a doorman propped on a barstool outside an otherwise unassuming doorway. The 2 longest-running venues are: **Szoda** in District 5; and **Szimpla** in the Jewish district, Kazinczy utca 14, T01-321 5880, www.szimpla.hu. **Tuzraktar**, Tuzolto utca 54-56, District 9, www.tuzraktar.hu, is the place for VJ festivals, avant-garde art, jazz and performance, while **WestBalkan**, Kisfaludy utca 36, District 8, T01-371 1807, is an open-air drink and dance hall.

Classical and opera

The city has fistfuls of concert venues from the **National State Opera** house and the art nouveau **Liszt Ferenc Academy**, to the state-of-the-art Russell Johnson- designed **National Concert Hall** at the Palace of Art, Komor Marcell u 1, T01-455 9000, www.muveszetek palotaja.hu, home of the National Philharmonic Orchestra. Tickets are available from T06-30 30 30 999, www.tex.hu, www.eventim.hu, www.ticket express.hu, or www.musicmix.hu.

Festivals

There's a quick marching parade of week-long festivals throughout the year, from the highbrow opera, ballet and folklore-themed **Budapest Spring Festival**, www.festivalcity.hu, to glass-clinking champagne and wine fests, and Central Europe's answer to Woodstock or Glastonbury: the island festival of **Sziget**, www.sziget.hu.

Copenhagen

What can we say about Copenhagen, capital of the land that gave us Lego, Lurpak and the egg chair? To say it is 'understated chic' hardly raises the blood pressure. We know it's Scandinavian and that hints at the sensual and the liberated. An existentialist philosopher called Kierkegaard hailed from the city, and isn't there some statue of a mermaid that keeps getting decapitated? All this is true but it hardly opens a window on the city's soul. Surprise is the bonus that comes with a city that is not presented in tourist cellophane. Sightseeing here becomes a more personal odyssey and Copenhagen's world-class museums and art galleries, the city's ever-so-literate awareness of architecture and design, and the everyday style and pace of life all become something to be discovered and experienced as new.

Arts & culture
★★★

Eating
★★★★

Nightlife
★★★★

Outdoors
★★★

Romance
★★★

Shopping
★★★★

Sightseeing
★★★

Value for money
★★

Overall score
★★★

At a glance

Rådhuspladsen is Copenhagen's Times Square, the **Tivoli Gardens** are to the south and the capital's major shopping street, **Strøget**, starts at its northeast corner. **Slotsholmen**, the historical heart of Copenhagen, lies in an oblong-shaped island enclosed by narrow canals northeast, a 10-minute walk away. North of Slotsholmen, another 10-minutes on foot, is **Nyhavn**, a pedestrianized street facing a 17th-century canal with a happy medley of cafés and restaurants. Immediately west of Central Station, multicultural and semi-gentrified **Vesterbro** is good for accommodation. The artificial **lakes** on the northern perimeter of the city and **Nørrebro** reveal the sharp edge of contemporary Copenhagen, while the 'free city' of bohemian **Christiania** lies on the Island of Christianshavn to the east of the centre.

Just living is not enough. One must have sunshine, freedom, and a little flower.

Hans Christian Andersen

★ *Don't leave town without watching the stunning firework display at Tivoli Gardens on Wednesdays and Saturdays.*

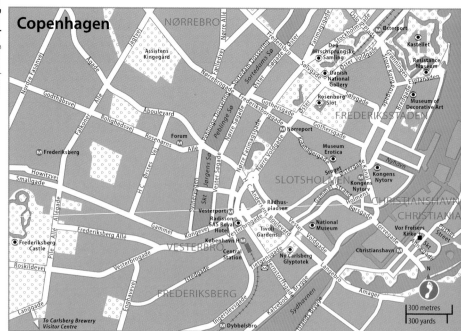

◉ Sights

Rådhuspladsen and around

The wide open space of Rådhuspladsen is best explored before mid-morning, with only the gentle buzz of commuters and the late 19th and early 20th-century buildings looking down on you. Nearby is one of Copenhagen's must-see galleries **Ny Carlsberg Glyptotek** ① *Dantes Plads 7 (Tietensgade 25 till Jun 2006), T33-41 81 41, www.glyptoteket.dk. Tue-Sun 1000-1600. Kr 20, Sun and Wed free.* Like other world- class museums, there is too much to take in on a single visit; amongst other things, there's extensive ancient Near East and Mediterranean collections and 19th-century French Impressionists galore. The most hyped street in Copenhagen, **Strøget**, hums by lunchtime; its cafés, restaurants and cobbled squares heaving with people and street performers. To get away from the crowds, explore the

Rådhuspladsen

narrow side streets where the Copenhagen of medieval times developed. For a more tangible feel of the past, move on a few centuries and delve about in the streets around the university and some grand 19th-century churches. There is a studious feel to this part of town but for more bustle, head back to Rådhuspladsen in the evening and the twinkly lights of Tivoli.

Tivoli Gardens

① *Vesterbrogade 3, T33-15 10 01, www.tivoli.dk. Mid Apr-late Sep Sun-Wed 1100-2300, Thu, Sat 1100-2400, Fri 1100-0100; early Nov-late Dec Mon-Thu 1100-2200, Fri 1100-2300, Sat 1000-2300, Sun 1000-2100. Kr 68.*

The tweeness of Tivoli, Denmark's most visited attraction (most visitors are Danes), encourages Disneyfication. However, a glimmer of the original Orient-inspired magic still pervades. When twilight descends, the Turkish facade of *Restaurant Nimb* is subtly illuminated, while outside is the silent fountain inspired by the concepts of Niels Bohr, the Danish winner of the Nobel Prize for physics. The Chinese- style Pantomime Theatre plays host to a genuine ghost of *commedia dell'arte*, there is an ancient roller coaster and smaller echoes of times past that are worth seeking out, like the 1949 spiral lamp of the designer Poul Henningsen near Tivoli Lake.

◉ Travel essentials

Getting there Copenhagen **International Airport**, T32-31 32 31, flight information T32-47 47 47, www.cph.dk, is 9 km from the city and 12 mins from Central Station by train every 20 mins (Mon-Fri 0500-2400, Sat 0530- 2400, Sun 0630-2400, Kr 25.50). Some stop at Nørreport, where a metro links with Kongens Nytorv for accommodation around Nyhavn. A city bus service, 250S, costs about the same as the train but takes 25 mins. Night bus N96 runs every 30 mins-1 hr to the centre (Kr 45). A taxi, from outside the arrivals hall, will cost about Kr 180-200.

Getting around Public transport tickets cover buses, S-Tog trains and the metro, within designated zones. The basic ticket costs Kr 17 and covers travel of any kind for up to 1 hr within any 2 zones (which covers most of the sights and places of interest). Tickets and maps showing the zones are available from machines or ticket offices in train stations and from bus drivers. If you intend to do a lot of travelling about the city you can buy a *klippekort* valid for 10 rides (2 zones Kr 105, 3 zones Kr 145) or a 24 hr unlimited travel card (Kr 100). Another alternative is to buy a **Copenhagen Card** which offers unlimited travel in greater Copenhagen and free admission to some museums and sights. It's valid for 24-72 hrs and costs Kr 215-495. It is also easy to get

around the various sights on foot. From Central Station it takes about 30 mins to walk the length of Strøget and reach Nyhavn. From around Istedgade or Vesterbrogade it takes 20 mins to reach Slotsholmen.

Tourist information Wonderful **Copenhagen** tourist office, T70-22 24 42, www.visitcopenhagen.dk, is on the corner of Vesterbrogade and Bernstorffsgade, close to Central Station. May-Jun Mon-Sat 0900-1800; Jul-Aug Mon-Sat 0900-2000, Sun 1000-1800; Sep-Apr Mon-Fri 0900-1600, Sat 0900-1400. There is a smaller tourist office at the airport.

Exchange rate Danish Kroner (Kr). £1 = Kr 11.03. €1 = Kr 7.47.

National Museum

ⓘ *Ny Vestergade 10, T33-13 44 11,*
www.natmus.dk. Tue-Sun 1000-1700.
Kr 50, Wed free.

Denmark's National Museum lays claim
to four floors of world cultural history
with more than a modicum of
justification. The emphasis is on
Denmark but there is an expansive
ethnographical collection as well as a
floor devoted to Near East and Classical
antiquities. Highlights include some
astounding 3000-year-old artefacts,
Viking treasure of silver ornaments,
jewellery, coins and skin cloaks, an
Eskimo hunter's anorak made of
sealskin and a metope from the outer
frieze of the Parthenon purchased by a
Danish naval officer in the 17th century.

Nyhavn and around

Nyhavn caters to hedonists and
consumers as well as museum lovers.
It successfully manages to do both in
the unique **Museum Erotica**
ⓘ *Købmagergade 24, T33-12 03 11,*
www.museumerotica.dk, May-Sep
1000-2300, Oct-Apr 1100-2000, Kr 69.

Tivoli

Nyhavn

Prestigious stores are to be found
along **Østergade**, where Strøget
begins its long, shop-laden route to
Rådhuspladsen, and the small streets
that lie to the north of Østergade are
filled with specialty stores and
restaurants. A more populist
atmosphere characterizes the sunny
side of Nyhavn, facing the eponymous
canal, where a cluster of eateries draws
in the crowds. Around the corner from
Nyhavn on stately **Bredgade**, the
mood abruptly changes once again
amidst the many reminders of
inherited affluence. **Frederiksstaden**,
has more than a fair share of
18th-century palaces and churches
plus some absorbing museums
(the **Resistance Museum**
ⓘ *Churchillparken, T33-13 77 14,*
*www.natmus.dk,*and the Danish
Museum of Decorative Art
ⓘ *Bredgade 68, T33-18 56 56,*
www.kunstindustrimuseet.dk, and
the remains of an old fortress,
the Kastellet. To the west of
Frederiksstaden lies the 16th-century,
much-visited **Rosenborg Slot**
ⓘ *Øster Voldgade, T33-15 32 86,*
www.rosenborgslot.dk.

Vesterbro and Frederiksberg

Although the area immediately behind
the railway station has plenty of hotels
and sex shops, Vesterbro is not tourist
land and a stroll down **Istedgade**
offers a window on contemporary
Copenhagen. Recent renovation work
is gentrifying parts and an ethnic
dimension is added by immigrants
from Asia and Africa. The tree-lined
boulevards and elegant gardens of
snooty Frederiksberg further west feel
very different. The best approach is by
way of stately **Frederiksberg Allé**
which branches off Vesterbrogade and
terminates at a grand park and gardens.
Places of interest here are as diverse as
the areas themselves, including:
Carlsberg Brewery Visitor Centre
ⓘ *Gamle Carlsberg Vej 11, T33-27 13 14,*
Tue-Sun 1000-1600, Kr 40; 18th-century
summer royal pad **Frederiksberg
Castle** ⓘ *Roskildevej 32, T36-16 22 44,*
guided tours last Sat of month at 1100,
Kr 25; and Arne Jacobsen's
still-controversial 1960s glass tower
Radisson SAS Royal Hotel
ⓘ *Hammerischsgade 1, T33-42 60 00.*

Carlsberg Brewery Visitor Centre

Christiania came into existence over 30 years ago, when hippies, activists and others began moving into a site of abandoned military buildings and set about creating an alternative way of living. Over the years, Christiania has experienced some tumultuous encounters with state authorities, from exasperated officials demanding taxes, to invasion by brigades of riot-suited police. Now an official "social experiment", Christiania has become a major attraction for visitors intrigued by the prospect of an alternative lifestyle flourishing in the heart of a modern bourgeois state. Between 650 and 1,000 people work or live here, in homes most have designed and built themselves, free of government taxes. In recent years a major clean-up campaign has put a stop to the open selling of marijuana on the streets of Christiania. Police patrols create a troubled atmosphere at times, but mainstream Danes seem to look on with bemused toleration. A poll in 1996 showed over 60% of the country's population agreed that Christiania should be preserved while only 20% wanted it closed down.

Nørrebro and the lakes

As in Vesterbro, there's a workaday, multicultural feel to Nørrebro. Young professionals are gentrifying the area and Palestinians, Turks, Asians and other immigrants are bringing a tang of cosmopolitanism to street life. Across the bridge, on the city side of the lakes, are two top-notch art galleries: the esteemed **Danish National Gallery** ⓘ *Statens Museum for Kunst, Sølvgade 48, T33-74 84 94, www.smk.dk, Tue-Sun 1000-1700, Wed 1000-2000, closed public holidays, Kr 50, free Wed*, with major works of European art; and tucked away behind it, the lesser-known but highly rewarding **Den Hirschsprungske Samling** ⓘ *Stockholmsgade 20, T35-42 03 36, www.hirschsprung.dk, Wed-Mon 1100-1600, Kr 35, free Wed*, a treasure trove of Danish art from the last two centuries.

Christiania and around

Christiania, much more than a social laboratory in alternative living, is a bustling and buzzing area. The place fascinates Danes as much as foreigners and a tour of to this multi-faceted community that mixes anarchists with hard-nosed dealers, and canny careerists with 21st-century hippies is recommended. A makeshift look to the entrance area and a few down-and-outs don't make for an auspicious start, but it all livens up considerably once you find **Pusher Street**. Along this street and running off it on both sides are cafés, bars, restaurants and stalls selling ethnic jewellery and political T-shirts. A few years ago you would have seen 20 different types of cannabis on sale on these stalls but now the best you'll get is some skunk seed to take home. Further west on Sankt Annægade is the baroque splendour of **Vor Frelsers Kirke** (Church of Our Saviour) ⓘ *0900-1700, free*, completed in 1696. Its 1752 spiral tower, built in pine and covered with copper, has a wacky external staircase that twists around the tower (Kr 20) to the top.

● Sleeping

The main hotel areas are Vesterbro and Frederiksberg, where smart and comfortable double rooms can be found for below Kr 1000. Classier hotels tend to be around Nyhavn and Kongens Nytorv.

€€€ Radisson SAS Royal Hotel, Hammerichsgade 1, T33-42 60 00, www.radissonas.com. You wouldn't think so from the outside but the most stylish rooms in town are to be found here. Arne Jacobsen's original designs have been recently remodelled by Yasmine Mahmoudieh.

€€€-€€ 71 Nyhavn, T33-43 62 00, www.71nyhavnhotelcopenhagen.dk. 2 warehouses have been converted into this smart, 150-room hotel. Original beams lend a rustic touch to the luxury interior, including the bar and the above-average restaurant.

€€ DGI-byens, Tietgensgade 65, T33-29 80 70, www.dgi-byen.dk. A hotel that fulfils one's expectations of Scandinavian style and Danish modernism – sleek and uncluttered. Superb swimming pool and sports facilities adjoin the hotel.

€€ Hotel Bethel Sømandshjem, Nyhavn 22, T33-13 03 70. Characterful old seaman's hotel, cheap rooms are without a harbour view, but for a little more you get a spacious corner room with a grand view. Showers not baths, café and nearby Nyhavn nightlife.

€ Cab inn City, Mitchellsgade 14, T35-39 84 00, www.city@cabinn.dk. Pristine, budget rooms, tiny but perfectly formed with all you need contained in an amazingly small space. Very central, good coffee bar, 24-hr reception. Possibly the best value in town.

● Eating

Gammel Strand in Slotsholmen has some upmarket fish restaurants and cafés. Nyhavn offers a more democratic mood for wining and dining, while in Vesterbrogade there is everything from Danish bakeries and kebab-style eateries to specialist restaurants. Værnedamsvej, a street off Vesterbrogade, has a number of non-touristy places.

Ψ Ψ Ψ Noma, Strandgade 93, Christianshavn, T32-96 32 97, www.noma.dk. 1200-1400, 1800-2400. Set in a converted 18th-century warehouse overlooking the harbour this ultra-minimalist room is offset by the excellent and creative modern Scandinavian cuisine.

Ψ Ψ Ψ Truffle Café and Restaurant, Vestergade 29-31, T33-13 15 00. Mon-Sat 1130-2200, Sun 1130-1500. Superb variety of food in this slinky, new restaurant. The set meals for 2 in the café are almost half the price of those in the restaurant. Try sushi with a Kirin in a tall glass.

Ψ Ψ Nørrebro Bryghus, Ryesgade 3, Nørrebro, T35-30 05 30, noerrebro bryghus.dk. Mon-Wed, Sun 1100-2200, Thu-Sat 1200-0200. An old factory converted into a stylish restaurant and microbrewery with live music in the basement, superlative service in the great dining hall and the brewery itself, all sleek steel vats and pipes, gurgling away beside you. Inventive modern Californian-Danish food.

Ψ Ψ Nytorv Restaurant and Café, Nytorv 15, T33-11 77 06. 1100-2200. One of Copenhagen's oldest restaurants, this is the best place to try the much heralded open sandwich. Great for lunch when the place fills with

Danes enjoying one of the few places left that specializes in smørrebrød.

Ψ Rizraz, Kompagnistræde 20, T33-15 05 75. 1130-2400. A vast warren of a place with a huge vegetarian all-you- can eat Mediterranean buffet and tasty meat dishes. This could be the best value in town.

● Nightlife

Copenhagen boasts a large, ever-changing bar and club scene. Everything pretty much centres around Vesterbro, Nørrebro, Østerbro and the centre, and the great thing is that they are all close enough to sample a selection from several in any one night. The most popular club in town is **Vega** in Vesterbro with a nightclub at weekends, lounge bar, concert venue and a cocktail bar to choose from. In Nørrebro are 2 good places to choose from: **Rust**, another multi-venue place where good music takes precedence over the weekly cattle market, and **Stengade 30** the more underground version of the same. In Østerbrogade in the city centre **Park Café**, with its 3 dance floors, attracts an upwardly mobile crowd. Copenhageners don't start to kick their heels until at least 2400-0100, particularly at weekends, but Scandinavian-style lounge bars (**Ideal Bar** in Fredriksberg and **Stereo Bar** in Nørrebro among the best) with a warm, intimate and inviting atmosphere will keep you simmering until then. Special one-off and try-out club and bar nights are plentiful. The weekly *Copenhagen Post's In & Out* guide contains a good day-by-day rundown in English.

From struggling provincial backwater to the city that never sleeps, Dublin has been riding one hell of a roller coaster in recent years. Ireland's capital has regained a European presence that it last experienced in the 18th century. Every day planeloads of visitors arrive in this city ready to party. While Temple Bar ladles on the blarney as thick as the head on a pint of Guinness, the statue of the 19th-century nationalist Daniel O'Connell overlooks wood-panelled Edwardian pubs, designer bars and clubs, chic shops and high-tech arts centres. Yet, amid the sophisticated gloss, the fiddly-diddly music and the political wheeler-dealing is a city whose secrets are still waiting to be explored. And through the heart of it all snakes the Liffey: dark, unfathomable and just a little bit muddier than we'd like to admit.

Dublin

Arts & culture
★★★

Eating
★★★

Nightlife
★★★★

Outdoors
★★★

Romance
★★

Shopping
★★

Sightseeing
★★★

Value for money
★★

Overall score
★★★

At a glance

Georgian **Grafton Street**, south of the river and Trinity College is the centre of tourist Dublin. It's where you'll find most of the most significant sights and the city's best restaurants and hotels. **Temple Bar**, with its ancient, redeveloped streets lies to the northwest on the banks of the Liffey. South and west of the immediate city centre is an odd mishmash of areas, loosely defined as the **Liberties** and barely touched by the Celtic Tiger phenomenon. To the north of the Liffey the area round **O'Connell Street**, one of the city's oldest and grandest boulevards, and now cluttered with shop signs and statuary, is less tourist orientated than areas south of the river but has much to offer thanks to its powerful historical associations and impressive literary connections. You'll also find much of the city's least expensive accommodation here. Northwest of the Liffey is a relatively unvisited area with a long history, an

Good puzzle would be to cross Dublin without passing a pub

Leopold Bloom, as he wanders around Dublin in James Joyce's 'Ulysses'

ancient church, the city's Four Courts and **Smithfield market**. Further west still are the old **Collins Barracks**, now housing a branch of the National Museum, and, beyond that again, the **Phoenix Park**, the largest enclosed public space in Europe. Grand Victorian and Edwardian **Ballsbridge**, to the southeast of the centre, is the poshest part of Dublin with some good restaurants and lively bars.

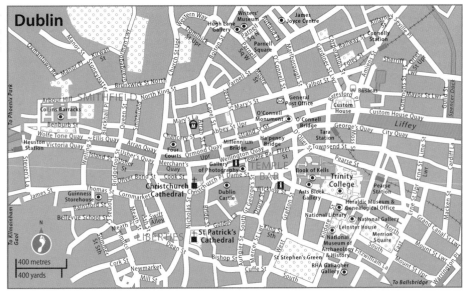

24 hours in the city

Begin your day with a full Irish breakfast, guaranteed to slow you down to the Irish pace of life for a few hours at least. Spend the morning marvelling at the collection of gold in the **National Museum**, followed by a quick peek at the Picasso in the **National Gallery** and a really classy lunch at *The Commons*. In the afternoon stroll around the shops and alleys of Temple Bar before hopping on a bus to the **Guinness Storehouse** to enjoy a bird's-eye view of the city – and a pint of Guinness to boot. In the evening head back to Temple Bar to sample modern Irish cuisine at *Eden*. After dinner enjoy a drink at *Oliver St John Gogarty's*, where you've a good chance of catching some traditional Irish music, or grab a cab over to the *Brazen Head*, Dublin's oldest bar. The next port of call for nightowls should be **Harcourt Street**, where the clubs get going around 2300. *Chocolate Bar*, *POD* and the *Red Box* are some of the hippest joints in town.

Trinity College

★ *Don't leave town without enjoying an impromptu folk session in one of Dublin's traditional pubs.*

European City Breaks Dublin

⊙ Travel essentials

Getting there Dublin International Airport, T01-8141111, www.dublin-airport.com, is 8 miles north of the city centre. **Aircoach** runs to and from from the City Centre to the airport 24 hrs, daily. Tickets can be bought on board and cost €6 (1-way) or €10 (return), journey time about 35 mins. This service stops at most of the major hotels around Dublin City. There is currently no train service from the airport to the centre. A taxi will cost about €25.

Getting around The centre of Dublin is easy enough to negotiate on foot but if you get tired, local buses run by **Dublin Bus**, T01-8734222, are frequent and cheap. Bus stops are green and fares (exact change only to the driver) start at €0.85 for a short hop within the city. A 1-day pass costs €5 (3- and 5-day passes

€10 and €15.50 respectively). An excellent bus map of the city is available free from Dublin Bus or the tourist office. Dublin Bus also operates the hop-on, hop-off Dublin City Tour which starts at *McDonalds* on O'Connell Bridge. The complete tour takes over an hour and visits 16 sights around the city. The bus ticket (€10) includes discounts at each of the sights and is valid for a day. The new electric tram system, the **Luas**, www.luas.ie, is designed to bring in commuters from the suburbs but the red line, from Connolly Street through the shopping streets north of the river and then along the quays to Phoenix Park and Heuston station, can be useful. Tickets are bought at the tram stop (a single ticket is valid for only 90 mins, a return for the whole day). The all-zone combi ticket

for bus and Luas costs €6 for 1 day. **DART** (Dublin Area Rapid Transit), Dublin's light railway system, links the coastal suburbs with the city centre and is useful for short hops between the south and north of the city and for transport to some suburban areas.

Tourist information Dublin Tourism Centre St Andrew's Church, Suffolk St, T01-605 7700. Jun-Sep Mon-Sat 0900-2030, Sun 1100-1700; Oct-May Mon-Sat 0930-1730. They supply accommodation advice and bookings, ferry and concert tickets, car hire, bureau de change, free leaflets and city-wide and Irish guidebooks for sale. **Temple Bar information centre**, 12 East Essex St, www.visit-templebar.ie.

👁 Sights

Trinity College

ⓘ *www.tcd.ie. Jun-Sep Mon-Sat 0930-1700, Sun 0930-1630; Oct-May Sun 1200-1630; closed for 10 days over Christmas and New Year. €7.50.*

Trinity College is a time capsule of smooth lawns, cobblestones, statuary and formal buildings, looking more like Oxford's dreaming spires than some of the Oxford colleges themselves do. It was founded in 1592 by Elizabeth I, in an attempt to prevent young Protestant intellectuals of the Pale going to Europe and discovering Catholicism. Its squares are dominated by the campanile tower, beside which is a Henry Moore statue, *Reclining Connected Form*. To the right is the finest building on the campus, the Old Library, home to the **Book of Kells**. There are two huge reproductions of pages from the book explaining the religious symbolism and the work which went into its manufacture. Across Fellowes Square is the **Arts Block**, built in 1980, and showing collections of conceptual and avant-garde art.

Oscar Wilde, Merrion Square

National Library

Kildare Street

Just south of Trinity College and tightly packed with museums and other places to visit, the area between **Merrion Square**, the Georgian heartland of Dublin (one-time home to Daniel O'Connell at No 58, W B Yeats at 82, and Oscar Wilde at No 1), and the main gate of Trinity is Dublin's tourist centre. At the corner of Leinster Street and Kildare Street the Kildare Street Club, as was, is now the **Heraldic Museum and Genealogical Office** ⓘ *2 Kildare St, T01-6614877, Mon-Fri 1000-1630, free.* Designed in 1861 by Deane and Son, the same firm that built the museum in Trinity College, there are exhibits of all kinds of coats of arms, coins, seals and whatnot. Heading up Kildare Street, you pass on your left the **National Library** ⓘ *Kildare St, T01-6030200, Mon-Wed 1000-2100, Thu-Fri 1000-1700, Sat 1000-1300, free.* It was designed in 1884-1890 by Deane and Son as part of the complex of the National Library and Museum and often holds exhibitions. The reading room is certainly worth a look, especially for fans of *Ulysses*. In

December 2000 the library purchased a draft manuscript of the Circe chapter of the novel, handwritten by Joyce.

Leinster House, further down Kildare Street, was built around 1745 by James Fitzgerald, Earl of Leinster as an escape from Parnell Square in north Dublin, which had become a little too nouveau riche for his liking. The house was eventually sold by his grandson to the Royal Dublin Society, which turned it into a museum and erected the two buildings on either side, as well as the School of Art and the National Gallery at the Merrion Square side of the estate. The building is now home to the Republic's two Houses of Parliament. ⓘ *T01-6183066. Tours Mon-Fri by prior arrangement only. You must show a passport to begin the tour.*

Further down Kildare Street is the **National Museum of Archaeology and History** ⓘ *T01-6777444, Tue-Sat 1000-1700, Sun 1400-1700, closed Mon, free.* The museum is full of the most wonderful things from Bronze Age gold hoards and a display of ancient Egyptian embalming techniques to an informative exhibition called *The Road to Independence.*

National Museum

Dublin Castle

ⓘ Dame St, T01-6777129,
www.dublincastle.ie. Mon-Fri 1000-1700,
Sat-Sun and bank holidays, 1400-1700.
€4.50. By guided tour only (40 mins),
last admission 1 hr before closing. Free
admission to Castle Yard, Chapel Royal
and Dubh Linn Garden.

It is difficult to surmise from the
hand-tufted carpets and 18th-century
plasterwork that this was once Dublin's
biggest stronghold, built in 1204 to
defend the city against the native Irish.
It must have looked the part too,
because apart from a Fitzgerald attack
in 1534 and an aborted attempt at
seizing it in 1641, the castle has seen
very little action. The most exciting
thing to take place here must have
been the night during the Black and
Tan War, when Michael Collins
infiltrated the records office. In 1922
the castle was officially handed over
to him as Commander in Chief of the
Irish Army. The guided tour explores
the still used State Apartments then
passes into the Upper Yard, where you
can see the Statue of Justice over the
gateway, unblindfolded and with her

National Gallery

back to the city she should have been
defending. Until she was mended
in the 1980s, her scales of justice
regularly tipped when they filled with
rainwater. From here you visit the
Undercroft, where you can see the
remains of Viking fortifications, part of
the old medieval city wall, the moat,
postern steps for deliveries, and a
dribble of the River Poddle itself. Also
in the castle is the **Chester Beatty
Library**, a priceless collection of
cultural and religious treasures.

Turning left out of the main gates of
the castle into Dame Street, you come
to **City Hall**, an outstanding piece of
Georgian architecture with the Story of
the Capital exhibition downstairs.

National Gallery

ⓘ Merrion Sq, T01-6615133,
www.nationalgallery.ie. Mon-Sat 0930-
1730 (Thu 2030), Sun 1400-1730. Free.

The big names of European art are well
represented here. There are works by
Caravaggio, Degas, El Greco, Fra
Angelico, Goya, Mantegna, Monet,
Picasso, Rembrandt, Tintoretto, Titian,
Velasquez and Vermeer for starters.

Dublin Castle

Then there is also a decent display of
English art and a marvellous collection
by Irish artists. Although the gallery
always functioned on a hand-to-mouth
basis, more prosperous times have seen
the opening of a new Millennium Wing
in 2002.

St Stephen's Green

Nowadays the city's playground, and
great for a picnic on a sunny day with
occasional music from the bandstand,
St Stephen's Green, south of Trinity
College, has had many incarnations
over the centuries. Until the 1660s it
was an expanse of open ground
where people grazed their cattle and
public executions took place. As the
surrounding area began to be
developed the green was partly
fenced in and became a park. In
1814 the public were excluded and
only residents of the grand houses
overlooking the park could use it.
In 1877 Lord Ardilaun, one of the
Guinness family, introduced a bill
to Parliament making it a public park
again and put up the cash to make
it happen.

St Stephen's Green

Temple Bar

Nowadays a vibrant tourist ghetto, the network of narrow lanes that criss-cross between the river and Dame Street and from Fishamble Street to Fleet Street is known as Temple Bar, after its 17th-century developer, Sir William Temple. The landmark to head for is **Ha'penny Bridge** over the River Liffey, a cast-iron footbridge built in 1816 and named for the toll levied on it until 1919. On the south side of the bridge **Merchant's Arch** leads into the hub of streets and alleys that define the area. Despite recent renovation and redevelopment, a few remnants of the old part of the city are still intact. Look out for **Sunlight Chambers**, on the corner of Parliament Street and Essex Quay, with multi-coloured terracotta reliefs displaying the benefits of soap.

The **Gallery of Photography** ⓘ *Meeting House Sq, T01-6714654, gallery@irish-photography.com, Tue-Sat 1000-1800, free,* is a carefully-lit, purpose-built venue with a permanent collection of 20th-century Irish photographs, plus changing monthly exhibitions by Irish

Ha'penny Bridge

and international artists and is well worth a look. The **Irish Film Centre** on Eustace Street shows art house films in a very post-modern conversion of an old Quaker Meeting House.

O'Connell Street and around

Most of the hyped tourist spots are in the southern half of the city but the north has lots to offer and fewer crowds; there is also a more genuine, earthy feel to it because it is less geared up to the tourist market. The area has strong historical and literary associations and some of the earliest Georgian buildings in the city, many of which are far more accessible to the public than snooty Merrion Square. Here too are the excellent **Hugh Lane Gallery** ⓘ *Charlemont House, Parnell Sq North, T01-8741903, www.hughlane.ie, Tue-Thu 0930-1800, Fri-Sat 0930-1700, Sun 1100-1700, closed Mon, free,* with its fine collection of modern art, and the attractive **Writers' Museum** ⓘ *18-19 Parnell Sq, T01-8722077, www.visit dublin.com, Mon-Sat 1000-1700, Sun, public holidays 1100-1700, later opening Jun-Aug, €6.25.*

◉ **Best of the rest**

St Patrick's Cathedral ⓘ *Patrick's Cl, T01-4539472, www.stpatricks cathedral.ie.* The national cathedral of the Church of Ireland and, despite its ugly exterior, the more interesting of Dublin's two cathedrals.
Guinness Storehouse ⓘ *St James' Gate, T01-4084800, www.guinness-storehouse.com. Daily 0930-1700; Jul-Aug 1930-2000. €14.* A temple to the famous Irish drink and brand.
Custom House ⓘ *Custom House Quay, T01-8787660. Mid Mar-Nov, Mon-Fri 1000-1230, Sat and Sun 1400-1700, Nov-mid Mar, Wed-Fri 1000-1230, Sun 1400-1700. €1.* Neoclassical architecture built to collect duties on boats arriving in Dublin.
General Post Office O'Connell Street's most famous building was gutted by fire and shelling in 1916 and suffered further damage in 1922 during the Civil War before being rebuilt in 1929. Still a functioning post office, inside there is a series of paintings depicting scenes from the 1916 uprising.
James Joyce Museum ⓘ *Sandycove, 13 km south of the centre, T01-2809265. Mar-Oct Mon-Sat 1000-1300, 1400-1700. Sun and public holidays 1400-1800. €6.50.* A Martello tower houses literary memorabilia associated with Joyce and *Ulysses*. More centrally, there's also a homage to be paid to the writer at the **James Joyce Centre** ⓘ *35 North Great George St, T01-878 8547, www.jamesjoyce.ie.*

Republican city

Built in 1792 and opened just in time to incarcerate any surviving rebels of the 1798 uprising, Kilmainham Gaol saw hundreds of men suffer and die for their belief in independence in the uprisings of 1798, 1803, 1848, 1867, 1916 and 1922. Most of the big names in Republican history spent time in here and some of them died here. The last man to walk out was Eamon de Valera at the end of the Civil War in 1923, whereupon the gaol was abandoned. Forty years later a voluntary group of history buffs decided to restore it. The work was completed by the state and Kilmainham was opened to the public. There is a museum covering the early 20th-century political history of Ireland as well as prison memorabilia and a guided tour. It takes you around the dungeons, tiny cells, the chapel where Joseph Plunkett was married three hours before his execution and the grim yard where *Connolly, Plunkett* and 15 other leaders of the 1916 uprising were executed. ① *Inchicore Rd, T01-4535984, www.heritageireland.ie. Apr-Sep daily 0930-1700; Oct-Mar Mon-Sat 0930-1600, Sun 1000-1700. €5.*

Sleeping

Hotel rooms in Dublin don't come cheap on the whole. Grafton St, Temple Bar and around form Dublin's chief accommodation area, and prices are pretty high at the 3-star hotel and upwards end. Guesthouses tend to be quite expensive and there are simply no B&Bs in the area. The O'Connell St area has a concentration of the more affordable guesthouses but the central location and proximity of the bus and a railway station, mean they tend to fill up most quickly. The top end of O'Connell St, around Parnell Sq, has some interesting possibilities. Ballsbridge, southeast of the city centre, has an excellent range of top-notch hotels, quality guesthouses and a cluster of interesting restaurants.

€€€ **The Clarence**, 6-8 Wellington Quay, T01-4070800, www.theclarence.ie. Owned by U2, the original wood panelling has been preserved amidst modish embellishments like leather-clad lifts, Egyptian cotton on the king size beds, and CD players in the individually designed bedrooms. Friendly staff, a bookless lounge called the *Study* and original artwork contribute to the strange mix of the spartan and the sybaritic. Room rates start from €330.

€€€ **Morrison**, 15 Ormond Quay, T01-8872400, www.morrisonhotel.ie. This classy building sits unobtrusively on the bank of the river and vies with *The Clarence* for Dublin's most hip hotel award. The new-fangled decor is refreshingly un-Irish and there are lots of other interesting touches about the place waiting to be noticed, not least of which is its

restaurant Halö. In the chic, air-conditioned bedrooms you'll find CD players, mood lighting, quality fabrics and original artwork. Breakfast not included in room rates.

€€ **Merrion Hall**, 56 Merrion Rd, T01-6681426, www.halpinsprivate hotels.com. A quiet, welcoming place with 4-poster beds, an ample lounge area, private gardens and a library of tourist literature. Award-winning breakfasts are served in the serene, sunny breakfast room.

€€-€ **Ariel House**, 50-54 Lansdowne Rd, T01-6685512. Listed, red-brick Victorian house, all non-smoking, car park, 3 mins on foot from the Lansdowne Rd DART station. Built in the 1860s, this is a classy guesthouse with a choice of rooms, all with a bath and shower, 3 with 4-poster beds. Americans, with good reason, adore the decor and antiques.

€ **Bewley's Hotel**, Merrion Rd, T01-6681111, www.BewleysHotels.com. Smart, spacious and comfortable accommodation in the Ballsbridge area. The red-brick Victorian building has been converted from a convent school and the original entrance opens into a roomy public area with the quality *O'Connell's* restaurant downstairs and a café. Aircoach stop is right outside. Rooms are around €99 for up to 3 adults or a family of 4.

€ **Castle Hotel**, 2-4 Gardiner Row, T01-8746949, www.castle-hotel.ie. One of our favourites, this is a lovingly restored Georgian building that offers so much more, and at better value, than some of the faceless hotels around town. Car parking available, elegant lounge and comfortable rooms. Michael Collins is said to have used room 201, originally No 23, when sleeping in one of his familiar safe houses during the War of Independence.

● Eating

While many of Temple Bar's restaurants are fun, fashionable and relatively inexpensive places to enjoy a meal, the area from St Stephen's Green to Merrion Square is where the real money tends to eat. Don't even look at the menus if you are on a tight budget, but for seriously fine dining and for splashing out on a treat, this is where many of the capital's best restaurants are to be found.

Ⓨ Ⓨ Ⓨ **Browne's Brasserie**, 22 St Stephen's Green, T01-6383939, www.brownesdublin.com. Book well in advance at this well-established and busy restaurant. All red plush and

white linen, it offers modern Irish cooking with lots of inventive sauces. A good place for brown enveloping at lunch time or a romantic dinner. Excellent value Sun lunch, 1230-1430.

Ⓨ Ⓨ Ⓨ **Peploe's**, 16 St Stephen's Green, T01-6763144. People seem to love or hate this place. It has been listed among the world's best places to eat by prestigious journals and has a growing band of addicted visitors. You can order simple inexpensive dishes in the wine bar or snuggle into the main restaurant for an imaginative and lovingly prepared meal. Book well in advance.

Ⓨ Ⓨ **Gallagher's Boxty House**, 20-21 Temple Bar, T01-6772762. Sells the eponymous filled potato pancakes,

❝❞ Pubs, bars and clubs are what Dublin does best.

plus lots more Irish-sourced things to eat. Vegetarians will do well here. It has a nice, old-fashioned country-kitchen feel to it, with newspapers and books to read.

Ⓨ Ⓨ **Little Caesar**, 5 Chatham House, Balfe St, T01-6718714. This Dublin institution has been around for 15 years, a very long time in the life of a Dublin restaurant, and, judging by the queues to get in, it hasn't lost its touch. It serves pizzas and pastas and some old favourites such as *bistecca alla griglia*.

Ⓨ Ⓨ **Mermaid Café**, 70 Dame St, T01-6708236. One of Dublin's better restaurants; has changing menus that show an American influence in the mussel and smoked fish chowder, the New England crab cakes and the

pecan pie with maple ice cream. The wine list is above average.

Ⓨ Ⓨ **Nico's**, 53 Dame St, T01-6773062. Ask anyone involved in the food business in Dublin where they like to eat and eventually this place crops up in the conversation. Good traditional Italian food, white cloths, chianti bottles and bustling waiters.

Ⓨ **Gruel**, 68a Dame St, T01-6707119. Very popular inexpensive restaurant, all bare boards and plain tables inside, which serves hearty hot meals such as beef hotpot and pan-fried sea trout as well as simpler filled rolls and soups.

● Nightlife

Pubs, bars and clubs are what Dublin does best. Venues around the city offer live traditional music and dancing, jazz nights, salsa nights, country nights, quiz nights, sports nights and just plain drinking nights. Tourists flock to Temple Bar, where you can party well into the early hours any night of the week. Elsewhere, the liveliest area is **South Great George's St** and **Camden St**, which from Thursday to Sunday seem to turn into a huge street party. **Harcourt St** is the centre of clubland. Most clubs serving drinks until 0200 and closing at about 0300.

Live music pours out of several pubs and bars in Dublin – a few places seeming to excel at supplying a seemingly inexhaustible selection of fresh young talent. The best bet is to check on noticeboards or the excellent and up-to-date *The Event Guide*. There are also several great venues for comedy and performing arts; especially in spring, during the film festival, and in autumn when there's an important theatre festival.

Edinburgh

Few cities make such a strong impression as Edinburgh. Scotland's ancient capital is undeniably one of the most beautiful cities in Europe, with a grandeur to match Paris or Prague, Rome or Vienna. Fittingly, such a setting provides the stage for the Edinburgh Festival, the biggest arts event on the planet. But Edinburgh is more than just the sum of its arts. Its Hogmanay party is the largest celebration in the northern hemisphere and the arrival of the new Scottish Parliament has brought confidence and vitality to a city that was always thought of as being rather straight-laced. Edinburgh's famous pursed lip has gone, replaced by a broad smile. The city is learning how to have fun, how to be stylish and, heaven forbid, how to be just a wee bit ostentatious.

Arts & culture
★★★★

Eating
★★★★

Nightlife
★★★

Outdoors
★★★★

Romance
★★★

Shopping
★★★

Sightseeing
★★★★

Value for money
★★★

Overall score
★★★★✓

At a glance

South of Princes Street is the **Old Town**, a medieval Manhattan of high-rise tenements running from the castle to the Palace of Holyroodhouse. This dark and sinister rabbit warren of narrow alleys and wynds is still inhabited by the ghosts of the city's grisly past. North of Princes Street is the elegant, neoclassical **New Town**, built in the late 18th and early 19th centuries to improve conditions in the city. The eastern New Town is bordered by **Broughton Street**, which forms one side of the so-called 'Pink Triangle', the pumping heart of the city's gay scene. Here you'll find hip bars and clubs as well as a neighbourly, laid-back atmosphere. Looming over the Pink Triangle is **Calton Hill** whose summit and sides are studded with sublime Regency terraces and bizarre monuments. The **West End** is a seamless extension of the New Town, with perfect neoclassical symmetry and discreet old money. Northeast of the city centre is

It is a precipitous city but it is still, in many ways, a hidden city with its catacombs and tunnels, and citizens who don't really want to be noticed...

Ian Rankin

Leith, Scotland's major port until the shipbuilding and fishing industries decanted south. Neglected and ignored for years, Leith has undergone a dramatic transformation and now warehouse conversions, gourmet restaurants, bars and bistros jostle for position along its waterside.

★ *Don't leave town without seeing the sun rise from the top of Arthur's Seat.*

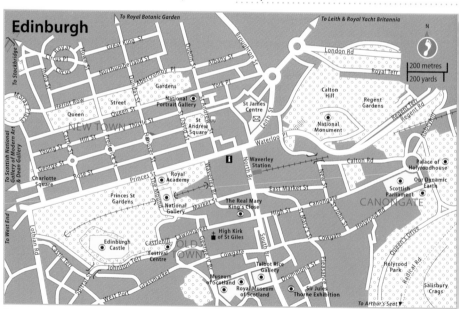

24 hours in the city

Plan your day over breakfast at *Café Hub*, then take a leisurely stroll down the length of the historic **Royal Mile** before landing back in the present with a bump at the controversial new **Scottish Parliament** building. Head back up the Royal Mile for lunch at *Off The Wall*, before stretching your legs with a walk up **Calton Hill** for the views. Afterwards, indulge in some indoor aesthetic appreciation at the **National Gallery of Scotland**, then hop on a bus down to Ocean Terminal for a fascinating tour of the **Royal Yacht Britannia**. From here it's a short stroll to **Leith** if you fancy an al fresco aperitif on the quayside, followed by a superb dinner at *Martin Wishart*. Then take a cab back to the centre for some late-night action in one of the **New Town**'s many bars.

Leith quayside

⊖ Travel essentials

Getting there Edinburgh International Airport, T0131-333 1000 (general enquiries), T0131-344 3136 (airport information), is 8 miles west of the city centre and takes 25-30 mins by road. An **Airlink** bus (www.flybybus.com) to and from Waverley Bridge leaves every 10-20 mins, takes 25 mins and costs £3 one way, £5 return. A taxi to the centre costs around £14-16.

There are direct trains to **Edinburgh Waverley** from London King's Cross (4½ hrs), Birmingham (5½ hrs) and Manchester (3½ hrs). Fares vary widely depending on the time of travel; for times, fares and bookings T08457-484950, www.thetrainline.co.uk. **Scotrail**, T08457-550033, www.scotrail.co.uk, runs the overnight Caledonian Sleeper service from London Euston (7 hrs).

Getting around Most of what you'll want to see lies within the compact city centre, which is easily explored on foot. **Public transport** is generally good and efficient. Princes Street is the main transport hub and you can get a bus to any part of the city from here. An excellent way to see the sights is to take one of the **guided bus tours** on board an open-top double-decker bus with a multilingual guide. These depart every 10-15 mins from Waverley Bridge, the first one leaving around 0900 and the last one between 1730 and 2000, depending on the time of year. Tickets are valid for the full day and you can hop on and off any of the company's buses at any of the stops. Tickets cost £8.50 from **Guide Friday Tours**, T0131-556 2244, www.guidefriday.com, or **Edinburgh Tour**, T0131-555 6363, www.edinburghtour.com.

Taxis are not cheap, costing from around £3 for the very shortest of trips up to around £8 from the centre to the outskirts. They also tend to be scarce at weekends so book ahead if you need one. **City Cabs** T0131-228 1211.

Tourist information Main tourist office, 3 Princes St, on top of Waverley Market, T0131-473 3800, www.edinburgh.org. Mon-Fri 0800-2000, Sat 0900-1730, Sun 1000-1600. It has a full range of services, including currency exchange, and will book hotel rooms, provide travel information and book tickets for various events and excursions. There's also a tourist information desk at the airport T0131-333 2167, in the international arrivals area. For details of entertainment listings in the city, pick up a copy of *The List* from any newsagent.

👁 Sights

Edinburgh Castle

ⓘ *www.historic-scotland.gov.uk. Apr-Oct 0930-1800; Nov-Mar 0930-1700. £9.80.*

The city skyline is dominated by the castle, sitting atop an extinct volcano, protected on three sides by steep cliffs. Until the 11th century the castle was Edinburgh, but with the development of the royal palace from the early 16th century, it slipped into relative obscurity. Though mobbed for much of the year, and expensive, the castle is worth a visit. It encapsulates the history of a nation, and the views from the battlements are spectacular. The highlight is the **Crown Room**, where the 'Honours of Scotland' are displayed, along with the Stone of Destiny, the seat on which the ancient kings of Scotland were crowned.

The Royal Mile

Running down the spine of the Old Town, from the castle to the Palace of Holyroodhouse, is the Royal Mile. The

Edinburgh Castle

Royal Mile

1984 regal yards comprise four separate streets: Castlehill, Lawnmarket, the High Street and the Canongate. Along its route is a succession of tourist attractions – some more worthy of the description than others – as well as many bars, restaurants, cafés and shops selling everything from kilts to Havana cigars. This is the focus of the city's tourist activity, especially during the festival when it becomes a mêlée of street performers, enthralled onlookers and al fresco diners and drinkers. One of the main points of interest is the medieval **High Kirk of St Giles**, conspicuously placed on the High Street.

Palace of Holyroodhouse

ⓘ *www.royal.gov.uk. Apr-Oct daily 0930-1800; Nov-Mar 0930-1630. £8.50.*

At the foot of the Royal Mile lies Edinburgh's royal palace. The present structure largely dates from the late 17th century when the original was replaced by a larger building for the Restoration of Charles II, although the newly crowned monarch never set foot in the place.

Scottish Parliament

ⓘ *www.scottish.parliament.uk. Tours every 15 mins; Apr-Oct Fri-Mon 1015-1715; Nov-Mar Mon and Fri 1015-1515. £3.50.*

Opposite the Palace of Holyroodhouse is the new parliament building, which finally opened in October 2004 after many years of delay and spiralling costs. Designed by visionary Barcelona architect, Enric Miralles, who died in 2000, the building is one of the most innovative pieces of architecture ever seen in the UK. It was awarded the Stirling Prize for architecture in 2005.

Holyrood Park

Edinburgh is blessed with many magnificent open spaces but Holyrood Park tops them all. The main feature is the 823 ft-high (237m) **Arthur's Seat**, the igneous core of an extinct volcano. It is a genuine bit of wilderness right in the centre of Scotland's capital and well worth the climb for the stupendous views. Another dominant feature on the skyline are the precipitous **Salisbury Crags**, directly opposite the south gates of Holyrood Palace.

Parliament building

Arthur's Seat

At the junction of The Mound and Princes Street are two of Edinburgh's most impressive neoclassical buildings, the National Gallery and the Royal Academy. The former houses the most important collection of Old Masters in the UK outside London and boasts many masterpieces from almost every period in Western art. On Queen Street is the **National Portrait Gallery**, a collection of the great and the good of Scottish history in a fantastical French Gothic medieval palace, modelled on the Doge's Palace in Venice. A free shuttle bus runs between them every 30-45 minutes from 1045 to 1600.

Museum of Scotland and Royal Museum of Scotland

ⓘ *Chambers St, T0131-247 4422, www.nms.ac.uk. Mon-Sat 1000-1700, Tue 1000-2000, Sun 1200-1700. Free.*

The Museum of Scotland is a treasure trove of intriguing and important artefacts, displayed chronologically from the basement up to the sixth floor. Though at times patchy and incomplete, it does help to take the mystery out of Scottish history and makes for a pleasurable few hours. Its elderly neighbour, the Royal Museum, holds an extensive and eclectic range of collections and includes everything from Classical Greek sculptures to stuffed elephants and Native North American totem poles, all housed in a wonderful Victorian building.

National Gallery and National Portrait Gallery

ⓘ *National Gallery, The Mound; Portrait Gallery, 1 Queen St. T0131- 624 6200, www.nationalgalleries.org. Daily 1000-1700, Thu till 1900. Free.*

Calton Hill

Calton Hill is another of Edinburgh's extinct volcanoes, at the east end of Princes Street, and well worth climbing for some of the best views in the city as well as the monuments at the top. These form the four corners of a precinct and make for a strange collection. The most famous is the **National Monument**, built to commemorate the Scots who died in the Napoleonic Wars.

National Portrait Gallery

European City Breaks Edinburgh

Botanic Gardens

Scottish National Gallery of Modern Art

ⓘ 75 Belford Rd, T0131-624 6200, www.nationalgalleries.org. Daily 1000-1700. Free.

About 20 minutes' walk from the West End is the Scottish National Gallery of Modern Art, featuring everything from the Impressionists to Hockney. It is particularly strong on Expressionism, with works by Picasso, Cézanne, Matisse, Magritte, Mondrian, Henry Moore, Kandinsky, Klee, Giacometti and Sickert all displayed as well as the big names from Fauvism, Surrealism, Abstract Expressionism and Cubism. Alongside these are the British greats like Francis Bacon, Helen Chadwick and Damien Hirst. Opposite, the **Dean Gallery**, houses one of the most complete collections of Dada and Surrealist art in Britain.

Water of Leith and the Botanic Gardens

If the weather's fair, one of the finest pleasures this city has to offer is the walk along the bucolic Water of Leith.

The Water of Leith Walkway runs from the western outskirts of the city, all the way to the docks at Leith, but the most beautiful section starts from below Belford Bridge, by the Scottish National Gallery of Modern Art and Dean Gallery, and takes you to the gorgeous **Royal Botanic Gardens** ⓘ Nov-Feb daily 1000-1600; Mar-Apr and Sep-Oct till 1800; May-Aug till 2000. Free.

Royal Yacht Britannia

ⓘ www.royalyachtbritannia.co.uk. Mar-Oct daily 0930-1630; Nov-Feb 1000-1530. £9. Britannia Tour bus from Waverley Bridge or buses 11, 22, 34, 35 and 36 from Princes St.

Housed at the Ocean Terminal in Leith, the Britannia is a fascinating attraction and shows the Windsors in a strangely downbeat manner. The relatively steep entrance fee may seem excessive, but it's well worth it. The tour offers a genuine insight into the lives of Britain's best-known family and the sight of Her Majesty's bedroom, more in keeping with a Berkshire guesthouse than a Head of State's private quarters, comes as a real shock.

Edinburgh

Also available

◉ Best of the rest

Our Dynamic Earth ⓘ Holyrood Rd, www.ourdynamicearth.co.uk. Apr-Oct daily 1000-1700, Nov-Mar Wed-Sun only. £8.95. Hi-tech virtual journey through time with strong environmental message.
The Real Mary King's Close ⓘ Warrinston's Close, High St, www.realmarykingsclose.com. Apr-Oct daily 1000-2100, Nov-Mar Sun-Fri 1000-1600, Sat 1000-2100, £7.45. Authentic and spooky insight into 17th-century town life.
Sir Jules Thorne Exhibition ⓘ 9 Hill Sq, T527 1600, www.rcsed.ac.uk. Mon-Fri 1400-1600. Free. Fairly grotesque but fun look through the keyhole of surgical history.
Talbot Rice Gallery ⓘ Old College, Tue-Sat 1000-1700 (daily during the festival), free, www.trg.ed.ac.uk. The University's collection of Renaissance paintings, housed in a wonderful neoclassical building.
Stockbridge One of the city's most beguiling corners, with a jumble of antique shops and second-hand bookstores.
Rosslyn Chapel ⓘ Mon-Sat 1000-1700, Sun 1200-1645. £5, www.rosslynchapel.org.uk. Seven miles south of the city centre, this magnificent 15th-century chapel features in the Da Vinci Code and is said to be the last resting place of the Holy Grail.
Cramond On the northwestern fringes of the city is this 18th-century coastal village. A lovely, wooded walk leads along the banks of the Almond river towards the Old Cramond Brig, where the Cramond Inn makes a fine spot for some liquid refreshment.

Every year Edinburgh plays host to the world's biggest arts festival, when the capital bursts into life in a riot of entertainment unmatched anywhere. Over a million tourists descend on the city to experience a brain-sapping variety of acts performed in a frightening variety of venues. The Edinburgh Festival is actually a collection of different festivals running alongside each other, from the end of July through to the beginning of September. The **International Festival** tends to be a fairly highbrow affair and features large-scale productions of opera, ballet, classical music, dance and theatre performed in the larger venues (box office: The Hub, Castlehill, www.eif.co.uk). **The Fringe** features everything from top-class comedy to Albanian existentialist theatre- performed in a lift (box office: 108 High St, www.edfringe.com). Also coming under the festival heading are the **International Jazz and Blues Festival** (www.jazzmusic.co.uk), **International Book Festival** (www.edbookfest.co.uk), **International Film Festival** (www.edfilmfest.org.uk) and **Military Tattoo** (www.edintattoo.co.uk). For details on all events and links to other websites see www.edinburghfestivals.co.uk.

Sleeping

Edinburgh has a huge selection of places to stay. Most of the upscale accommodation is in the New Town, West End and around Calton Hill. Many city centre hotels offer good deals during the low season, especially at weekends, and also offer a standby room rate throughout the year. You'll need to book well in advance during the festival or at Hogmanay. The tourist office has a free accommodation brochure or their Central Reservations Service, T0131-473 3855, centres@eltb.org, will make a reservation for a fee of £5. Also check www.laterooms.com for last-minute deals.

€€€ **The Glasshouse**, 2 Greenside Pl, T0131-525 8200, www.theeton

group.com. Luxury boutique hotel, entered via the original façade of a Victorian church. Most rooms have their own balconies and great views. Features a 2-acre roof garden with superb views and a rooftop bar. The rooms are stylish and contemporary, in keeping with the sleek glass exterior.
€€€ **Scotsman Hotel**, North Bridge, T0131-556 5565, www.scotsmanhotel.co.uk. The former offices of *The Scotsman* newspaper have been transformed into this state-of-the-art boutique hotel. Each room is distinctive and has been furnished with great attention to detail, with original art, DVD and internet. Services and facilities include valet parking, screening room, bar, brasserie and restaurant, breakfast room, private dining rooms and a health club and spa.

€€ **Bank Hotel**, South Bridge, T0131-556 9940, www.festival-inns.co.uk. 9 individually-themed rooms, each based on a famous Scot, from the poetry of Robert Burns to the designs of Charles Rennie Mackintosh, and all tastefully done. Well-situated and good value for this part of town.
€€ **Point Hotel**, 34 Bread St, T0131-221 5555, www.point-hotel.co.uk. Former Co-op department store now stylishly refurbished and a paradigm of chic and minimalist elegance. The suites are huge (some have jacuzzis), and rooms at the front have castle views. Handily placed for the castle and Royal Mile. Its ground-floor restaurant offers high-quality bistro food, and the bar and grill, *Mondobbo*, is equally stylish. Great value for such designer style.

€€ **Ricks**, 55a Frederick St, T0131-622 7801, www.ricksedinburgh.co.uk. 10 very sleek and stylish rooms accessed via a staircase at the rear of the bar-restaurant. Decor is subtle, furnishings unfussy and in-room entertainment includes CD and DVD players and minibar. Of all the new boutique hotels in town, this is the best value.

🍴 Eating

Edinburgh has a wide range of culinary options. Most of the upmarket restaurants are in the New Town, though there are also some excellent places to be found around the Royal Mile and in Leith, which has fish restaurants and dockside bistros. Most restaurants are open from 1200-1430 and 1800-2200 and are closed on Sundays, though many Indian, Chinese and Thai restaurants, bistros and brasseries serve food daily until around 0100. During busy periods such as the festival it's best to book ahead.

Breakfast
🍴 **Café Hub**, Castlehill, T0131-473 2015. Stylish, chilled-out café providing a soothing backdrop to the tasty and inventive food. Seating outside on the terrace in summer.
🍴 **Plaisir du Chocolat**, 251-253 Canongate, T0131-556 9524. A slice of genuine Gallic gastronomic greatness and the city's finest tearoom, offering some 180 varieties of tea, hot chocolate, cakes and various French fancies. They also do a fine *petit- déjeuner* wonderful (but not cheap at £15) weekend brunch. The épicerie across the road is great for tasty picnic treats.

🍴 **Valvona & Crolla**,19 Elm Row, T0131-556 6066. Great home cooking and the best cappuccino in town. The perfect place for a big Sat brunch and very popular. Authentic Italian deli out front.

Lunch
🍴 **The Grain Store**, 30 Victoria St, T0131-225 7635. High quality Scottish ingredients served with effortless aplomb. Exuberant menu features fish, game and meat. Attentive service and relaxed ambience. 2-course lunch for less than a tenner. A real find.

66 99 **Edinburgh has more pubs and bars per square mile than any other European city and the most liberal licensing laws in the UK.**

🍴 **Off the Wall**, 105 High St, T0131-558 1497. Combines the finest Scottish produce with flair and imagination. Vegetarians are also well-catered for and the puddings are luscious in the extreme. Great value set lunch.

Dinner
🍴 **Restaurant Martin Wishart**, The Shore, T0131-553 3557. Multi award-winning restaurant serving French-influenced cuisine at its very finest. A meal here is a truly memorable experience.
🍴 **The Tower**, Museum of Scotland, Chambers St, T0131-225 3003.

The place to be seen among the corporate set, the superb Scottish menu and magnificent views across the city skyline from the rooftop terrace are hard to beat. This is modern dining at its sophisticated best.

🌙 Nightlife

Edinburgh has more pubs and bars per square mile than any other European city and the most liberal licensing laws in the UK. Bars open till 2400 or 0100 any night of the week and till 0300 during the festival and the Christmas/New Year period. The prime drinking venue is **George St** and the streets running north and south of it. Another good destination is the area at the top of **Leith Walk** known as the "Pink Triangle". The club scene has improved dramatically and any self- respecting raver will be supplied with the latest dance floor tunes spun by some of the UK's top DJs.

For movie fans, the legendary **Filmhouse**, 88 Lothian Rd, T0131-228 2688, is the UK's most famous regional cinema and the hub of Edinburgh's International Film Festival. The café-bar is a good place to hang out. **Henry's Cellar Bar**, Morrison St, T0131-221 1228, is the best place to experience Edinburgh's vibrant jazz scene. The **Traverse Theatre**, Cambridge St, www.traverse.co.uk, is the city's most exciting theatre venue, commissioning works from contemporary playwrights from Scotland and throughout the world.

For all its reputation as one of the world's most beautiful cities, Florence can seem impenetrable to the first-time visitor: a city of cramped traffic, enormous groups of tourists, street-hawkers and markets selling enormous quantities of belts and aprons decorated with the anatomy of Michelangelo's David. But it's a city that people come back to. There's good Tuscan food and wine (if you know where to look), beautiful countryside all around and a history that includes the birth of the Renaissance. But it's the art and architecture that, rightly, are most celebrated. From Michelangelo's David and Botticelli's Venus to the marginally less well known but no less impressive cloisters in Santa Croce and frescoes in Santa Maria Novella, Florence has it all. And if you need a new belt there are few better places.

Arts & culture
★★★★★

Eating
★★★

Nightlife
★★

Outdoors
★★

Romance
★★★★

Shopping
★★★★

Sightseeing
★★★★★

Value for money
★★★

Overall score
★★★⯨

At a glance

Florence sits mostly on the northern bank of the river Arno. Many arrive in the city at **Santa Maria Novella**, the city's train station and main transport hub. The city centre spreads out southeast beyond it. To the immediate east, the area of **San Lorenzo** has streets crowded with market stalls. Just northeast of here is the **Galleria dell'Accademia**, home to many of Florence's statues. The **Duomo**, Florence's biggest landmark, lies a little further south, below which a regular grid of streets stretch towards the river and make up the heart of the antique district. At the western edge of this grid, **Palazzo Strozzi** is a hulking Renaissance building, while to the south **Piazza della Signoria** competes with the Duomo to be the city's centre point. It's surrounded by grand buildings including the **Palazzo Vecchio** and the **Uffizi**, Florence's great art gallery. Nearby the **Ponte Vecchio**, Florence's oldest bridge, leads to the enormous Palazzo Pitti and elegant Giardino di Boboli.

> This is a city of endurance, a city of stone

The Stones of Florence, Mary McCarthy

Also here are the churches of Santo Spirito and, up a steep hill, San Miniato al Monte. Back on the northern bank of the Arno, to the east of Piazza della Signoria, is the spectacular Gothic basilica of **Santa Croce** and an area of interesting narrow streets and considerably fewer visitors.

★ *Don't leave town without climbing the steep hill to San Miniato al Monte.*

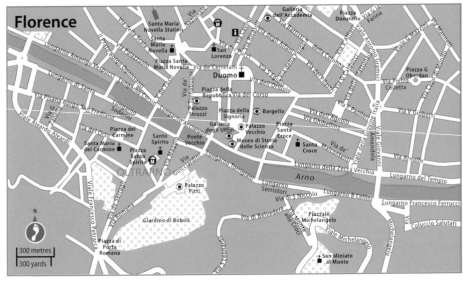

24 hours in the city

Start with a coffee and a pastry from a café (stand at the bar to drink it – many of Florence's cafés will charge you a small fortune to sit down) and allow a little time to wander across the **Ponte Vecchio** before the crowds descend too thickly. You can also stop off in **piazza della Signoria** for the obligatory photo of Michelangelo's David. If you plan to visit the Uffizi, start early to get a good place in the queue and allow the whole morning. Alternatively, the Galleria dell'Accademia, Bargello or museums and galleries of the Pitti Palace will give a taste of Renaissance art with less queuing time involved. Find a restaurant in the **Oltrarno** on the other side of the river for lunch and follow it up with a stroll in the **Giardino di Boboli**, or a climb up the hill to **San Miniato al Monte**. In the late afternoon, visit the spectacular **Duomo** and the Battistero and climb to the top of either the Campanile or the Cupola and survey the city from above, ideally with the sunshine glowing off the rooftops. Head to **Santa Croce** in the evening – if you can get there before it closes at 1730 have a look around the interior and the cloisters. Otherwise sit for a while on the steps while people gather for *aperitivi*

Santa Croce steps

before drinking one or two of your own. There are some good eating options around here, too, and you shouldn't miss an ice cream from *Vivoli*. If you want to keep going into the night, bars around Piazza Santa Croce are a good place to start, followed by a nearby club in which you can dance until dawn.

⊖ Travel essentials

Getting there Florence's **Amerigo Vespucci Airport**, T055-3061300, www.aeroporto.firenze.it, is 4 km from the centre of Florence. It is small and travelling to nearby Pisa or even Bologna may be cheaper (onward travel by train to Florence not is difficult from either). A taxi to the centre will cost you about €20, alternatively the **Vola in Bus** service (€4, every 30 mins, buy tickets on-board) connects with the railway station.

From Pisa's **Gallileo Galilei Airport**, T050-849111, www.pisa-airport.com,

Florence can be reached by train in about 1 hr 20 mins. Trains run every hour or so throughout most of the day. There is also a regular bus service to Florence. From Bologna's **Marconi Airport**, T051-6479615, www.bologna-airport.it, buses connect to the train station (a 30-min journey) every 15 mins, from where there are frequent trains (taking an hour or so) to Florence.

Getting around The city centre is small and doing anything other than walking has little to recommend it. Taxis can be found at ranks but they are

notoriously few and far between. Buses work reasonably well but traffic is often snarled up in jams. Cars are not allowed in some parts of the centre; even if you could get to the centre, trying to park is next to impossible.

Tourist information Azienda Promozionale Turistica, via Cavour 1, T055-290832, Mon-Sat 0815-1915, is helpful and has free maps as well as information on opening hours and prices. There are also offices at the train station and at the airport.

◉ Sights

Duomo and Battistero

ⓘ *piazza del Duomo, www.opera duomo.f renze.it. Duomo: Mon-Wed and Fri 1000-1700, Thu 1000-1530, Sat 1000-1645, Sun 1330-1645. First Sat of month 1000-1530. Free. Campanile: daily 0830-1930. €6. Cupola: daily 0830-1930. €6. Battistero: Mon-Sat 1200-1900, Sun 0830-1400. €3.*

Florence's tallest building is still its pink-and-white, marble-clad cathedral. Filippo Brunelleschi's dome was completed in 1463 and, at the time, was the biggest in the world with a span of 42 m. Brunelleschi constructed the octagonal ribbed dome without scaffolding, using bricks inside a marble skeleton.

Both the cupola (dome) and the separate campanile (bell tower) can be climbed – there are 414 steps to reach the tower; 463 steps to the top of the dome. The campanile was designed by Giotto in 1334 but not completed until after his death.

The interior of the Duomo doesn't quite match the extraordinarily beautiful exterior, although Vasari's

Piazza della Signoria

16th-century frescoes of the Last Judgement on the inside of the dome are suitably spectacular.

Just to the west of the Duomo, the **Battistero** (baptistry) may date to as early as the fourth century and is the city's oldest building. The interior has 13th-century mosaics and a font where Dante was baptized. The highlights, however, are the famous brass doors, by Pisano and Ghiberti. Those in situ are now copies – the originals are in the **Museo dell'Opera del Duomo**
ⓘ *piazza del Duomo 9, T055-2302885, Mon-Sat 0900-1930, Sun 0900-1340, €6.*

Piazza della Signoria

At the heart of the city, piazza della Signoria is a busy square which buzzes with tourists milling around the Renaissance and Roman statues and fountains. A replica of Michelangelo's *David* gets the most camera clicks but there is also the *Fontana di Nettuno* (Neptune Fountain) by Ammannati (1575) and the *Rape of the Sabine Women* by Giambologna (1583), carved remarkably from a single block of marble.

On the southern edge of the piazza, opposite the 14th-century, statue-filled Loggia dei Lanzi is the **Palazzo Vecchio** ⓘ *T055-2768224, Fri-Wed 0900-1900, Thu 0900-1400, €6. Originally the town hall, it also served as the residence of Duke Cosimo de Medici. Nowadays visitors can wander through some of its grand rooms.*

Galleria degli Uffizi

ⓘ *piazzale degli Uffizi, T055-2388651, www.polomuseale.firenze.it. Tue-Sun 0815-1850. €6.50.*

Some of the longest queues in the art world are to be found outside the Uffizi Gallery – allow several hours to get in. Booking ahead is highly recommended but even this is unlikely to mean you will be able to swan straight in.

Once inside the hallowed halls of Renaissance art, highlights include: Sandro Botticelli's *Birth of Venus*, Titian's *Venus of Urbino*, Artemisia Gentileschi's *Judith Beheading Holofernes*, Michelangelo's Holy Family, three Caravaggios, three Leonardos and two Giottos.

The Giorgio Vasari-designed building was finished in 1581, originally

Galleria degli Uffizi

Duomo

European City Breaks Florence

Excursion: Fiesole

In the hills to the northeast of Florence, Fiesole was once a more important power base than Florence itself and still likes to think of itself as a little bit superior. Certainly a little cooler, Fiesole is also more laid-back and has great views down over Florence in the valley below as well as some sights of its own. The town has a duomo which dates back to the 11th century as well as the archeological remains of a Roman theatre. The **Museo Archeologico** ⓘ *summer daily 0930-1900, winter Mon and Wed-Sun 0930-1700, €6.20*) contains pieces that were uncovered at this site. The winding walk along via Vecchia Fiesolana to San Domenico is a scenic one but many choose not to move far from the central piazza Mino, which has plenty of good bars and restaurants. Bus No 7 goes between Santa Maria Novella train station in Florence and Fiesole every 15 minutes.

intended to be offices (hence the name) of Florentine magistrates. It suffered significant damage as a result of a car bomb in 1993.

Ponte Vecchio

Best known for the jewellers' shops which line its sides, the Ponte Vecchio is the only Florentine bridge which

Ponte Vecchio

survived the Second World War. There have been shops on the bridge since it was built in 1345 – possibly originally in order to escape taxes. These days the shops themselves are expensive tourist traps but the bridge remains one of the city's iconic symbols.

Palazzo Pitti and Giardino di Boboli

ⓘ *piazza Pitti. Tue-Sun 0815-1850 (closing time of gardens varies with dusk). Combined ticket to all museums and gardens valid for 3 days, €10.50. Various other ticket combinations from €4.*

During Florence's brief position as capital of Italy in the 19th century, the Palazzo Pitti was the main royal residence. Before that it was the home of the Medici family, for centuries the ruling power in Florence.

Started in 1457, the huge building was originally built by a banker, Luca Pitti. A conscious effort to outdo the

Medicis, the enormity of the project practically bankrupted the Pitti family and the Medicis moved in in 1550. Already grandiose, the place has been further extended since then, the most recent additions being wings added in the 18th century.

The contemporary palace contains several museums. The **Galeria Palatina** ⓘ *T055-2388614*, contains many great

Pitti Palace Museum

works of Renaissance art, including paintings by Titian, Botticelli and Veronese. The **Appartamenti Monumentali** are examples of overblown opulence, and there are also museums dedicated to costume, porcelain and gold and silver.

Behind the Palazzo Pitti, the **Giardino Boboli** is a large formal garden offering a peaceful, relaxed and often pleasantly cooler counterpoint to the stresses of the city centre. The gardens are the setting for musical and theatrical events in summer.

San Miniato al Monte
ⓘ *via Monte alle Croci, Summer 0800-1930, winter 0800-1200, 1500-1800. Free.*

High on a hill to the southeast of the city centre, the church of San Miniato is one of Italy's most beautiful Romanesque buildings. Construction began in 1013 and it has changed little in the last 1000 years. The striking exterior is decorated with green and white marble. Inside the choir is raised above the crypt, creating a two-tier design, all of which is bathed in light.

San Miniato al Monte

Santa Croce

The nave is inlaid with mosaics and the walls have faded frescoes.

Just down the hill, **piazzale Michelangelo**, an otherwise unremarkable car park, has great views down the Arno and across the city. The place fills with tourists and local couples around sunset.

Santa Croce
ⓘ *piazza Santa Croce, T055-2466105. Mon-Sat 0930-1730, Sun 1300-1730. €4.*

Containing the tombs of several famous Florentines, including Michelangelo, Galileo and Machiavelli, the Gothic basilica of Santa Croce is one of Florence's most important.

To the right of the altar, **Giotto's frescoes** of the Bardi and Peruzzi chapels are the highlights of the interior. Brunelleschi's 15th-century **Secondo Chiostro** (second cloister) is serenely beautiful and the **Capella dei Pazzi** (also by Brunelleschi) is another fine example of Renaissance architecture. There is a statue of Dante outside the basilica and a funerary monument to him inside, although he was actually buried in Ravenna.

Santa Maria Novella
ⓘ *piazza Santa Maria Novella, T055-215918. Mon-Thu and Sat 0900-1700, Fri and Sun 1300-1700. €2.50.*

Built by the Dominicans in the 13th and 14th centuries, the church of Santa Maria Novella holds a startlingly colourful **fresco cycle by Ghirlandaio**, illustrating the life of John the Baptist. Masaccio's *Trinità* is famous for its pioneering use of perspective, and other highlights include the **Chiostro Verde**, so-called because of the green pigment used by the artist of the frescoes here, Paolo Uccello. The Romanesque-Gothic façade (by Leon Battista Alberti) was added in 1470.

Galleria dell'Accademia
ⓘ *via Ricasoli 60, T055-2388609. Tue-Sun 0815-1850. €6.50 (Apr-Jul €8.50). Summer also Tue 1900-2200, free.*

Famously containing Michelangelo's masterful statue of David, sculpted (when the artist was 29 years old) in 1504, the Accademia also holds unfinished Michelangelo sculptures intended for the tomb of Pope Julius II.

San Lorenzo

Best of the rest

Capella Brancacci ⓘ *piazza del Carmine, T055-2382195. Mon and Wed-Sat 1000-1700, Sun 1300-1700. €4*. This small chapel contains a selection of Masaccio's expressive 15th-century frescoes, belonging to the church of Santa Maria del Carmine.

San Lorenzo ⓘ *piazza San Lorenzo, T055-216634. Mon-Sat 1000-1700. €2.50*. In the middle of Florence's market district and so surrounded by Leonardo aprons and fake designer belts, San Lorenzo was the Medici's church in the 15th century. Brunelleschi, Michelangelo and Donatello all worked on it and it remains one of the city's most important buildings.

Oltrarno. One of the most satisfying areas of the city to wander around, the Oltrarno has a more laid-back feel than the rest of Florence. **Piazza Santo Spirito** has a few market stalls and full-blown markets on some days of the week.

Bargello ⓘ *via del Proconsolo 4, T055-2388606. Tue-Sun 0815-1350. €4*. Built in 1255, the Bargello was later used as a prison but now holds Renaissance sculpture, including masterpieces by Michelangelo, Donatello and Sansovino.

Museo di Storia della Scienza ⓘ *piazza dei Giudici 1, T055-265311, www.imss.fi.it. Jun-Sep Mon and Wed-Fri, 0930-1700, Tue and Sat 0930-1300; Oct-May, Mon and Wed-Sat 0930-1700, Tue 0930-1300, €6.50*. Renaissance from a scientific viewpoint.

Sleeping

Hotels in Florence tend to be expensive and, with notable exceptions, service can be below standard – the city's popularity means that it is a seller's market and standards tend to suffer.

€€€ **Gallery Hotel Art**, vicolo dell' Oro 2, T055-268557, www.lungarno hotels.com. A contemporary luxury hotel near the Ponte Vecchio, Gallery Hotel Art is a part of the Lungarno group and has a well-stocked library and a trendy bar. The place is decorated in muted tones and holds exhibitions of photography and art.

€€€ **JK Place**, piazza Santa Maria Novella 7, T055-2645181, www.jkplace.com. A real fire and antique furniture meet hip design in coffee and caramel tones in this 20-room hotel on piazza Santa Maria Novella. There's an immaculate roof terrace, cakes are served in the courtyard and you'd be hard-pushed not to feel eminently fashionable, in a refined Florentine kind of way.

€€ **Casa Howard Florence**, via della Scala 18, T06-69924555, www.casahoward-florence.com. The elegant recipe of the well-known Rome hotel has been repeated in Florence – a handful of individually designed (and loosely themed) rooms creating an intimate and homely feel. The owners have a personal and idiosyncratic style, with plenty of quality fabrics and artefacts from around the world.

€€ **Torre Guelfa**, borgo Santi Apostoli 8, T055-2396338. Draped 4-poster beds, wooden floors, a roof terrace (at the top of the eponymous 13th-century tower) with views over the Florentine rooftops and large antique-filled communal areas make Torre Guelfa good value and its location, near the Ponte Vecchio, makes it an even better choice.

€ **Orchidea**, borgo degli Albizi 11, T055-2480346, www.hotelorchidea florence.it. A small, friendly place with 7 rooms on one floor of a palazzo just to the east of the Duomo. Some of the large, simple rooms overlook an internal garden. It tends to fill up quickly, so book ahead.

€ **Pensione Scoti**, via Tornabuoni 7, T055-292128, www.hotelscoti.com. Almost opposite Palazzo Strozzi, Pensione Scoti is a smart, friendly, antique place with frescoes and large, simple, old-fashioned rooms.

€ **Residenza Johanna**, via Bonifacio Lupi 14, T055-481896, www.johanna.it. The cheapest of a group of 5 *residenze* in Florence (the others are Johanna II, Johlea I and II and Antica Dimora Firenze). Johanna is especially good value, with simple but classy rooms. Service is friendly, though guests are left to themselves after 1900, when staff go home.

Eating

An abundance of good quality fresh produce is the heart of Tuscan cuisine and Florence's restaurants do well from it. Eating out is not especially cheap, although there are still some traditional trattorias to be found which cater more to a local market than the tourists.

♥♥ **Alla Vecchia Bettola**, Vila e Ariosto 32-33, T055-224158. Communal eating on benches at marble-topped tables is the style at this excellent traditional trattoria just off piazza Tasso near Santo Maria del Carmine. A daily changing menu offers top Tuscan food.

Cibreo Trattoria, via dei Macci 122, T055-2341100. Closed Sun. Also known as *Il Cibreino*, this is the little sibling of the altogether smarter *Cibreo* next door. It's cheaper and the style is more rustic, but the food is the same inventive, occasionally idiosyncratic take on Tuscan classics.

Fuori Porta, 10/r via del Monte alle Croci. Perfectly placed for those who plan to visit San Miniato al Monte but never make it up the hill, Fuori Porta is a wine bar which serves excellent light meals too. The outside tables are popular and inside you can gaze on (and of course consume) some of the enormous selection of wine on offer.

Benvenuto, via della Mosca 16, T055-214833. Closed Sun. Simple but reliably good (and reliably good-value) Tuscan food in the centre of Florence.

Da Nerbone, 1st fl Mercato Centrale di San Lorenzo, T055-219949. Closed Sun. Well-known for its tripe rolls (see *Tripperia da Sergio e Pierpaolo*, below), Nerbone also has some excellent cheese and meat and, at lunchtime, pasta, salads, and minestrone.

Il Pizzaiolo, via dei Macci 113, T055-241171. Closed Sun. Authentic Neapolitan pizza place in Santa Croce, Il Pizzaiolo fills up quickly in the evenings with those eager for their mouth- watering discs of tomato and mozzarella. In a city not renowned for its pizzas, this is a beacon of excellence.

Osteria Santo Spirito, piazza Santo Spirito 16, T055-2382383. A friendly and colourful place in the corner of the attractive piazza, which has attempted to reinvent the traditional osteria in a contemporary style. Popular with travellers.

Tripperia da Sergio e Pierpaolo, via dei Macci. To the east of the city centre some of Florence's most traditional food is served from Italy's most traditional agricultural vehicle – with no compromises to tourism or mad cow disease. From a specially adapted *ape* usually to be found at lunchtimes outside *Cibreo Trattoria*, the wonderful world of tripe is cooked and served fresh to an increasingly young and fashionable Florentine crowd. And, to wash it down, you can help yourself to a plastic cup of wine. It's very good value and it tastes better than you might expect.

Vivoli, Via Isole delle Stinche 7, T055-292334. Closed Mon. Quite rightly one of Italy's most celebrated gelaterias, serving ice-cream of the highest quality in generally old-fashioned flavours.

Nightlife

Bars and clubs

Much of Florence's nightlife takes place around piazza Santa Croce with other lively pockets in the Oltrarno. Clubs loosen up a little and move outside in the heat of summer but for the rest of the year, well-dressed chic predominates.

Aperitivi, usually drunk between 1900 and 2100, are often accompanied by generous buffets of complimentary snacks. Drinks are correspondingly more expensive but at places like **Negroni**, via dei Renai 17, you can just about nibble your way to an evening's sustenance.

After *aperitivi*, cocktails (or, increasingly, wine bars) take over, followed by dancing the night away at locations such as **Maramao**, via dei Macci 79, usually a refined rather than a raucous experience.

Fiorentina reborn

Twice Italian champions and six times cup winners, Fiorentina were, for a long time, big fish in the Italian football pond. But in 2002 they were declared bankrupt and became one of the biggest casualties of a financial crisis in Italian football. However, Fiorentina have also shown how the Italian system can be worked effectively: having been reborn as 'Florentia Viola' and re-admitted to the lower leagues, they proceeded to work their way back up through the ranks, conveniently being allowed to skip one division. The Viola bought back the rights to their old name and in 2004 won a play-off against Perugia to re-enter *Serie A* for the 2004-2005 season. The club plays at the 47,282- seater **Stadio Artemio Franchi** *viale Manfredo Fanti, T055-5030190, www.acffiorentina.it.*

Live music

The pop, rock and jazz scene has become livelier in recent years, belying Florence's conservative reputation. Record shops are the best places to find out what's going on. There's also plenty of good, traditional classical music around – tourist information offices have details of upcoming concerts. **Accademia Bartolomeo Cristofori**, via di Camaldoli 7/r, T055-221646, www.accademiacristofori.it, has baroque concerts. For opera and ballet head to the **Teatro del Maggio Musicale Fiorentino**, via Solferino 15, T055-27791, www.maggiofiorentino.com.

Glasgow is hard to define. This spontaneous free spirit has cast off its industrial past to become a modern, design-conscious city with an energy and exuberance that is simply not found anywhere else in Scotland. It is often compared to Manhattan, with its grid of streets, its tall, narrow buildings and its wisecracking citizens. It also has an air of Celtic edginess like Liverpool, a distinctive city swagger like London and a lingering sense of Victorian civic pride like Manchester. The city that reinvented itself in the 1980s is at it again, following the discovery of St Valentine's relics in a Gorbals church. Meet Glasgow, the "City of Love", with its very own love festival on the 14th of February. It gives a whole new meaning to the 'Glasgow kiss'.

Glasgow

Arts & culture
★★★

Eating
★★★★

Nightlife
★★★★

Outdoors
★★★

Romance
★★

Shopping
★★★★

Sightseeing
★★★

Value for money
★★★

Overall score
★★★✦

⊙ Sights

City Centre

The heart of the city is **George Square**. Here you'll find the tourist office and the two main train stations (Central Station and Queen Street) all within a couple of blocks. The grid-plan of streets to the east of George Square as far as the High Street forms the **Merchant City**, the city's erstwhile trade centre, characterized by its many tobacco warehouses and elegant Palladian mansions. Money has been poured into the area's restoration and regeneration and it has now been reclaimed by the professional classes as a fashionable place to eat, drink and play.

Only a stone's throw from here is the city's **East End**, downbeat by comparison but offering a genuine slice of pure Glasgow, especially in

George Square

The Barras ① *Sat-Sun 1000-1700*, a huge flea market spread out around the streets and alleys south of Gallowgate. Close by is the **People's Palace** ① *T0141-5540223, Mon-Thu and Sat 1000-1700, Fri and Sun 1100-1700, free*, a folk museum giving a real insight into the social and industrial history of this

great city. At the top end of the High Street is the early Gothic **Cathedral** ① *T0141-5526891, www.historic-scotland.gov.uk, Apr-Sep Mon-Sat 0930-1800, Sun 1400-1700, Oct-Mar Mon-Sat 0930-1600, Sun 1400-1600, free*, the only complete medieval cathedral on the Scottish mainland.

Pedestrianized **Buchanan Street** is the city centre's main thoroughfare, running north from St Enoch Square to Sauchiehall Street. Amongst its most notable features is **Princes Square**, an über-stylish art nouveau shopping mall. Head several blocks west along St Vincent Street to find the magnificent Roman Classical **St Vincent Street Church**, designed in 1859 by Alexander 'Greek' Thomson, the city's other architectural genius. Shamefully, it's now on the World Monument Fund's list of the 100 most endangered sites. Due north, past Blythswood Square and uphill from Sauchiehall Street, at 167

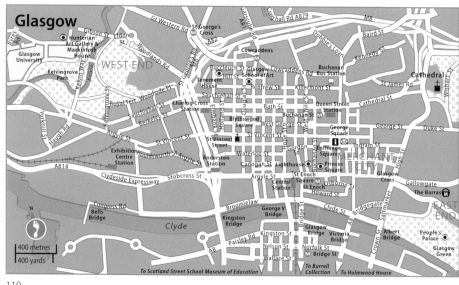

Renfrew Street, is the city's defining monument, the **Glasgow School of Art** ⓘ *T0141- 3534526, www.gsa.ac.uk, guided tour Apr-Sep daily 1030, 1100, 1130, 1330 and 1430, Oct-Mar Mon-Sat 1100 and 1400, £6.* Designed by Charles Rennie Mackintosh and completed in 1907, the school is regarded as his architectural masterpiece.

West End

On the other side of the M8 motorway, which cuts a swathe through the city, is the West End, an area of grand Victorian townhouses and sweeping terraces. Here, opposite Glasgow University, is the **Hunterian Art Gallery** ⓘ *Mon-Sat 0930-1700, free,* which holds an important collection of European paintings as well as a huge collection of works by the American painter, James McNeill Whistler. Attached to the gallery is the **Mackintosh House**, a stunning reconstruction of the interior of the Glasgow home of Charles Rennie Mackintosh and his wife, Margaret MacDonald, from 1906 to 1914.

University Avenue continues west to meet **Byres Road**, which runs north to

Hunterian Art Gallery

meet Great Western Road, passing Hillhead Underground. Supporting a large student population, the streets and lanes around here are where you'll find many of the city's best bars, cafés and restaurants.

Burrell Collection

ⓘ *T0141-6497151, www.glasgow.gov.uk. Mon-Thu and Sat 1000-1700, Sun 1100-1700. Free. Pollokshaws West train station. Bus 45, 47, 48 and 57 all stop on Pollokshaws Rd, opposite the main entrance to the park.*

Three miles southwest of the centre, in Pollok Country Park, is Glasgow's top tourist attraction, the Burrell Collection. Among the 8500 art treasures on view are ancient Greek, Roman and Egyptian artefacts, a huge number of dazzling oriental art pieces, and numerous works of medieval and post-medieval European art. There's also an impressive array of paintings by Rembrandt, Degas, Pissaro, Bellini and Manet amongst many others. The Burrell can easily be reached from the city centre by train or bus. A taxi from the city centre costs £6-7.

◉ Best of the rest

Tenement House ⓘ *145 Buccleuch St, 1 Mar-31 Oct, daily 1300-1700, £5.* Time-capsule of the first half of the 20th century. **Scotland Street School Museum of Education** ⓘ *Shields Rd, Mon-Thu and Sat 1000-1700, Fri and Sun 1100-1700, free.* Another of Rennie Mackintosh's great works. **Holmwood House** ⓘ *61-63 Netherlee Rd, Cathcart, T0141-6372129, Apr-31 Oct, daily 1200-1700, phone in advance, £5.* Trains to Cathcart from Central station. Designed by Alexander 'Greek' Thomson. A bit out of the way but a work of genuine originality and international importance. **The Lighthouse** ⓘ *Mitchell Lane, T0141-2216362, Mon, Wed, Fri and Sat 1030-1730, Tue 1100-1700, Thu 1030-1700, Sun 1200-1700, £3.* Designed by Rennie Mackintosh as a newspaper office, and now housing Scotland's Centre for Architecture, Design and the City, with a Interpretation and Review Gallery and Viewing Tower.

Buchanan Street

⊖ Travel essentials

Getting there Glasgow International Airport, T0141-8871111, www.baa.co.uk/glasgow, is 8 miles west of the city. The Citylink bus No 905 goes to the centre every 10 mins 0600-1800, (£3.30 single, £5 return, journey time 25-30 mins). A taxi from the airport to the city centre costs around £17. **Glasgow Prestwick**, T01292-511000, www.gpia.co.uk, is 30 miles southwest of the city. It is used by Ryanair from London Stansted, also for flights from Paris Beauvais, Dublin, Franfurt Hahn, Stockholm and Brussels. Trains to and from Central Station leave every 30 mins (taking 45 mins; £2.70 single with your Ryanair ticket, otherwise £5.40). Glasgow has 2 main train stations: Central station is the terminus for all trains to southern Scotland, England and Wales; and Queen Street serves the north and east of Scotland.

Getting around The best way to get around the city centre is by walking. If you want to explore the West End or South Side, you'll need to use public transport – which is generally good, efficient and reasonably priced. The best way to get from the city centre to the West End is to use the city's **subway** (stations are marked with a huge orange 'U' sign). There's also an extensive suburban **train** network run by Strathclyde Passenger Transport (SPT), www.spt.co.uk. **Strathclyde Travel Centre**, St Enoch Centre Sq, T0141-2264826, Mon-Sat 0830-1730, provides a free *Visitor's Transport Guide* with a particularly useful map of the city.

Tourist Information VisitScotland Glasgow, 11 George Sq, T0141-2044400, www.seeglasgow.com. May daily 0900-1800; Jun and Sep daily 0900-1900; Jul-Aug daily 0900-2000; Oct-Apr Mon-Sat 0900-1800. They can help you find somewhere to stay.

⊖ Sleeping

€€€ **One Devonshire Gardens**, 1 Devonshire Gdns, T0141-3392001, www.onedevonshiregardens.co.uk. Highly-acclaimed hotel which is still the very last word in style and comfort.

€€€-€€ **The Art House**, 129 Bath St, T0141-2216789, www.arthousehotel.com. Stylish, sleek and individual hotel in a refurbished former education authority building. Well located and good value.

€€ **Groucho Saint Judes**, 190 Bath St, T0141-3528800, www.saintjudes.com. Intimate and stylish boutique hotel with fine restaurant. It's a good place for a romantic break.

€€ **Malmaison**, 278 West George St, T0141-5721000, www.malmaison.com. Chic, stylish urban rooms for smart 30-somethings, with a good brasserie.

€ **Rab Ha's**, 83 Hutcheson St, T0141-5720400, www.rabhas.com. A Merchant City institution best known for its food. 4 stylish, light, bright contemporary rooms, crisp sheets and white bathrobes.

⊖ Eating

††† **Rogano's**, 11 Exchange Pl, T0141-2484055. Designed in the style of the Cunard liner, Queen Mary, this place looks like the set of a Hollywood blockbuster with prices to match, but the seafood is truly sensational.

†††-†† **The Ubiquitous Chip**, 12 Ashton La, T0141-3345007. The city's favourite restaurant. Superb Scottish cuisine, especially venison and seafood.

†† **Café Gandolfi**, 64 Albion St, T0141-5526813. The first of Glasgow's style bistro/brasseries and still comfortably continental, relaxed and soothing. Good place for a leisurely late breakfast.

†† **Fratelli Sarti**, 121 Bath St, T0141-2040440. A Glasgow institution. Good value food in authentic Italian surroundings. Their pizzas are delicious.

†† **Mother India**, 28 Westminster Terr, Sauchiehall St, T0141-2211663. Exquisite Indian cooking at affordable prices. Friendly and informal atmosphere. Strong vegetarian selection. Cheap set lunch and good banquet menus.

⊖ Nightlife

Glasgow is bursting at the seams with bars and pubs to suit all tastes, from ornate Victorian watering holes to the coolest of designer bars. One of the best areas is the **West End**, with its large student population. The city centre has a great choice too, especially along **Bath St** and around the **Merchant City**. Glasgow's club scene, much of which is found in the city centre, is amongst the most vibrant in the UK. Opening times are usually 2300-0300. Entry costs vary from £2-5 for smaller mainstream clubs and £5-10 for the bigger venues, up to £20 for some of the special club nights with top class DJs. For something a little more highbrow, don't miss a night out at the **Citizens' Theatre**, 119 Gorbals St, T0141- 4290022, www.citz.co.uk, which is home to some of the UK's most exciting and innovative drama.

Istanbul

With over 25 centuries of uninterrupted history, including periods as the capital of two world empires – one Christian, the other Muslim – Istanbul is an undisputed cultural heavyweight. Castles, mosques, churches, seminaries, bazaars and palaces, plus some great museums: it has them all. Add to that a superb backdrop, cleaved by the waters of the Continent-dividing Bosphorus and the Golden Horn, with minarets and domes puncturing the skyline and the taste of salt in the air. The cosmopolitan human landscape is no less beguiling, as modernity and tradition, east and west, rub shoulders and Istanbul finds its feet as a cool European city with a vibrant café-culture and fancy restaurants. Be prepared – Istanbul will surprise, amaze, entertain and confound you, all in the space of an afternoon.

Arts & culture
★★★★

Eating
★★★

Nightlife
★★★

Outdoors
★

Romance
★★★★

Shopping
★★★★★

Sightseeing
★★★★★

Value for money
★★★★

Overall score
★★★☆

At a glance

Home to the Byzantine Emperors and Ottoman Sultans, **Sultanahmet** is Istanbul's historic heart. If you are only visiting for a few days, much of your time will be spent here. The area has a concentration of the city's main sights within a short stroll of its most atmospheric accommodation – think boutique Ottoman. Within walking distance are the **Grand Bazaar** and the teeming streets of **Eminönü** (where the Bosphorus ferries dock) and the **Spice Bazaar**. It's easy to spend several weeks exploring this part of the city, although a lot more awaits north of the Golden Horn. Across the Galata Bridge, in what was the European quarter in Ottoman times, **Galata** and **Beyoglu** have many of the city's best bars and restaurants. Formerly seedy and run-down, the narrow backstreets off pedestrianized **Istiklal Caddesi**, Istanbul's main shopping street, are dotted with atmospheric eateries, galleries and bars. At the north end of Istiklal Caddesi is **Taksim Square**, centre of the modern city but with little of interest besides its bland modern hotels. A short cab ride north is Nisantasi, an upmarket shopping district ideal for a bout of retail therapy. Down beside the Bosphorus, a string of suburbs are great to explore. The cobbled streets of **Ortakoy** lead to a waterside square overlooked by lively cafés and bars. Beyond the continent-spanning Ataturk bridge, things get progressively more exclusive, as you head towards the upmarket Bosphorus 'village' of **Bebek**, with its diminutive mosque, cafés and restaurants over-looking the expensive yachts moored offshore. Nearby, is the Ottoman castle of Rumeli Hisar, built in preparation for the conquest of Constantinople while a string of equally bucolic villages lining the Asian shore can be reached by ferry.

★ *Don't leave town without taking a trip on the Bosphorus.*

If one had but a single glance to give the world, one should gaze on Istanbul.

Alphonse de Lamartine,
French poet and statesman, 1790-1869

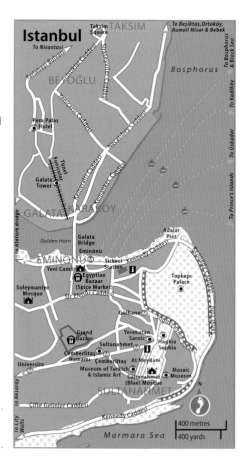

European City Breaks Istanbul

24 hours in the city

Galata Bridge

Have a lazy breakfast on your hotel roof terrace while drinking in the fantastic view. If your lodgings are one of the few in the Old City that don't have one, then try the *Hotel Uyan*. Be enthralled by the soaring symmetry of the Sultanahmet (Blue) Mosque, before jumping on a tram to shopaholic heaven – the Grand Bazaar. With lightened wallet and bag of souvenirs in hand, weave your way down through the backstreets to Eminönü and the Spice Market. Take refuge from the hustle and a late lunch in the *Pandeli Restaurant*. Afterwards, wander past the fishermen on the Galata bridge before catching the Tünel funicular up to Galata and the other main shopping hub of Istanbul, Istiklal Caddesi. The Genoese watchtower in Galata is a great place to enjoy the sunset and a well-earned beer. After dark, jump in a taxi to Ortaköy, where in summer you can dine alfresco on the main square. Alternatively, the bars and clubs of Beyoglu await those wanting to imbibe or boogie into the wee small hours.

⊖ Travel essentials

Getting there Ataturk Airport, www.ataturkairport.com, is 25 km west of the city centre. The journey by taxi into Sultanahmet or Taksim, takes 35-60 mins depending on the traffic, and costs TRY 18-25 (taxis are metered). **Havas** operate an airport bus into Taksim (every 30 mins, TRY 6.5). For Sultanahmet, get off at Aksaray and get a taxi or jump on the tram.

Getting around To get around the Old City all you need is your feet and an occasional ride on the modern **tram**, which passes Aksaray, Beyazit and the Covered Bazaar, Sultanahmet Square, and Topkapı Palace (Gülhane) before terminating in Eminönü. Tokens can be bought at each station and cost TRY 0.75.

The 19th-century **funicular railway**, known as the Tünel climbs steeply up to Istiklal Caddesi from the north side of the Galata Bridge (straight on at the end of the bridge and then bear left at the first main junction). Tokens can be bought from the ticket booths in either station, TRY 0.60. There's also a picturesque little tram that will take you the length of Istiklal Caddesi, from Tünel to Taksim Square, without stopping. For longer journeys **taxis** are fast and cheap, but avoid road travel during rush hour.

Ferries regularly cross the Bosphorus from Eminönü and Karaköy to the suburbs of Uskudar and Kadiköy on the Asian shore. Tickets cost TRY 0.75 and the crossing takes about 15 mins. There are also 3 daily cruises up and down the Bosphorus to the Black Sea. These depart at 1030 and 1330 from Eminönü's "Bogaz Hatti" pier, with an extra sailing at 1200 during the summer months. Tickets cost TRY 5 and the trip takes over 3 hrs, including a stop for lunch.

Tourist information The most convenient offices are in the arrivals hall at Ataturk Airport, T0212-663 0793; Sultanahmet Sq, at Divan Yolu 3, T0212-518 1802; and in Sirkeci Station, Eminönü, T0212-5115888. They can provide maps, brochures and information on current events. For listings and city information buy a copy of *Istanbul: The Guide*.

Exchange rate Turkish New Lira (TRY). £1 = TRY 2.4. €1 = TRY 1.6.

Visas These can be bought at the airport before you go through customs. Remember to have cash ready to pay for it; euros and pounds sterling accepted.

⦿ Sights

Topkapı Palace
ⓘ *Topkapı Sarayi, Sultanahmet.*
Wed-Mon 0900-1700. TRY 12; Harem
Tour TRY 15; Treasury TRY 10.

Home of the Ottoman sultans and
centre of their empire, the Topkapı
Palace is one of the world's most
important historical collections, as well
as one of most popular sights in the
whole country. Each year tens of
thousands wander through its many
halls, apartments and pavilions.
Entered through the imposing
Imperial Gate (Bab-i Humayun), the
palace sprawls over a series of large
courtyards, with the Harem, inviolate
residence of the Sultans, their wives
and concubines, at its core. Things can
get very crowded so it is wise to visit
early in the day and buy your ticket for
the Harem tours, which depart every
30 minutes, as soon as you arrive. With
so many other things to see, you
should allow at least half a day for your
wanderings. Highlights include the
palace kitchens and the dazzling
artefacts in the Imperial Treasury.

Topkapı Palace

Haghia Sophia

Haghia Sophia
ⓘ *Sultanahmet Meydani. Tue-Sun*
0900-1900. TRY 12.

The pinnacle of Byzantine architectural
achievement was built in AD 537 at the
behest of Emperor Justinian, eager to
prove the pre-eminence of his "New
Rome". Towering over the city's
rooftops and topped by a whopping
30-m-wide dome, the cathedral
enthralled Byzantine visitors then and
continues to do so today. Despite a
sacking by the Crusaders in 1204, its
conversion into a mosque in 1453, then
into a museum in 1934, the building
has a great collection of precious and
ancient Christian mosaics, some only
recently rediscovered beneath Ottoman
plaster. But it is the venerable
atmosphere that can't help but impress.

Sultanahmet Mosque
ⓘ *Daily 0900-1900. Free.*

Gracefully cascading domes and sharp,
soaring minarets, the Sultanahmet
Mosque, better known as the **Blue
Mosque**, rises evocatively above the

well-kept gardens of Sultanahmet
Square. Built by Sultan Ahmet in 1616,
it was the last of the great imperial
mosques, an architectural milestone
marking the beginning of the Ottoman
Empire's long, inexorable decline.
Controversially, the Sultan had six
minarets built, instead of the usual four,
an act that many saw as a mark of
disrespect to the Mosques of the
Prophets in Mecca, which were also
graced with a half-dozen towers. As a
functioning mosque you enter through
a special entrance and must be
appropriately dressed – shawls can be
borrowed to cover exposed arms and
female heads at the door. Inside, the
walls are gaudily decorated with 20,000
patterned Iznik tiles, hence the
building's western name.

Museum of Turkish and Islamic Art
ⓘ *At Meydani 46, Sultanahmet,*
T0212-5181805. Tue-Sun 0900-
1700. TRY 4.

Overlooking what was once the
Byzantine Hippodrome, an arena where
ceremonies, parades and chariot races
were held and which is now known as

Sultanahmet Mosque

Poorer Palace?

Istanbul's most famous hotel is the Pera Palas (Mesrutiyet Caddesi 98, Tepebasi, Beyoglu), built in 1892 to accommodate travellers stepping off the glittering Orient Express. The visitor's book is filled with the names of heads of state, politicians, poets, movie stars and spies: Greta Garbo, Mata Hari, Alfred Hitchcock and Jackie Onassis among them. Agatha Christie penned part of *Murder on the Orient Express* while staying, and Ataturk, the country's founder and first president, rested his head in room 101, which is kept as a mini-shrine to the great man. Small brass plaques on many of the doors identify other famous occupants. Curiosity value aside, little of the Pera Palas' original splendour survives and the high room rates are not justified by the limited facilities and rather plain rooms. It's far better to come for a look around and a drink at the hotel's long bar.

At Meydani, the museum has an interesting collection covering the Middle East and Central Asia, from earliest Islamic times through to the present day. The exhibits are well labelled, organized chronologically and geographically and housed in a 16th century palace constructed by Ibrahim Paşa, influential Grand Vizier to Suleyman the Magnificent before he was strangled at his master's behest.

Grand Bazaar

ⓘ www.grand-bazaar.com.
Mon-Sat 0830-1930.

Grand Bazaar

With over 5000 shops connected by a maze of covered streets and passageways, the Grand Bazaar is the largest retail area of its kind in the world. Surrender yourself to the inevitability of getting lost and just wander, browsing shops selling clothes, carpets, gold and silver, household goods and souvenirs, stopping to practice your haggling skills. Each type of shop is concentrated in a particular area, with silver and antique merchants occupying the Ic Bedestan, the historic heart of the bazaar. If you need a break there are several cafés within the bazaar.

Çemberlitaş Hamamı

ⓘ www.cemberlitashamami.com.tr.
0600-2400. TRY 12-20, plus 10% tip.

The prefect antidote to a day's sight-seeing is a steam-clean, followed by a massage in one of the city's many Turkish baths. Built in 1584 by master architect Mimar Sinan, and with separate sections for men and women, the Çemberlitaş Hamamı is one of the most atmospheric, as well as being close to the Grand Bazaar and Sultanahmet. Towels and cloths to wrap around you while bathing are provided, and refreshments are also available.

Egyptian Bazaar and Eminönü

ⓘ Mon-Sat 0800-1900.

Also known as the **Spice Market**, this busy arcade lined with shops selling spices, imported foods, souvenirs and herbal remedies, such as the somewhat dubious "Turkish Viagra", gets its name from a time when it was endowed with the custom duties from Cairo. The market is part of the **Yeni Camii** (New Mosque) complex, which is surrounded by the bustling district of Eminönü. Bosphorus ferries dock at the quayside and the air is filled with the sound of

Çemberlitaş Hamamı

European City Breaks Istanbul

itinerant traders hawking their wares from the pavements and the smell of juicy kebabs.

Istiklal Caddesi and Beyoglu

In Ottoman times Beyoglu was home to the city's Greek, Armenian and European communities and many of their churches and consulates remain. With the departure of these communities after the establishment of the Turkish Republic, the area fell on hard times, though it has been enjoying a renaissance in recent years. Bohemian Beyoglu's narrow streets, running off the main shopping thoroughfare of Istiklal Caddesi, have lots of great restaurants, cafés and bars.

Ortaköy

Ortaköy is the first of the Bosphorus "villages" on the European shore. Cobbled streets lined with cafés, shops and market stalls lead down to a small square overlooked by the baroque **Mecidiye mosque**, which

Egyptian Bazaar

Istiklal Caddesi

looks like a wedding cake when lit up at night. On sunny days, the cafés are crowded, as are the bars at night. Further north, some of the city's most upmarket nightspots overlook the straits.

Rumeli Hisar and Bebek

ⓘ *Tue-Sun 0900-1630. 25E bus from Eminonu or 40 bus from Taksim.*

In preparation for his attack on Constantinople in 1453, Sultan Mehmet had castles built on either side of the Bosphorus to prevent supply ships reaching the city. The larger of these was Rumeli Hisar, on the European shore north of Bebek, overlooking a bend in the Bosphorus. Today you can walk the restored 15-m thick battlements and take imaginary pot-shots at passing ships. There are several good little cafés nearby or stroll along the coastal path to the genteel Bosphorus "village" of Bebek, which attracts a well-heeled crowd.

☻ Best of the rest

Mosaic Museum ⓘ *Arasta Sokak, Sultanahmet. Tue-Sun 0900-1630. TRY 5.* Byzantine mosaics displayed in situ where they were unearthed.
Yerebatan Sarayi ⓘ *Yerebatan Caddesi 13, Sultanahmet. Daily 0900-1800. TRY 10.* Underground cistern featured in *From Russia With Love.*
Suleymaniye Mosque ⓘ *Tiryakiler Çarşısı, Suleymaniye. Daily 0900-1900.* To some, the finest mosque in the city.
Galata Tower ⓘ *Galata Sq. Daily 0900-2000. TRY 5.* A medieval Genoese watchtower with a great view.
City Walls The historic walls have recently been restored and you can walk much of their 6.5 km length, although it's best not to do it alone.
Dolmabahçe Palace ⓘ *Dolmabahçe Caddesi, Besiktas, 0900-1600. TRY 10.* Ostentatious home of the last Ottoman sultans in the twilight years of the empire.
Nisantasi An upmarket shopping and residential district north of Taksim, which has designer clothes stores and domestic chains aplenty.
Akmerkez ⓘ *Nispetiye Caddesi, Etiler. Daily 1000-2200.* One of the city's swankiest shopping malls.
Leander's Tower ⓘ *(Also called the Maiden's Tower) Salacak Caddesi. 1200-1900.* Get the ferry from Eminönü to Uskudar, from where there's a ferry to the tiny tower-topped island with café and spectacular views.

Excursion: Prince's Islands

Off Istanbul's Asian shore are a collection of nine islands, which were a place of exile in Byzantine and Ottoman times, later becoming home to wealthy families from the city's Greek and Armenian minorities. The islands are graced with many beautiful wooden houses, churches and a Greek Orthodox monastery. They also remain blissfully car-free, with horse carts the only means of transport. The largest, **Buyukada**, is the most interesting and you can explore it by rented bicycle or hire a horse-drawn phaeton. A tour of the island takes a couple of hours on foot, taking in Leon Trotsky's home – he wrote History of the Russian Revolution while living here – and the hill-top St George's Monastery. There is a beach club on the far side of the island with a small beach for cooling off. Ferries depart from Eminönü's Adalar Pier regularly for the hour-long crossing. Tickets cost TRY 3.5.

Sleeping

Istanbul has an excellent choice of accommodation from budget hotels to atmospheric Ottoman boutique places and luxury international chains. Prices are competitive in comparison to other European cities, although there are plenty of places to pamper yourself if you wish. Booking in advance is advisable at any time of year as the most popular hotels fill up quickly. Many of the city's top-notch beds are found along the Bosphorus.

€€€ **Ciragan Palace**, Ciragan Caddesi 32, Beşiktaş, T0212-2583377. Operated by the German Kempinski chain, this 5-star on the edge of the Bosphorus incorporates an Ottoman palace and has the city's finest swimming pool, as well as a spa and several excellent restaurants.

€€€ **Four Seasons**, Tevfikhane Sokak 1, Sultanahmet, T0212-6388200, www.fourseasons.com. Formerly a prison, this is now one of Istanbul's most exclusive and luxurious hotels. Its 54 high-ceilinged rooms have every possible mod-con and there is an excellent restaurant too.

€€ **Empress Zoe**, Adliye Sokak 10, Sultanahmet, T0212-5182504. Incorporating the ruins of a 15th-century Turkish Baths, the Zoe is exquisitely decorated throughout, with modern frescoes and wall hangings and small but comfy and well-furnished rooms. There is a scenic roof terrace bar and a lovely garden.

€€ **Sultan Ahmet Palace Hotel**, Torun 19, Sultanahmet, T212-4580460, www.sultanahmet.com. Great location, 36 rooms, 5 with private balcony, Turkish bath in each room, minimum 2 nights, free airport transfer and also children under 6 free.

€€ **Yesil Ev**, Kabasakal Caddesi 5, Sultanahmet, T0212-5176785. Housed in a restored Ottoman mansion on Sultanahmet Square, you can't beat the Yesil Ev (which means "Green House") for location or atmosphere. The accommodation is slightly faded and creaky, though, and don't expect a lift either. The garden café is a tranquil haven in summer.

€ **Hotel Uyan**, Utangac Sokak 25, Sultanahmet, T0212-516 4892. A good budget hotel in a converted corner house with clean en suite rooms. The scenic roof terrace has stunning views.

€ **Side Hotel**, Utangac Sokak 20, Sultanahmet, T0212-517 2282. A well-managed place with a selection of simple pension rooms, or more expensive hotel rooms, most with their own bathrooms.

Eating

Istanbul's restaurant scene has come on leaps and bounds in recent years, with a crop of talented new Turkish chefs adding to the existing mix of traditional *meyhane* (the city's equivalent of a taverna), kebab houses and fish restaurants. Dining out is generally good value for money, though prices in some of the top-notch establishments are on a par with prices in other European cities. Alcohol is available in all but a few of the city's dining spots.

For a great evening out visit the raucous area of Kumkapi, on the coast south of Beyazit and the Grand Bazaar, which is crowded with meze and fish restaurants, where diners are entertained by gypsy street musicians. The *meyhane* of Nevizade Sokak, reached down the Balik Pazari from Istiklal Caddesi, are very popular with local diners.

Breakfast

† **Fes Café**, Halıcılar Caddesi 62, Grand Bazaar, T0212-528613. At the heart of the bazaar, this trendy café is a good spot for a cappuccino and a snack.

† **Kaffeehaus**, Tünel Sq 4, Beyoglu, T0212-2454028. In a courtyard opposite the top Tünel station, this atmospheric café has tables outside or a cosy interior for the winter.

Lunch

†† **Haci Abdullah**, Sakizagaci Caddesi 17, T0212-2938561. In a sidestreet off Istiklal Caddesi, this is the grandfather of the Istanbul restaurant scene, having been serving Ottoman/Turkish

cuisine for over 110 years. It's also known for its pickles and preserves which are displayed in colourful jars along the walls. No alcohol served.

†† **Pandeli**, Misir Carşısı (Egyptian Bazaar), Eminönü, T0212-5273909. This atmospheric restaurant, housed in vaulted rooms above the entrance to the Spice Market, serves local Turkish dishes at lunchtime only.

66 99 Istanbul has to be one of the great shopping cities of the world, up there, in its own way, with New York and Milan.

Dinner

†† **Imroz**, Nevizade Sokak 19, T0212-2499073. One of the best fish and meze restaurants on a street crowded with excellent *meyhane*.

†† **Refik**, Sofyali Sokak 10-12, Asmalimescit, T0212-2432834. A quintessential backstreet *meyhane* with an excellent selection of meze and meat or fish. There are tables on the street in summer.

Nightlife

You certainly won't be bored after dark in Istanbul. Beyoglu has a diverse collection of bars and clubs, catering for tastes from jazz to Turkish folk and techno. Pick up a copy of *Time Out - Istanbul* for details of the best nightspots. **Babylon**, Seybender Sokak 3, Asmalimescit, Beyoglu, www.babylon-ist.com. A live venue which hosts top international and

Turkish acts, as well as club nights.

If you want to see where Istanbul's rich and famous strut, visit one of the super-clubs overlooking the Bosphorus in Kuruçeşme. Try **Reina**, Muallim Naci Caddesi 44, Kuruçeşme, but dress up and be prepared for a vertiginous bar bill.

Ataturk Cultural Centre, Taksim Sq, T0212-2515600. This is the city's premier performing art venue, hosting concerts, ballet and opera.

Shopping

Istanbul has to be one of the great shopping cities of the world, up there, in its own way, with New York and Milan. The **Grand Bazaar** is of course a good place to start, but there are other areas to check out including **Arasta Bazaar**, beside Sultanahmet Mosque, for carpets, handicrafts and Iznik tiles. The **Istanbul Handicraft Centre** on Kabasakal Caddesi 7, Sultanahmet Sq, has artisans on site producing various traditional Ottoman crafts.

Istaklal Caddesi, the city's main drag, has a mix of department stores, clothing shops like Mavi Jeans and some good bookshops. For antiques, the Beyoglu district of Çukurcuma, east of Istiklal Caddesi, is dotted with little treasure-troves, though remember there are restrictions on exporting real antiquities. **Nişantaşi** has international and home-grown fashion labels along Abdi Ipekci Caddesi and Tesvikiye Caddesi.

Across the Bosphorus in **Kadiköy**, the city's largest street market is held on Tue and Sun along Kusdili Sokak. Ask for the "Salı Pazarı", then follow the crowd.

With its back to Europe, and its soul circa 1498, scrupulously low-key Lisbon has long taken a back seat while its neighbours strutted their stuff. During nearly 50 years of solitude, Salazar smothered the city in a conservative mantle but now it has emerged from its cocoon. Thanks to European funding, a stint as City of Culture in 1994 and Expo 98 that saw the arrival of futurist Parque das Nações, Lisbon is flourishing. But appropriately, given Portugal's sea-faring, imperialist history, old and new worlds sit comfortably side by side in Lisbon. While gilded *Lisboetas* emerge from riverside warehouse conversions, arthritic trams still chug up ludicrous gradients, zigzagging through squat dwellings, hole-in-the-wall grocers and chunks of ancient Roman walls.

Lisbon

Arts & culture
★★★

Eating
★★★

Nightlife
★★★★

Outdoors
★★★

Romance
★★★

Shopping
★★★

Sightseeing
★★

Value for money
★★★★

Overall score
★★★

At a glance

Square and spare, Lisbon's downtown, **Baixa**, is the city's commercial nexus, a grid of thrusting thoroughfares built in the wake of the 1755 earthquake. Pedestrianized **Rua Augusta** is the Rambla-esque central promenade which funnels south to handsome **Praça do Comércio**, Lisbon's Whitehall and medieval city gateway. To the north, Baixa's main square and the city's central reference point is **Rossio**. To the west, straddling one of Lisbon's seven hills, is gentrified **Chiado**. North of Rossio is **Avenida da Liberdade**, Lisbon's Champs-Elysées. This ends in **Praça Marques de Pombal** beyond which is Lisbon's largest park **Parque Eduardo VII** and further north, the unassailable **Museu Calouste Gulbenkian**. West of Chiado, **Bairro Alto**, has always been Lisbon's Latin quarter. Chiado's backyard to the west is the earthy neighbourhood of **São Bento** which gives way to smarter **Estrela** and further west still, streets climb to haughty, diplomatic **Lapa**. East of

Our lips meet easily across the narrow street

Federico de Brito

Baixa is **Alfama**, a maze of medieval, Moorish streets and where it all began. A few kilometres west of Baixa, stretching along the Tagus, **Belém** sees Portugal's imperial triumphs made stone. To the northeast, suburban sprawl gives way to sleek modernism at **Parque das Nações**, site of Expo 98.

★ *Don't leave town without visiting the Antiga Pastelaria de Belém, the cathedral to Lisbon's famed custard tart, the* pastel de nata.

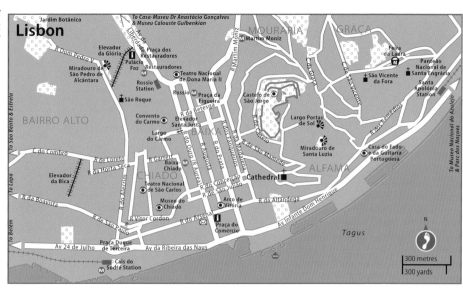

⊙ Sights

Baixa and Rossio

Surrounded by whizzing traffic, all roads seem to lead to Rossio, Baixa's central square, formally known as Praça Dom Pedro IV. The neoclassical **Teatro Nacional de Dona Maria II**, built in 1846 by Fortunato Lodi, occupies the north side of the square. During the 18th century this was the site of the Palace of the Inquisition. To the northwest stands the interlocking horseshoe arches of **Rossio station**, designed in 1887 and betraying a late 19th-century nostalgia for the period of the Discoveries. Adjacent to Rossio, **Praça da Figueira** retains more endearing old world charm.

Southbound from Rossio, **Rua Augusta** is lined with touristy pavement cafés, international chain stores and leather emporiums. This climaxes with the over-arching splendour of the **Arco de Vitória**,

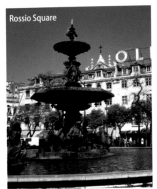
Rossio Square

gateway to **Praça do Comércio** – the culmination of an enlightened despot's vision for a model city and designed to out-pomp the most regal of Europe's squares. The showpiece is a bronze equestrian statue of King Dom José I and, on the north side of the square, nestling beneath the arcaded colonnades is one of Lisbon's most famous literary landmarks, **Café Martinho do Arcado**.

On Rua Santa Justa, just south of Rossio, **Elevador de Santa Justa** ⓘ *0900-2100, €1.20,* is one of Lisbon's most iconic and memorable images. Designed by an apostle of Eiffel, Raoul Mesnier du Ponsard, the 45-m vertical wrought-iron structure was built to link the Baixa with Largo do Carmo, via a 25-m walkway.

Alfama

Alfama is Lisbon's spiritual heart. It's the old Moorish quarter where ribbons of alleyways coil into blind alleys and crooked alcoves. Dominating the skyline is the iconic, if a little Disneyfied, **Castelo de São Jorge**. Ancient trams take you to **Miradouros de Santa Luzia** and **Largo Portas de Sol** from where the view of city below is breathtaking. The pristine baroque **Panteão Nacional de Santa Engrácia** and the twin bell towers of the **Igreja de São Vicente da Fora** rise amidst clusters of squat houses stacked on top of each other. Encircling the

⊖ Travel essentials

Getting there Lisbon's **Portela Airport**, T21-841 37 00, www.ana-aeroportos.pt, is 6.5 km from the city centre. The **AeroBus** is the cheapest and most convenient way to reach the city centre, departing every 20 mins (0745-2045) making stops en route, including Saldanha, Marquês de Pombal, Praça dos Restauradores, and arriving in Rossio in around 20-25 mins, before terminating at Cais do Sodré railway terminal. A ticket costs €2.35 and is valid on the **Carris** transport network for the remainder of that day. Buses 8, 22, 44 and 83 also operate 0600-2130 to the centre, and bus 45 runs until 0010 from outside the Cais de Sodré terminal. Bus 5 links the airport to Oriente Station. A taxi to the centre should cost €12-15 but always try to fix a fare before leaving.

Getting around Most of the main sights of the Baixa, Bairro Alto, Chiado and Alfama, can be reached on foot. But an efficient network of orange **buses** is run by **Carris**, T21-361 30 00, www.carris.pt. A *simple* (1-way) ticket bought on board costs €1. Bright yellow Carris booths provide maps of routes. Lisbon's **metro**, with 4 lines, is fast and efficient. It's best used if you are going to the north and west of the old city. A helter-skelter ride on one of Lisbon's ancient emblematic **trams** is the most enjoyable way to get around. Tram 28 is an unofficial tourist tram. A single journey costs €1.20 (you can buy tickets on board). The new super tram No 15, runs from Praça da Figueira to Belém and then on to Ajuda Palace. The new rechargeable card,

"7 Colinas" costs an initial €0.50 which can then be credited with passes that cover the bus, tram and metro network (1 day, €3; 5 days €12.10), or pre-pay tickets, only valid on buses and trams (5 journeys €3.30-4.95, 10 journeys €6.15-9.25). **Taxis** are cheap. A trip from Rossio to the northern reaches of the city should be no more than €5. Fares are higher after 2200. There are taxi ranks close to the Baixa-Chiado Metro station and Largo de Camões, or call **Radio Taxis**, T21-79 27 56.

Tourist information Ask me Lisbon, Praça do Comércio, and in Palácio Foz, Praça dos Restauradores. They can be very busy but they have specialist information on sports and the arts, as well as guides to the palaces and museums in the city and surrounding areas.

church on Saturday or Tuesday is the "thieves' **flea market**, Feira da Ladra; buy your own piece of crumbling Lisbon, a fireman's T-shirt, or a traditional basket. Surrounded by seafood restaurants, tour group orientated fado houses and neighbourhood grocers, the **Casa do Fado e da Guitarra Portuguesa** ⓘ *Largo do Chafariz de Dentro, 1, T21- 882 34 70, 1000-1800, €2.50*, tells the history of the national song, while a short bus ride away set in the tranquil Madre de Deus Convent the **Museu Nacional do Azulejo** ⓘ *Rua de Madre de Deus, 4, T21-810 03 40, Tue 1400-1800, Wed-Sun 1000-1800, €3, free on Sun 1000-1400*, houses the finest collection of *azulejo* tiles in the country. (For more authentic exposure to the Portugal's art forms, wander around earthy **Mouraria** to the north, the cradle of fado, or **Graça**, to the northwest, where fragments of lustrous 16th-century *azulejos* peel from façades.)

Chiado

In Chiado 19th-century old-world elegance prevails. **Rua Garrett** is studded with high fashion boutiques

Café A Brasileira

Elevador da Glória

and art nouveau jewellery stores. The literary legacy of cryptic genius Fernando Pessoa, still hangs in the air, his spirit immortalized in stone at *Café A Brasileira*. But, devastated by fire in 1988, Chiado has been born again and now SoHo-style wrought-iron architecture is juxtaposed with the rococo elegance of the **Teatro Nacional de Sao Carlos** ⓘ *Rua Serpa Pinto, 9, T21-325 30 45, www.saocarlos.pt*.

From Rua Garrett, Calçada do Sacramento leads to the peaceful **Largo do Carmo**, site of one of the most enigmatic buildings in the city, the cadaverous **Convento do Carmo** ⓘ *T21-347 86 29, Oct-Apr Mon-Sat 1000-1700, May-Sep Mon-Sat 1000-1800, €2.50*. Heading south along Rua Serpa Pinto towards the river, the **Museu do Chiado** ⓘ *T21-343 21 48, Tue-Sun 1000-1800, €3, free on Sun 1000-1400*, is one of the finest exhibition spaces for Portugal's 19th- and 20th-century artists.

Bairro Alto

In Lisbon's 'High Town' peeling doorways reveal sleek bars, gritty *tascas* and fado houses. Seductive samba

mingles with deep techno and black-shawled divas sing out the nation's woes. Here you'll also find baroque magnificence in the Jesuit **Igreja de São Roque** ⓘ *Largo Trindade Coelho, T21- 323 53 81, Tue-Sun 1000-1700, museum €1.50, free Sun*, and exotic gardens at the **Jardim Botânico** ⓘ *Rua da Escola Politécnica, May-Oct 0900-2000, Nov-Apr daily 0900-1900, €1.50*. Connecting the Baixa with Bairro Alto, the **Elevador da Glória** chugs up to the stunning Miradouro de São Pedro de Alcântara.

Belém

Belém, spreading west along the banks of the inky blue Tagus, is a tremendous heap of 15th- and 16th-century marvels, built to celebrate Vasco da Gama's discovery of the sea route to India. The **Mosteiro dos Jerónimos** ⓘ *Praça do Império, T21-362 00 34, Oct-Apr Tue-Sun 1000-1700, May-Sep Tue-Sun 1000-1830, church free, cloisters €4.5, free Sun 1000-1400*, astounds with its sublime cloister where fantastical sea creatures and maritime emblems writhe in milky stone. By the river, the **Torre de Belém** ⓘ *Av de Brasília,*

Monument to the Discoveries, Belem

Excursion: Sintra

Poets have raved and pagans have revelled in the Elysian Fields of Sintra, recaptured from the Moors in 1147. It's a truly ethereal landscape where castles rise from the mists of emerald mountain ranges. On sloping terraces, carpeted with lush pine forests, erupts a rhapsody of Bavarian kitsch in the form of the slapstick **Palácio da Pena** ⓘ *T21-910 53 40, 1 Jul-15 Sep 1000-1900; 16 Sep-30 Jun 1000-1730, last entry 30 mins before closing, closed Mon, €6,* the epitome of 19th-century decadence. In the valley, the cobblestone streets of quaint **Sintra Vila**, the old quarter, fan into Moorish courtyards, festooned with flowers and palms – all very chocolate box, but nonetheless alluring. The tourist magnet is the sublime **Palácio Nacional** ⓘ *Largo Rainha D Amélia, T21-910 68 40, Thu-Tue 1000-1730, last admission 30 mins before closing, €4,* steeped in Arabian mythicism, Shakespearean dramas and the imprint of cavorting kings. Sintra is about 30 km from Lisbon. Trains run from Sete Rios every 15 minutes, journey time is around 45 minutes (€2.80 return trip). The Scotturb bus No 434 runs a circular service every 20 minutes from Sintra train station through Sintra Vila and then up the mountain to the Palácio da Pena (€3.70). It takes a good hour to walk up to the palace. The Tourism Office at Sintra Station is open 0900-1900

T21-362 00 34, Tue-Sun 1000-1700, €3, free Sun 1000-1400, looks more like a chess piece washed ashore than a defensive fortification. Belém is one of the loveliest places in the city. There are breezy riverside walkways, super-sleek yachts, primary coloured fishing boats, and kites and frisbies flying across expansive parks. There's also the exceptional **Design Museum** ⓘ *Centro Cultural de Belém, Praça do Império, T21-361 28 80, www.ccb.pt, 1000-1900, closed Mon, €3.50,* which opened in 1999 to universal acclaim.

Museu Calouste Gulbenkian

ⓘ *Av da Berna, 45a, T21-782 34 61. Tue-Sun 1000-1800. €3, free Sun. Metro São Sebastião.*

The broad avenues of the *Estados Novos* (New States) which stretch beyond **Parque Eduardo VII** bear the imprint of fascist Prime Minister Salazar (1936-1970). Yet nestling between thrusting 1940s office blocks and monolithic apartment buildings are fine examples of

elegant prize-winning architecture. The **Casa-Museu Dr Anastácio Gonçalves** ⓘ *Av 5 de Outubro, 6 e 8, T21-3540 823/09 23, www.cmag- ipmuseus.pt, Tue 1400-1800, Wed-Sun 1000-1800, €2, Metro Saldanha/Picoas,* is a decorative art museum worth visiting for its swirling art nouveau façade alone. But Lisbon's number one attraction, as monumental in its scope as in its quality, is the **Museu Calouste Gulbenkian**, lying in its own serene, 17-acre garden and

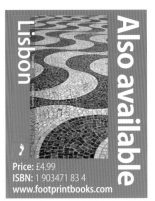

Price: £4.99
ISBN: 1 903471 83 4
www.footprintbooks.com

housing an outstanding collection of Western and Eastern art of the major periods from 2800 BC onwards.

Parque das Nações

This industrial wasteland has been transformed into a modernist playground, united by the theme "The Oceans, a Heritage for the Future". Cable cars glide up to the highest lookout point in the city, the **Torre de Vasco da Gama** ⓘ *Cais das Naus, T21-891 80 00, 1000-2000 (but closed until end 2006), €2.49.* The **Oceanarium** ⓘ *T21-891 70 02, www.oceanario.pt, Mar-Oct 1000-2000, Nov-Mar 1000-1900 last entry an hour before closing, €10,* is the largest in Europe and there also the **Interactive Science museum** (Pavilhão do Conhecimento Ciência Viva) ⓘ *Alameda dos Oceanos, T21-891 71 00, www.pavconhecimento.pt, Tue-Fri 1000-1800, Sat-Sun and holidays 1100-1900, €6.*

⊜ Sleeping

The most idiosyncratic places to stay are in Alfama, with its charming guesthouses, arty *pensões* and a couple of sleeker 4-star options. Bairro Alto is good if you want to be at the heart of the night-time action. Many rooms overlook Rossio and Praça da Figueira, but this area is noisy. Avenida da Liberdade has most of the really swanky options.

€€€ **Le Meridien Park Atlantic**, Rua Castilho, off Parque Eduardo VII, 149, T21-381 87 00. Contemporary rooms and the highest standards. Sweeping views out over the Tagus.

€€ **Hotel Lisboa Plaza**, Travessa Salitre 7, off Av da Liberdade, T21-321 82 18, www.heritage.pt. A warm hotel with an understated, luxurious atmosphere and a home-from-home feel.

€€ **Hotel Metrópole**, Praça do Rossio, 30, T21-321 90 30, www.almeidahotels.com. Unrivalled views over Rossio, a stately 1920s classic with characterful rooms. Great value.

€ **Pensão Ninho das Águias**, Costa do Castelo, 74, Alfama, T21-885 40 70. Just below the walls of Castelo de São Jorge and one of the best *pensãos* in the city. Comfortable rooms, some with private bathrooms. Proud owner Luís is utterly charming and devoted to the history of the place and the city in general.

€ **Pensão Residencial Santa Catarina**, Rua Dr Luís de Almeida e Albuquerque, 6, T21-346 61 06. Temple to 1960s kitsch 10 mins from the bars and restaurants of Bairro Alto on a tranquil and picturesque street.

⊘ Eating

Chiado offers Portuguese traditional cuisine, Alfama is fado tour group territory and Bairro Alto has hip food, soul food, Portuguese staples and polycultural delicacies. Dinner is eaten late; in Bairro Alto restaurants stay open until around 0200.

♦♦♦ **Gambrinus**, Rua Portas de Santo Antão 23e 25, Baixa, T21-342 14 66. Daily 1200-0130. One of Portugal's best seafood restaurants and a local institution. Tantalizing flavours, served by knowledgeable and friendly staff.

♦♦ **Alfaia**, Travessa da Queimada 22, Bairro Alto, T21-346 12 32. Daily 1200-1630, 1830-0200, closed Sun lunch. A refined Bairro Alto restaurant with international style cuisine and superb traditional Portuguese dishes. Very popular at weekends. Booking advised.

♦♦ **Bota Alta**, Travessa da Queimada 35, Bairro Alto, T21-342 79 59. 1200-1430, 1900-2245. Closed Sat lunch and Sun. Eccentric wood-panelled tavern with a faultless repertoire of Portuguese classics, favourites include steak in red wine and cod with port and sausages.

♦♦ **Casa do Alentejo**, Rua das Porta de S Antão 58, Baixa, T21-340 51 40. 1200-1430 1900-2200. Pass through the Arab Patio to this gem serving delicacies from the Alentejo region.

♦ **Antiga Pastelaria de Belém**, Rua de Belém 90. Daily 0800-2300. An average of 10,000 salivating locals come to worship each day at the shrine of the most famous bakery in Portugal. Unquestionably the best way to spend €0.75 in Lisbon.

♦ **Café A Brasileira**, Rua Garrett, Chiado. Daily 0800-0200. The best place for a *bica* and *pastel de nata*. The former stomping ground of Lisbon's literati is now a popular gay meeting point.

♦ **Café Martinho da Arcada**, Praça do Comércio, 3, T21-886 62 13. Closed Sun. The oldest café in Lisbon, opened in 1782, and an essential stop on the trail of Fernando Pessoa. There's an expensive restaurant or you can simply order a *bica*, a *pastel de nata*.

⊕ Nightlife

Bairro Alto is the best place to kick start an evening. The lattice of cobbled streets holds hundreds of drinking spots, restaurants, clubs and shops. Start along the main drag, Rua da Atalaia, and explore down-to-earth *tascas*, sleek gay joints (**Frágil**, **Sétimo Céu**), jazz bars (**Catacombas**), loungy clubs (**Suave**, **Clube da Esquina**) and funky discos (**Bicaense**) that come to life after 2200. The Miradouro de Santa Catarina has the best views, either on the terrace or at the new **Noo Bai** rooftop bar. **B.leza** has the best African rhythms, with live music and tight dancing every night in Largo Conde Barão. Av 24 de Julho holds the larger, more commercial venues, like **Kremlin** or **Kapital** with 3 storeys of pop-rock and house. Further down, under 25th April Bridge, is **Docas** – renovated warehouses on a marina with latino sounds and tall drinks. Finally, *the* nightclub of Lisbon, **Lux**, (www.luxfragil.com, in the docks opposite Santa Apolonia train) is spacious and high-tech and offers the best of national and international DJs, concerts, performance and video.

Finding authentic **fado** is tricky. Repackaged for tourists it has become the antithesis of its primordial essence. Still, it is possible to stumble across raucous amateur *fado vadio*, where there's no formal programme, only an orgy of emotional catharsis.

Ljubljana

You'd be forgiven for not being entirely sure where Ljubljana is. The tiny Slovenian capital only recently caught the eye of international travellers. But like an awkward teenager who's suddenly discovered she's pretty, Ljubljana is basking in her new-found attention. The feel today is one of self-assured sophistication – the tight grid of cobbled streets and baroque townhouses is filled with trendy bars, slick museums, fashion-conscious boutiques and stylish restaurants. In summer, life spills outdoors and jazz and late-night chatter drifts out over the mint-green River Ljubljanica. Some good museums and an animated cultural scene add to the air of refinement, although the delicious (and ludicrously cheap) beer is set to become a major draw. Just be sure to get here soon – before the stag parties do.

Arts & culture
★★★

Eating
★★★

Nightlife
★★

Outdoors
★★★★

Romance
★★★★

Shopping
★★

Sightseeing
★★★

Value for money
★★★★★

Overall score
★★★✦

◉ Sights

The social and historical heart of the city is **Prešernov trg**; just a few metres from the banks of River Ljubljanica, it's a lively hub where locals congregate in open-air cafés. Flanking the north of the square is the rust-red Franciscan church, with the proud statue of France Prešeren, Slovenia's greatest poet. Stroll southeast from Prešeren's feet and you'll come to Ljubljana's most photographed landmark, **Triple Bridge**, designed by Jože Plečnik, grand architect and the city's equivalent to Barcelona's Gaudi. The three-pronged bridge crosses the narrow river to the Old Town. Turn left on the other side towards the elegant **Market Colonnade**, also designed by Plečnik, a grand curve of pale stone filled with food shops. The two squares fronting it are taken over by a bustling

Triple Bridge

daily **market**, and at the far end stands the portly bulk of **St Nicholas's Cathedral** ⓘ *daily 0600-1200, 1500-1800*, (look out for the rather spooky brass doors); the inside is awash with frescoes. **Dragon Bridge** curves back over to the left bank, but retracing your steps brings you to

Mestni trg, or Town Square, known for its baroque Town Hall and the ornate **Fountain of the Three Carnolian Rivers**, created in 1751 by Francis Robba. The cobbled streets of the **Old Town** wind south from here, past Shoemaker's Bridge, site of a Sunday **flea market**, with **Ljubljana Castle** ⓘ *May-Sep daily 0900-2100, Oct-Apr 1000-1800, SIT 790*, towering to the left. Turn left onto Ulica Na Grad and follow the steep path to the top of **Castle Hill**; a funicular is being planned, and a tourist train runs from Prešernov trg if you'd rather not walk. The castle itself is an impressive medieval hulk, with panoramic views from its tower and a 3D multimedia show of the city's history inside. Back on the other side of the river, **Kongresni trg** is a leafy square flanked by the University Building and the Slovene Philharmonic, from where it's a quick stroll to the brand

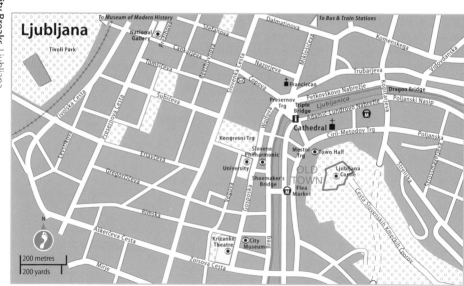

new **City Museum** ⓘ *Tue-Sun 1000-1800, free*. The displays are still being developed, but the stunning conversion of the Auersperg Mansion is worth a visit for the building alone. Northwest of here is the **National Gallery** ⓘ *Tue-Sun 1000-1800, SIT 800*, an ugly post-modernist lump tacked onto a Hapsberg-era edifice, filled with excellent examples of Slovenian impressionists, including Ivan Grohar and Ivana Kobilca. Two blocks west is **Tivoli Park**, a lush summer playground of rolling lawns and forests; the **Museum of Modern History** ⓘ *Tue-Sun 1000-1800, SIT 800*, housed in the bubblegum-pink Sequin Castle, has good displays on 20th century Slovenia.

⊖ Sleeping

€€€ Grand Hotel Union, Miklosiceva 1, T01-3081270, www.gh-union.si. The city's grande dame and the most elegant place to stay in Ljubljana. Great central location and fabulous views towards the castle.

€€ City Hotel, Dalmatinova 15, T01-2349140, www.cityhotel.si. A modern business hotel close to Preserrnov trg, with functional rooms and a huge breakfast buffet.

€ Celica, Metelkova 8, T01-2309700, www.hostelcelica.com. An excellent hostel in a converted military prison, with dorms and doubles in the old cells. It's stylish and comfortable, with a great café and chill-out area downstairs.

⊙ Eating

🍴🍴🍴 **Gostlina As**, Čopova 5, T01-4258822. A romantic fish restaurant with candlelit tables under plane trees and a cosy, vaulted interior. There's no menu;

Mestni trg and Cathedral

the waiters tell you what's on offer and recommend a wine to accompany it.
🍴🍴🍴 **Gostlina Sokol**, Ciril Metodov trb 4, T01-4396855. A labyrinthine Slovenian restaurant attracting its share of tour groups but serving authentic local food, including sausages and dumplings from the interior, and fresh trout from the Julian Alps.
🍴🍴 **Julija**, Stari trg 9, T01-4256463. A trendy bistro with gilded mirrors and art-deco posters, packed with fashionable locals. There's a good range of French and Italian dishes, including a delicious risotto.
🍴 **Ljubljanski Dvor**, Dvorni trg 1, T01-2516555. Serving over 100 varieties of superb crispy-based pizzas, including a wide choice for veggies, this place has a sunny deck overlooking the river.
🍴 **Zvezda Café**, Kongresni trg. A famous café serving a delectable array of cream cakes, tortes and pastries, with views over the grassy square.

⊖ Nightlife

During the summer, locals flock to the bars and cafés lining the Ljubljanica River, and it's a matter

of finding a table wherever you can. Ljubljana's young and hip take to the city's clubs from around 2400 – the scene changes rapidly, but a long-standing favourite is the **Bacchus Center**, Kongresni trg, T01-241 8242.

Chamber recitals
Between July and September the open-air Krizanke theatre hosts the **Ljubljana Summer Festival**, www.festival-lj.si, with weekend jazz performances and concerts from the Slovenian Philharmonic.

⊖ Travel essentials

Getting there Aerodrom Ljubljana, T04-2061000, www.lju-airport.si, is 23 km from the city centre. Buses run from the main bus terminal to the airport from Mon-Fri 0520-2010, and Sat-Sun 0610-1910, taking 45 mins. A taxi to the centre costs around SIT 7500.

Getting around The best way of getting around Ljubljana is on foot; all the sights are within easy walking distance of each other. Bicycles are available for rent from Plečnikov trg square, the main railway station, Tivoli railway station and Bavarski dvor square, Apr-Oct only. Buses run throughout the city and out to the suburbs, but the route map and schedule is confusing. There is a flat fare of SIT 300 which should be dropped into the box by the driver. Alternatively, tokens can be bought from newsagents kiosks.

Tourist information The main office is Adamič Lundrovo nabrežje 2, T01-3061215, www.ljubljana-tourism.si. Jun-Sep daily 0800-2100, Oct-May daily 0800-1900. It stocks free maps and city guides, and can book accommodation.

Exchange rate Slovenian Tolar (SIT). £1 = SIT 354.11 €1 = SIT 240.99.

European City Breaks Ljubljana

London

Somewhat to its own surprise, London is still one of the world's great cities. It's not the loveliest in the world, nor the most antique, romantic, or mysterious. Far from exotic, it's not the richest, largest, or even the most happening place on the planet either. Notwithstanding all of this, it's still impossible to resist. Civilized, improvised, sophisticated and alive, London wins all comers over in the end. A workaday, endlessly surprising mess, very much the capital of the UK, and very British, it's also a global town that has grown up thanks to other nations. Neither ancient nor modern, though erudite and grand, much of it hardly feels like a proper city at all. It's not Gotham or even Paris. The Romans, who founded Londinium in the first century AD, failed to impose any kind of order on its street plan, and no one has succeeded since. In fact London's streets, despite their enormous extent, are small, haphazard and human in scale. But they hold a world of artistic wonder within their mixed-up planning. London still does tradition, with its Tower, Buckingham Palace and Trooping the Colour, but there's a new London too: the London Eye, Tate Modern, Millennium Bridge, even the ill-fated Millennium Dome, and the new-found self-confidence afforded by the successful Olympic bid. With such magnificent trees, river views and murky weather, with its thriving culture and driven soul, like nowhere else on earth this teeming muddle works its way into your heart.

Arts & culture
★★★★★

Eating
★★★★★

Nightlife
★★★★★

Outdoors
★★★

Romance
★★★★

Shopping
★★★★★

Sightseeing
★★★★★

Value for money
★★★

Overall score
★★★★✦

London hotels

FROM

£50

per double room per night

All deals are subject to availability so check online now or call 0207 437 4370

London hotels, hostels, B&Bs & Apartments
all at guaranteed lowest rates

LONDONTOWN.com™
Your Best Friend in London

Check your hotel's LondonSurvey™ rating before you book.

See what previous customers thought about their London hotel experience by checking the LondonSurvey™ ratings. LondonSurvey™ is a continuous, independent survey of London accommodation, sightseeing and entertainment products and services.

LondonSurvey™ ratings are available at:

A LondonMarketing consumer product

At a glance

Trafalgar Square is the centre of London. **The Strand** runs east out of the square from **Whitehall** and **Westminster**, the seat of central government, to the **City**, east of St Paul's Cathedral. Just north of the Strand is **Covent Garden** and, to the northwest of Trafalgar Square, **Leicester Square** and **Shaftesbury Avenue** are the showbiz centre of the West End with **Chinatown** next door. **Soho** is the West End's late-night party zone, with **Oxford Street** forming its northern boundary. West of Regent Street, **Mayfair** remains the swankiest end of town with the gentleman's clubland and royal stamping ground of **St James's** next door. Beyond Piccadilly Circus, **Piccadilly** heads west to Hyde Park Corner with panache. West of here, **Knightsbridge** and **South Kensington** boast luxury shopping and a trio of great museums. **Regent's Park** and **London Zoo** are northeast of Hyde Park, above **Marylebone** with its low-brow tourist attractions around **Baker Street**.

> ❝❞
>
> New York is a great city, no question, but it will never be as pretty as London
>
> *Woody Allen*

Bloomsbury, to the east, is the academic heart of London, home to the British Museum. Further east are **Holborn**, with its Law Courts, and buzzing **Clerkenwell**. South of the river, **Southwark**, **Bankside** and **Borough** are laden with attractions and reached from St Paul's across the Millennium Bridge, or along the river from the **South Bank** and the London Eye. Out in the East End, some of London's most happening nightlife is in **Shoreditch**, **Hoxton**, **Brick Lane** and **Spitalfields**, while **Greenwich**, across the river from **Docklands** has the National Maritime Museum and Royal Observatory.

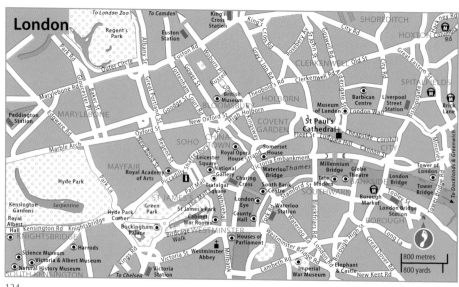

24 hours in the city

View from Waterloo Bridge

In order to see as much of London as possible in a day, it's best to avoid public transport. An easy three-mile stroll takes in several of the major sights. From **Trafalgar Square**, walk down Northumberland Avenue to the Embankment and cross over the Golden Jubilee footbridge to the **South Bank**, from where there are great views of Big Ben and Houses of Parliament. Unless you want a closer look at the attractions of **County Hall**, turn left to walk along the river, past the Royal Festival Hall and **Waterloo Bridge**, to **Tate Modern** and Shakespeare's **Globe Theatre** before heading over the Millennium Footbridge to **St Paul's Cathedral**. After a look around St Paul's, the restaurants and clubs of **Clerkenwell** and **Smithfield** or **Shoreditch** are close at hand for an evening's entertainment.

★ *Don't leave town without taking a walk over Waterloo Bridge – preferably at sunset.*

⊖ Travel essentials

Getting there London Heathrow Airport, T0870-000 0123 (Heathrow Travelcare T020-8745 7495), is 15 miles west of central London. Piccadilly Line tube trains run every 5-9 mins (roughly 0630-0100), journey time 50 mins. Heathrow Express, T0845-600 1515, www.heathrowexpress.co.uk, runs to Paddington Station, every 15 mins (0510-2340), journey time 15 mins, £12 single, £22 return. A black cab costs £45-50 (45 mins-1 hr). **London Gatwick** Airport, T0870-000 2468, 28 miles south of the capital. Gatwick Express, T0845-850 1530, to and from London Victoria every 15 mins (hourly at night), £10.50 single, £20 return. Taxi around £70, about 1 hr. **London Luton Airport**, T01582-405100, 30 miles north of central London. Regular trains to and from London Bridge, Blackfriars, Farringdon and King's Cross stations. A taxi takes 50 mins and costs around £55. **Stansted Airport**, T0870-000 0303, 35 miles northeast. Stansted Express, T08458-500150, every 15 mins to Liverpool Street, 45 mins, £13 single, £23 open return. A taxi takes 1-1½ hrs and costs about £75.

There are 4 main train stations: King's Cross from Scotland and northeast England; Euston from the northwest; Paddington from Wales and the west; and Waterloo International for **Eurostar**, www.eurostar.com, from France and Belgium. For train times and ticket prices call **National Rail Enquiries** T08457-484950, or www.qjump.co.uk.

Getting around London's public transport is fairly efficient, though expensive. At the time of writing, fares on the London Underground (Tube) and London buses were set to increase significantly for those not using the Oyster charge card system. A single tube fare in Zone 1 (most of central London) will rise to £3, and single bus fares to £1.50. Daily travelcards which can be used on both buses and the tube

currently cost £6 (peak) and £4.70 (off-peak). For 24-hr information on all forms of public transport call T020-7222 1234, or visit www.tfl.gov.uk. Bus and tube are the most commonly used forms of transport. The tube is generally faster but buses are good if you want to do some sightseeing as you get about town. Car drivers should note that a congestion charge (£8) is in operation in central London Mon-Fri 0700-1830. For more details, visit the website above.

Tourist information Britain and London Visitor Centre (BLVC), 1 Lower Regent St, SW1, (Piccadilly Circus tube) Mon 0930-0630, Tue-Fri 0900-0630, Sat-Sun 1000-1600; Jun-Sep Sat-Sun 1000-1700. **London Information Centre**, in the middle of Leicester Sq, T020-7292 2333, www.londontown.com, daily 0800-2300. **Corporation of London Information**, St Paul's Churchyard, south side of the cathedral, T020-7332 1456, Apr-Sep daily 0930-1700; Oct-Mar Mon-Fri 0930-1700, Sat 0930-1230.

⦿ Sights

Trafalgar Square
ⓘ *Tube Charing Cross, Leicester Sq.*

Trafalgar Square is the centre of London, avoided by Londoners whenever possible, unless to make their voices heard at demonstrations and celebrations. It's the breadth of Whitehall approaching from Westminster and Parliament to the south that explains the prominence of the square in London's geography. This is where the administrative offices of government meet the people. **Nelson's Column**, **Landseer's lions** and the two large fountains give the square some dignity, inspiring a sense of occasion. The pedestrianization of the north side of the square has transformed access to the **National Gallery** ⓘ *T020-7747 2885, www.nationalgallery.org.uk, daily 1000-1800, Wed 1000-2100, free, guided tours from Sainsbury Wing Level 0 daily at 1130 and 1430, also Wed 1800 and 1830, Sat 1230 and 1530*, one of the world's most comprehensive collections of fine art with more than 2000 Western European paintings

Trafalgar Square

Tower of London

dating from the 13th century to 1900. Along with the **National Portrait Gallery** ⓘ *T020-7306 0055, ext 216, www.npg.org.uk, Mon-Wed, Sat-Sun 1000-1800, Thu -Fri 1000-2100, free*, behind it, these two treasure houses are the best reasons for a visit here.

Westminster Abbey
ⓘ *Information and tours T020-7654 4834, www.westminster-abbey.org. Mon-Fri 0930-1645 (last admission 1545), Sat 0930-1445 (last admission 1345). Sun entry is for services only. Tube: Westminster.*

A surprisingly small church for one of such enormous significance to the Anglican faith and British state, Westminster Abbey's charm lies in its age (the oldest part is 13th century). That said, once inside, the length and especially the height (over 100 ft) of the nave are awe-inspiring. Highlights include the **Coronation Chair**, made to order for the 'Hammer of the Scots', Edward I, and used to crown every English monarch except three since 1308; **Henry VII's Chapel** (or Lady Chapel), dating from the early 16th century; and **Poet's Corner**, with its

monuments to Shakespeare, Chaucer and other poets and actors, as well as scientists, architects and historians.

Tower of London
ⓘ *T0870-756 7070, www.tower-of-london.org.uk. Mar-Oct Tue-Sat 0900-1800, Sun, Mon 1000-1800; Nov-Feb Tue-Sat 0900-1600, Mon, Sun 1000-1600. Last admission 1 hr before closing. £14.50 or £13.50 in advance. Tube: Tower Hill.*

Londoners traditionally dislike the tower. After all, it wasn't built to protect them 900 years ago, but to subdue them, a role it played until the mid-19th century. Nowadays many have their revenge by either ignoring the place or dismissing it as a tourist trap. In fact it's less a trap than a treat, making an enormous effort to elucidate its wealth of historical associations and bring the old buildings to life with a mix of bare Norman stonework and 21st-century three-dimensional virtual tours. Highlights include the **Royal Armouries** and, behind the **White Tower**, in the Waterloo Barracks, the **Crown Jewels**. Nearby, the entertaining neo-Gothic extravagance of **Tower Bridge** keeps the isolated fortress company.

St Paul's Cathedral

St Paul's Cathedral

ⓘ T020-7236 4128, www.stpauls.co.uk.
Mon-Sat 0830-1600 (phone to check
before visiting). £8 including cathedral
crypt and galleries. Organ recitals Sun
1700, free. Tube: St Paul's.

Standing proud at the top of Ludgate
Hill is St Paul's Cathedral. At least the
fifth church on the site, it was started
in 1675, and took about 35 years to
complete. Hemmed in on all sides
over the centuries, Wren's relatively
colossal church still impresses. The
redevelopment of Paternoster Square
has opened up new views of the place,
reflecting its newly cleaned Portland
stone in plate-glass office blocks, while
the **Millennium Bridge** now provides a
neat approach from Tate Modern. It's
definitely well worth climbing up to the
Golden Gallery for the tremendous
wraparound open-air views.

British Museum

ⓘ T020-7323 8000, www.thebritish
museum.ac.uk. Sat-Wed 1000-1730,
Thu-Fri 1000-2030 (late view of main
floor and some upper floor galleries only);
Great Court Mon-Wed 0900-2100,

British Museum

Tate Modern

Thu-Sat 0900-2300, Sun 0900-1800. Free
(donations appreciated), prices of
temporary exhibitions vary. Tube:
Tottenham Court Rd.

With its new slogan 'illuminating
world cultures', the British Museum
now comes closer to that ideal in
spectacular style. Architect Norman
Foster's redevelopment of the central
Great Court, opened in December
2000, turned the museum's
long-hidden central quadrangle into
the largest covered square in Europe,
rechristened the Elizabeth II Great
Court. A beautiful canopy made up of
a latticework of 3312 unique panes
of glass now wraps itself around the
dome of the round **Reading Room**,
free-standing once again at the heart
of the museum. On entering the
Great Court from the south, pick up
a floorplan and get your bearings.
It would be quite impossible to see
everything in one day: apart from the
guided and audio tours, it's well worth
finding out from the information desk
when and where the informative and
free daily 50-minute 'EyeOpener'
Gallery Talks are taking place.

Tate Modern

ⓘ Ticket bookings T020-7887 8888;
information T020-7887 8008,
www.tate.org.uk. Sun-Thu 1000-1800,
Fri-Sat 1000-2200 (last admission
45 mins before closing). Free (charges for
special exhibitions around £7). Tube:
Southwark or Blackfriars.

Tate Modern has been one of the
most spectacular and popular new
additions to London in years. The
converted Bankside Power Station
now houses the Tate's collection of
international modern art from 1900 to
the present. An extraordinary great solid
box of brick with a single free-standing
square chimney front centre, the power
station was decommissioned in 1986
and left desolate until Swiss architects
Herzog and de Meuron were appointed
to adapt the building to its new role. The
immense **Turbine Hall** is an astonishing
space for specifically commissioned
artworks on a grand scale and the rest of
the main collection is permanently
arranged around four themes: Still Life,
Landscape, the Nude and History. Free
guided tours leave from level 5 at 1100
(Nude), at 1200 (History), from level 3 at
1400 (Still Life), and at 1500 (Landscape).

London Eye

London Eye and South Bank

ⓘ *T0870-500 0600, www.ba-london eye.com. May-Sep Mon-Thu 0930-2000, Fri-Sun 0930-2100; Jun Mon-Thu 0930-2100, Fri-Sun 0930-2200; Jul-Aug daily 0930-2200; Oct-Dec daily 0930-2000. £12.50, private capsule £375 (advance booking available on the web). Tube: Westminster or Waterloo.*

The British Airways London Eye is the vast spoked white observation wheel beside Westminster Bridge that has become one of the most welcome recent additions to the London skyline. Well over 100 m in diameter, it's visible from unexpected places all around the city. There's no denying its novelty value, or even perhaps its beauty. The half-hour 'flight' in one of its surprisingly roomy capsules, moving at a quarter-metre a second, provides superb 25-mile views over the city and is neither vertiginous nor at all boring. On a clear day you can see all of London and beyond.

Just upstream from the Eye, the magisterial **County Hall** now houses the highly acclaimed **London Aquarium** ⓘ *T020-7967 8000, www.london aquarium.co.uk, daily 1000-1800 (last admission 1700), £9.75*, and the **Saatchi**

London Aquarium

Science Museum

Gallery ⓘ *T020-7823 2363, www.saatchi-gallery.co.uk, Sun-Thu 1000-1800, Fri-Sat 1000-2200, £9*, with its provocative contemporary art collection.

Downstream from County Hall stands the **South Bank Centre**, the largest arts complex of its kind in Europe. Apart from the main **Royal Festival Hall**, it also houses an exhibition space, the Poetry Library, more concert halls, the National Theatre and National Film Theatre as well as the cutting-edge **Hayward Gallery** ⓘ *T020-7928 3144, www.hayward.org. uk. Mon, Thu, Sat-Sun 1000-1800, Tue-Wed 1000-2000, Fri 1000-2100. £9.*

South Kensington Museums

ⓘ *Science Museum: T0870-870 4868, www.sciencemuseum.org.uk. Daily 1000-1800. Free. Natural History Museum: T020-7942 5000, www.nhm.ac.uk. Mon-Sat 1000-1750, Sun 1100-1750. Free. V&A Museum: T0870-906 3883. Daily 1000-1745, till 2200 Wed and the last Fri of the month. Free. Tube: South Kensington.*

Although such a short distance apart on the Cromwell Road heading towards Knightsbridge, the temptation to 'do' all three of these great museums in a day

ⓞ Best of the rest

Royal Academy of Arts ⓘ *Piccadilly, T020-7300 5678. Mon-Thu, Sat-Sun 1000-1800, Fri 1000-2030.* Attention-grabbing exhibitions of contemporary art.
Cabinet War Rooms ⓘ *King Charles St, T020-7930 6961; winter 1000-1800, summer 0930-1800 (last admission 1700). £10.* The nerve centre of Churchill's morale-boosting war effort.
London Zoo ⓘ *Regent's Park, T020-7722 3333, www.zsl.org. Summer daily 1000-1730, winter daily 1000-1630 (last admission 1 hr before closing). £14.*
Museum of London ⓘ *150 London Wall, T020-7600 3699, events T020-7814 5777, www.museumoflondon.org.uk. Mon-Sat 1000-1750, Sun 1200-1750. Free.* A refreshing visual approach to the social history of the city.
Imperial War Museum ⓘ *Lambeth Rd, T020-7416 5000, www.iwm.org.uk. Daily 1000-1800. Free.* Dedicated to the history and consequences of all 20th-century warfare.
Somerset House ⓘ *Strand, T020-7845 4600, www.somerset-house.org.uk. Daily 1000-1800 (last admission 1715). 1 collection £5, any 2 collections £8, all 3 £12.* An ice rink in winter and year-round fine art and antiques in the Courtauld and Gilbert Collections or Hermitage Rooms.
Tate Britain ⓘ *T020-7887 8000, www.tate.org.uk/britain. Daily 1000-1750, free, but special exhibitions £10.* Ancient and contemporary British art.

should definitely be resisted. Even two could prove too rich a treat. The **Science Museum** prides itself on being one of the most forward-thinking, interactive and accessible museums in the country. The Wellcome Wing in particular is worth visiting with its four floors dedicated to displaying cutting-edge science incorporating an IMAX cinema and the first Virtual Voyage simulator in Europe.

The **Natural History Museum** is housed in the extraordinary old orange and blue terracotta building on Cromwell Road. This academic research institution has become seriously fun-packed. Divided into Life Galleries and Earth Galleries, it tells the history of our planet with a not entirely successful combination of venerable artefacts and playschool attractions. Children and adults are sure to learn something about the natural world whether they want to or not. It never disappoints.

The **Victoria and Albert Museum** is one of the world's greatest museums. Surprisingly, considering its grand façade on Cromwell Road, it wears that greatness lightly. It was founded in 1857 with the intention of educating the populace in the appreciation of

St James's Park

decorative art and design by exhibiting superb examples of what could be achieved in that field. Never a narrowly nationalistic enterprise, its remarkable collection was gathered, like the British Museum's, from all corners of the globe.

Buckingham Palace and St James's Park

ⓘ *T020-7766 7300, www.royal collection.org.uk. Aug-Sep daily 0930-1830. £12.95. Tube: Green Park, St James's Park, Hyde Park Corner.*

The Queen's official London residence is open to the paying public for two months of the year and, despite the high admission prices, long queues and disappointing tour, it attracts thousands of people from all over the world. Next door to the visitors' entrance to the palace, and open year round, the **Queen's Gallery** ⓘ *T020- 7766 7301, daily 1000-1730 (last admission 1630), £7.50,* displays changing selections from the Queen's collection of Old Masters and portraiture, an extraordinary array founded by Charles II. The **Changing of the Guard** on the forecourt of Buckingham Palace happens daily at

1130 from 1 April to the end of July and alternate days the rest of the year.

St James's Park, stretching out east from the palace, is the finest and most carefully laid out of the Royal parks (others include Hyde Park, Green Park, Regent's Park and Kensington Gardens). A wander around reveals surprising but carefully orchestrated vistas at every turn. From April to September guided tours are given by its warden.

Greenwich

ⓘ *Cutty Sark DLR or overland train from Charing Cross or London Bridge to Greenwich train station.*

Greenwich has been attracting visitors for centuries. Home to the beleaguered Millennium Dome, it has many more successful attractions which draw tourists and Londoners alike. Most especially the **National Maritime Museum** ⓘ *Park Row, T020-8858 4422, www.nmm.ac.uk, daily 1000-1700, free,* the **Royal Observatory** ⓘ *T020-8858 4422, www.rog.nmm.ac.uk, daily 1000-1700, free,* and the tea clipper **Cutty Sark** ⓘ *King William Walk, T020-8858 3445, www.cuttysark.org.uk, daily 1000-1700, £4.50.*

Natural History Museum

Sex and clubs and rock'n'roll

Soho has long been associated with sex and vice. Central London's notorious one square mile district was home to some 300 prostitutes in the 1950s and when they moved elsewhere in the 1960s the number of strip clubs and drinking clubs increased dramatically. The most famous, *Raymond Revuebar*, is still doing business, though most have now closed. From the late 1960s Soho became the centre of the porn industry. While pornographic publications were whipped over from the continent in Danish Bacon lorries, the Obscene Publications Squad (OPS) was being bribed to turn a blind eye. But in 1972 a new commissioner of the Metropolitan Police was appointed to clean up Soho and the OPS was suspended. In the early 1980s new legislation requiring all sex shops to be licensed came into effect.

Soho was also one of the centres of British bohemia. Its drinking clubs are still famous: *The Colony Room*, on Dean Street, has always been a favourite haunt of hard-drinking British artists, from Francis Bacon to Damien Hirst, and the *Groucho*, once the epitome of Thatcherite excess, still serves the inflated egos of medialand. Soho also has mighty impressive music credentials: *Ronnie Scott's* was the first outlet in the capital for modern jazz, while the *Marquee* (now closed) played host to the Yardbirds and the Rolling Stones. Its dance clubs, such as *The Wag* and *Beat Route* were at the cutting edge of late 1970s/early 1980s music. Soho's most recent incarnation as the capital's big, gay heart, only confirms its status as London's Left Bank or Greenwich Village.

Sleeping

Accommodation doesn't come cheap in London – even at the budget end – but if it's luxury, pampering and romance you're after you'll be spoilt for choice. We've left out the really obvious big-hitters like *Claridge's*, *The Dorchester* and *The Savoy* in favour of more intimate, cosy or romantic options. All are centrally located.

€€€ **Dukes**, St James's Pl, SW1, T020-7491 4840, www.dukeshotel.com. With 89 comfortable, old-fashioned rooms and a health club, this is a very discreet luxury small hotel with a cosy bar that mixes devastating martinis.

€€€ **Hazlitt's**, 6 Frith St, W1, T020-7434 1771, www.hazlittshotel.com. Many people's London favourite with 23 individual period rooms of great character, in memory of the London essayist. No restaurant or bar but plenty nearby in the liveliest streets of Soho.

€€€ **The Rookery**, Peter's Lane, Cowcross St, T020-7336 0931, www.rookeryhotel.com. A renovated old-fashioned townhouse hotel with 33 rooms in an antique building with a crow's nest of a penthouse. Owned by the same people as *Hazlitt's*.

€€€ **St Martin's Lane**, 45 St Martin's Lane, WC2, T0800-634 5500, www.morganshotelgroup.com. Formerly Ian Schrager's media favourite, designed by minimalist Philippe Starck, with a restaurant doing classic French and modern European on the side, the awesome *Light Bar* and the *Seabar*.

€€ **Aster House**, 3 Sumner Pl, SW7, T020-7581 5888, www.asterhouse. com. Sweet little guesthouse with 14 rooms, a garden and conservatory.

€€ **The Claverley**, 13-14 Beaufort Gdns, SW3, T020-7589 8541, www.claverleyhotel.co.uk. Comfortable and classy small hotel. All rooms different, with marble bathrooms, decorated in a romantic English way. Breakfast included.

€€ **Malmaison**, 18-21 Charterhouse Sq, EC1, T020-7012 3700, www.malmaison.com. With 97 differently shaped rooms, this hotel is comfortable, easygoing but quite flash.

€€ **Number Sixteen**, 16 Sumner Pl, SW7, T020-7589 5232, www.number sixteenhotel.co.uk. 42 rooms in 4 small townhouses. Elegant privacy and the most salubrious (and expensive) of the set in this dainty little stucco street. Another of the successful Firmdale group's operations.

€€ **Tophams Belgravia**, 28 Ebury St, SW1, T020-7730 8147, www.tophams.co.uk. A charming, small country house-style hotel, family-run with very friendly service.

ⓘ Eating

London's restaurant scene continues to mature at a heady rate. The range of excellent food on offer in almost every setting and price bracket can be baffling. A good meal has become an essential part of a top night on the town. That said, the city does remain a notoriously expensive place in which to eat out compared to much of Europe. Compensation of a kind can be found in the sheer variety of different cuisines available – from Africa to Yemen via Poland and New Zealand; and in the quality of the fresh ingredients appearing on menus across the capital.

¶¶¶ **Andrew Edmonds**, 46 Lexington St, W1, T020-7437 5708. Excellent modern European cooking at reasonable prices is served up in a cosy, candlelit atmosphere. Booking ahead strongly recommended.

¶¶¶ **Hakkasan**, 8 Hanway Pl, W1, T020-7907 1888. Probably the funkiest Chinese in the capital, with its blue-lit banquettes and stylish decor and a Michelin star to boot.

¶¶¶ **Moro**, 34-36 Exmouth Market, EC1, T020-7833 8336. A modern Spanish restaurant that has been wowing the area's hipsters for some time with its artful way with super-fresh ingredients.

¶¶¶ **Nobu**, 19 Old Park Lane, W1, T020-7447 4747. Robert de Niro et al's venture at the super-fashionable *Metropolitan Hotel*. Stuff your face on some ultra-light Japanese-cum-South American food. Book up to a month in advance for dinner reservations.

¶¶ **The Eagle**, 159 Farringdon Rd, T020-7837 1353. One of the first pubs to go gastro, cooking up excellent modern European food.

¶¶ **Joe Allen**, 13 Exeter St, WC2, T020-7836 0651. Quite hard to find but definitely worth the effort. The American menu served up in this traditional basement diner never fails to please a host of theatre-going regulars as well as tourists in the know.

¶¶ **St John**, 26 St John St, T020-7251 0848. Especially good offal and freshly baked bread are served up in a stark former smokery celebrating 'nose to tail' eating.

¶ **India Club**, 143 Strand, WC2, T020-7836 0650. Closed Sun. Pay up to £10 for old-style curries at formica tables on linoleum floors with yellow walls. A very Indian institution, since 1950. Bring your own booze.

¶ **Lahore Kebab House**, 2 Umberston St, E1, T020-7488 2551. Daily till 2330. A 30-year-old family-owned restaurant set deep in the Pakistani and Bangladeshi quarters of East London. Delicious and authentic Pakistani dishes on offer. Basic, informal and a multi-cultural crowd. Bring your own alcohol.

ⓘ Nightlife

Bars and clubs

Traditional pubs survive across town, some with genuinely extraordinary Victorian interiors (**The Salisbury**, 90 St Martin's Lane, W1), but many are just straightforward local boozers doing what they've always done (**The Coach and Horses**, 29 Greek St, W1, **The Dog and Duck**, 18 Bateman St, W1). Music bars are still jumping into the wee small hours, particularly in Shoreditch (**Big Chill Bar**, Dray Walk, off Brick Lane, E1, **Shoreditch Electricity Showrooms**, 39a Hoxton St, N1) and the gay bars in Soho (**Freedom**, 60 Wardour St, W1). And then there are the hundreds of candlelit wine bars, swish brasseries and elegant hotel bars, sweaty dives and designer cocktail lounges. Many of the best clubs are around Old Street and Shoreditch.

Cinema

British Film Institute London IMAX, South Bank, Waterloo, T0870-787 2525.

Curzon Mayfair, 38 Curzon St, T020-7465 8865. Generally shows middle to highbrow mainstream movies on its one screen.

The Electric Cinema, Portobello Rd, W11, T020-7229 8688. The epitome of cinema-going chic and is accordingly priced.

ICA Cinema, Nash House, The Mall, SW1, T020-7930 3647. The place for very rare or independent films, especially 'world cinema'.

National Film Theatre (NFT), South Bank, SE1, T020-7928 3535. Home to the British Film Institute and the obvious starting point for any cinephile's London visit.

Markets

London's markets are often most evocative of the spirit of the city. A brief run-down of the main ones goes like this: **Berwick Street**, W1, (Mon-Sat 0900-1700) for fabrics and food; **Borough**, SE1, (Fri 1200-1800, Sat 0900-1600) for organic food; **Brick Lane**, E1, (Sun 0700-1300) for just about everything; **Camden**, NW1, (Sat-Sun 0900-1700) for furniture, gifts, clothes, accessories and general mayhem; **Columbia Road**, E1, (Sun 0800-1400) for flowers; **Leather Lane**, EC2, (Mon-Fri 1030-1400) for cheap clothes, accessories, fruit and veg; **Portobello Road**, W11, (Sat 0800-1800) for antiques, second-hand clothes and bric-a-brac; **Spitalfields**, E1, (Sun 1100-1500) for clothes, books, organic food, jewellery and bric-a-brac.

Portobello Market

Classical music and dance

Barbican Centre, T020-7638 8891, www.barbican.org.uk. Home of the London Symphony Orchestra.

Royal Albert Hall, Kensington Gore, T020-7589 8212. A grand setting for just about any and every type of entertainment spectacular.

Royal Opera House, Bow St, T020-7304 4000, www.royaloperahouse.org. Exorbitant prices (up to £115), though seats available in the gods for under £20. Also home to the Royal Ballet.

Sadler's Wells and **Lilian Baylis Theatre**, Rosebery Av, T020-7863 8000. Superb state-of-the-art base for dance and opera.

South Bank Centre, including **Royal Festival Hall**, **Purcell Room**, and **Queen Elizabeth Hall**, T020-7960 4242. The Royal Festival Hall holds large-scale symphonic orchestral and choral concerts, while the smaller Queen Elizabeth Hall and smaller still Purcell Room stick to chamber music.

Wigmore Hall, 36 Wigmore St, T020-7935 2141, www.wigmore-hall.org.uk. World-class chamber music and song, lunchtimes at 1300 and evenings.

Jazz, rock and pop

Astoria, 157 Charing Cross Rd, T020-7434 9592. Arguably London's most eminent rock and pop venue.

Brixton Academy, 211 Stockwell Rd, T020-7771 2000. Attracts big rock and pop acts but not over-large.

The Jazz Café, 3 Parkway, Camden, NW1, T020-7916 6060. An eclectic mix of world, funk and folk, as well as jazz.

Ronnie Scott's, 47 Frith St, W1, T020-7439 0747. Still smokin' like a train and often needs to be booked in advance.

Theatre

The heart of theatre is still the West End. Though criticized for pandering to the bottom denominator, competition for audiences has led some producers become more adventurous. However, smaller theatres are still often a better bet and include: **Almeida** Almeida St, T 020-7359 4404; **Donmar Warehouse**, 41 Earlham St, T020-7369 1732; **Haymarket Theatre Royal**, Haymarket, T020-7930 8800; and **Royal National Theatre**, South Bank, T020-7452 3000. The half-price West End ticket booth is in Leicester Square.

○ Shopping

The difficulty is knowing where to begin. **Oxford St** and **Regent St** have *Selfridges, Hamleys, Liberty* and other large department stores and big brand shops. **Tottenham Court Rd** is the place to go for computers and other electronics. Head to **Charing Cross Rd** and **Bloomsbury** for new and second-hand books and **Soho** and **Carnaby St** for urban streetwear and style accessories. **Covent Garden** is good for clothes, specialist foods, toys, toiletries and gifts. **Bond St** and **Mayfair** are the place to go for high fashion and expensive jewellery. For bespoke boots, hats, suits, smoking requisites, wine and other clubby male accessories, go to **St James's** and **Savile Row**. **Clerkenwell** is good for crafts and independent designers. **Knightsbridge** has more high street fashion and, of course, *Harrods*.

Chelsea and **Notting Hill** are good for one-off, independent fashion labels (as well as second-hand clothes), music, book and gift shops. See also Markets above.

Lyon

In Lyon, it's all about the food. Forget sightseeing – to get a real feel for what the city's all about, step into its restaurants. Lyon has more eateries per capita than any other city in the world. Here, people swap recipes over breakfast, quarrel about chefs at lunch and debate Michelin stars over dinner. From some of the best restaurants in France to the simplest *bouchons*, you'll struggle to have a bad meal. And to walk off all that food, France's second largest city has a staggeringly beautiful Renaissance centre – so impressive that it was awarded UNESCO World Heritage Site status in 1998. Its history dates from Roman times, but its wealth came from the silk industry and Lyon still thrives today as a couture centre. Only in France can the concepts of high fashion and high calories marry so well.

Arts & culture
★★★

Eating
★★★★★

Nightlife
★★★

Outdoors
★★

Romance
★★

Shopping
★★★

Sightseeing
★★

Value for money
★★★★

Overall score
★★★

> The pig is nothing but an enormous dish which walks while waiting to be served.

Charles Monselet, chef

At a glance

The **Presqu'île**, wedged between the Rhône and Sâone rivers, is the centre of the city, focussed on the smart **Bellecour** area (centre of which is the vast place Bellecour) and **Perrache**, the area around the main train station. Just south of here is the Musée des Tissus, a highlight and an excellent introduction to the city's status as a silk capital. To the north is the Musée des Beaux-Arts, and the area of **La Croix-Rousse**, once home to silk weavers and becoming a fashionable hot spot today, while to the east, on the other side of the Rhône, is the modern and commercial part of town. Sights here include the Centre d'Histoire de la Résistance et de la Déportation, L'Institut Lumière and the Musée d'Art Contemporain. On the western banks of the Sâone is **Vieux Lyon** (Old Lyon), the Renaissance centre of the old town, the most atmospheric part of the city and the reason that Lyon is a UNESCO World Heritage Sight. Here, the cobbled lanes creep up towards **Fourvière**, the hill upon which the Romans founded Lugdunum. For an excellent overview of the city's layout, head to the terrace of the basilica at the top of Fourvière, which offers panoramic views over Lyon.

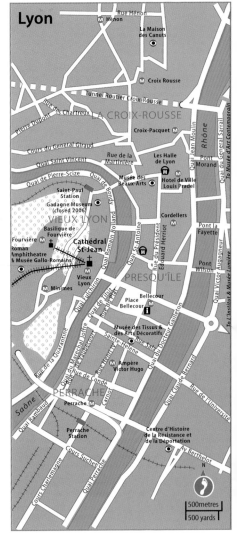

★ *Don't leave without rising early and seeing celebrity chefs haggling over cured ham and goldleaf-dusted chocolates at Les Halles de Lyon.*

◉ Sights

Place Bellecour

Place Bellecour

This vast square – one of the largest in the country – lies at the heart of the centre, in the middle of Presqu'île and midway between the Rhône and Sâone rivers. In the centre is a statue of Louis XIV dressed in Roman garb on horseback, surrounded by pale gravel, grand façades and posh shops. This is also the site of the tourist bureau.

Musée des Beaux-Arts

ⓘ *T04-7210 1740. Sat-Tue and Thu 1000-1800, Fri 1030-2000. €6. Métro Hôtel de Ville. Buses 1, 3, 6, 13, 18, 19, 44.*

Housed in the grand Palais Saint-Pierre, this museum holds a vast fine arts collection, second in France only to the Louvre. The collection includes pieces from ancient Greece, Rome and Egypt, continues through the Middle Ages and culminates in an excellent selection of France's finest 19th-century painters including Monet, Renoir and Gauguin.

There's a pleasant café and the museum is all but deserted during the week.

Musée des Tissus

ⓘ *T04-7838 4200, www.musee-des-tissus.com. Tue-Sun 1000-1730. €5. Métro Ampère Victor Hugo.*

The history of Lyon's status as a silk capital is chartered in this surprisingly fascinating museum, spread across 30 rooms filled with fabrics and costumes from around the world. Included are

rare examples of Persian carpets, Coptic tapestries and silks from Italy, China and Japan, as well as some of the finest silks produced in Lyon. Parts of the museum were closed at time of writing, and will re-open in October 2006. Next door is the reasonably diverting **Decorative Arts Museum** ⓘ *1000-1200 and 1400-1730; same ticket)*, with objets d'art and household goods from the 17th and 18th centuries.

Centre d'Histoire de la Résistance et de la Déportation

ⓘ *T04-7273 9906. Wed-Sun 0900-1730. €3.80. Métro Jean Macé; tram T2, stop Centre Berthelot.*

Located in old Gestapo headquarters, this harrowing museum is a dark tour through the times of Nazi occupation, resistance and deportation during the Second World War. Lyon was a hotbed of anti-fascism, and where resistance hero Jean Moulin was arrested and tortured – the old torture cells today house displays, including the film of the trial of Klaus Barbie, head of the Gestapo.

European City Breaks Lyon

⊖ Travel essentials

Getting there Lyon Saint Exupéry Airport, T0826-800826, www.lyon.aeroport.fr, is about 25 km east of the city centre. The **Satobus**, T04-3725 3732, www.satobus.com, is a regular shuttle service between the airport and the city centre, leaving every 20 mins from 0500-2340. A 1-way ticket costs €8.40. Taxis are available from outside the terminal building; the 40-min journey should cost around €40. The airport also has its own TGV station, which connects to the national rail network, from where you can get into central Lyon.

Getting around The centre of town is easily explored on foot but there's also an integrated public transport system, with 4 métro lines, 2 tram lines, a bus network and 2 funiculars, all run by **Transport en Commun Lyonnais (TCL)**, T0820-427000, www.tcl.fr. A single ticket, which is valid on all the metros, buses and trams, costs €1.50, and must be validated before travel (valid for 1 hr). A pack of 10 tickets costs €11.90. A day pass costs €4.20, and a City Pass, lasting 1 month, costs €43.40. The funicular runs on separate tickets, costing €2.20 for a return ticket.

Tourist information The Lyon Convention and Visitors Bureau, T04-7277 6969, www.lyon-france.com, is on place Bellecour. It's open Apr-Oct Mon-Sat 0900-1900, Sun 1000-1800, Nov-Mar Mon-Sat 1000-1800, Sun 1000-1730). **Lyon City Card**, valid for 1, 2 or 3 days, is issued by the tourist bureau and provides free transport and entry to museums, free guided tours and reductions at theatres and concerts. 1 day costs €18, 2 days costs €28, and 3 days costs €38.

Vieux Lyon

ⓘ *Métro Vieux Lyon*

The delightful Renaissance quarter, reached across a series of bridges, granted the city its UNESCO World Heritage Site status and is the most enjoyable area to wander around today. Vieux Lyon feels somehow more Italian than French, with cobbled lanes lined with pastel-coloured Renaissance façades, a huge number of which are given over to bustling restaurants, cafés and boutiques. Many of the roads are chopped up by *traboules*, tunnel-like alleys built to protect silks being carried by weavers, and used by resistance fighters during the Second World War. Although the main attraction here is simply to wander about, there are a handful of sights, including the **Gadagne Museum** (incorporating the Musée Historique de Lyon and the Musée de la Marionnette, but closed for restoration until winter 2006/spring 2007) and the **Théâtre de Guignol** ⓘ *T04- 78289257, www.guignol-lyon.com,* where you can see the famous local marionettes doing their thing.

The enormous **Cathédral St-Jean** is on place St-Jean, from where the

Musée des Beaux-Arts

Vieux Lyon

funicular (€2.20) whisks visitors to the top of **Fourvière hill** (the gardens here are a lovely spot for a picnic) topped by the extravagant **Basilique de Fourvière**, a close imitation of Sacré Coeur in Paris. Although the interior is rather overbearing, the views from here over the city are tremendous. Nearby are the city's roman remains including an impressive ruined amphitheatre, and the **Musée Gallo-Romains** ⓘ *Tue-Sun 1000-1700/1800, €3.80.*

La Croix-Rousse

The old silk weaver's district, on the north of Presqu'île, is rapidly undergoing a transformation. What is still to some extent a working class district is rapidly becoming the city's trendy new hot spot, with its alleys quickly filling up with cutting-edge boutiques and restaurants. This part of town is also riddled with *traboules* (narrow passages between houses), although many are now closed to the public for safety reasons. **La Maison des Canuts** ⓘ *Tue-Sat 1000-1830, free,* is an old cooperative, where you can watch weavers at their looms and buy a variety of silk products.

L'Institut et Musée Lumière

ⓘ *T04-78781895, www.institut-lumiere.org. Tue-Sun 1100-1830. €6*

The home of the famous Lumière brothers, to the southeast of the centre, charts their inspiring photographic inventions and the birth of film. Included in the four floors of exhibits is the world's first cinematograph, which projected a film for the first time in 1895. Visitors can watch various screenings, and this is also the site of a film festival.

Musée d'Art Contemporain

ⓘ *T04-72691717, www.moca-lyon.org. Wed-Sun 1200-1900. €3.80. Bus 4 or 47.*

The contemporary arm of the Musée des Beaux-Arts lies out in the east of town in a modern extension to a 1930s building. The focus here is on installation art including sound, video and interactive pieces, with regularly changing exhibitions. The museum also hosts the annual biennial arts festival, held at the end of every second year (next one in 2007).

La Croix-Rousse

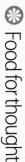

Food for thought

Lyon is the self-proclaimed – and undisputed – gastronomic capital of France, with more restaurants per head than anywhere else in the world. Its traditions are rooted in its surroundings; the region is rich in fowl, fresh fish and dairy cows, and surrounding it are the vineyards of Beaujolais and the Côtes du Rhône. This abundant natural larder is plundered by an army of celebrated chefs, who are the hot topics of conversation and speculation amongst locals. Top of the pile is legendary **Paul Bocuse**, with no less than three Michelin stars, the inventor of nouvelle cuisine and today reigning supreme over five restaurants. Other kings of the kitchen include **Pierre Orsi** (the French swoon over his foie gras ravioli) and **Jean-Paul Lacombe**, although new chefs such as **Nicolas le Bec** are snapping at their heels.

Bouchons

But some of the finest eating experiences in Lyon can be had in its simplest establishments, the *bouchons*. Traditionally catering for silk workers, these serve the best of Lyon's specialities, such as *quenelles*, a poached pike mousse served with béchamel sauce, and kidneys with Madeira sauce and andouillette (chitterling) sausage. Just don't expect to leave Lyon slimmer than when you arrived.

✪ Sleeping

It's always a good idea to book ahead because the high number of business travellers coming to Lyon means that rooms get booked up both during the week and at weekends.

€€€ **La Tour Rose**, 22 rue du Boeuf, T04-7837 6910, www.slh.com. A small, opulent hotel in the Old Town, set across 3 grand 15th- and 18th-century mansions with 12 suites, each with exposed beams, grand furniture and Lyonnaise silks. The famous restaurant, headed by Philippe Chavent, is housed in a renovated chapel.

€€€ **Villa Florentine**, 25 Montée St Barthelémy, T04-7256 5656, www.villaflorentine.com. This 18th-century convent has wide-reaching views over the city from its peaceful hilltop location, with an excellent restaurant and 29 plush rooms, filled with an odd mix of antiques, chintz and modern pieces.

€€ **Collège Hotel**, 5 place Saint-Paul, T04-7210 0505, www.college-hotel.com. Stylish hotel with quirky school theme, in the centre of the Old Town. The 39 pure-white minimalist rooms have flat-screen TVs. Breakfast is served at old school desks surrounded by blackboards and bookcases.

€€ **Hotel Bayard**, 23 place Bellecour, T04-7837 3964, www.hotelbayard.com. A homely hotel in the centre of town, with a mix of modern and traditional rooms, some of which have original parquet floors, canopies over the beds and rickety antique furniture – rooms 2 and 4 are the most appealing.

€ **Hôtel du Théâtre**, 10 rue de Savoie, T04-78423332, www.hotel-du-theatre.fr. A friendly hotel overlooking place des Célestins, with simple, spotless rooms, some with French windows and views of the theatre.

✪ Eating

As you may have gathered by now, you'll eat extremely well in Lyon. Bear in mind that it's a good idea to book head at many of these restaurants, however, as locals understandably like to eat out.

Breakfast

Le Canut sans Cervelle, 4 bis, rue Belfort/Dumenge, T04-7830 1020. Serves a popular brunch on Sun in its attractive Croix-Rousse location.

Le Pain Quotidien, 13-15 rue Quatre Chapeaux, T04-7838 2984. A trendy Belgian chain serving delicious breads, pastries and yoghurts, as well as their decadent trademark home-made chocolate spread.

Lunch

Brasserie Georges, 30 cours de Verdun, T04-7256 5454, www.brasseriegeorges.com. Cavernous art-deco interior, with soaring ceilings, red banquettes and bustling waiters. Good standard fare, such as onion soup and Lyonnaise sausages.

Café Chantecler, 151 boulevard de la Croix-Rousse, T04-7828 1369, www.cafe-chantecler.com. A good value, old-fashioned brasserie and bar with a bohemian feel, which brews its own beers. It's an excellent choice for lunchtime specials served on its outdoor terrace.

Dinner

L'Auberge du Point de Collonges, 40 quai de la Plage, Collonges-au-Mont-d'Or, T04-7242 9090, www.bocuse.fr. One of the finest restaurants in France, 4 km from Lyon. The 3 choices of menu (including the wonderfully-named Menu Bourgeois) offer superb traditional cuisine. Book several weeks in advance and be prepared to pay heftily for the privilege.

Les Terrasses, Villa Florentine, 25 Montée St Barthélémy, T04- 7256 5656. One of the best fine dining options in the city. Chef Stéphane Gaborieau is also a Michelin star holder

for his superb food. Set menus include the self-explanatory scallop menu, and the traditional Voyage Gourmand including duck liver with sweetbreads, squid stewed with lobster and Dordogne veal.

Restaurant Nicolas Le Bec, 14 rue Grolée, T04-78421500. A Michelin-star chef, but a relative newcomer on Lyon's culinary scene, Le Bec's stylish, airy restaurant feels more contemporary than many others. His menus change monthly, and include a surprisingly affordable lunchtime *prix fixe* menu. For dinner, expect odd, but delicious, combinations such as lobster with coco beans, beef braised in sea urchin stock, or hare in game sauce with hibiscus.

Happy Friends Family, 29 rue du Boeuf, T04-7240 9147. Don't be put off by the name; this fashionable place has some of the best modern food in the city. Fusion cooking, with a mix of French, oriental and spicy north African cuisines. Book ahead.

Le Sud, 11 place Antonin-Poncet, T04-7277 8000, www.bocuse.com. Lyon's kitchen heavyweight, Paul Bocuse, owns 4 "neobrasseries" (Le Nord, Le Sud, L'Est and L'Ouest). Le Sud has an appropriately Mediterranean menu.

Chabert et Fils, 11 rue des Marronniers, T04-78370194. A typical Lyonnaise *bouchon* (a bistro-style restaurant serving hearty local dishes) in a narrow Old Town sidestreet. The warm, bustling atmosphere draws in the crowds with traditional dishes such as tripe cooked with onions, or chicken livers with thyme.

Le Bouchon des Carnivores, rue des Marronniers, T04-78429769. Another *bouchon*, just opposite, is this

meat-oriented restaurant, with a cheerful yellow interior smothered in posters and pictures of bulls. Roast beef served with morels comes recommended.

Nightlife

The streets of the Old Town get very busy with young folk in the evenings, particularly around **place Bertras** where there is a wide choice of bars and late-night cafés. The up-and-coming area of **Croix Rousse** is also getting popular, with trendy bars and pubs.

More sedate, but no less popular, is the excellent **Opéra National de Lyon** ① T0826-305525, www.opera-lyon.com. Housed in an 18th-century building on place de la Comédie, it has a changing programme and good value last minute tickets available on the actual day of performances.

Shopping

Lyon's position as a fabric and silks capital continues today, and all major designers have outlets here. Clothes shops and international chains can be found along the pedestrian thoroughfare on Presqu'île, between **rue Victor Hugo** and **rue de la République**. For fresh fruit, meat and cheese, head nighter to the covered market at **Les Halle de Lyon** or the open-air market on the banks of the river at **quai St-Antoine**, held every morning. There is also a book market here on Sundays. Just off place Bellecour is **rue Auguste Comte**, lined with some excellent little antique shops.

European City Breaks Lyon

Madrid

Madrid is not a city of half-measures: Europe's highest, youngest, sunniest capital likes to boast *Desde Madrid al Cielo* ('from Madrid to Heaven'), with its matter-of-fact assumption that when you've seen Madrid, the only place left is Heaven. The city is as famous for what it lacks as for what it boasts – there's no great river, no architectural marvels, no immediate picture-postcard charm. But what it does have, it has in spades: a fabulous collection of western art held in the Prado, the Thyssen and the Reina Sofía; a crooked old centre where almost every alley is stuffed with excellent tapas bars and restaurants; a famously intense blue sky; and an even more intense nightlife that makes most other cities look positively staid.

Arts & culture
★★★★★

Eating
★★★★

Nightlife
★★★★★

Outdoors
★

Romance
★★

Shopping
★★★

Sightseeing
★★★★

Value for money
★★★

Overall score
★★★✦

At a glance

The leafy, elegant **Paseo del Prado** sits on the eastern side of the city, where the three big museums – the Prado, the Centro de Arte de Reina Sofía, and the Thyssen-Bornemisza – are conveniently clustered. West of here is **Puerta del Sol**, Madrid's crossroads, and the cheerful, bohemian barrio of **Santa Ana** which slopes downhill back towards the Prado. **Plaza Mayor**, west down Calle Mayor is the grand heart of old Madrid. The area around it, sprinkled with old palaces and monasteries, is known as **Hapsburg Madrid**. To the west is the enormous Bourbon **Palacio Real** and the city's beautifully restored Opera House. South of Plaza Mayor is are the edgy, multicultural, traditionally working class districts of **La Latina** and **Lavapiés** with a great flea market on Saturdays. North of the **Gran Vía**, **Chueca** and

It is not the bustle of a busy people;
it is the vivacity of cheerful persons,
a carnival-like joy, a restless idleness,
a feverish overflow of pleasure...

Edmondo de Amicis

Malasaña are sweetly old-fashioned by day and unstoppably wild by night. Swanky **Salamanca**, east of here, is an elegant 19th-century grid scattered with upmarket restaurants and designer boutiques.

★ *Don't leave town without checking out the Reina Sofía's glossy new extension.*

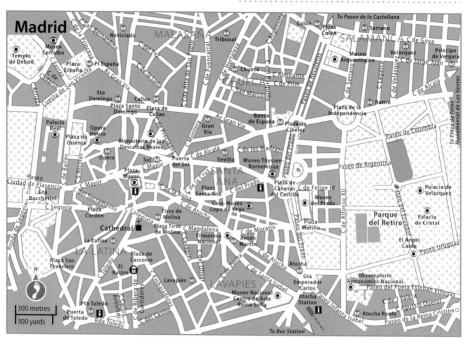

24 hours in the city

Plaza de Oriente

Have breakfast on the **Plaza de Oriente**, with views of the Palacio Real. Spend a few hours seeing the highlights at one of the big three museums – the Goyas at the **Prado**, Picasso's *Guernica* at the **Reina Sofía** or the Italian Primitives at the **Thyssen**. Trawl around the old-fashioned tapas bars in the **Plaza Santa Ana** for lunch, followed by a siesta under the trees in the **Parque del Retiro**. Take a look at some of the new galleries springing up in trendy **Chueca** or go shopping at its quirky fashion boutiques. Soak up the atmosphere at a traditional restaurant like *Casa Paco* followed by flamenco at *Casa Patas*. Alternatively, check out the Madrid club scene: celebrity-spot at *Suite*, or hop onto a podium at Coppelia. Finish up with some traditional *churros con chocolate* at the *Chocolatería San Ginés*.

⊖ Travel essentials

Getting there Madrid's **Barajas Airport** is 15 km northeast of the city (airport information T91-305 83 46). There are 2 bus lines from the airport (departures from Terminals 1 and 2): No 101 for Canillejas (on the metro) and the more convenient No 200 for Av de América (also on the metro). Departures are frequent (daily 0520- 2330) and journey time 20-50 mins depending on traffic. The metro is also a cheap way to get into the city centre and takes roughly 40-50 mins. Metro and bus cost the same (see below) but if you'll be using public transport during your stay it's best to get a **Metrobús ticket** (see below) Taxi ranks are outside all arrival halls. A taxi into the city costs €20-25.

Getting around Almost all Madrid's sights are clustered in the centre, an enjoyable stroll from each other. However, if you're in a hurry, the **buses** and **metro** are cheap, efficient and user-friendly. Just a few places – the museums dotted around the Salamanca district and the Ventas bullring, for example – are a bit further afield but they are all accessible by public transport. A single ticket for 1 trip by bus or metro costs €1.15, but the **Metrobús ticket** (which can be shared) costs €.80 for 10 journeys. You can buy metro and bus tickets at stations and the Metrobús ticket is also sold at tobacconists (or *estancos*). You can pick up free bus and metro maps from tourist offices, metro and bus stations, or at www.ctm-madrid.es. The **city information line**, T010 (English spoken), has transport information. There are a few good bus routes for sightseeing: **No 2** from Plaza España, along the Gran Vía to the Retiro. **No 3** for an overview of the centre; get on at Puerta de Toledo, past the Opera, the Puerta del Sol, the Gran Vía, and finish up in Chueca just in time for a cocktail. **No 5** from Puerta del Sol up Paseo de la Castellana (the one street in Madrid you definitely don't want to stroll along) to Plaza de Castilla. **No 21** down Pintor Rosales in the northeast of the city, through Chueca and out to the bullring at Ventas.

Tourist information The main office is at C del Duque de Medinaceli 2, T91-429 37 05, Mon-Sat 0900-1900, Sun 0900-1500. Other branches: Atocha train station, T91-528 4630, daily 0900-2100; Barajas Airport, Terminal 1, T91-305 85 56, Mon-Fri 0800-2000, Sat 0900-1300; Chamartín train station, Gate 16, T91-315 99 76, Mon-Sat 0800-2000, Sun 0800- 1400; Mercado Puerta de Toledo, Ronda de Toledo 1, T91-364 18 76, Mon-Sat 0800-2000, Sun 0800-1400. They can provide a basic map of the city and a copy of *En Madrid What's On*, a pocket-sized magazine with helpful local information and listings. There's also a free English-language monthly newspaper *InMadrid*, with plenty of bar and club listings. The tourist information line is T902-100 007. Useful websites include: www.madrid.org, www.descubremadrid.com and www.esmadrid.com.

👁 Sights

Museo del Prado

ⓘ *T91-330 28 00,*
www.museoprado.mcu.es. Tue-Sun
0900-2000 (last admission 30 mins before
closing). €6, free on Sun. Metro Banco de
España. A special ticket, the Abono Paseo
del Arte (€7.66), gets you into the Prado,
Reina Sofía and Thyssen-Bornemisza

The Prado museum houses one of the
world's greatest art collections – a
dazzling display of European art
spanning seven centuries. When it
opened in 1819, it was one of the very
first public art museums, infused with
the spirit of the Enlightenment, and
shored up by royal whim (Queen Isabel
of Braganza had been impressed with
the Louvre and wanted one for Spain).
The collection is enormous, with several
thousand works of art, and the sheer
scale can make it a daunting prospect.
It might be worth picking out some
highlights or favourite painters rather
than trying to see it all in one go. The
museum's strength is its magnificent
collection of Spanish masterpieces
from the 12th to the 19th centuries,

Museo del Prado

Palacio de Cristal, Parque del Retiro

including works by Velázquez, Zurbarán
and Goya. The Casón del Buen Retiro,
which holds the museum's collection
of 19th-century art, was undergoing
renovations as this book goes to press.

Museo Thyssen-Bornemisza

ⓘ *T91-420 39 44, www.museo*
thyssen.org, Tue-Sun 1000-1900. €6.
Metro Banco de España.

Facing the Prado across Plaza de
Cánovas del Castillo is the **Thyssen-
Bornemisza** which perfectly
complements its 'big brother'. It plugs
the gaps left by the Prado with its vast
collection of western European art
spanning eight centuries and offers a
dazzling selection of early 20th-century
masters from Braque to Kandinsky to
whet your appetite for the Reina Sofía.

Museo Nacional Centro de Arte Reina Sofía

ⓘ *T91-467 50 62, www.museoreinasofia.*
mcu.es, Mon, Wed-Sat 1000-2100, Sun
1000-1430. €3.01, free Sat 1430-2100 and
Sun from 1000-1430. Free guided visits Mon,
Wed at 1700, Sat at 1100. Metro Atocha.

Housed in a former hospital close to
Atocha station, at the end of Paseo
del Prado, Reina Sofía has been
beautifully remodelled to hold the
nation's collection of 20th-century art.
It's a graceful, light-filled building set
around a quiet, interior courtyard, with
a pair of panoramic glass lifts which
are almost an attraction in themselves.
The second and fourth floors are
devoted to the permanent exhibition
and the first and third floors are used
for temporary exhibitions which are
usually excellent. The undoubted
highlight is Picasso's celebrated
Guernica, whose sheer scale and
emotional power cannot fail to impress.

Parque del Retiro

ⓘ *Metro Banco de España/Retiro.*

This dreamy expanse of manicured
gardens, lakes, shady woods and
pavilions was once the garden of the
Palacio Real del Buen Retiro and is the
perfect escape from the city bustle.
At the centre is a vast lake (*estanque*),
with a sprinkling of cafés and boats for
hire. At the southern end of the park,
take a peek at the bizarre *Angel Caído*
(Fallen Angel), one of only three

Plaza Santa Ana

monuments in the world to Satan, caught midway in his fall from Paradise. Ricardo Velázquez designed the elegant **Palacio de Velázquez** and **Palacio de Cristal** in 1882. The pavilions are now used for the Reina Sofía's temporary art exhibitions.

Plaza Santa Ana

ⓘ *Metro Antón Martín.*

This square, flanked by bars, restaurants, theatres and hotels, has been the heart of the *Barrio de los Literatos* for centuries. It's been overhauled a dozen times and the latest restoration confirms Madrid's predilection for public squares. Although not especially pretty, the square's charm lies in its vibrancy and constant animation; the pavements are lined with dozens of tapas bars complete with turn-of-the-20th-century fittings, and it's one of the most popular places in Madrid for a tapas crawl (*tapeo*). On summer nights the pavements are dense with tourists, locals walking their dogs and elderly *Madrileños* sitting on benches. There are few reminders that this neighbourhood was once home to

Plaza Mayor

Palacio Real

Cervantes, Lope de Vega, Quevado and other great writers of the Golden Age, but you can visit Lope de Vega's delightful home, the **Casa-Museo Lope de Vega** ⓘ *C Cervantes, 11, T91-429 92 16, Tue-Fri 0930-1400, Sat 1000-1400, closed Sun. Tour by guided visit only (in Spanish) €2.*

Plaza Mayor

ⓘ *Metro Sol.*

The Plaza Mayor is vast, a huge cobbled expanse surrounded by elegant arcades and tall mansions topped with steep slate roofs. When it's bright and sunny, it's packed with terrace cafés, souvenir shops and sun-worshipping tourists; the only time you might catch a *Madrileño* here is on a Sunday morning when a stamp and coin market is held under the arcades. Building of the square started in 1617 to designs by Felipe II's favourite architect, Juan de Herrera. This was the ceremonial centre of Madrid, a magnificent backdrop for public spectacles, coronations, executions, markets, bullfights and fiestas. (It is riddled with the subterranean torture chambers of the

Inquisition, who used the square for *autos-da-fé,* the trial of suspected heretics.) Before the square was built, a market was traditionally held in front of the **Casa de la Panadería**, the old bakery, which is now the most eye-catching building on the square. It was repainted in 1992 by Carlos Franco who covered it with a hippy-trippy fresco of floating nymphs. Arched passages lead off from here to some of the most important streets of 17th-century Madrid – **Calle Toledo**, **Calle Mayor**, and **Calle Segovia** – as well as several which still echo the trades which were once carried out here, like **Calle Cuchilleros**, the Street of the Knife-Sharpeners, which incorporates part of the old city walls. This is where you'll find the traditional *mesones* (inns), which grew up to cater to merchants and travellers arriving at the city gates. *Casa Botín* opened in the 16th century and claims to be the oldest restaurant in the world.

Palacio Real

ⓘ *C Bailén s/n, T91-454 88 03, www.patrimonionacional.es. Oct-Mar Mon-Sat 0930-1700, Sun 0900-1400; Apr-Sep Mon-Sat 0900-1800, Sun*

El Rastro

0900-1500. €8 (€9 with guided tour in English). Free to EU passport holders on Wed. Metro Opera.

In 1734, after a fire destroyed the original Moorish alcázar, Felipe V saw an opportunity to create something altogether grander and commissioned the most prestigious architects of the day to create this monumental pile. Built on a staggering scale – thankfully, earlier plans for a palace four times the size of the current one were rejected – it's no surprise that Juan Carlos I and his family have chosen to live in the more modest surroundings of the Palacio de Zarzuela on the outskirts of Madrid. The Royal Palace is still used for official functions and can be closed at short notice – if two flags are flying instead of just one, the King is at home and you won't be allowed in.

El Rastro

① C Ribera de Curtidores. Metro Tirso de Molina or Puerta de Toledo.

South of Plaza Mayor, the neighbourhoods of La Latina and Lavapiés have traditionally been home to Madrid's poorest workers and most desperate

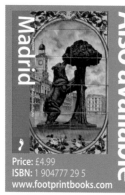

Gran Via

immigrants. It's here that Madrid's famous flea market takes place every Sunday morning. Stalls wind all the way up **Calle Ribera de Curtidores** and sell everything from tacky clothes and souvenirs to leather goods, underwear, arts and crafts and kites. The street name means Tanner's Alley and recalls the pungent trades which took place down here out of sight (and smell) of the smart neighbourhoods at the top of the hill. 'Rastro' refers to the sticky trail of blood left when the meat carcasses were hauled through the streets. The neighbourhood is still a little shabby and run-down, although it's in the process of regeneration and half the streets seem to have been dug up. The surrounding shops are mainly devoted to antiques and bric-a-brac, although you'll still find plenty of leather goods too. Though the days of a bargain are long gone the atmosphere is wonderful and carries on long after the stall-holders have packed up and everyone heads to the surrounding bars for tapas and a well-earned cold beer. Watch out for your bags though, the Rastro is notorious for pickpockets.

◉ Best of the rest

Museo Cerralbo *① C Ventura Rodríguez 17, T91-547 36 46. Tue-Sat 0930-1500, Sun 1000-1500, Aug Tue-Sat 0930-1400. €2.40.* 19th-century palace with opulent furnishings, crammed with treasures from the collection of the 17th Marqués de Cerralbo. **Monasterio de las Descalzas Reales** *① Pl de las Descalzas Reales 3, T91-454 88 00, www.patrimonionacional.es. Guided tour only (usually in Spanish) Tue-Thu, Sat 1030-1245, 1600-1745, Fri 1030- 1245, Sun and holidays 1100-1345. €5.* A 16th-century convent for blue-blooded nuns, with a remarkable collection of tapestries and other artworks. **Templo de Debod** A 2000-year-old gift from the Egyptians, in a cool, shady park spreading along the western flank of the city just a few minutes' stroll north of the Plaza de España. **Museo de Arqueológico** *① C Serrano 13, Salamanca, T91-577 79 12, www.man.es, Tue-Sat 0930-2030, Sun 0930-1630. €3.01, free Sat afternoon and Sun. Metro Serrano.* The most comprehensive archaeological museum in Spain, with a vast collection spanning several millennia. **Plaza de Toros Monumental de las Ventas** *① C Alcalá 237, Pl de las Ventas, T91-725 18 57. Museum open Mar-Oct Tue-Fri 0930-1430, Sun, hols and bullfight days 1000-1300; Nov-Feb Mon-Fri 0930-1430. Free. Metro Ventas.* The 'Cathedral of Bullfighting' built in the 1930s, with capacity for 25,000 spectators.

Pedro Almodóvar arrived in Madrid in the late 1960s; he was just 16 but he already knew that he wanted to be a film-maker. Franco had closed Spain's only film school, so he started making shorts on super-8. In 1978, three years after Franco's death and the year Spain signed a new democratic constitution, he made his first full-length film and began work on *Pepi, Luci, Bom*. The Movida Madrileña was just getting into its stride: the city's youth, making up for decades of repression, turned music, fashion, design and art upside-down. No one knew the city's anarchic subculture better than Almodóvar and Madrid has been as much a recurrent feature of his work as the faces of his band of favourite actresses – 'las chicas de Almodóvar' – who appear regularly in his movies. In 2000, Almodóvar hit the big time winning an Oscar for *Todo Sobre Mi Madre* (All About My Mother). The subversive director had become the toast of the Hollywood establishment. In 2004 he released *La Mala Educación* (Bad Education), based on his experiences of sexual abuse by the priests who taught him at school. Apparently, he remains as relevant as ever. In Santa Ana just off Plaza Antón Martín, the **Cine Doré**, now the Filmoteca Nacional, made an appearance in the recent *Hable con ella* (Talk to her).

Sleeping

Strangely, Madrid has few hotels which are truly charming. There are a few enterprising places with bright, modern decor and internet access but finding accommodation here is no longer as easy as it once was; book as far in advance as possible and bring some industrial strength earplugs – Madrid is very noisy.

€€€ **Hotel Urban**, Cra de San Jerónimo 34, T91-787 7770, www.derbyhotels.com. Metro Sevilla. Currently the city's hottest hotel, in a striking glassy contemporary building, with ultra-luxurious rooms, a pool, gym, sauna and excellent restaurant.

€€€ **Orfila**, C Orfila 6, Salamanca, T91-702 77 70, www.hotelorfila.com. Metro Alonso Martínez. A luxurious 19th-century mansion offering discreet 5-star luxury. Has a beautiful, flower-scented terrace, a charming salón de té, and a renowned restaurant.

€€ **Galiano**, C Alcalá Galiano 6, Salamanca, T91-319 20 00, www.hotel galiano.com. Metro Colón. Delightful, antique-filled hotel housed in a (much modernized) former palace, with spacious rooms and a leafy, central location.

€€ **Hotel Mario** (formerly HH Campomanes), C Campomanes 4, T91-548 85 48, www.room-mate hoteles.com. Metro Opera. Ultra-slick minimalist decor throughout, charming staff, perfect central location and a very reasonable price. Highly recommended.

€ **Hostal Cervantes**, C Cervantes 34, Santa Ana, T91-429 83 65, www.hostal-cervantes.com.

Metro Antón Martín. A big favourite. Friendly owners have made it feel like a home from home. There's a cosy lounge, each room has been decorated with pretty blue prints and all have en suite bathrooms.

€ **Hostal Madrid**, C Esparteros 6, between La Puerta del Sol and La Plaza Mayor, T91-522 00 60, www.hospedajemadrid.com. Metro Sol. Welcoming hostal with modern, attractive rooms decorated with pine or wrought iron furniture. En suite bathrooms.

€ **Monaco**, C Barbieri 5, T91-522 46 39. Metro Chueca. This enjoyably louche former brothel is now distinctly shabby, even dilapidated, but still worth checking out. To really soak up the atmosphere, ask for rooms 20 or 123.

✪ Eating

While there isn't much around the Paseo del Prado, the streets around the Plaza Santa Ana – just 5 mins' walk from the Prado – are densely packed with all kinds of bars and restaurants. There are lots of traditional restaurants around the Plaza Mayor (although it's best to avoid the touristy ones on the square), as well as excellent gourmet tapas bars. Some of the cheapest and best tapas bars are in La Latina and Lavapiés.

Cafés and tapas bars

Café de los Austrias, Pl de Ramales 1, T91-559 84 36. Metro Opera. Daily 0900-0100, Fri-Sat until 0300. Old-fashioned café/bar and a perfect spot to while away an afternoon.
El Jardín Secreto, C Conde Duque 2, T91-541 80 23. Metro Plaza de España. Mon-Thu 1730-0100, Fri-Sat 1800-0230, Sun 1700-2400. Magical café with a scattering of shells, candles and drapes.
Taberna Las Dolores, Pl de Jesús 4, T91-429 22 43. Metro Antón Martín. Daily 1100-0100, Fri-Sat until 0200. Beautiful, century-old tiled tapas bar – one of the most *típico* in the city.

Restaurants

† † **La Taberna del Alaberdero**, C Felipe V, T91-547 25 77. Metro Opera. Daily 1300-1600, 2100-2400. Just off the Plaza de Oriente, this celebrated restaurant serves exquisite Basque cuisine; splash out on the 5- course *menú de degustación*. A wide variety of tapas and *raciones* available in the bar.
† † **Zalacaín**, C Álvarez de Baena 4, T91-561 48 40. Mon-Fri 1300-1600 and 2100-2400, Sat 2100-2400. Madrid's most celebrated restaurant, holder of

all kinds of stars and awards under the direction of chef Benjamin Urdiain. The Basque cuisine is complemented by a refined setting, perfect service and a spectacular wine list.
† † **Casa Paco**, Pl Puerta Cerrada 11, T91-366 31 66. Metro La Latina. Mon-Sat 1330-1600 and 2000-2400. A resolutely old-fashioned tiled bar with a restaurant at the back. Dignified waiters in long aprons serve traditional sizzling grilled meats and good wines.
† † **Palacio de Anglona**, C Segovia 13, T91-366 37 53. Metro La Latina. Fri and Sat until 0200. Fashionable restaurant in 19th-century palace, with sleek, pared-down decor. Grilled meats and pasta.
† **Champañería Gala**, C Moratín 22, T91-429 25 62. Metro Antón Martín. Mon-Thu 1330-1530 and 2030-0030, Fri and Sat 1330-1630 and 2030-0200. Valencian rice dishes, including fantastic paella, served in a beautiful, glassy patio.
† **La Isla del Tesoro**, C Manuel Malasaña 3, T91-593 14 40. Metro Bilbao. Daily 1330-2330. A wonderfully romantic spot; it's vegetarian and the *menú del día* (€8.90) features the cuisine of a different country each day.

✪ Nightlife

The giddy days of the Movida may be gone but it's still possible to start dancing on Fri night and not stop until Mon morning. Some of the best clubs include: *Low Club* on Fri at **De Nombre Publico** (Pl Mostenses 11); *Ohm* on Sat and Sun at **Bash** (Pl de Callao 4); and *The Room* on Fri at ultra-stylish **Stella** (C Arlabán 7). At the beautiful 19th-century **Palacio Gaviria** (C Arenal 7) you can tango or salsa during the week and there's dance music and electro-pop at

weekends. The Paseo de Castellano is famous for its summer terrazas where you can drink and dance outside. Madrid also has hundreds of *discobares* spread all over the city. Santa Ana and Huertas get packed, especially in summer, and though not especially fashionable *barrios*, you are guaranteed a good time. The streets around Plaza de la Paja, in the Plaza Mayor and Los Austrias area, are packed with fancy tapas joints but there's also a healthy sprinkling of down-to-earth bars. There are some very funky bars tucked away in the formerly run-down neighbourhoods of La Latina and Lavapiés. To the north of Gran Vía are two formerly run-down neighbour-hoods which have become the focal point of the city's heady nightlife. Chueca is the heart of the gay district and stuffed with some ultra-stylish places (**Acuarela**, C Gravina 10, **Star's Café**, C Marqués de Valdeiglesias 5, **El Liquid**, C Barquillo 8), while Malasaña is popular with students and younger people looking for a good time. For the latest, visit www.clubbingspain.com.

✪ Shopping

As a general guide, you can find almost anything you want in the streets around C Preciados: department stores, chain stores, individual shops selling everything from hams to traditional Madrileño cloaks. The northwestern neighbour-hoods of Argüelles and Moncloa, particularly C Princesa, are also good for fashion chains. Smart Salamanca has plenty of designer boutiques and interior decoration shops. Chueca is full of hip, unusual fashion and music shops.

The epitome of style and sleek design, Milan's often grey, polluted streets are an unlikely backdrop for its population of models, designers and chic businessmen. This is a functional modern Italian metropolis of football, Berlusconi, money and separatist politics where industriousness is held in high esteem. Milan, however, is a city with hidden beauty. The city's courtyards, if you can get a glimpse of them, are famously attractive. The most beautiful spot in the city is on the roof of the cathedral and there is a lively Milanese cultural life, too – from the grand opera of La Scala to hip modern music venues. As a city, Milan goes against what its fashion industry might suggest: in the end it's what's inside that matters.

Milan

Arts & culture
★★

Eating
★★★★

Nightlife
★★★★

Outdoors
★★

Romance
★★

Shopping
★★★★★

Sightseeing
★★

Value for money
★★

Overall score
★★★

◉ Sights

The **Duomo** ⓘ *T02-8646 3456, daily 0645-1845, free; access to roof 0900-1900, €5 lift, €3.50 steps,* is the epicentre of the city with the cathedral to the gods of shopping, the grand Galleria Vittorio Emanuele II, right beside it. Started in 1386, the mammoth cathedral was not completed until Napoleon ordered the addition of the façade in the 19th century. Intricately Gothic, the pale marble building has over 3000 statues, many on tall slender spires, best appreciated from the roof. Inside, a nail purportedly from Christ's cross hangs from the ceiling.

The **Galleria Vittorio Emanuele II**, to the northern side of the piazza del Duomo, connects with the piazza della Scala. A vast, cross-shaped, vaulted arcade, it was opened by the eponymous first king of Italy in 1867.

Duomo

It is now filled with pricey cafés and equally expensive shops. Milanesi come here to strut and tourists come to marvel at the enormity of the place and, near the centre, to spin on the balls of the mosaic bull (a symbol of nearby Turin) for good luck.

Radiating out from here are several pedestrianized shopping streets, such as **corso Vittorio Emanuele II**, though the highest concentration of designer togs is the **Quadrilatero della Moda**, an area to the northeast encompassed by via Monte Napoleone, via Manzoni, via della Spiga and via Sant'Andrea. Further in the same direction is the Giardini Pubblici, with the **Galleria d'Arte Moderna** ⓘ *T02-7600 2819, Tue-Sun 0900-1730, free,* where works by Van Gogh, Picasso and Matisse hang in Napoleon's one-time residence, Villa Reale. Further northeast still is the train station.

To the northwest of the Duomo is the hulk of the **Castello Sforzesco** ⓘ *T02-8846 3700, various museums Tue-Sun 0900-1730, €3, free Fri after 1400,* with the **Parco Sempione** beyond.

Between the castle and the Giardini Pubblici the area of **Brera** has some of the city's oldest and most interesting streets and an excellent gallery in the

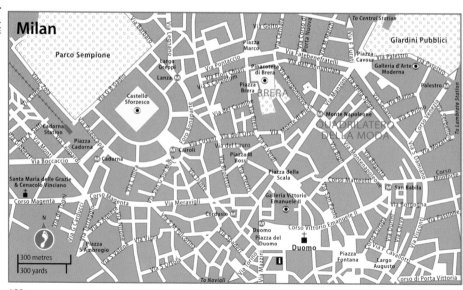

Pinacoteca di Brera ⓘ *T02-8942 1146, Tue-Sun 0830-1930, €5.* Highlights include paintings by Raphael, Caravaggio and Bellini.

The **Cenacolo Vinciano** (Leonardo da Vinci's *Last Supper*) ⓘ *T02- 8942 1146, Tue-Sun 0815-1900, €8, telephone booking obligatory at least 1 day in advance,* is in the Church of Santa Maria delle Grazie, to the west of the centre. The already enormous popularity of Leonardo's innovative and dramatic masterpiece has been enhanced by the success of *The Da Vinci Code* and it's advisable to book as far as possible in advance. If you don't have a booking your best chance is to get there early and hope someone who has booked doesn't show up.

To the south of the centre, the **Navigli** is an area with remnants of the canal system of Milan's past which has become one of the best in the city for eating, drinking and shopping.

● Sleeping

Many of the cheaper places to stay are in the area east of the station. Central hotels tend to be on the

Galleria Vittorio Emanuele II

Castello Sforzesco

expensive side and often cater to a business clientele.

€€€ Straf, via San Raffaele 3, T02-805081, www.straf.it. A minimalist 21st-century design hotel in slate, brass and glass, a stone's throw from the Duomo.

€€ Antica Locanda Leonardo, corso Magenta 78, T02-4801 4197, www.leoloc.com. A smart and friendly place west of the centre, with wooden floors, a garden and contemporary art.

€€ Antica Locanda Solferino, via Castelfidardo 2, T02-657 0129, www.anticalocandasolferino.it. Stylish 19th-century bohemian hotel in the laid-back Brera area of town.

€€ Ariston, Largo Carrobbio 2, T02-7200 0556, www.aristonhotel.com. Bio-architecturally redesigned, the Ariston purifies the Milanese air and even the carpet glue is non-toxic. Bicycles are available for guests to use and it's only 400 m from the Duomo.

€€-€ Hotel Charly, via Settala 76, T02-204 7190, www.hotelcharly.com. Bargain elegance in 2 adjacent villas with a garden, within reach of the station. The cheapest rooms lack en suite bathrooms.

ⓔ Eating

The Brera area has many of Milan's best restaurants. The Navigli, to the south, has traditional, down-to-earth places.

₶₶₶ Corso Como 10, corso Como 10, T02-653531, closed Mon. A complex incorporating a café, photography gallery (Galleria Carla Sozzani, www.galleriacarlasozzani.org), a bookshop, and fashion and perfume boutiques, Corso Como 10 really comes into its own in the evenings when the who's who of Italian fashion troop into its courtyard garden to consume trendy food at its restaurant. It's also good for breakfast.

₶₶ Al Pont de Ferr, ripa di Porta Ticinese 55, T02-8940 6277, closed Sat-Sun in winter, Sat-Sun lunch in summer. A traditional, good-value, canalside osteria lined with wine bottles. Offers country cooking and a good range of cheeses.

₶₶ Joia, via P Castaldi 18, T02-2952 2124, www.joia.it. Closed Sun. A rarity in Italy – a hip and inventive vegetarian restaurant, despite the ludicrous names of the dishes.

Fashion Quadrilateral

⊖ Travel essentials

Getting there Malpensa Airport, T02-7485 2200, www.sea-aeroporti milano.it, Milan's biggest airport, is connected to the central station by bus every 20 mins (€5 one-way, journey time around 50 mins); buy tickets in arrivals or online. A taxi will cost around €75, or you can travel by train every 30 mins (€9, 40 mins to Cadorna station). **Linate airport**, T02-7485 2200, www.sea-aeroporti milano.it, the most central, is connected to the centre by city bus 73 from San Babila station every 10 mins (€1, about 30 mins). Alternatively, Starfly buses run between Linate and the central

station every 30 mins (€2.50). A taxi to or from the centre costs about €15. **Orio al Serio**, www.orioaeroporto.it, just outside Bergamo and used by Ryanair, has 2 bus connections to Milan, either to Lambrate station (with Zani Viaggi, €6, 50 mins' journey, approximately every hour, buy tickets in arrivals) or to the central station (with Autostradale, €6.70, around an hour's journey, every 30 mins, buy tickets on the bus). Alternatively you can take a local bus into the attractive town of Bergamo and catch a train from there (hourly, €3.90, around an hour's journey).

Getting around Much of the city centre's main sights are within easy walking distance of the Duomo. Alternatively, the metro is an efficient way of getting to and from the station, or down to the Navigli. There are 4 colour-coded lines, red, blue, green and yellow. Single tickets (€1) allow travel on buses and trams for 75 mins but only one metro journey. Day tickets (€4) give the freedom to use any mode of transport.

Tourist information The main tourist information centre, T02-7252 4301, www.milanoinfotourist.com, is in piazza del Duomo, on the southern side of the Duomo.

---

† **Latteria San Marco**, via San Marco 24, T02-659 7653. Closed Sun. A small traditional place in an ex-dairy in Brera serving an ever-changing menu of Milanese food. It's popular with locals and good for lunch. No bookings so be prepared to wait.

† **Spontini**, via Spontini 4, T02-204 7444, closed Mon. With lots of oil and copious mozzarella, the enormously thick and tasty pizza slices in this popular and noisy place only come in 2 versions – big and bigger. Good beer on tap and handy for hotels near the station.

☾ Nightlife

Bars and clubs

At *aperitivo* time, many bars compete with each other by offering ever more generous buffets of free nibbles with your drink and these can sometimes constitute a meal in themselves. Later on, Milan has a wider selection of nightclubs than most Italian cities, as well as some hip bars. Club opening hours vary with demand and the

seasons but most stay open until at least 0400. Bars tend to close between midnight and 0200. The best areas for bars are **Brera** (the most leftfield), **Navigli** (the cheapest, good on summer evenings when the area is closed to traffic) and **Corso Como** (the hippest). Notable nightspots include the immaculately smart and hip **Café Atlantique**, viale Umbria 42, www.cafeatlantique.com; and the lively left-wing *centro sociale* **Leoncavallo**, via Watteau 7, www.leoncavallo.org. In summer much of the nightlife decamp to Idroscalo, a lake near Linate airport.

Opera

La Scala, T02-7200 3744, www.teatro allascala.org. Probably the world's most famous opera house, has a Dec-Jul opera season, with classical concerts at other times. Tickets, from around €70 upwards, can be booked online. The tourist information office produces the bilingual monthly *Mese Milano*, with details of events and concerts.

◯ Shopping

The line between Milanese street and catwalk is a fine one and it's not hard to spot the fashion set striding with hauteur and the latest look around the city centre. The most famous area for Milan's designer clothing industry is the **Quadrilatero d'Oro** (Golden Square), an area just to the north of piazza della Scala. Quadrilatero has all the big names from Armani to Zenga and should be visited just for some window gazing even if you have no intention of making any purchases.

There are, however, other parts of the city also worth visiting for the shops where you might well be encouraged to part with some cash: the more leftfield **Navigli** is a good area for picking up some bargains, as is **corso Buenos Aires**, east of the station. And if the clothes don't do it for you, on **via Durini** there's some pretty slick Italian designer kitchen-ware, furniture and lots else to fill your home with.

Munich

Munich knows how to have a good time. This is, after all, the beer capital of Europe. But while the merriment continues year-round in the city's bounteous beer halls, Munich manages somehow to shake off its hangover and retain a surprisingly sensible reputation for hard work and innovation. This is the home of BMW and Siemens, and is the location of some of Germany's finest museums, art galleries and theatres, lending it a rather refined and prosperous air. All this marries well with its elegant Bavarian palaces and grand churches, and its trustworthy character has given it the honour of hosting the first game of the 2006 World Cup. But look past the sharp suits and flash cars and you'll find another beer hall pounding with oompah music – an appealing reminder of Munich's mischievous side.

Arts & culture
★★★★

Eating
★★★

Nightlife
★★★

Outdoors
★★★★

Romance
★★★

Shopping
★★★

Sightseeing
★★★

Value for money
★★

Overall score
★★★

At a glance

Munich's centre radiates out from **Marienplatz**, the Gothic heart of the **Altstadt** (Old Town). Just to the north is the **Residenz**, a former palace, surrounded by grand town houses, churches, theatres and elegant shops, while to the east is **Platzl**, home to the city's most famous beer hall, the Hofbräuhaus. Further east is **Museumsinsel** (Museum Island), an island on the Isar River, site of the Detaches Museum. Back at Marienplatz, the **Viktualienmarkt**, a bustling outdoor food market, sprawls to the south of the square, while to the west is the main pedestrian shopping district, leading to **Karlsplatz** and on to the main train station. A few blocks to the north of the station is a cluster of excellent art galleries, known collectively as the **Pinakothek**, while to the south is the **Theresien-wiese**, the purpose-built area that holds the huge tents of the Oktoberfest each year. Munich's best-known suburb is **Schwabing**, the

"O' Zapft is!"

The mayor's declaration at the start of Oktoberfest, meaning the first beer barrel is tapped and it's time to start drinking.

lively student district, stretching to the north of the centre. The tranquil, grassy **Englischer Garten** can also be found here. Further north still is **Olympiapark**, site of the 1972 Olympics, and out to the west are the sculpted grounds of **Schloss Nymphenburg**, Munich's summer palace.

★ *Don't leave town without sitting in the dappled sunshine of a beer garden tucking into a Weisswurst and frothy glass of Augustiner beer.*

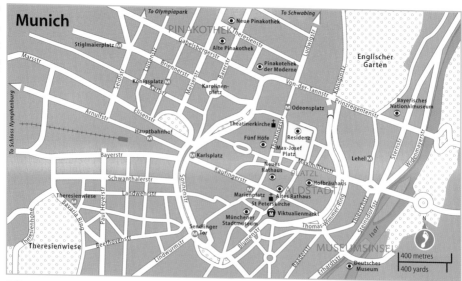

● Sights

Marienplatz

ⓘ *S-Bahn/U-Bahn Marienplatz, bus 52 to Marienplatz, Tram 19 to Theatinerstrasse.*

The pulsing heart of Munich is this broad square, centred around the **Mariensäule**, a column from 1638, topped by a statue of the Virgin Mary. Flanking the entire north side is the brooding, gargoyled façade of the **Neues Rathaus** (New Town Hall), which holds the tourist office and has an 85-m tower offering impressive views of the city. The area in front of the tower is packed with tourists at 1100, 1200 and 1700 daily, when the rather tuneless glockenspiel springs into action. Elsewhere on the square is the **Fischbrunnen** (Fish Fountain) and the **Altes Rathaus** (Old Town Hall), which was almost entirely destroyed during the Second World War. Its rebuilt bulk today houses the **Spielzeugmuseum** (Toy Museum) ⓘ *daily 1000-1730, €3*, a vast collection of antique toys. Every

Marienplatz

December, a traditional Christmas market takes place on the square.

Overlooking Marienplatz from the west are the unmistakable domed towers of the Gothic **Frauenkirche** (Cathedral Church of Our Lady); the Alps can be seen from the top of the south tower on a clear day. South of the square is **St Peterskirche** (St Peter's Church) and the **Viktualienmarkt**, a huge open-air food market selling sausages, cheeses, fruit and vegetables.

Münchener Stadtmuseum

ⓘ *Sankt-Jakobs-Platz 1, T089-23322370, www.stadtmuseum-online.de. Tue-Sun 1000-1800. €4. S-Bahn/U-Bahn Marienplatz.*

Just to the east of Viktualienmarkt is this excellent local history museum, which covers Munich from its official foundation in 1158 through to the present, and also includes sections on fashion, musical instruments, puppets and film, with a cinema showing German and arthouse films.

Residenz and around

ⓘ *Residenzstr 1, T089-290671, www.schloesser.bayern.de. Daily Apr-Oct 0900-1800, Nov-Mar 1000-1600. €6 (€9 with Schatzkammer) S-Bahn/U-Bahn Odeonsplatz, bus 52 to Marienplatz.*

Munich's most photographed sight is this magnificent Renaissance palace, the seat of Bavaria's rulers, the Wittelsbachs, until 1918. It is split into two sections: one open in the morning, the other in the afternoon, so you'll need a full day to

---

⊖ Travel essentials

Getting there Flughafen München, T089-97500, www.munich-airport.de, is 28 km northeast of the city centre. The Airport Bus runs to the city centre every 20 mins and takes 45 mins. The S-Bahn (lines S1 and S8) connects the airport to the main train station and takes around 35 mins.

Getting around Munich has an excellent integrated public transport system, including underground (**U-Bahn**) and overground (**S-Bahn**) trains, **trams** and **buses**. The Altstadt is easily explored on foot but the wider city will require you to jump on a train or tram. One ticket system covers all

public transport; tickets can be bought from machines at U-Bahn/S-Bahn stations and from some bus and tram stops. A day ticket costs €4.50 for the inner city or €8 for a 'partner' ticket for 2 people. Tickets can also be bought for 3 days (€11 for 1 person or €18.50 for 2). Alternatively, a single trip ticket costs from €1.10, depending on the distance travelled. All tickets must be validated in the blue machines before travel. Strip tickets are useful for more than one trip; two strips need to be validated for each zone crossed.

Tourist information The main Munich Tourist Offices, T089-2339 6500,

www.muenchen-tourist.de, are in the main railway station (Mon-Sat 0930-1830, Sun 1000-1800) and in the Neues Rathaus on Marienplatz (Mon-Fri 1000-2000, Sat 1000-1600).

Munich Welcome Card is a 1- or 3-day ticket that provides free public transport in the city centre as well as discounts of up to 50% on over 30 attractions. Cards cost €6.50 for 1 adult for 1 day, or €11 for 2 people, rising to €16 and €23.50 respectively, for 3 days. Welcome Cards can be bought from the main tourist office on Marienplatz, and from dedicated kiosks at the train station and the airport.

163

take it all in. A total of 130 rooms are filled with art, period furnishings and decorations, including the ancestral portrait gallery and the extravagant royal apartments. The highlight is the **Antiquarium**, a vast, arched hall resplendent with rococo swirls and murals. A separate ticket allows entry to the **Schatzkammer**, the royal treasury, crammed with jewellery and artworks from the late Greco-Roman period to the Middle Ages.

To see their modern-day counterparts, head just south to **Maximilianstrasse**, where Munich's well-heeled spend their dosh in glamorous boutiques. At the other end of Max-Joseph Platz is the baroque façade of **Theatinerkirche**, its ochre walls and green dome lending a splash of colour to the pale stone surroundings.

Deutsches Museum

ⓘ *Museumsinsel 1, T089-21791, www.deutsches-museum.de. Daily 0900-1700. €7.50. U-Bahn Fraunhofer-strasse, S-Bahn Isartor, Tram 17 to Isartor or Tram 18 to Detaches Museum.*

Claiming to be the world's largest science and technology museum, this

Residenz

Deutsches Museum

is certainly a gargantuan collection, covering everything from seafaring and space probes to the car industry and chemistry. The 50,000 sq m museum can be exhausting, but it is a sure-fire hit with children.

Pinakothek

ⓘ *www.pinakothek.de.*

This series of art galleries is exceptional and regarded as one of the finest in Europe. The **Alte Pinakothek** ⓘ *Barer Str 27, T089-2380 5216, Tue 1000-2000, Wed-Sun 1000-1700, €5, U-Bahn Königsplatz*, is a vast treasure trove of German art from the Middle Ages to the end of the rococo period. Its highlight is the exceptional collection by Dürer: look out for *The Four Apostles*, and his defining self portrait from 1500.

The **Neue Pinakothek** ⓘ *entrance on Theresienstr, T089-23805195, Thu-Mon 1000-1700, Wed 1000- 2000, €6, U-Bahn Theresienstrasse*, holds a fine collection from the late 18th century to the early 20th century, including the private collection of King Ludwig I.

Open since 2002 and worth visiting for its architecture as much as for its

collections is the newest addition, the **Pinakothek der Moderne** ⓘ *Barer Str 40, T089-2380 5360, www.pinakothek -der-moderne.de, Tue, Wed, Sat-Sun 1000-1700, Thu-Fri 1000-2000, €9, U-Bahn Theresienstrasse or Odeonsplatz.* The airy concrete and glass structure has works by Dalí, Picasso and German greats such as Beckman and Polke, as well as architecture and design exhibits.

Englischer Garten

Wedged between the Altstadt and Schwabing is the Englischer Garten, a large city park of rolling lawns and lakes. Don't be shocked by the nude sunbathers during summer – Munich is known for its liberal views on nudity. Bare sunbathing aside, the park is a wonderful area for a stroll or picnic. The **Chinesischer Turm**, a pagoda-shaped tower, is a good landmark, set above a popular beer garden.

At the southeast corner of the park is the **Bayerisches Nationalmuseum** ⓘ *T089-2112401, www.bayerisches-nationalmuseum.de. Tue-Wed and Fri-Sun 1000-1800, Thu 1000-2000, €3, U-Bahn Lehel.* Although at times

Neue Pinakothek

Oktoberfest – the world's largest beer festival attracts a staggering – often literally – over 6 million visitors each year, who manage to knock back around 6 million litres of beer over two weeks. The festival actually begins in September, to much pomp from various processions and brass bands, and takes over the 'Wiesn' – the nickname for the Theresienwiese to the southwest of the city centre. Fourteen vast tents spring up along custom-built avenues, surrounded by around 200 fairground rides and sideshows. Each tent is filled with rows of wooden tables where visitors down litre-sized Steins of beer and link arms to the pounding of oompah bands. The best time to visit is at lunch, when the tents are busy but not packed and it's possible to enjoy a big meal in relative peace (roast chicken and plates of sausages are the norm). In the evening, the pace picks up, the tents get crammed, and revellers take to dancing on the tables. Outside, the fairground rides do their best to churn the stomachs of those stumbling between tents. Although the festival attracts a fair contingent of Brits and Aussies, the majority of visitors are still Bavarian – you'll still see plenty of punters in Lederhosen and feathered caps. For more information: **www.oktoberfest.de**.

rambling, it provides a worthwhile overview of the region's history. Exhibits include a fine collection of porcelain from Nymphenburg and art nouveau glassworks.

Englischer Garten

Schloss Nymphenburg

ⓘ *T089-179080, www.schloesser. bayern.de. Daily Apr-Oct 0900-1800, Nov-Mar 1000-1600. €5 museum only or €10 for museum and Marstallmuseum. Tram 17, bus 51.*

Northwest of the city centre is the summer residence of the Wittelsbachs, built in the Italian style from 1664. The main building includes the **Schönheitsgallery** (Gallery of Beauties) collected by Ludwig I, which is filled with portraits of many of the women that he considered beautiful. The **Steinerner Saal** has an elaborate frescoed ceiling and the **Marstall-museum**, housed in the court stables, includes the coronation coach of Emperor Karl VII.

Most attractive, however, are the beautiful formal gardens and pavilions surrounding the palace. Take some time to stroll around and get a feel for the place.

Schloss Nymphenburg

😊 Sleeping

Prices for accommodation tend to be high and, be warned, they rise further during Oktoberfest, when most hotels and guesthouses get booked up months in advance.
€€€ **Bayerischer Hof**, Promenadeplatz 2-6, T089-21200, www.bayerischerhof.de. Munich's leading hotel since 1841, Bayerischer Hof has a great central location, with a grand marble lobby and huge rooms, many with 4-poster beds. There's also a roof garden with pool and spa, several bars and a nightclub.
€€ **Acanthus Hotel**, An der Hauptfeuerwache 14, T089-2 607364, www.acanthushotel.de. Traditional, small, family-run hotel, 10 mins' walk from the Altstadt. Rooms are floral with new bathrooms, and staff are a good source of information on the city.
€€ **Advokat**, Baaderstr 1, T089-216310, www.hotel-advokat.de. Claiming to be Munich's first boutique hotel, the Advokat is stylish and low-key, with pistachio-coloured rooms and scathingly cool staff. Excellent breakfasts served in the trendy café-bar.
€€ **Hotel Uhland**, Uhlandstr 1, T089-543350, www.hotel-uhland.de. Friendly guesthouse in a beautiful neo-renaissance villa on a quiet street close to the Oktoberfest site. Extremely helpful staff, free bikes for rent, and cosy rooms – some with waterbeds.
€ **Euro Youth Hotel**, Senefelderstr 5, T089-59908811, www.euro-youth-hotel.de. Pleasant youth hostel with spotless, comfortable rooms, 50 m from the main train station. Some double rooms have private bathrooms. The Globetrotters Bar serves good breakfasts and cut-price Augustiner beer on tap.

🍴 Eating

ᵚᵚᵚ **Tantris**, Johann-Fichte-Str 7, T089-3619590, www.tantris.de. One of the city's finest restaurants, with a moodily-lit interior, cool retro touches and a stylish lounge bar upstairs. The menu is a mix of contemporary French and Italian, with some good value (but not cheap) lunchtime menus.
ᵚᵚ **Seven Fish**, Gärtnerplatz 6, T089-23000219, www.sevenfish.de. Californian-style seafood is served in this airy, bare-brick and blue-themed restaurant. Expect interesting twists, like swordfish with vanilla, or lemongrass crème bruleé.
ᵚ **Brotzeitstüberl**, Viktualien Markt. In the heart of the outdoor food market, this beer garden is a real social hub in summer, when locals flock here for a bout of people-watching, a cold beer and plate of the local Weisswurst and sweet mustard. Closes at 1900.
ᵚ **Fraunhofer**, Fraunhoferstr 9, T089-266460. Students flock to this refreshingly tourist-free beer hall for big portions of good Bavarian food and the usual selection of beers. There's live music some nights, and a small theatre at the back.
ᵚ **Hofbräuhaus**, Platzl, T089-29013610, www.hofbraeuhaus.de Munich's most famous beer hall has been serving for over 4 centuries, although it's suffered from its popularity and can feel very touristy. Still worth a quick visit to soak up a bit of history – and half a litre of excellent beer, of course.
ᵚ **Tresznejewski**, Theresienstr 72, T089-282349, www.tresznjewski.de. Hugely popular brasserie serving big bowls of pasta, steaks, burgers and salads. Transforms into a cocktail bar from midnight.

🌙 Nightlife

Munich's nightlife has something of a split personality. On the one hand, the city is famous for its down-to-earth beer halls, where locals gather for their huge litre-glasses of beer and spill out into leafy beer gardens in summer. On the other hand, Munich has a thriving yuppie class with a correspondingly flash nightlife scene, focussing on cocktail lounges and thumping clubs dotted around the centre and suburbs. The studenty area of **Schwabing** has good laid-back bars, while the gay and lesbian bar scene is based around **Gärtnerplatz**. Also worth seeing are some of the jazz and classical music venues; the city has three first-rate symphony orchestras, 11 major theatres and numerous fringe theatres. A good source of information is the monthly *Go München* magazine, www.gomuenchen.com, which also produces *München Geht Aus*, a useful guide to restaurants and bars.

🛒 Shopping

The main shopping district is the pedestrian zone in the Altstadt. **Kaufingerstrasse** runs between Marienplatz and Karlsplatz and is lined with chain shops and department stores. The best place for food is the large open-air **Viktualienmarkt**, where you can stock up on fresh fruit and vegetables, cheeses, cakes and deli items. The city's smartest (and most expensive) boutiques are along **Maximilianstrasse**; close-by is fashionable **Theatinerstrasse** and **Fünf Höfe**, a series of smart courtyards filled with shops. For more off-the-wall purchases, head to the second-hand shops in **Schwabing**.

Naples

Naples, wedged between the world's most famous volcano and the deep blue sea, is beautiful and ugly in equal measure. A world away from the genteel islands of Ischia and Capri that grace its bay, the city can be intimidating: anarchic and only sporadically law-abiding, the traffic is terrible and peace and quiet is hard to find. But it's an extraordinarily vivacious city, the pizzas are fantastic, music is ingrained in its culture and the treasure trove of sights hidden away in its narrow streets is overwhelming. More like Marrakech than Milan, ask an Italian from the north about Naples and they will throw up their hands in despair. But probe these gentrified folk a little more and they may tell you with something approaching admiration about the Neapolitan Renaissance, the cultural rebirth of a once-grand city.

Arts & culture
★★★★

Eating
★★★

Nightlife
★★

Outdoors
★

Romance
★★★

Shopping
★★

Sightseeing
★★★★

Value for money
★★★★★

Overall score
★★★

◉ Sights

Santa Lucia

The grandest part of the city is around the giant and slightly barren **piazza del Plebiscito**. With its curved colonnade and vast, imposing space dotted with kids playing football, Vesuvius can be glimpsed between the grand 17th- and 18th- century buildings. The **Palazzo Reale** ⓘ *T848-800288, daily except Wed, 0830-1930, Royal Apartments €7.50, palace courtyard and gardens, free,* was built at the beginning of the 17th century for Spanish viceroys and extended by the Bourbons in the 18th century. Behind the church on the hill of **Monte di Dio**, tightly packed housing is stacked on the area where the original Parthenope was founded in around 680 BC by Greeks from nearby Cuma. **Via Chiaia**, running north of the hill, is

Piazza del Plebiscito

one of Naples' smartest shopping areas. In piazza Trento e Trieste, **Teatro di San Carlo** ⓘ *T081-7972331, www.teatrosancarlo.it, daily 0900-1830, €5, tours daily 0900 and 1900 except during performances,* is Naples' great opera house. If you like castles, **Castel dell Ovo** ⓘ *Mon-Sat 0830-1900, Sun 0830-1400, free,* jutting out into the bay is worth a wander round. And **Borgo**

Marinari, the collection of houses and (mainly) restaurants and bars surrounded by jetties beside the castle, is heaving on summer evenings.

Centro Storico

This is the true heart of Naples; its dark, narrow streets greasy, irregularly paved and overflowing with scooters, people and noise. Now a UNESCO World Heritage Site, the area still follows the ancient Greek and Roman layout of Neapolis, with three main east-west streets, or *decumani*. Long, straight **Spaccanapoli** ('Split Naples', vias Benedetto Croce, San Biagio dei Librai and Vicaria Vecchia), was once the *decumanus inferior* of the Greek city, while **via dei Tribunali** was the *decumanus major*.

The most interesting part of Spaccanapoli begins at piazza del Gesù, with late 16th-century **Gesù Nuovo** ⓘ *T081-5518613, daily 0630-1300, 1600-1900.* Its brutal armoured exterior

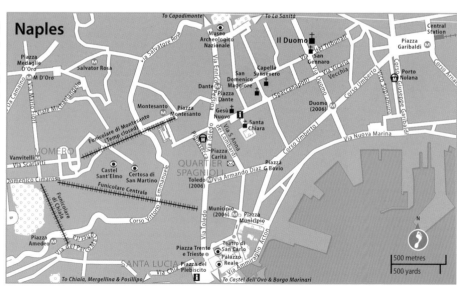

gives little hint of its spectacular interior. Next up, away from the chaotic plethora of bars, restaurants and small shops, are the city's inconceivably peaceful and colourfully tiled 14th-century cloisters of **Santa Chiara** ⓘ *via Santa Chiara 49/c; Church T081-7971235, www.santachiara.org, Mon-Fri 0930-1300, 1430-1730, Sat-Sun 0930-1300; Museum/cloister T081-5521597, www.santachiara.info, Mon-Sat 0930- 830, Sun 0930-1430, €4.*

Other highlights of the Centro Storico include three 17th- and 18th-century spires, looking like enormously elongated wedding cakes: **Guglia dell'Immacolata**, piazza del Gesù, **Guglia di San Domenico Maggiore**, in a piazza of the same name, and **Guglia di San Gennaro**, in piazza Riario Sforza, adjacent to the Duomo. The 13th-century **Duomo** ⓘ *via del Duomo, Mon- Fri 0800-1230, 1630-1900, Sat 0800-1230, 1630-1930, Sun 0800-1330, 1700-1930,* is slightly less of a focus than it might be in other Italian cities but it is still an exceptionally grand edifice. Its chapels are especially interesting, one holding the famous remains of San Gennaro, the city's patron saint. Another, the fourth-century Cappella

Santa Chiara cloisters

di Santa Restituta, is one of the city's oldest buildings. Under the building, in the *Scavi del Duomo,* some fascinating ancient remains have been unearthed.

Cappella Sansevero ⓘ *via de Sanctis 19, T081-5518470, www.museo sansevero.it, Wed-Sat and Mon 1000-1800, Sun 1000-1330, €5,* originally built 1590 but remodelled in the 18th century, is also worth a visit for some virtuoso allegorical marble sculptures, notably *Disillusion,* by Francisco Queirolo (1704-1762) and an amazingly lifelike *Veiled Christ* (1753) by Giuseppe Sanmartino.

Amongst other numerous places to wander, **via San Gregorio Armeno**, running north perpendicular to Spaccanapoli, is worth a visit. All year round shops spill their wares out onto the pavements: thousands upon thousands of figures, some tinier than others, vie for space with models of baskets of fruit, mini electrically pumped water-features and the occasional mechanized man-drinking-beer, or butcher-chopping-meat. Above you, angels, suspended from ceilings and doorways, stare down lovingly.

Quartieri Spagnoli and Via Toledo

Via Toledo, Naples' bustling high street, runs between piazza del Plebiscito and piazza Dante. To its west, the narrow streets of the Quartieri Spagnoli are one of the city's poorest areas, and the Camorra heartland. There's a fascinating **market** every day up via Pignasecca and towards piazza Montesanto, while via Toledo heads north to the **Museo Archeologico Nazionale di Napoli** ⓘ *piazza Museo 19, T081-4401466, www.marketplace.it/museo.nazionale/, 0900-2000, closed Tue, €6.50.* From enormous grandiose marble statues to small homely paintings, and from erotic oil-lamps to a mosaic made of a million pieces, this is a staggering collection and gives an amazing idea of the look and feel of the ancient Roman world.

Mercato di Porta Nolana

Just to the west of the Circumvesuviana Terminal this extraordinary piece of Neapolitan theatre spills out every morning onto via Cesare Carmignano and via Sopramuro. It's a heady mix of

Via San Gregorio Armeno

Naples & the Amalfi Coast

Also available

Price: £6.99
ISBN: 1 904777 30 9
www.footprintbooks.com

Pompeii and Herculaneum

✳ There's a reason that **Pompeii** is the most famous of Vesuvius' victims. It may not be as well preserved as Herculaneum, but its sheer scale is staggering. Here is an entire Roman town, once home to as many as 20,000 people, ruined yes, but in many ways extraordinarily intact; a city stopped dead in its tracks in AD 79. Much of the wonder of the place is to be had simply by wandering around, looking into ordinary houses and some of the most striking parts are the most ordinary: tracks on the roads where carts have worn down the stones, shop signs advertising their wares, mosaics warning you to "beware of the dog". ⓘ *T081-8575347, www.pompeiisites.org, Apr-Oct 0830-1930, last entrance 1800, Nov-Mar 0830-1700, last entrance 1530. €10. 3-day ticket for Pompeii, Herculaneum, Oplontis and Stabia €18.*

House of Neptune, Herculaneum

Deep below the level of the surrounding contemporary city, **Herculaneum** is extraordinarily well preserved: much more than Pompeii's mixture of ash and pumice, Herculaneum's mud solidified and sealed in the town below, preserving organic substance and the upper storeys of houses. ⓘ *Corso Resina 6, Ercolano, T081-7390963. Apr-Oct 0830-0730, last entry 1800; Nov-Mar 0830-1700, last entry 1530. €10.*

---

fish, fruit and veg, pirated DVDs, bread, olives, contraband cigarettes, extraordinarily cheap beer, toy helicopters and fishing rods.

La Sanità and Capodimonte

Beyond the Museo Archeologico the road continues to the fine, green Parco di Capodimonte, where the **Palazzo Reale di Capodimonte** ⓘ *via Capodimonte, T081-7499111, Thu-Tue 0830-1930, €7.50 (1400-1700 €6.50)*, houses the Bourbon and the Farnese art collections. On a bus there you might not even notice Dickensian La Sanità. Home to the city's ancient catacombs, it lies below, and is bypassed by, the bridge built by the French in 1808.

Chiaia, Mergellina and Posillipo

To the west of the centre the genteel Caracciolo seafront curves around to the yacht-filled marina of Mergellina,

View from Certosa di San Martino

beyond which the exclusive residential area of Posillipo rises. Chiaia in particular is a more laid-back area of bars, cafés and restaurants and some green spaces, notably the **Villa Comunale** park.

Certosa di San Martino

ⓘ *largo San Martino 5, T081-5585942. Thu-Tue 0830-1930. €6.*

Perched high above Naples in Vomero with exceptional views is this 14th-century Carthusian monastery. It now contains the excellent **Museo di San Martino**, and is one of Naples' most satisfying sights, containing interesting paintings, an elegant cloister, an exhibition of *presepi*, one of Naples' most spectacular churches and terraced gardens. The hulking **Castel Sant'Elmo** is next door.

Travel essentials

Naples Airport, T848-888777, T081-7896259, www.gesac.it, is 5 km from the centre. 3S buses run to piazza Garibaldi (central train station) every 20 mins 0600-2330 (€1); Alibus run every 30 mins to piazza Garibaldi and piazza Municipio, by the port (€3). A taxi to the Centro Storico will cost around €20.

Getting around The city is a fairly manageable size and, despite the crazy traffic, walking is the best way to get around the Centro Storico. There are also useful **bus** routes: R2 goes from piazza Garibaldi along corso Umberto I to piazza Trento e Trieste; R3 from piazza Carità to Mergellina past piazza Trento e Trieste and the Chiaia seafront; R4 north from the port to the Museo Archeologico. Linea 2 of the **metro** is useful for connecting piazza Garibaldi to Montesanto, Chiaia (piazza Amadeo), Mergellina. www.anm.it has timetables and plenty of information on getting around the city. Tickets cost €1 each but it's also possible to buy a day-ticket (*Giornaliero*) for €3 (€2.50 at weekends). Four **funicular railways** go to Vomero, Centrale (via Toledo to piazza Fuga), Chiaia (via del Parco Margherita to via Cimarosa), Montesanto (piazza Montesanto to via Morghen, closed at the time of writing) and Mergellina (via Mergellina to via Manzoni). The **Circumvesuviana**, T081-7722444, runs from Naples' piazza Garibaldi around the bay to Sorrento every 30 mins, stopping at Torre Annunziata (for Oplontis), Pompeii ('Pompei Scavi') and Herculaneum ('Ercolano') along the way. A daily return ticket costs €6.40.

Tourist information Azienda autonoma di soggiorno, cura e turismo, piazza del Gesù, T081-5523328. Mon-Sat 0900-2000, Sun 0900-1500. **Osservatorio Turistico-Culturale del Comune**, Portico di San Francesco di Paola, piazza Plebiscito, T081-2471123. Mon-Fri 0900-1900, Sat 0900-1400. The useful bilingual monthly publication *Qui Napoli*, is free and full of up to date information.

Sleeping

€€€ Miramare, via N Sauro 24, T081-7647589, www.hotelmiramare.com. Art nouveau-style with a roof terrace and elegantly decorated rooms.

€€ Caravaggio, piazza Riario Sforza 157, T081-2110066, www.caravaggio hotel.it. Modern rooms in a 17th-century building. Cosy feel and staff are amiable.

€€ Soggiorno Sansevero, piazza S Domenico Maggiore 9, T081-790 1000, www.albergosansevero.it. In the heart of the Centro Storico, large rooms in a handsome old *palazzo* at a good price.

€ Albergo Bellini, via San Paolo 44, T081-456996. This small, exceptionally welcoming and good-value hotel has an old-fashioned feel and is popular with travellers.

€ Donnalbina7, via Donnalbina 7, T081-19567817, www.donnalbina7.it. Minimalistic, classy and chic but also welcoming and cosy, Donnalbina7 offers the best value in the city.

Eating

††† **Pizzeria Brandi**, salita Sant'Anna di Palazzo ½, T081-416928. 1230-1500, 1930-0100. Inventors of the ubiquitous pizza Margherita. Also has an excellent selection of traditional Neapolitan food.

† **Da Michele**, via Sersale 1, T081-5539204. Mon-Sat 1000-2400. The purists' pizzeria supreme. There are two choices: Margherita or Marinara, and service is lightning quick.

† **La Cantina di Via Sapienza**, via Sapienza 40/41, T081-459078. Mon-Sat 1200-1530. Great home cooking in a popular lunch-only local restaurant. A delicious bowl of *Penne Aum Aum*, with aubergine, tomato and mozzarella, is only €2.90.

† **La Vecchia Cantina**, vico San Nicola alla Carità 14, T081-5520226. Mon and Wed-Sat 1200-1600, 1900- 2200. Busy, traditional family place with lots of good fish dishes and exquisite *torta caprese*.

† **Osteria della Mattonella**, via G Nicotera 13, T081-416541. Mon-Sat 1300-1500, 1930-2330. Tucked away up the hill from the piazza del Plebiscito. You may need to knock on the door and wait to be let in. Fast, friendly and informal service combined with fairly simple but delicious Neapolitan fare.

† **Caffè Letterario Intra Moenia**, piazza Bellini 70, T081-290720. Daily 1000-0200. A literary café with a decent menu and a cultured atmosphere. Exhibitions, literary meetings, concerts and poetry evenings happen here and there's also internet access.

Nightlife

Areas which buzz until late are: around **piazza Bellini** and via Benedetto Croce in the Centro Storico; **Borgo Marinari** (in summer), by the Castel dell'Ovo; **Chiaia**, mainly to the west of piazza dei Martiri; and **Mergellina**.

Bar Gambrinus, via Chiaia 1 (piazza Trento e Trieste), T081-417582, 0800-0130, is Naples' most refined bar and worth a visit for the luscious Liberty interior and the exceedingly good cakes.

New York

Despite the protestations of other world cities, New York is the planet's urban epicentre (hence its inclusion in this book). Koreatown is just one block away from Little Brazil, Little Italy jostles for elbow room with Chinatown, which, in turn, merges into the Hispanic Lower East Side. This makes the city very open to visitors who can pick out a little corner to claim as home, even if temporarily. And following the economic and emotional slump the city saw after September 11th 2001, New York's communities seem to be even more tight-knit these days. For the visitor, New York's appeal is different from other world-class cities: it's the lights that hold back the night, the zany characters on the streets, the neck-wrenching buildings and the exhilarating pace. A tranquil moment here is undoubtedly fleeting but it is the inexhaustible energy that makes the city inimitable. In no other place can you find more top-notch culture, architecture, food, entertainment, excitement and glamour – all caught within the confines of a tight grid of streets. Perhaps it's so frenetic because visitors and locals alike simply feel there's not enough time to sample everything that this extraordinary city has to offer. Its streetwise citizens believe that anyone who chooses to live elsewhere must, in some sense, be kidding.

Arts & culture
★★★★★

Eating
★★★★★

Nightlife
★★★★★

Outdoors
★★

Romance
★★★★

Shopping
★★★★★

Sightseeing
★★★★★

Value for money
★★

Overall score
★★★★

At a glance

New York City consists of five boroughs: Manhattan, Brooklyn, Queens, the Bronx and Staten Island. Manhattan Island, the city's heart, is divided (at least in the minds of its inhabitants) into **Uptown** and **Downtown**. Downtowners, technically those living below 14th Street, regard themselves as the cutting-edge, liberal darlings of New York. Those living Uptown, anywhere alongside Central Park, claim to be genteel, while being labelled as a bit staid and unadventurous by their southern neighbours. During the week, **Midtown** is the centre point of it all, bringing the two together. **Broadway** threads from north to south, distinguishing the more laid-back west side from the more upscale east and often intersecting drastically varied neighbourhoods. Starting in the south, **Lower Manhattan** has stunning views of the Statue of Liberty, Ellis Island and is the site of Ground Zero. North of here, **SoHo** and **Tribeca** are the stomping ground of models, movie stars and well-to-do artists. **Chinatown** and **Little Italy** snuggle up to each other along with super-cool

There is more sophistication and less sense in New York than anywhere else on the globe.

Don Herold, American cartoonist, 1889-1966

Nolita (north of Little Italy). Next comes boho **Greenwich Village** with the edgy, glamorous **Meatpacking District** and the centre of gay New York, **Chelsea**, to the north and grimy-chic **Lower East Side** to its east. **Union Square**, the entrance to Downtown, sits between 14th and 17th Streets, bordered by Broadway and Park Avenue South. North of the square, **Flatiron** district houses creative and media types between 17th and 23rd Streets. **Midtown** with its clear-cut grid is the business centre of the city. Once-shabby **Hell's Kitchen,** around Eighth and Ninth Avenues, now teems with artists and yuppies, who enjoy its ethnic restaurants and its close proximity to **Central Park**. Tidy and uppity **Upper East Side** stretches up from 59th Street to 96th Street. Although this area may reek of old money, its famed Museum Mile won't disappoint. **Upper West Side**, bordered by the sprawling green sanctuary of Central Park, is home to New York's cultural elite, while fast-gentrifying **Harlem**, north of Central Park, is rich in culture, music, cuisine and art. **Brooklyn**, easily accessible from Downtown, has its own New York jive, **Queens** is its less-glamorous northern neighbour, home to JFK and La Guardia airports and the **Bronx**, on the mainland to the north, is well worth a visit for baseball or zoo fans.

Lower East Side

New York

To Harlem
To The Cloisters
E 96th St
Guggenheim Museum
E 90th St
CENTRAL PARK
Neue
E 86th St
Galerie
MUSEUM MILE
Metropolitan Museum of Art
UPPER WEST SIDE
W 86th St
West 79th St
79th St Transverse
E 79th St
American Museum of Natural History
The Lake
UPPER EAST SIDE
Whitney Museum of American Art
E 72nd St
Westside Hwy
W 72nd St
West Dr
Central Park W
East Dr
Frick Collection
ROOSEVELT ISLAND
Central Park S
E 60th St
W 57th St
E 57th St
Carnegie Hall
Museum of Modern Art
MIDTOWN
Rockefeller Center
Grand Central Station
Chrysler Building
HELL'S KITCHEN
Lincoln Tunnel
W 42nd St
Times Square
E 42nd St
Queens Midtown Tunnel
Port Authority Bus Station
New York Public Library
12th Av
W 30th St
Penn Station
Macy's
Empire State Building
E 34th St
East River
Dia Center for the Arts
W 23rd St
E 23rd St
CHELSEA
FLATIRON
Franklin D Roosevelt Dr
MEATPACKING DISTRICT
Union Square
W 14th St
E 14th St
GREENWICH VILLAGE
EAST VILLAGE
Hudson River
Washington Square
LOWER EAST SIDE
Bleecker St
WEST VILLAGE
Lafayette St
Holland Tunnel
SOHO
NOLITA
Canal St
Delancey St
Grand St
LITTLE ITALY
CHINATOWN
NEW JERSEY
TRIBECA
Broadway
City Hall
Manhattan Bridge
World Trade Center Site
Park Row
Fulton St
Brooklyn Bridge
Wall St
BROOKLYN HEIGHTS
800 metres
800 yards
LOWER MANHATTAN
State St
To Statue of Liberty
To Staten Island

24 hours in the city

Kick off any New York visit with a strong coffee and a visit to **Lower Manhattan**. Get there early, before the crowds turn up, and take the free **Staten Island Ferry** over and back for astounding views of the city. If you're feeling energetic, walk through **Chinatown** on the way to a leisurely brunch at *Café Lebowitz* or *Café Gitane*. Afterwards, stroll the streets of **Greenwich Village**, browse the galleries and shops in **SoHo**, rummage through **Hell's Kitchen** flea market or enjoy great views of the Hudson River from the Hotel Gansevoort's rooftop *Plunge* bar. Then, head northeast to be awed by the dizzying skyscrapers of **Midtown**. The shops of **Fifth Avenue** are temptingly close but save some cash for a sunset drink Downtown. After dinner at *Koi*, pay a brief visit to **Times Square**, either to catch a Broadway show or just to ogle at all those neon lights and pandemonium. You can sip a fancy cocktail as you people watch at the *Blue Fin* bar or peer down on the crowds from the sophisticated surroundings of the *Ava Lounge* on top of Dream Hotel. Later, head to *Bungalow 8* in **Chelsea** for some classy clubbing.

Alternatively, if it's Sunday, get up early and stroll up to **Central Park**. The museums along the east side make a welcome change from hectic Midtown, but choose just one if you're short on time. The **Metropolitan Museum of Art** is worthy of several hours, but the **Frick Collection**, **Guggenheim Museum** and **Whitney Museum** are each possible in an hour or two. Stop at *Serafina's* (Madison Avenue and 79th Street) for lunch or take coffee and cakes at the Viennese *Café Sabarsky* inside the Neue Galerie. Later, take in a comedy show, such as the *Upright Citizens' Brigade*, or hear some jazz in **Harlem** or **Greenwich Village**.

★ *Don't leave without watching the sun set over all those skyscrapers from the top of Rockefeller Center.*

◉ Sights

Statue of Liberty

ⓘ *T212-363 3200, www.nps.gov/stli.*
Circle line ferry from Battery Park daily
0900-1700 in winter, 0845-1845 in
summer. Admission to Liberty Island
free. Ferry tickets $11.50 (sold at
Castle Clinton).

Brainchild of the French statesman
Edouard de Laboulaye, who wanted to
honour the friendship between France
and the USA, New York's most
recognized symbol carries even more
significance these days due to the gap
in the Manhattan skyline. Modern-day
Ms Liberty and her torch now seem
more emblematic of the struggle for
harmony than the promise of

Chinatown

opportunity. Sculptor Frederic-August
Bartholdi was responsible for building
it and Gustav Eiffel helped design a
metal framework to support the base
of the structure.

World Trade Center site

ⓘ *Subway 1, 2 to Chambers St.*

Visiting the World Trade Center site will
give you a sense of the enormity of
what is missing but there's little actually
to see from the viewing platform, apart
from a big open pit, a few signs of
construction and street vendors, still
capitalizing on tourists' morbid
fascination by selling souvenirs nearby.

Chinatown

ⓘ *Subway J, M, N, R, Z, 6 to Canal St.*

The colourful pagoda-style storefronts
aligning **Canal Street** are the most
popular destination for shoppers hoping
to take home some discounted goods.
There are extensive collections of
counterfeit goods, unique Asian imports

◉ Travel essentials

Getting there **JFK International Airport**,
T718-244 4444, www.panynj.gov/aviation/
jfkframe, is 15 miles from Manhattan.
Transportation to the city is available from
all terminals, just outside the baggage
reclaim area. Taxis are the easiest way but
charge a flat rate of $45 plus toll and tip,
bringing the total up to $55 or so. A
cheaper option are the various buses
which circle around the terminals and
charge about $15 single/$27 return. The
journey into the city takes about an hour.
The **AirTrain JFK** which links to the subway
takes about an hour and costs $7 single.

Newark International Airport, T973-
961 6000, www.newarkairport.com, is 16
miles from Manhattan across the Hudson
River. The **Newark Airport Train** is the
best way to get to Manhattan. A free
monorail takes you to the airport station
and, once on board, it's a 20-min journey
to Penn Station ($14). Otherwise, take
the **Olympia Airport Express**, T212-964
6233, which runs every 15-20 mins to
Grand Central Terminal, Penn Station

and Port Authority. Tickets ($13/22
single/return) can be purchased near
baggage claim or outside by the bus.

Getting around The **Metropolitan
Transportation Authority**, T718-330
1234, www.mta.info, operates New York's
buses and subway. Maps and other
information are available on their website.
A **MetroCard** allows unlimited use of the
subway and MTA buses for a day, a week
or a month and can be bought with cash
or card from subway vending machines or
ticket booths. Pay-per-use MetroCards are
also available. A $10 MetroCard is valid for
6 journeys.

The **subway** system encompasses a
massive area without zones or fare
restrictions; for $2 you can travel to any
of the 5 boroughs as far as the end of the
line. The system can seem complicated
at first but it's logical once you get the
hang of it. Letters or numbers are used to
distinguish the trains and colours are
used to denote different lines, with
stations named after their street location.

'Express' trains only call at major stops,
while 'local' trains stop at each station.

Staten Island Ferry, T718-727 2508,
runs from the terminal on South St at the
end of Whitehall St in Lower Manhattan.
It runs 24 hrs daily, every 15-20 mins
(every hour at night), with less frequent
services at weekends.

Inexpensive compared to most other
major cities, New York's yellow **taxis** are
easy to hail and loved by most city
dwellers. Fares start at $2.50 until 2000
or $3 thereafter.

Tourist information NYC Official
Visitor Information Center, 810 Seventh
Av between 52nd St and 53rd St,
T212-484 1222, www.nycvisit.com. Mon-Fri
0830-1800, Sat-Sun 0830-1700 and holidays
0900-1700. It provides free maps, brochures
and discount coupons to sights and
theatres. It also has a MetroCard vending
machine. **Times Square Visitors Center**,
1560 Broadway, between 46th St and
47th St, T212-869 1890, daily 0800-2000,
also has free city and theatre information.

and pop-culture kitsch, not to mention jewellery, T-shirts, pashminas, dishes, paper lanterns, slippers, toys and just about anything else you might want. Further north at the markets on **Grand Street**, Chinese-Americans and other savvy New Yorkers shop for fish, fruit and vegetables. Countless restaurants serve up dim sum and Cantonese and Szechwan delicacies at affordable prices, while nightlife options include clubs and karaoke bars.

West Village and Chelsea

ⓘ *Subway 1, 9 to Christopher St.*

Considered the most liberal part of Manhattan, **Christopher Street** is the focal point for the city's gay community. Wander just off Christopher Street, however, and the country-like streets taper off into some seriously off-grid sections of town, creating a village atmosphere that was central to New York's literary and artistic development from the 1830s onwards. Stroll around the West Village to see the row houses on **Barrow**, **Bedford** and **Grove Streets**, between Seventh Avenue and Hudson Street. The 9½-ft wide house at 75½ Bedford Street is allegedly the narrowest

Grand Central Station

in the village and is situated on one of its loveliest corners. Some well-known people lived here including the poet Edna St Vincent Millay, Cary Grant and Margaret Mead. At 86 Bedford Street is a former Prohibition speakeasy, known to locals as *Chumley's*. Hudson Street intersects many of the leafier thoroughfares and is a good stopping point for a drink or meal. Dylan Thomas frequented the *White Horse Tavern* at 11th and Hudson streets and died after leaving the bar one night in 1953.

To the south of Washington Square, cafés, bars and souvenir shops line **Bleecker Street**, some more appealing than others. *Caffe Reggio*, 119 MacDougal Street, claims to own the first ever espresso machine to arrive in the USA. Writers and poets made this area famous but now the scene is rather touristy. However, among the tacky shops are some outstanding bars and music venues, notably the *Blue Note*.

The **Chelsea Historic District** contains some of the area's best architecture from the 1800s, including dignified blocks of townhouses, elegant apartment buildings and the peaceful General Theological Seminary and its

Bleecker Street

garden. Among the myriad galleries of Chelsea's warehouse district is the pioneering **Dia Center for the Arts** ⓘ *548 West 22nd St, T212-989 5566, www.diachelsea.org, Wed-Sun 1200-1800, $6*, the first gallery to open in Chelsea in 1974. Internationally recognized artists, such as Andy Warhol and minimalist Sol LeWitt got their early breaks here.

Midtown

In Midtown, hordes of tourists mix with workers in business suits and, by night, the neon blitz of **Broadway** puts on a show. Midtown, flashy, austere and impersonal, is also home to some of the most eye-catching buildings including the **Chrysler Building** ⓘ *405 Lexington Av, T212-682 3070*, the **Empire State Building** ⓘ *5th Av at 34th St, www.esbnyc.com, daily 0930-2400, last elevator 2315, $11*, **Grand Central Terminal**, and the **New York Public Library** ⓘ *5th Av and 42nd St, T212-930 0830, www.nypl.org, Tue-Thu 1100-1930, Fri-Sat 1000-1800*.

These architectural icons are dotted between 59th Street and legendary **42nd Street**. The streets in this area

MOMA

contain some of the world's ritziest restaurants and hotels, not to mention the magnetic pull of **Fifth Avenue** shops and the tourist razzle-dazzle of **Times Square**. Not to be missed is the recently expanded **Museum of Modern Art (MOMA)** ⓘ *11 West 53rd St, T212-708 9400, www.moma.org, Sat-Thu 1030-1700 (except Tue when closed); Fri 1030-2000. $20 (free Fri 1600-2000).*

Museum mile

ⓘ *Metropolitan Museum of Art: 1000 5th Av at 82nd St, T212-535 7710, www.metmuseum.org. Tue-Thu and Sun 0930-1730, Fri-Sat 0930-2100. Suggested donation $15. Frick Collection: 1 East 70th at 5th Av, T212-288 0700, www.frick.org. Tue-Sat 1000-1800, Sun 1300-1800. $12. Guggenheim Museum: 1071 Fifth Av at 89th St, T212-423 3500, www.guggenheim.org. Sat-Wed 1000-1745, Fri 1000-2000. $15.*

You could spend days exploring Museum Mile, stretching along Central Park's eastern border. But if you only have a weekend, try and get to at least one of these: The **Met** has one of the world's most impressive art

Central Park

collections from Greek and Roman, to African, Asian, Oceanic, American and modern. The **Frick**, with its collection of European artwork, porcelain and sculpture, mostly dating from the Renaissance to the end of the 19th century, is arguably the most pleasing destination on Museum Mile. Frank Lloyd Wright's striking funnel-shaped **Guggenheim** houses important works by major 20th-century artists as well as fine Impressionist and Post-Impressionist pieces.

Central Park

ⓘ *59th St to 110th St between 5th Av and Central Park West, T212-360 3456, www.centralpark.org.*

Most New Yorkers insist that Central Park is the finest planned urban space in the world. You will see plenty of them jogging, rollerblading, cycling, boating, picnicking, playing baseball and badminton and, of course, people-watching within its borders. If you're visiting in summertime, there's also likely to be a concert, play or some other event taking place here. Check on the park website.

⊚ Best of the rest

Harlem Since the 1920s, this neighbourhood has been the centre of black culture in New York, producing some of the best in music, art, dance and politics. The area's recent regeneration has seen not only the arrival of Starbucks, but also the fast gentrification of brownstone houses and Bill Clinton's office space on 125th Street.

Brooklyn Bridge ⓘ *walkway begins at Centre St in front of the Municipal Building, Subway 4, 5, 6 to Brooklyn Bridge – City Hall.* The magical structure with its twin Gothic towers and cathedral-like arches, rises gracefully 83 m above the East River. Walking across the bridge between Brooklyn and Manhattan is, for many, the perfect Sunday afternoon activity. In Brooklyn Heights, follow the 'promenade' along the waterfront for jaw-dropping views of Lower Manhattan to leafy Montague Street, where there are plenty of relaxed cafés and restaurants.

The Cloisters ⓘ *Fort Tyron Park at 190th St, T212-923 3700, www.metmuseum.org; Mar-Oct Tue-Sun 0930-1715, Nov-Feb Tue-Sun 0930-1645; $15 suggested donation; Subway A to 190th/ Dyckman St, bus M4 to The Cloisters,* is the site where the 12th-century French chapter house, the Spanish Fuentaduena Chapel and other Gothic and Romanesque chapels were reassembled in the 1930s. Now, shadowy, vaulted passageways and Gregorian chant set the mood for a superb collection of medieval artefacts.

● Sleeping

The swanky, classic hotels featured in so many New York films are abundant in Midtown, along with identikit hotel chains and branches of the YMCA, while quirkier boutique places seem to have cropped up everywhere, especially in SoHo and around Union Square. Most hostels are clustered around the Upper West Side. The website www.nycvisit.com has links to hotel specials offered by big chains, www.hotres.com has details of $99 room deals in the city.

$$$ **Dream Hotel** (formerly the Majestic Hotel), 210 W 55th St between, T212-247 2000, www.dreamny.com. Subway N, Q, R, W to 57th St. The facelift on the already plush hotel includes a circular aquarium in the lobby, and a modern, lounge-like feel to the hotel. Buzzy Italian restaurant *Serafina* is attached and the *Ava* bar on the penthouse level is still one of New York's best rooftop bars.

$$$ **Hotel ThirtyThirty**, 30 E 30th St, T212-689 1900, www.3030nyc.com. Subway 6 to 28th St. The stark, clean, designer decor consistently makes this one of the most popular and reasonably priced boutiques in the city. Within easy walking distance of Union Square, Downtown or Midtown, you'd have to spend a great deal more for the same style elsewhere.

$$$-$$ **The Lucerne**, 201 W 79th St at Amsterdam Av, T212-875 1000, www.thelucernehotel.com. Subway 1 to 79th St. The building's historic façade and its Upper West Side location make this hotel desirable. Service is friendly, but head to *Nice Matin*, the French bistro downstairs, for ambiance.

$$ **Abingdon Guest House**, 13 Eighth Av, T212-243 5384,

www.abingdonguesthouse.com. Subway A, C, E, L to 14th St. Classy, romantic and cosy guesthouse in the heart of the West Village. 4-poster beds and fireplaces. For the location, it's really a bargain but the Abingdon is quiet and wants to stay that way.

$$ **Chelsea Hotel**, 222 W 23rd St, T212-243 3700, www.chelseahotel.com. Subway C, E, 1, 2 to 23rd St. The Chelsea Hotel has been home to many writers and artists including Dylan Thomas, Mark Twain, Tennessee Williams and Arthur Miller, but it is most famous as the place where Sid Vicious murdered Nancy Spungen.

> **❝❞ quirkier boutique hotels seem to have cropped up everywhere, especially in SoHo and around Union Square.**

It's a bit tattered these days but still retains its lively and artsy persona. The velvety, candlelit Serena bar lures cocktail-drinkers downstairs.

$$ **Gershwin Hotel**, 7 E 27th St, T212-545 8000, www.gershwinhotel.com. Subway N, R, 6 to 28th St. This funky, arty place seems more like an upscale hostel than a hotel, with its eclectic furniture and red façade. A bargain in a central location, just off Fifth Av. Variety of rooms and dorms.

$$ **Larchmont Hotel**, 27 W 11th St, T212-989 9333, www.larchmonthotel.com. Subway F, V to 14th St, L to Sixth Av. A beaux arts building and one of the better bargains in the city on one of the prettiest streets in Greenwich Village, near Washington Square Park. Clean, sparse rooms share

bathrooms but robes and slippers are provided. Breakfast included.

$$ **Maritime Hotel**, 363 W 16th St, T212-242 4300. Subway A, C, E to 14th St. A portholed, maritime building perfectly poised on the edge of the busy Meatpacking District. Here trendy types stay for slightly cheaper prices than the equivalent in SoHo.

$ **Carlton Arms Hotel**, 160 E 25th St at 3rd Av, T212-679 0680, www.carltonarms.com. Subway 6 to 23rd St. Small, clean, cheerful hotel, in a residential area bordering Gramercy Park. Popular, so book early.

● Eating

A culinary tour of New York will take you to all corners of the city, so keep your tastebuds primed for all sorts of gastronomic delights. Every style of cuisine can be found here: Greek and Lebanese, Japanese and Korean, Indian and Vietnamese, Ethiopian and French, Italian and Caribbean. Downtown eateries tend to attract a young, laid-back clientele, Uptown restaurants are more upscale in appearance and price. Reserve tables in advance, or be prepared to wait during busy periods.

$$$ **Balthazar**, 80 Spring St, T212-965 1414. Mon-Thu 0730-1200, Fri-Sun 0730-0200. Subway N, R, W to Prince St, 6 to Spring St. The beautiful bar, trendy scene and mouth-watering bread make this one of the best brunches in town, but come early. Dinner is good too, but getting a table may require some good fortune.

$$$ **Gramercy Tavern**, 42 E 20th St, T212-477 0777. Mon-Thu 1200-1430, 1730-2200, Fri 1200-1400, 1730-2300, Sat 1730-2300, Sun 1730-2200. Subway N, R, W, 6 to 23rd St. If you

want to splash out just once, leave it for the tasting menu at this classy American restaurant run by celebrity chef Tom Colicchio. For a slightly cheaper taste of the superlative cuisine, consider eating in the more casual bar area in the front.

$$$ **Koi**, 40 West 40th St, T212-921 3330. Mon-Fri 0730-1100, 1200-1430, 1800-2300, Sat 0730-1100, 1730-2300, Sun 0730-1100, 1800-2000. Subway B, D, F, V to 42nd St-Bryant Park. Set in the fashionable Bryant Park Hotel, this popular celeb-ridden spot features some of the best Japanese food in town. Try the rock shrimp tempura or the crispy rice with spicy tuna.

$$$ **River Café**, 1 Water St, T718-522 5200, Mon-Sat, 1200-1700, 1730-2300, Sun 1130-1500, 1730-2300. Subway A, C to High St. The most famous restaurant in Brooklyn is also one of the city's most romantic, with sparkly views of Manhattan that help justify the price. Fairy lights, flowers and seafood are all on offer here under the Brooklyn Bridge.

$$ **Cafeteria**, 119 Seventh Av, T212-414 1717. Open 24 hrs. Subway 1, 9 to 18th St. Buzzing all day and night with a techno vibe, this white minimalist restaurant serves satisfying sandwiches, salads and meat loaf.

$$ **Florent**, 69 Gansevoort St, T212-989 5779. Mon-Wed 0900-0500, Thu-Sun 24 hrs. Subway A, C, E to 14th St. This classic diner, the backdrop to many films, is the place to be seen eating burgers and steak frites in the small hours.

$$ **Katz's Delicatessen**, 205 E Houston St, T212-254 2246. Sun-Tue 0800-2200, Wed-Thu 0800-2300, Fri-Sat 0800-0300. Subway F, V to Lower East Side-Second Av. The king of New York's delis. Come here for corned beef

or pastrami sandwiches big enough to feed a family. The systematic ordering makes for a raucous but entertaining event, and you may spot some well-known New Yorkers in the queue.

$ **Ñ**, 33 Crosby St, T212-219 8856. Sun-Thu 1700-0200, Fri-Sat 1700-0400. Subway 6 to Spring St. This tiny and wonderful tapas spot bursts with flavour and even hosts a flamenco band on Wed nights.

$ **Supper**, 156 E 2nd St, T212-477 7600. Sun-Thu 1100-0100, Fri-Sat 1100-0200. Subway F, V to Lower East Side-Second Av. Rustic yet hip, this chandeliered Italian restaurant pleases locals with its 'priest stranglers' (tubes of pasta with ricotta, mozzarella and red sauce) and asparagus parmesan.

$ **Trailer Park**, 271 W 23rd St, T212-463 8000. Daily 1200-0100. Subway C, E to 23rd St. The velvet Elvises make this the perfectly kitschy environment for juicy burgers and BLTs served in plastic baskets.

☺ Nightlife

Bars and clubs

New York's nightlife comes in many forms and lasts from dusk till dawn. Although the bar-lounge-club combination continues to be popular, New York has also seen a revival in large-scale clubbing. Venues where hundreds can dance are opening in abandoned warehouses in Chelsea around 10th and 11th avenues, with owners hoping to attract an older, more sophisticated clientele whose party spirit isn't necessarily fuelled by drugs. Head to the Lower East Side and East Village for local DJs and live bands or to the Meatpacking District for everything from biker hangouts to

wine bars. Uptown is generally quieter, but it does have some rowdy sports bars and a few chic clubs.

Arlene's Grocery, 95 Stanton St, T212-359 1633. Subway F to 2nd Av. Indie bands with a rock and roll slant feature nightly at this unpretentious, small Lower East Side spot popular with locals.

Brandy Library, 25 N Moore St, T212-226 5545. Subway 1, 9 Franklin St; A, C, E to Canal St. This comfortable bar feels like a friend's living room with a fireplace, cosy chairs and relaxed atmosphere. It also has an extensive wine and brandy list.

Brooklyn Brewery, 79 N 11th St, T718- 486 7422. Subway L to Bedford Av. This laidback Williamsburg brewery and bar has great happy hour specials on the weekends.

Marquee, 289 10th Av, T646-473 0202. Subway C, E to 23rd St. This West Chelsea 'ultralounge' is where swanky people go to dance in stylish decor and sip expensive cocktails.

Plunge, 18 Ninth Av, T212-660 6736, Subway A, C, E to 14th St; L at Eighth Av. Prepare to queue, but the Hotel Gansevoort's slick rooftop lounge/bar offers spectacular views of the Hudson River and Manhattan.

Zinc Bar, 90 W Houston, T212-477 8337. Subway A, C, B, D to W 4th St. This cool and cosy candlelit jazz joint hosts Brazilian, Latin, African and other world music.

Cinema

New York has a moviehouse to suit any taste, including a commendable number of independent and arthouse cinemas. Tickets for new releases should be bought in advance by calling T212-777 FILM or by booking online at www.moviefone.com.

Two significant film festivals take place each year, the **New York Film Festival** in October and the **Tribeca Film Festival** in May. The latter was first organized by Robert De Niro and others to help boost Lower Manhattan after September 11th and has, so far, been a great success. There's also free, open-air cinema at the **HBO Bryant Park Summer Film Festival** starting in June and many other important film debuts, premieres and events throughout the year.

Comedy

New York comedy has had a huge revival in recent years, with fringe performers now making a good showing at big venues and unconventional shows attracting local crowds to the smaller clubs. Check out the experimental comedians, musicians and performance artists at **Moonwork**, Greenwich Village Center, 219 Sullivan St, T212-254 3074, www.moonwork.com, and the unique brand of entertaining improvisation offered by the **Upright Citizens' Brigade**, 307 W 26th St, T212-366 9176, www.ucbtheatre.com. Subway C, E at 23rd St. Most comedy shows charge a small admission and a 2-drink minimum.

Live music

Aside from the few listings below check weekly magazines and local press. Don't miss Central Park's free summer concerts for rock, classical, opera, funk and more.
Apollo Theater, 5253 W 125th St at Frederick Douglass Blvd, T212-531 5337. Subway A, B, C, D to 125th St. The famous amateur nights still fill

up the house, though the performances tend to lean more towards hip-hop and comedy shows these days.
Café Carlyle, Carlyle Hotel, 35 E 76th St, T212-570 7189. Subway 6 to 77th St. This chic 90-person cabaret venue is the perfect place to hear Woody Allen's Mon night jazz band. Book at least a week in advance.
Carnegie Hall, 154 W 57th St, T212-247 7800, www.carnegiehall.org. Subway A, C, B, D, 1, 9 to 59th St-Columbus Circle, N, R, Q, W to 57th St. For classical music, Carnegie Hall

66 99 Although the bar-lounge-club combination continues to be popular, New York has also seen a revival in large-scale clubbing.

promises superb acoustics and a beautiful setting.
Village Vanguard, 178 Seventh Av, T212-255 4037. Subway 1, 2 to Christopher St-Sheridan Sq. Regarded by many as the best jazz venue in New York.

Theatre

Choose from the large, well-funded Broadway shows staged in ornate theatres or the offbeat and cosier Off Broadway and Off-Off Broadway venues, where audiences are much smaller but productions are of high quality. Tickets for big hits on Broadway and long-running productions can cost between $35 and $200.

○ Shopping

It's not surprising so many visitors come to the city to max out their credit cards. New York's shops tempt even the most budget-conscious with their huge choice. Uptown and West Village's designer shops and Midtown's department stores (**Bergdorf Goodman**, 745 Fifth Av **Barneys**, 660 Madison Av; **Bloomingdales**, 1000 3rd Av and now also in SoHo; **Henri Bendel**, 712 Fifth Av at 56th St; **Macy's**, 151 W 34th St) flash their expensive goods from swanky window displays, while Downtown has smaller boutiques, discount stores, bric-a-brac and offbeat speciality shops. Fifth Avenue, from 23rd St down to 14th St, features many of the chains found in shopping malls throughout the USA. Unexpected delights, too, can be found from the scrumptious food hall at **Grand Central Terminal** to the fabulous, kitschy weekend **Hell's Kitchen Flea Market** (39th St between Ninth and Tenth Avs, Sat- Sun, dawn to dusk). For fashionistas there's everything from punk to posh, couture to camp, thrift and second- hand to designer heaven. Vintage gear can be found in the East Village, the Lower East Side and Nolita, especially at the new bazaar-style **Emerge NYC** where shoppers buy directly from new designers (65 Bleecker St between Broadway and Lafayette St) while high-end designers have taken over the Meatpacking District.

Most shops are generally open 7 days a week, Mon-Sat from about 1000 until at least 1800, with shorter hours on Sun. Before you go mad with your credit card, don't forget the whopping 8.25% **sales tax** that is tacked on to all purchases.

Paris

Not a city for the fainthearted, Paris engulfs the senses with its vibrant culture, architectural marvels, world-class galleries, stylish shopping, smoky wine bars and fantastic food. With a list like this, it's hardly surprising that the city has a reputation for arrogance; something that could be called merely confidence in itself as both a historical showpiece and a fearless innovator. While it holds tight to its traditions, this modern city continues magically to evolve. Its essence is an effortless balance of old and new, of traditional elegance and creative innovation. It is Notre Dame through cherry blossom from the quai de la Tournelle and rollerblading under potted palm trees beside the Seine; and more than ever before, Paris of the 21st century is a feisty brew of peoples from around the world. Old-fashioned French flavours have not been lost, or even submerged – men in berets still play *boules* on the quai de la Seine and bourgeois Madames still feed tasty titbits to their poodles from the restaurant table. But now there are more ingredients in the city mix, more viewpoints. (It is estimated that 20% of the two million people living in central Paris are immigrants.) Twirling seductively to her own special tempo, with the rest of Europe gawping from the sidelines, Paris confidently expects to lead the way but is also not afraid to go against the prevailing wind, from the French Revolution to trenchant opposition to foreign intervention in Iraq.

Arts & culture
★★★★★

Eating
★★★★★

Nightlife
★★★★

Outdoors
★

Romance
★★★★★

Shopping
★★★★★

Sightseeing
★★★★

Value for money
★★

Overall score
★★★★

At a glance

Central Paris is divided into 20 numbered districts (*arrondissements*) and is bisected by the River Seine. At its heart are two small islands – **Île de la Cité** (home to Notre Dame Cathedral) and **Île St Louis**. This is intricate, romantic Paris. On the **Left Bank** of the Seine (*Rive Gauche*), **St Germain** still has a high concentration of publishing houses and bookshops but tourist chatter has largely replaced debates on Existentialism and Surrealism. The **Latin Quarter**, to the east, is home to the Sorbonne, while the imposing seventh *arrondissement*, to the west, has a number of key landmarks, including the **Eiffel Tower**, **Les Invalides** and the **Musée d'Orsay**. Southwest is **Montparnasse**, once a place of wild entertainment.

North of the Seine on the **Right Bank** (*Rive Droit*), the **Louvre** is a big pull for tourists who buzz around

We'll always have Paris...

Rick (Humphrey Bogart), 'Casablanca', 1943

the place du Carrousel snapping the glittering **Pyramide** and the **Jardin des Tuileries**. From here, the **Champs-Elysées**, long synonymous with wealth, sweeps up to the **Arc de Triomphe**. To the east of the Louvre are three adjoining *quartiers*: **Les Halles**, **Marais** and **Bastille**, while, to the north, **Montmartre** sits prettily on a hill, more like a village that anywhere else in the city and home to the fanciful **Sacré Coeur**. Thanks to some canny facelifts the working-class districts of **Belleville** and **Ménilmontant**, to the east, are now the hip places to be once the sun goes down.

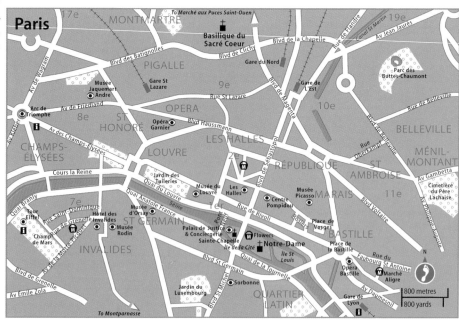

24 hours in the city

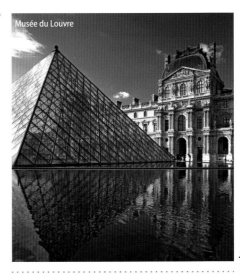
Musée du Louvre

Get up early and head to the Île de la Cité for **Notre Dame** and the **Sainte-Chapelle**. Linger at the flower market, grab a delicious sorbet from **Berthillon**, then cross the Pont Neuf to the Left Bank. After a caffeine and philosophy fix in *Café de Flore*, visit the beautiful **Musée Rodin** or browse for books, antiques and fashion around **place St-Germain-des-Prés**. Treat yourself to lunch at *Ze Kitchen Gallerie* or *Les Bookinistes*, in preparation for one of the great museums: the **Louvre** or the **Musée d'Orsay**, perhaps. In the late afternoon, head for the **Marais** for window shopping or **Montmartre** for the view. After dark, *Brasserie Flo* is great for dinner, followed by jazz at *New Morning*. Alternatively, succumb to the lure of the lit-up **Eiffel Tower** or join the beautiful people, drinking the night away at the bars along **rue Oberkampf**.

★ *Don't leave town without checking out the sculptures at the Musée Rodin.*

⊖ Travel essentials

Getting there Eurostar (www.eurostar.com) runs at least 10 trains daily from London Waterloo to **Paris Gare du Nord**. (A few services stop in Calais and Lille en route.) **Charles de Gaulle Airport**, aka Roissy, www.paris-cdg.com, is 23 km northeast of Paris. The best way into the centre is by the RER B train to Châtelet-Les-Halles (45 mins/€8) from Terminal 2 (there's a free shuttle connection from Terminal 1). There is also the **Roissybus**, T08-36 68 77 14 (45 mins/€8) to rue Scribe, near the Opéra Garnier, or regular **Air France** buses to Porte Maillot, the Arc de Triomphe, the Gare de Lyon and Gare Montparnasse. To reach the city from **Orly Airport**, 14 km south, the best bet is the **Air France** bus to Les Invalides and Montparnasse (40 mins/€7.50). Or take the free bus to RER Pont de Rungis and catch the **Orlyrail** train to the city centre (50 mins/€5.15). The RATP **Orlybus** runs to Denfert-Rochereau

(30 mins/€5.50). Ryanair flies to **Paris Beauvais Airport** to the northwest of the city. A shuttle bus to Porte Maillot takes 1 hr 15 mins and costs €13 each way. **Paris Airports Service**, T01-55 98 10 80, will pick up from your hotel and charge €25 per person to the airport (half the cost of a taxi).

Getting around Note that the last two digits of a Paris postcode indicate the *arrondissement*. Central Paris is walkable but you will almost certainly want to use the **metro** system at some point. There are 16 numbered lines, plus the small cable car (*funiculaire*) up to Sacré Coeur. Trains run daily 0530-0030. Numbered **buses** ply the streets daily 0630-2030, with a select few operating a reduced service past midnight. There are fewer buses on Sun. Maps of routes and approximate timetables are posted at each bus stop. Always validate your ticket in the machine at the front of the bus when you board. **Tickets** within

Zones 1 and 2 (which cover all of central Paris) are valid for buses, the metro and RER urban rail. A single costs €1.40; a carnet of 10 tickets is better value at €10.70. Tickets are sold at metro stations and some tobacconists. There are also a number of **passes** available: *Paris Visite* is valid for 1, 2, 3 or 5 consecutive days (€8.35, €13.70 €18.25 or €26.65) and can be used throughout Paris and its regions, including Disneyland Paris and Versailles. The pass comes with a little booklet of vouchers for discounts at certain sights.

Tourist information
Paris Convention and Visitors Bureau, 120 av des Champs Elysées, 75008, T08-92 68 31 12, www.paris-tourist office.com. Summer daily 0900-2000; winter Mon-Sat 0900-2000, Sun 1100-1900. There are other branches of the Paris Tourist Office at the Gare de Lyon (Mon-Sat 0800-2000) and the Eiffel Tower (summer daily 1100-1840).

◉ Sights

Île de la Cité and Notre Dame
ⓘ *6 place du Parvis-de-Notre-Dame, 75001. Church, T01-42 34 56 10; daily 0745- 2100; free. Towers, T01-53 10 07 00; summer daily 0845-1845; winter daily 1000-1645; €5.50. Metro Cité.*

The island's most famous landmark and France's most famous place of worship is the indomitable Notre Dame Cathedral, built to replace and surpass a crumbling earlier church, on a site where a Roman temple to Jupiter once stood. It took more than 170 years to complete, after Pope Alexander III laid the first stone in 1163. The building has a spectacular Gothic façade with a rose window at its western end and magnificent flying buttresses at its eastern end. The nave is at its best when the sun shines through the stained-glass windows, washing it with shafts of light in reds and blues. Place du Parvis Notre Dame is an epicentre of tourist activity but the gardens at the rear and to the south are comparatively calm. Walk all the way round to appreciate the flying buttresses and the cherry blossoms in spring.

Notre Dame

Les Invalides

Since the early 19th century there has been a colourful and sweet-smelling **Marché aux Fleurs** at place Louis-Lépine, towards the centre of the island (on Sundays the market also sells caged birds and small pets). **Île de la Cité** was once the seat of royal power and much survives from the original medieval palace complex on the western part of the island, namely the Conciergerie, the Palais de Justice (still the city's law courts) and the glittering jewel of **Sainte-Chapelle** ⓘ *4 blvd du Palais, 75001, T01-53 73 78 51, daily 0930-1730, €5.50,* a chapel built by King Louis IX to house his precious religious relics. Here, too, are the legendary sorbets at **Berthillon** (closed Mon-Tue). **Pont Neuf**, the best-loved of all the city's 36 bridges (inaugurated in 1607), straddles the Seine at the western end of the island.

Tour Eiffel
ⓘ *Champ de Mars, 75007, T01-44 11 23 11, www.tour-eiffel.fr. Sep-Jun 0930-2245; Jul-Aug 0900-0030. Lift to Level 1 €4.10, Level 2 €7.50, Level 3 €10.70; stairs to Levels 1 and 2, €3.80. Metro Bir Hakeim.*

Gustav Eiffel won a competition to design a 300-m tower for the Universal Exhibition of 1889. The resulting **Eiffel Tower** was originally reviled by Parisians and was only meant to stand for 20 years; now it's the city's most identifiable landmark. The highest viewing platform is at 274 m and, on a clear day, you can see for more than 65 km. On the first level, there's a bistro, a small museum and a post office; on the second level, there are souvenir shops and the gourmet *Jules Verne* restaurant. To avoid long queues (at least an hour), visit early in the morning or late at night, when the tower is lit up like a giant Christmas tree.

Les Invalides
Metro Invalides, Latour Maubourg

The seventh *arrondissement* exudes extravagance from every pore. Expect 19th-century elegance and grandeur rather than quaint backstreets and curiosities. The avenues, mansions and monuments here loudly proclaim their importance. Wander rues de Grenelle, St Dominique and Cler, east of the Champ-de-Mars to discover where high society shops and dines.

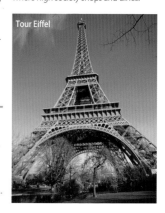
Tour Eiffel

Musée Rodin

Sitting splendidly amid the broad avenues, is **Hôtel des Invalides** ⓘ *129 rue de Grenelle, 75007, T01-44 42 38 77, www.invalides.org, daily 1000-1800 (till 1700 in winter), closed first Mon of month, €7.50, Metro La Tour- Maubourg, Varenne,* Louis XIV's hospice for war veterans. The vast Army Museum now charts French military history from prehistoric times to the present.

Around the corner, **Musée Rodin** ⓘ *77 rue de Varenne, 75007, T01-44 18 61 10, www.musee-rodin.fr, summer Tue-Sun 0930-1745, winter Tue-Sun 0930-1645, €5,* is housed in the light and airy 18th-century Hôtel Biron – the sculptor's last home. There are over 500 of Rodin's sculptures here, as well as works by Camille Claudel (his model and lover) and Rodin's own collection of paintings, including work by Van Gogh.

Musée d'Orsay
ⓘ *Quai Anatole-France, 75007, T01-40 49 48 48, www.musee-orsay.fr. Tue-Wed, Fri-Sat 1000-1800, Thu 1000-2145, Sun 0900- 1800 (last entry 45 mins before closing). €7.50, Sun €5.50, extra for temporary exhibitions. Metro Solferino.*

This 1900 train station-turned-art gallery is worth visiting almost as much for the building as for the great Impressionist treasures it holds. The enormous space is enhanced and illuminated by a vaulted iron-and-glass roof. There are decorative arts and Rodin sculptures on the middle level, with the most popular works, by the likes of Monet, Cézanne, Degas and Signac, on the upper level. Visit during the week to avoid the crowds.

Jardin du Luxembourg
ⓘ *rue Guynemer and blvd St Michel, 75006, T01-42 34 20 00. Summer daily 0730-1 hr before sunset, winter 0815-1 hr before sunset. Metro Notre Dame des Champs. RER Luxembourg.*

The lovely Luxembourg gardens cover more than 23 ha of the Left Bank. Their centrepiece, in front of the Luxembourg Palace, is the octagonal pool, surrounded by wide paths, formal flowerbeds and terraces. On the eastern side of the garden, accessed by boulevard St Michel, is the Médicis Fountain, an open-air café and ice-cream sellers. From April to August there are free daytime musical concerts at the bandstand.

Jardin du Luxembourg

◉ Best of the rest

Île St Louis ⓘ *75001. Metro Pont Marie, Sully Morland.* This island on the Seine is like stepping into a film set for the 17th century.
Musée Picasso ⓘ *Hôtel Salé, 5 rue de Thorigny, 75003, T01-42 71 25 21. Wed-Mon 0930-1800 (until 1730 in winter). €6.70. Free 1st Sun of month. Metro Saint Paul, Chemin Vert, St Sébastien-Froissart.* A chronological journey through the artist's life, including a gem from the blue period.
Canal St Martin ⓘ *75010, 75019. Metro République for quai de Valmy, Stalingrad for quai de la Seine.* The canal was built in the 19th century as a shortcut on the Seine. Its most attractive sections have footbridges and barges.
Musée Jacquemart-André ⓘ *158 blvd Haussmann, 75008, T01-45 62 11 59, www.musee-jacquemart-andre.com. Daily 1000-1800. €8, Metro Miromesnil.* In 1872 the portrait artist Nélie Jacquemart painted Edouard André. Nine years later they were married and living in this magnificent mansion on boulevard Haussmann.
Cimetière du Père Lachaise ⓘ *16 rue Repos, 75020, T01-43 70 70 33, 6 Nov-15 Mar, daily 0800-1730, 16 Mar-5 Nov, 0800-1800. Free. Metro Père Lachaise, Gambetta.* The most celebrated cemetery in France and last resting place for the likes of Jim Morrison, Edith Piaf, Frédéric Chopin, Honoré de Balzac and Oscar Wilde to name but a very few.

In the western section, towards rue Guynemer, there is an adventure playground and a puppet theatre. Photo exhibitions are often suspended along the garden's iron railings. Bartholdi's Statue of Liberty here is a smaller model of the one given to the United States in 1885.

Musée du Louvre

ⓘ *Palais du Louvre, 75001, T01-40 20 51 51/53 17, www.louvre.fr. Fri-Mon 0900-1800, Wed-Thu 0900-2145. €8.50, €6 after 1500. Free first Sun of month. Those with tickets can avoid queuing and enter via Passage Richelieu. Metro Palais Royal.*

Paris's foremost art gallery is as vast as it is famous. It was constructed as a fortress in the 12th century, lived in as a palace by the late 14th century, rebuilt in the Renaissance style in the 16th century and finally converted into a museum by Napoleon. The wonderful glass pyramid entrance by I M Pei was added in 1989. Today the four floors of the three wings (Sully, Denon and Richelieu) hold some 350,000 paintings, drawings, sculptures and other items, dating from 7000 BC to the mid-19th century. Highlights include *Vénus de*

Centre Pompidou

Milo (2nd century BC), Rubens' *Life of Marie de Médici*, Italian sculpture in the Michelangelo Gallery and, of course, the crowd-pulling *Mona Lisa*.

Champs-Elysées and Arc de Triomphe

ⓘ *place Charles de Gaulle, 75008, T01-55 37 73 77. Summer daily 0930-2300, winter daily 1000-2230. €7. Free first Sun of month. Metro Charles de Gaulle-Etoile.*

The Champs-Elysées has been an international byword for glamorous living since the 19th century. The eponymous avenue is Paris's 'triumphal way', leading from the vast **place de la Concorde** to the **place Charles de Gaulle**, site of the **Arc de Triomphe**. The arch has always been the focus of parades and celebrations: Napoleon's funeral procession was held here in 1840, as were the victory celebrations of 1919 and 1944, and it's the finishing point of the Tour de France cycle race. In recent times Parisians have been snooty about the surrounding tackiness but it now seems that the down days of the Champs Elysées are coming to an end. Culturally and commercially, the area is

undergoing a mini-makeover, with an influx of new restaurants, designer shops and exhibition centres.

Les Halles

Trendy boutiques, hip hang-outs, historic squares, aristocratic-mansions-turned-museums, the *Rive Droite* is fashionable and, in parts, smart. It has its low points too – the eyesore of Forum des Halles and brazenly drunken rue de Lappe in Bastille – but the good far outweighs the questionable. The **Centre Pompidou** ⓘ *place Beaubourg, 75004, T01-44 78 12 33, www.centrepompidou.fr, daily 1100-2200 (Thu till 2300), €7-9 for exhibitions, €10 internet day ticket, permanent exhibitions free on the first Sun of the month, Metro Rambuteau,* is an architectural masterpiece of the late 1970s that brought a buzz to the surrounding area. The multicoloured fun continues with the funky fountains in neighbouring place Igor Stravinsky, and there are plenty of galleries along rue Beaubourg and rue Quincampoix.

Marais

Metro Chemin Vert, St Sébastien Froissart.

Sandwiched between Les Halles and the Bastille is the **Marais**, everybody's favourite place for aimless wandering, thanks to its winding medieval streets, charming tea rooms and bars, and ultra-fashionable shops. The highlight is **Place des Vosges** ⓘ *Metro St Paul*, a beautiful 17th-century square of arcaded buildings. Rue des Rosiers, a resolutely Jewish street, is packed with bakeries, kosher restaurants and falafel takeaway joints, while the city's unabashedly gay centre is around rue Vieille-du-Temple and rue des Lombards.

Shopping is an essential part of the Paris experience, even if it is only of the window variety. Inventive presentation is an art form here, especially among the city's specialist food retailers. **Place de la Madeleine** is renowned for its gourmet shops, including **Fauchon**, Nos 28-30, T01-47 42 60 11, Monday to Saturday 0930-1900, a Parisian institution that sells cheese, wine, pastries, chocolates and more. There are also treats to be found on **Île St Louis**. The architectural appeal of Parisian shops is demonstrated by the city's impressive department store buildings and by **Les Galeries** – the 19th-century covered shopping arcades between boulevard Montmartre and rue St Marc. The traditional hotspots for gold-card holders are **rue du Faubourg St Honoré, avenue Montaigne, rue de la paix** and **place Vendôme**. More recently, designer names have joined the bookshops and antique shops around **place St-Germain-des-Prés**. Smaller, cheaper boutiques are to be found around the **Marais**, the **Bastille** and **Abbesses**. Streets with the winning combo of morning food markets (every day except Monday) and wonderful speciality shops include **rue Cler, rue de Buci, rue Lepic** and **rue Mouffetard**.

Fauchon

Bastille

Metro Bastille.

The winds of regeneration that the Pompidou Centre blew into Les Halles, brought the new **Opéra Bastille** to the Bastille just over a decade later. This gritty, working-class area has

Sacré Coeur

emerged as an after-dark hotspot and bastion of designer outlets but it still clings to its revolutionary credentials: raucous protests and demonstrations are a common sight on place de la Bastille. For a glimpse of the grittier side of life, away from trendy rue de la Roquette and rue du Fauboug St Antoine, head to the **Marché Aligre** ⓘ *place d'Aligre, 75012, Tue-Sat 0800-1300, 1600-1930, Sun 0800-1300, Metro Ledru Rollin,* and the surrounding streets, where old-style bars full of cigarette butts and sullen, red-faced locals are still the norm.

Basilique du Sacré Coeur

ⓘ *Parvis du Sacré Coeur, 75018, T01-53 41 89 00. Daily 0600-2230 (dome and crypt 0900-1730). Church free, dome €5. Metro Anvers, Lamarck-Caulaincourt, Abbesses plus funiculaire.*

It was the Romans who first erected a place of worship on top of this hill to the north of the city. They beheaded Denis, the first bishop of Paris, here in the third century AD. He was sainted as a result and the hill became the 'Mont des Martyrs' for early Christians. The current basilica – a glorious flurry of domes or a fanciful abomination, depending on your point of view – was designed by Paul Abadie and financed largely by national subscription. It took nearly 40 years to build, finally being consecrated in 1919, and now attracts some five million visitors each year. Inside, a golden Byzantine mosaic of Christ by Luc Olivier Merson hovers beatifically over the high altar. The spiral staircase to the dome is worth tackling, if you're partial to a long view, but you can enjoy a similar panorama from the steps of the basilica – along with the crush of tourists, hustlers and pigeons.

⊜ Sleeping

Hotels near the big sights are expensive, but there are popular, mid-priced options on rue Saint-Dominique, squeezed between the Eiffel Tower and Les Invalides. The bustling streets of Marais or St Germain also have some good hotels. There are romantic corners on Île St Louis and in Montmartre, while Bastille and Oberkampf are good for night owls.

€€€ Hôtel Bourg Tibourg, 19 rue du Bourg Tibourg, 75004, T01-42 78 47 39, www.hotelbourgtibourg.com. Metro St Paul, Hôtel de Ville. This wonderful Marais hotel is a Costes/Jacques Garcia masterpiece. The French designer has lived in the Marais for over 20 years. The rooms are exquisitely intimate and de luxe, seamlessly combining French and Oriental influences.

€€€ Pershing Hall, 49 rue Pierre Charron, 75008, T01-58 36 58 00, www.pershinghall.com. Metro George V. Ultra-modern hotel designed by Andrée Putman. Minimalist in the extreme but also luxurious.

€€ Hôtel Beaumarchais, 3 rue Oberkampf, 75011, T01-53 36 86 86, www.hotelbeaumarchais.com. Metro Filles du Calvaire, Oberkampf. Primary colours are the defining feature of this buzzing 33-room hotel.

€€ Hôtel Danemark, 21 rue Vavin, 75006, Montparnasse, T01-43 26 93 78, www.hoteldanemark.com. Metro Vavin. An elegant and welcoming hotel on a lively street, lined with little cafés and shops. Rooms are cosy and at least one of the bathrooms has a jacuzzi.

€€ Hôtel des Deux-Îles, 59 rue St Louis en l'Île, 75004, T01-43 26 13 35, www.hotel-ile-saintlouis.com. Metro

Pont Marie. Welcoming and comfortable. Specify if you want a bath rather than a shower.

€€ Hôtel des Écoles, 19 rue M le Prince, 75006, T01-46 33 31 69, hotel_des_ecoles@hotmail.com. Metro Odéon. Atmospheric and 'compact': 11 small rooms, small beds and possibly the smallest lift in Paris. All rooms have shower or bath.

€€ Hôtel des Marronniers, 21 rue Jacob, 75006, T01-43 25 30 60, www.paris-hotel-marronniers.com. Metro St-Germain-des-Prés. This is in the heart of animated St Germain but is set back from the street so it's not too noisy. The rear courtyard has tables for breakfast or afternoon tea.

€€ Hôtel des Tuileries, 10 rue Saint-Hyacinthe, 75001, T01-42 61 04 17, www.hotel-des-tuileries.com. Metro Pyramides. An 18th-century house converted into a hotel. The 26 rooms are individual, comfortable and homely. The reception room showcases Louis XVI-style furniture.

€€ Hôtel du Vieux Marais, 8 rue du Plâtre, 75004, T01-42 78 47 22, www.vieuxmarais.com. Metro Hôtel de Ville. A family-run hotel for the past 30 years, the Vieux Marais has 30 rooms, equipped with Poltrona Frau furniture and gleaming bathrooms.

€ Grand Hôtel Lévêque, 29 rue Cler, 75007, T01-47 05 49 15, www.hotel-leveque.com. Metro École Militaire, La Tour Maubourg. Hotel in a market street, offering clean rooms, most with en suite loo and shower. Recently renovated, so reservations essential.

€ Hôtel Esmeralda, 4 rue St-Julien-le-Pauvre, 75005, T01-43 54 19 20. Metro St Michel. A budget option with character. Try to ignore the wonky bedside tables, the curling wallpaper and the decrepit breakfast room.

❷ Eating

Breakfast

⍦ Le Comptoir du Commerce, 1 rue des Petits Carreaux, 75002, T01-42 36 39 57. Mon-Sat 0800-2400, Sun 1200-1900. Metro Sentier. Pine walls and shutters and comfy cushioned seating create a country kitchen ambience. Good range of breakfasts.

⍦ Café de Flore, 172 blvd St Germain, 75006, T01-45 48 55 26. Daily 0730-0100. Metro St Germain. Renowned for decades as an unofficial philosophical forum, the Café de Flore still retains its air of intellectualism, although today's thinkers need deeper pockets than their forebears.

Lunch

⍦⍦⍦ Le Dauphin, 167 rue Saint Honoré, 75001, T01-42 60 40 11. Daily 1200-1430, 1930-2230. Metro Palais Royal. Hearty fare from southwest France served in an elegant setting. The house speciality is *la parilladas* – meat, fish or vegetables on a hot plate.

⍦⍦ Les Bookinistes, 53 quai des Grands Augustins, 75006, T01-43 25 45 94. Mon-Fri 1200-1430, 1900-2300, Sat 1900-2300. Metro St Michel. One of Guy Savoy's bistros, this place serves popular modern French cooking and overlooks Notre Dame. Healthy-sized portions of quality food, from delectable sea bass to melt-in-the-mouth scallops.

⍦⍦ Ze Kitchen Gallerie, 4 rue des Grands Augustins, 75006, T01-44 32 00 32. Mon-Fri 1200-1500, 1900-2300. Metro St Michel. One of the places that's got the tongues of fashionable gourmets wagging in recent times. Inspirational and inventive, with a real emphasis on the nutritious as well as the delicious. The lunchtime menu ranges from €21-32, including a glass

of wine and coffee. Booking essential.
† **Pause Café**, 41 rue de Charonne, 75011, T01-48 06 80 33. Mon-Sat 0800-0200, Sun 0900-2000. Metro Bastille, Ledru-Rollin. The relaxed atmosphere, large terrace and good, reasonably priced food have made this a very popular lunch spot.

Dinner
††† **La Fermette Marbeuf**, 5 rue Marbeuf, 75008, T01-53 23 08 00, www.fermettemarbeuf.com. Daily 1200-1500, 1900-2330. Metro Franklin D Roosevelt. An art nouveau extravaganza with ceramic panels featuring animals and flowers. When booking your table, ask to be placed in the back room, under the glass roof with its delicate stained-glass panes.
†† **Brasserie Flo**, 7 cour des Petites-Ecuries (enter 63 rue du Fg St Denis), 75010, T01-47 70 13 59. Daily 1200-1500, 1900-0130. Metro Château d'Eau. Excellent food in a wonderful panelled art nouveau dining room. Classic Flo dishes include oysters in a champagne sauce and steak tartare.
† **Le Café Noir**, 65 rue Montmartre, 75002, T01-40 39 07 36. Daily 1200-0200. Metro Sentier. A down-to-earth corner café with large windows, red formica tables, mirrors and pictures.

◑ Nightlife

For up-to-the-minute info on what's on check the listings magazines *Pariscope* or *L'Officiel des Spectacles*.

Bars and clubs
Paris has something to suit every taste, from authentic wine bars with red-faced old soaks propping up the zinc counter, to swish and swanky venues fit for glamorous celebrities. The **Bastille** is always a popular nightspot, although it can be overrun with tourists. **Oberkampf** is just as lively, but cheaper and more authentic. Nearby **rue St Maur** is tipped to be the new Oberkampf. A lot of clubs double as live music venues some nights of the week. Many bars also serve food, albeit a limited menu, and there are a growing number of cross-over places. **Man Ray** (34 rue Marbeuf, 75008, www.manray.info, Metro Franklin Roosevelt), is a classic example of a fine restaurant that is also a bar and has DJs, while **Café Cheri(e)**, 44 blvd de la Villette 75019, Metro Belleville, is a trendy nightspot known locally as a great alternative to a full-blown club.

❝❞ Jazz-lovers will find everything they could wish for at New Morning.

Dance and opera
National and international dance troupes regularly come to Paris to perform. **Opéra Garnier**, Palais Garnier, place de l'Opéra, 75009, T08- 36 69 78 68, www.opera-de-paris.fr, Metro Opéra, is the principal base of the Ballet de l'Opéra National de Paris, and the best place to see classical ballet and opera favourites. **Opéra Bastille**, place de la Bastille, 75012, T08-36 69 78 68, www.opera-de-paris. fr, Metro Bastille, veers toward more contemporary choices, but for ground- breaking shows, with dazzling sets and musical effects, look no further than **Opéra Comique**, 5 rue Favart, 75002, T01-42 44 45 46, Metro Richelieu-Drouot.

Music
Jazz-lovers will find everything they could wish for at **New Morning**, 7-9 rue des Petites-Ecuries, 75010, T01- 45 23 51 41, www.newmorning.com, Metro Château d'Eau.

If you want a taste of good old-fashioned and newly fashionable chansons, head to **Au Lapin Agile**, 27 rue des Saules, 75018, T01-46 06 85 87, www.au-lapin-agile.com, Metro Lamarck Caulaincourt. Shows are held Tue-Sun at 2100 and admissionis €24, including one drink. Alternatively, **L'Olympia**, 28 blvd des Capucines, 75009, T01-55 27 10 00, www.olympiahall.com, Metro Opéra, is the home of chanson, where Johnny Halliday and Edith Piaf once performed. It still pulls the crowds for a broad range of performers.

L'Elysée Montmartre, 72 blvd de Rochechouart, 75018, T01-55 07 06 00, www.elyseemontmartre.com, Metro Anvers, features acts from all musical backgrounds – Talvin Singh to the Cinematic Orchestra. Things start late, so be prepared to sit on the floor and drink beer for a good while.
La Maroquinerie, 23 rue Boyer, 75020, T01-40 33 30 60, Metro Gambetta, features world acts, from accordion to flamenco troupes, indie rock and Middle Eastern oud players.

For classical music keep an eye out for concerts in the auditoriums at the **Louvre**, T01-40 20 84 00, and the **Musée d'Orsay**, T01-40 49 47 17, as well as the concerts, mainly of chamber music, held in churches, including **Sainte-Chapelle**. For a contemporary classical sound, the **Cité de la Musique**, 221 av Jean-Jaurès, 75019, T01-44 84 45 45, www.cite-musique.fr, Metro Porte de Pantin, has an exciting and varied programme.

Visitors get rather poetic when they first clap eyes on Prague. The 'Golden City', the 'Belle of Bohemia' and the 'City of a Thousand Spires' certainly has a lot to live up to, but the reality matches the hype. Prague remained blessedly unharmed during the two World Wars, and the Velvet Revolution of 1989 came to pass without a single shot being fired. This translates into a beautiful city with a stunning showpiece centre: winding, medieval lanes flanked by elegant Gothic, baroque and art nouveau façades. As you wander through Europe's largest castle or over famous Charles Bridge, it's hard to imagine that Prague was off limits to western visitors as little as two decades ago. But time moves quickly in this part of the world: the Czech Republic has been a member of the EU since May 2004 and a new veneer of sophistication is spreading through the capital. Locals aren't surprised; Prague was, after all, at the vanguard of European culture for much of the 19th and early 20th centuries. Vestiges of this past are the main draws today; from the cobbled streets of Staré Město and the haunting atmosphere of the Jewish cemetery to the smoky cellar bars and the graceful concert halls that launched some of Europe's greatest composers. The essence of Prague, however, is something less tangible; getting lost in the medieval Old Town on a foggy evening, or watching the sun set over terracotta roofs and soaring church spires is, quite simply, poetry.

Arts & culture
★★★★

Eating
★★

Nightlife
★★★

Outdoors
★★

Romance
★★★★★

Shopping
★★

Sightseeing
★★★★

Value for money
★★★

Overall score
★★★

At a glance

The Vltava River, running from south to north through the city centre, neatly splits up the area in which visitors spend most (if not all) of their time. On the right bank is **Staré Město** (Old Town), at the heart of which is **Staroměstské náměstí** (Old Town Square), famous for its astronomical clock. North of here is the old Jewish district of **Josefov**, edged by **Parízská** boulevard. The winding, narrow streets of the Old Town fan out south of Old Town Square, opening up in the southeast at **Václavské náměstí** (Wenceslas Square), site of the 1989 Velvet Revolution. This is the main hub of **Nové Město** (New Town), Prague's business and commercial district. To the north is the busy square, **Náměstí Republiky**, while, to the south, the wide streets hold many of the biggest hotels, restaurants and department stores. Further east is the residential district of **Vinohrady**, once the royal vineyards.

On the other side of the river is **Malá Strana** (Lesser Quarter). This area of 18th-century town

Prague doesn't let go

Franz Kafka

houses and palaces is quieter and even more atmospheric than the Old Town, its streets rolling up towards **Hradčany**, the castle district. Hradčany is completely dominated by the magnificent castle complex, with the central road of **Nerodova** (always full of tour groups trudging to the castle) running back down into **Malá Strana**. To the south is the green expanse of **Petřín**, a tranquil, leafy hill topped by a little model of the Eiffel Tower.

★ *Don't leave town without sipping a cup of Prague grog – hot rum with water, lemon and sugar.*

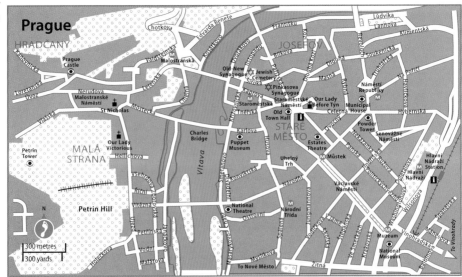

24 hours in the city

Astronomical clock

Start early with a coffee in **Old Town Square** to beat the crowds – the astronomical clock begins its daily whirrings at 0900. Look into the brooding hulk of **Our Lady Before Týn** before striking north along Parízská and into the **Josefov** district. Take a look at the **Old-New Synagogue** and the exhibitions in the **Pinkasova Synagogue** before strolling through the eerily atmospheric **Jewish Cemetery**. For a snack or early lunch, stroll back along Parízská which is lined with cafés and restaurants. Veer west and you'll hit the river and picture-postcard **Charles Bridge**, with its buskers and views of the red-roofed houses of Malá Strana creeping up towards the castle. Once across the bridge, wander along the cobbled lanes centering on **Malostranské náměstí**, the area's busiest square. Lunch at trendy *Square*, before the stiff climb up to the castle. You'll need a good few hours to stroll around the complex, after which you'll have earned a Czech beer at one of the little, smoke-filled pubs in Malá Strana.

Continue the traditional theme for dinner at *U Medvídků*, back in the Old Town, before checking out the live jazz at *AghaRTA*, Zelezna 16. Or, catch the Prague Symphony Orchestra at the **Municipal House**.

⊖ Travel essentials

Getting there Ruzyně Airport, www.csl.cz, is 20 km northwest of the centre. Buses run every 20 mins to the city centre, taking 20 mins. No 119 runs to Dejvicka metro station, No 100 to Zlicin metro, and No 179 to Nove Butovice metro. **CEDAZ**, T220-114296, runs a minibus shuttle to Náměstí Republiky (CZK 90 per person) every 30 mins daily 0600-2130. Private CEDAZ buses can be booked for up to 4 people and cost CZK 480. Taxis from outside the airport terminal should cost around CZK 400-450 to the centre.

Getting around The Old Town is very easy to walk around, as is Malá Strana – although the climb to the castle might be too steep for some. **Dopravní Podnik** (DP), T296-191817, www.dp-praha.cz, runs Prague's limited metro system, extensive **tram** and **bus** network, as well as a **funicular train** to the top of Petř ín hill. The metro system has 3 lines: A (green), B (yellow) and C (red), running daily 0500-2400. Trams operate daily 0430-2400; buses run at similar times. Tram Nos 51-59 and bus Nos 502-514 and 601-603 run at night. The funicular runs daily 0900-2320. Tickets need to be bought before boarding and are available from DP Information offices, some metro stations, tourist information centres and newsstands. The single ticket system is complicated, so visitors are better off buying a 1-, 3- or 7-day pass (CZK 100, CZK 200, CZK 250 respectively). Tickets must be validated in the machines at stops and in metro stations before travel.

Tourist information Prague Information Office, T12444, www.pis.cz, has several outlets. At the time of writing, a new office was due to open in Lucerna Passage, Vodickova 36. There is also an office in the Old Town Hall (Apr-Oct Mon-Fri 0900-1900, Sat and Sun 0900-1800; Nov-Mar Mon-Fri 0900-1800, Sat and Sun 0900-1700) and in Hlavní nádraží railway station (Apr-Oct Mon-Fri 0900-1700, Sat and Sun 0900-1600; Nov-Mar Mon-Fri 0900-1800, Sat and Sun 0900-1500). The **Prague Card** is a 3-day admission card to 40 monuments and museums, and can be purchased with or without travel on public transport. 3 days with transport costs CZK 810; 3 days without is CZK 590.

Exchange rate Czech Koruna (CZK). £1 = CZK 43.78. €1 = CZK 29.70.

⊙ Sights

Pražský hrad (Prague Castle)
ⓘ *T224-373368, www.hrad.cz. Castle grounds daily Apr-Oct 0500-0000; Nov-Mar 0600-2300. Buildings daily Apr-Oct 0900-1700; Nov-Mar 0900-1600. Combined ticket CZK 350. Tram 12, 18, 20, 22 or 23, metro Malostranská.*

Prague Castle has dominated the city's skyline for over a thousand years. Its sprawling complex merits at least half a day's exploration. The first evidence of a castle here dates back to AD 880 and, over the following millennium, the site became the monarchic and spiritual powerhouse of the country. Today it feels like a walled town and is reputedly the world's largest castle, its courtyards linking the palace, cathedral, several churches, museums, galleries and a monastery, all beautifully lit up an night.

Your first port of call should be **St Vitus' Cathedral** (Chrám sv Vita), the seat of the Archbishop of Prague. The interior of this magnificent Gothic structure is delicately lit by a series of mosaic-style stained-glass windows.

Prague Castle and Malá Strana

Saint Vitus' Cathedral

Look out for **St Wenceslas's Chapel**, resplendent with over a thousand semi-precious stones.

The **Old Royal Palace** (Starý královský palác) is worth seeing for the soaring, empty expanse of Vladislav Hall. It once hosted coronation celebrations; today presidents of the Republic are sworn in here. Wander around the rest of the palace before exiting by **St George's Basilica** (sv Jiří), with its beautifully preserved Romanesque interior, where chamber music recitals are held. Next door is the old monastery, now a gallery.

Behind the monastery is **Golden Lane** (Zlatá Ulička), a cobbled street, lined with 16th-century cottages, today filled with craft shops. (The Prague-born writer, Franz Kafka, briefly stayed at No 22.) At the end of the lane is the **Toy Museum** (Muzeum hraček) ⓘ *daily 0930-1730, CZK 60*, filled with traditional wooden toys and, oddly, hundreds of Barbie dolls. Opposite is **Lobkovicz Palace** (Lobkovický palác) ⓘ *Tue-Sun 0900-1700, CZK 40*, with its rambling historical collection. Also worth exploring are the castle gardens, particularly the peaceful **Royal Gardens**, which have beautiful views.

Malá Strana
ⓘ *Tram 12, 18, 20, 22 or 23, metro Malostranská.*

This wedge of land between the castle and Vltava River, often bypassed by visitors, is a delightful, atmospheric area of cobbled lanes and crumbling baroque façades. At its heart is **Malostranské náměstí**, a busy square fringed with grand, neoclassical houses and elegant colonnades. In the centre is the baroque **St Nicholas church** (Sv Mikuláš chrám) ⓘ *0900-1700, CZK 50*, built in the early 18th century. Its prominent green dome and tower quickly became a major Prague landmark. The inside is quite overwhelming, awash with hectic, multicoloured frescoes.

Petřín
ⓘ *Tram 6, 9, 12 or 20 to Újezd.*

A steep funicular railway, dating from the 1891 Jubilee Exhibition, climbs up green and leafy Petřín hill. At the top of the funicular, pause awhile to soak up the views, then follow the path along the old city wall, which passes a rose garden and observatory, to the **Petřín Observation**

Petřín

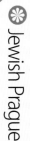

Jewish Prague

Before the Nazi occupation from 1939-1945, Prague's Jewish population was a thriving community, numbering some 50,000. Today, the number has dwindled to around 4,000. The focal point of the community remains the Josefov district, named after Emperor Josef II, whose 1781 reforms helped bestow civil rights to the Jewish community. The original ghetto actually dated back to the 13th century, although much of it was cleared in a huge late-19th century development project. This drove out the poorer sections of the community and transformed the winding old alleys into smart boulevards, lined with elegant mansions. With the arrival of the Nazis came forced removals, both to a new ghetto in Trezín, 60 km from the city, and, later, to concentration camps; a staggering two thirds of the population is thought to have died in camps before the end of the war. Ironically, what was left of the old ghetto was spared demolition by Nazi forces thanks to Adolph Hitler's chilling wish to preserve the area as an "exotic museum of an extinct race".

Tower (Petřínská rozhledna) ① *May-Aug daily 1000-2200, Sep-Apr Mon-Fri 1000-1900, Sat-Sun 1000-1700, CZK 50.* This 60-m high structure is a small-scale version of the Eiffel Tower, also dating from the Exhibition, with a viewing platform offering fabulous views over rooftops, broken by the soaring silhouettes of dozens of spires. Next door is a small neo-Gothic castle featuring a mirror maze (same times and prices as the tower).

Charles Bridge (Karlův most)

Prague's oldest bridge was founded in 1357 by Charles IV and, for many centuries, was the only link between the right and left banks. Today, it is best known for its dozens of statues, although most of these were added in the 18th century. The car-free bridge is thronged with tourists and buskers at all times of day but, at night, the bridge empties out and takes on a fairytale quality, never more so than in winter, with snowflakes drifting over the water.

Old Town Square (Staroměstské náměstí)
① *Tram 17 or 18, metro Staroměstská.*

All roads in Bohemia once led to Staroměstské náměstí, still Prague's most important and jaw-dropping square, a vast cobbled expanse flanked by brightly painted baroque houses. Centrepiece is the Town Hall, home to the extraordinary **Astronomical clock** (Orloj) in a tower to the right. Crowds

Karlův most

Staroměstské náměstí

gather on the hour (0900-2100) to watch the figures shuffle out from little doors. They portray various saints, as well as representations of death, vanity, history and greed – the latter is a dodgy depiction of a Jew clutching money bags, albeit minus his beard, which was removed at the end of the war.

Behind the Town Hall is the looming, blackened church of **Our Lady Before Týn** (Panna Marie pred Týnem), its Gothic hulk hiding a surprisingly pretty baroque interior. In winter, a **Christmas market** selling mulled wine, souvenirs and wooden toys is held on the square.

Josefov
ⓘ *Tram 17 or 18, metro Staroměstská.*

Prague's old Jewish ghetto is one of the most atmospheric quarters of the city. It's no longer the warren of old streets depicted by Kafka, but the main sights – four synagogues and the cemetery – remain. A good starting point is the **Old-New Synagogue** (Staranová synagoga) ⓘ *Cervená 2, Sun-Thu 0930-1800, Fri 0900-1300, CZK 200*, a squat structure dating from 1275. It still functions as a synagogue, making it the

Old-New Synagogue

Municipal House

oldest still in use in Europe. The other sights in Josefov are visited as part of the **Jewish Museum** (Zidovské Muzeum) ⓘ *T221-711511, www.jewish museum.cz, Sun-Fri Apr-Oct 0900-1800, Nov-Mar 0900-1630, CZK 300*. The most striking is the **Old Jewish Cemetery** (Starý zidovský hrbitov). Used from 1439 to 1787, it is the oldest and largest Jewish cemetery in Europe. It is a poignant, mysterious place, with hundreds of ancient headstones bristling from the ground at haphazard angles. The adjoining **Pinkas Synagogue** (Pinkasova sinagoga) holds a moving Holocaust memorial, with chilling pictures drawn by children from the Trezín ghetto outside Prague, most of whom were later transported to concentration camps.

Republic Sqaure (Náměstí Republiky)
ⓘ *Tram 3, 5, 14, 24 or 26, metro Náměstí Republiky.*

This busy square, in the east of Nové Město is worth visiting for the **Municipal House** (Obecní dům), the city's finest art nouveau building. An exuberantly decorated cultural centre,

it was opened in 1912 on the site of King's Court. There's a restaurant and opulent café on site, as well as the Smetana concert hall. Next door is **Powder Tower** (Prasná brána) ⓘ *daily 1000-1800, CZK 50*, one of a series of towers that once fortified the Old Town and were used to store gunpowder. The sharply pointed, medieval tower is the starting point of the 'Royal Mile', along which Bohemian kings once marched towards their coronation. You can climb to the top for views over Staré Město.

Wenceslas Square (Václavské náměstí)
ⓘ *Tram 3, 9, 14 or 24, metro Muzeum or Můstek.*

Site of the most important political protests in the city for the last 150 years, this sloping space is more like a long, divided avenue than a square. Most famously, it was the backdrop to the 'Velvet Revolution' of 1989, when half a million people gathered to protest against the government. At the southern end of the square is a statue of St Wenceslas, as well as the vast **National Museum** (see Best of the rest box).

National Museum

⊚ Best of the rest

National Museum (Národní muzeum) ① *T224-497111, www.nm.cz, daily 1000-1800, closed on first Tue of every month, CZK 100.* This hulking, neo-renaissance building houses an enormous collection of almost 14 million items of natural history, art and music.

Puppet Museum (Marionette Muzeum) ① *Karlova 12, T222-220928, www.puppetart.com, daily 1200-2000.* Impressive collection of wooden puppets and a marionette theatre with regular performances (phone for times and tickets). This is also the headquarters of the international puppetry organization, UNIMA.

Church of Our Lady Victorious (Chrám Panny Marie Vítězné) ① *www.pragjesu.info, Mon-Sat 0930-1730, Sun 1300-1700.* Home of the *Infant Jesus of Prague*, a 14th-century wax statue, measuring 28 cm, that was presented to the Carmelites in 1628 and is revered in Catholic countries around the world. Its spangly outfits are changed regularly by the nuns.

⊙ Sleeping

Prague is crammed with characterful guesthouses and hotels; those in Staré Město tend to be more expensive, while those in Malá Strana are quieter.

€€€ Hotel Aria, Triziste 9, T225-334111, www.ariahotel.net. As implied by the name, this is one for music-lovers. It's a baroque hotel with a contemporary interior and composer-themed rooms, a comprehensive CD library, a musical director on hand to advise on concert venues in Prague, a music salon and a roof-top café.

€€€ Hotel Josef, Rybná 20, Josefov, T221-700111, www.hoteljosef.com. Prague's most stylish hotel is a minimalist haven of glass, calm white lighting and the odd splash of colour. Rooms have groovy touches like DVD players and Sony Playstations. Models and rock stars make this their first port of call.

€€€ U Pava, U Luzického semináre 32, T257-533360, www.romantic hotels.cz/upava. Characterful, historical hotel on a leafy street in Malá Strana. Rooms have heavy curtains, thick rugs on wooden floors, painted, restored ceilings and patches of over-the-top original frescoes on the walls. Views of the castle or over the old town.

€€ Dum u Velke Boty, Vlašská 30/333, T257-532088, www.dumuvelke boty.cz. A welcoming family-run outfit on a quiet square in Malá Strana with attractive, antique-filled rooms. There's art on the walls, simple brass beds and parquet floors. Charles Bridge is a 10-min walk away, and the owners are a great source of local information.

€€ U Karlova Mostu, Na Kampe 15, T257-531430, www.archibald.cz. Atmospheric, old-fashioned house just 50 m from Charles Bridge. Cosy rooms with wooden floors and stencilled walls; the room in the attic has a lovely beamed ceiling.

€€ U Zlatého Jelena, Celetná 11/Štuparská 6, T222-317237. Simple, airy rooms with parquet flooring, brass beds and tall windows, just a few steps from Old Town Square. Ask for a room overlooking the quiet courtyard. The staff are friendly and the breakfasts (included in the price) are substantial.

€ Betlem Club, Betlémskeé městi 9, T222-2215745, www.betlemclub.cz. Good-value hotel on a quiet square, a short walk from Old Town Square. The rooms are small and comfortable, with dark wood furniture – some of it incongruously modern. Breakfast is served in a vaulted cellar.

⊙ Eating

The restaurant scene in Prague has improved immeasurably in recent years; for one thing, pork is no longer the key ingredient in all dishes. Although a traditional meal in a *pivnice* (pub) remains an essential part of a visit to Prague, there are now also a number of top-notch restaurants serving international cuisine.

Breakfast

¶ **Au Gourmand**, Dlouhá 10, T222-329060. Upmarket French boulangerie in the Old Town, serving a delicious selection of pastries, cakes, snacks and Italian coffees in a cool, tiled interior.

¶ **Café Imperial**, Na Poříčí 15, T222-316012. Gorgeous high-ceilinged Hapsburg-era café, with tiled walls, rickety furniture and excellent coffee – served with free doughnuts in the mornings. Breakfasts are big plates of eggs and sausages, and there are more substantial meals throughout the day.

Lunch

¶¶ **Nebozízek**, Petrínské sady 411, T257-315329, www.nebozizek.cz. Brilliant views from this traditional restaurant half-way up the funicular to Petřín, with a bright glass-covered terrace. Good salads and Bohemian onion soup, plus fresh fish and hearty game dishes.

¶¶ **Square**, Malostranské náměstí 5, T296-826104. What was once a favourite hang-out of Kafka's is today an elegant restaurant, with vaulted ceilings and a well-heeled clientele who come for the Italianesque menu.

Dinner

¶¶ **Kampa Park**, Na Kampě 8b, T296-826102. This is Prague's most sophisticated restaurant, with a heated terrace that overlooks the river. It has a contemporary menu, complemented by a 150-strong wine list. The cooking is sublime: expect things like langoustine ravioli followed by baby chicken with chanterelles and chorizo.

¶¶ **U Maltézských rytírů**, Prokopská 10/297, T257-530075. Snug, Gothic cellars with formal high-backed chairs and white linen tablecloths. This place feels either romantic or cold, depending on how busy it is, but the food is great – there's a melt-in-the-mouth chateaubriand and a good choice of game dishes.

¶ **U Medvídků**, a Perštýň 7, T224-211916. This wood-panelled, smoke-filled and genuinely old-fashioned beer hall attracts a mix of local regulars and tourists. The food is traditional Czech stodge – pork, dumplings and sauerkraut – perfect for soaking up a few jars of the delicious on-tap Budvar.

✪ Nightlife

The English-language *Welcome to Prague* publication, produced by the tourist office, has basic seasonal information on up-to-date events. Tickets for most venues can be bought online at www.ticketpro.cz or www.ticketportal.cz.

Bars and clubs

Traditional Prague nightlife revolves around top-notch beer and smoky pubs (*pivnice*), such as **Baráčnická rhychta** (Tržiště 23) in Malá Strana or **Kozicka** (Kozi 1) in Staré Město. The local beer is the main draw, thanks to famous names such as *Pilsner Urquell*, *Staropramen* and *Budvar*. One drawback of these good-value brews, however, is that they attract a profusion of stag parties from the UK. Many bars and pubs now ban such groups from their premises altogether.

Beer aside, many bars offer nightly live music; the jazz scene is thriving

❝❞ the jazz scene is thriving and it suits the vaulted, smoky cellars of the Old Town particularly well.

and it suits the vaulted, smoky cellars of the Old Town particularly well. The **Prague Jazz Festival** is held every autumn at **AghaRTA**, Zelezna 16, www.arta.cz.

A number of stylish cocktail bars have sprung up around town in recent years, not to mention dodgy Irish-themed pubs, mostly aimed at tourists. To find some of the best of the former, head to the streets around the north of Old Town Square. Most of the city's nightclubs are yet to undergo a 21st-century style makeover but they continue to pull in the punters until the wee small hours.

Music, ballet and opera

Music is the lifeblood of the city, and you can barely walk a step without hearing classical strains wafting out of a church, concert hall or home. Music-lovers flock to Prague every May for **Prague Spring**, T257-312547, www.festival.cz, one of the world's leading classical music festivals. It has been running since 1946 and attracts scores of symphony, philharmonic and chamber orchestras. It begins every year on 12th May with a performance of Smetana's *Má vlast* (*My Country*) and closes three weeks later with Beethoven's *9th Symphony*.

High-quality concerts can be enjoyed at other times of year, too. Prague's classical music venues are among the most beautiful buildings in the city. The Prague Symphony Orchestra plays at the **Municipal House**, on Námeští Republiky (see above), while the illustrious Czech Philharmonic performs at the splendid **Rudolfinum**, Alsovo nabr 12, T227-059244, www.rudolfinum.cz.

Performances of opera and ballet are held amid the neo-Renaissance magnificence of the **National Theatre** (Národní divadlo), Národní trída, T224-933782, www.narodni-divadlo.cz; at the opulent **State Opera**, Legerova 75, www.czechopera.cz, and at the **Estates Theater** (Stavovské divadlo), Ovocný trh, T224-215001, www.stavovskedivadlo.cz. The latter, a beautiful cream and pistachio building, is Prague's oldest theatre and hosted the premieres of Mozart's *Don Giovanni* and *La Clemenza de Tito* in the 18th century. *Don Giovanni* remains one of the most popular operas performed here to this day.

European City Breaks Prague

Reykjavík is the coolest of cities. And that's not just because it's the most northerly capital in the world. Set in an expanse of lava fields, close to both the largest desert and biggest glacier in Europe, this remote outpost is so far off the European map it has virtually been granted a licence to be quirky, unconventional and ground-breaking in its music, architecture, sculpture and even lifestyle. With a population of only around 113,000, it is hardly a teeming metropolis but what it lacks in size, Reykjavík more than makes up for in the brio and creativity of its youthful population. This restless energy is reflected in powerful, subterranean forces of nature which, with typical ingenuity, have been harnessed to make life more bearable in this harsh, unforgiving environment.

Reykjavík

Arts & culture
★★★

Eating
★★

Nightlife
★★★★

Outdoors
★★★★★

Romance
★

Shopping
★

Sightseeing
★★

Value for money
★

Overall score
★★☆

At a glance

The bohemian old town of Reykjavík, known as **101**, is situated between two water features: the harbour and the pond. In between you'll find the heart of the city, **Austurvöllur Square**, with the historic Alþing parliament building and cathedral. Follow the main street, **Austurstraeti**, and you reach Lækjatorg Square, from where the buses leave and the roads radiate. Across the road and up the hill is **Laugavegur**, the city's busiest street, buzzing with shops, bars and cafés. Down by the harbour – at weekends – you'll find the flea market where you can try specialities such as dried cod or putrefied shark meat (only for those with strong stomachs). Towering above the city is the soaring steeple of **Hallgrímskirkja**, always useful for finding your bearings. The other dominant feature on the city's skyline is **Perlan** (the Pearl), which sits above the city's hot water tanks. To the east of 101 is **Laugardalur Valley** where you'll find the city's largest thermal swimming pool, the botanical gardens, zoo and one of the city's best sculpture

What angered the gods, when the lava flowed, on which we are standing now?

Kristni saga, Snorri goði

museums. Just beyond the city itself is the vast emptiness of Iceland's weird and wonderful volcanic countryside. Even if you only have a few days, it's worth making the effort to get out of the city.

★ *Don't leave town without taking a walk along the harbour to see the viking boat sculpture, Sólfar, meaning 'Sun Voyager'.*

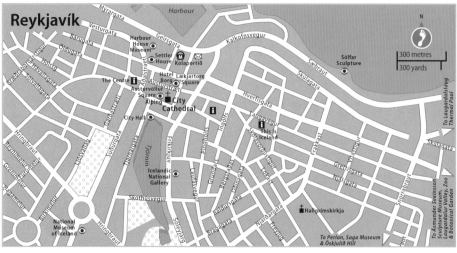

Reykjavik more than a city break…

ICELAND

FLY DRIVES

CITY BREAKS

ESCORTED TOURS

ACTIVITY

WEEKENDS

SPECIAL INTEREST

WHALE WATCHING

FESTIVE TREATS

NATURE BREAKS

TAILOR-MADE

For details see our
summer or winter
Arctic Experience brochures

Iceland specialists offering a wide
range of year round holidays

24 Hour Brochure Line on 01737 218801

www.discover-the-world.co.uk/iceland

DISCOVER
THE WORLD

⊙ Sights

Austurvöllur Square

Although Lækjatorg Square is the actual centre, Austurvöllur is the real heart of the city. The grassy square was originally six times bigger than it is today and thought to be the site of Ingólfur Arnarson's farm – Reykjavík's first settler. Today it's a popular meeting place, surrounded by cafés and bars. The small church (1787) is actually the modest **city cathedral**; next to it is the **Alþing** (Parliament House), overlooked by a stern-looking statue of **Jón Sigurdsson** who led Iceland to independence from Denmark in 1944. In the corner of the square is **Hotel Borg**, a graceful art deco hotel, frequented by the rich and famous. Surprisingly, the Icelandic rock revolution of the 1980s began here and the hotel became a mecca for the city's young punks.

Austurvöllur Square

Aðalstræti

This is the oldest street in Reykjavík and recent archaeological excavations have revealed the impressive remains of what is thought to be one of the very first settler houses, dating from AD 874-930. The site is due to open as a museum in 2006, www.citymuseum.is,

and is located under the *Hotel Centrum*. The city's oldest surviving house, dating from 1752, is at Aðalstræti 10; it's now a bar-bistro called *Viðalín*.

Tjörnin and around

The town pond, Tjörnin, is popular with young and old alike who come for a stroll or to feed the ducks and greylag geese. It was created millions of years ago at the end of the last Ice Age as a sand and gravel bar was built up by the pounding waves of Faxaflói Bay. The futuristic building that seems to rise right out of the pond is the **City Hall** ⓘ *Mon-Fri 0800-1900, Sat-Sun 1200-1800, free*. Inside is a large relief map of Iceland, a café and a small information desk. On the east side of the pond is the **Icelandic National Gallery** ⓘ *Fríkirkjuvegur 7, T515-9600, www.listasafn.is, Tue-Sun 1100-1700, closed Mon, ISK 500, free on Wed*, which shows exhibitions from around the world and has a small

⊙ Travel essentials

Getting there **Keflavík International Airport**, T425-0600, www.airport.is, is 48 km from Reykjavík. The reliable **Flybus** meets all incoming flights and drops you at your hotel or guest house, ISK 1150, 45 mins. For organized trips to Iceland, contact: **Discover the World Ltd**, 29 Nork Way, Banstead, Surrey, SM7 1PB, T01737-214214, www.discoverthe world.co.uk/iceland.

Getting around 101 Reykjavík is small enough to walk around on foot and a stroll around town won't take you more than 20 mins. To walk to Laugavegur Valley or Öskjuhlíð Hill takes about 30 mins, or there are regular buses.

The yellow **straeto** city buses operate Mon-Fri 0700-2400, Sat-Sun 1000-2400. They are reliable and

efficient, running every 20 mins, less frequently at weekends. A single fare costs ISK 220. Lækjatorg Sq is the main bus terminal for local travel, where you can pick up route maps and timetables. Reykjavík is well suited to cycling as it is mainly flat. Bike rental is available from guest houses and a number of places across town for around ISK 1500 a day. If you want to get out of the city, it's probably best to hire a car (**ALP Car Rental**, T562-6060) or take a tour.

Tourist information The tourist season runs from Jun-Sep, after which many hotels shut down. Reykjavík's main tourist office is **The Centre**, Aðalstræti 2, T590-1500, www.visitreykjavik.is. Jun-Aug daily 0830-1800, Sep-May Mon-Fri 0900-1700, Sat-Sun 1000-1400.

They provide all the information you could possibly need and can arrange tours, car hire and concert tickets. There's a bureau de change, internet access and tax refund centre here.

Also useful is **This is Iceland**, Laugavegur 20, T561-6010, www.this.is/ iceland, a friendly and helpful information centre offering free internet and tour booking service. It's easy to spot with a red canoe across the front wall.

The **Reykjavik Card** is an economical way of seeing the major museums and swimming pools as well as being a free bus pass. It costs ISK 1200 for 24 hrs, ISK 1700 for 48 hrs and ISK 2200 for 72 hrs. Available from the tourist office.

Exchange rate Icelandic Kronur (ISK). £1 = ISK 106.12. €1 = ISK 71.65.

sculpture garden. On the opposite side of the pond you can see the street of **Tjarnargata** with its colourful early-20th-century timber houses.

National Museum of Iceland

ⓘ *Suðurgata 41, T530-2200, www.nat mus.is. 1 May-15 Sep, daily 1000-1700, 16 Sep-30 Apr, Tue-sun 1100-1700. ISK 600. Wed free.*

South of the pond the National Museum is the best place to get a sense of 1200 years of Icelandic history. Tangible exhibitions and multimedia displays provide a fascinating insight into the Icelandic culture and how the nation has developed from the times of the earliest settlers to the present day. The exhibitions cover diverse aspects of the country's history, such as mythology, the construction of early Viking buildings, the adoption of Christianity, the Reformation and the Census of 1703. It is well worth a visit.

Old Harbour

Replaced by Sundahöfn as the main centre for commercial fishing vessels,

Sólfar (Sun Voyager)

Hallgrímskirkja

the old harbour has a certain charm (if you don't mind the lingering smell of fish) and remains busy with an influx of small fishing boats every now and then. Each weekend the **Kolaportið flea market** is held in the old customs building by the quay. Locals flock to browse through piles of bric-a-brac and second-hand clothes, and it's a good place to taste some Icelandic delicacies such as dried cod.

Just behind the customs building is the **Harbour House Museum** ⓘ *Tryggvagata 17, T511-5155, www.listasafnreykjavikur.is, daily 1100-1800, Thu till 1900, ISK 500, free on Mon*, which houses diverse exhibitions by Icelandic and foreign artists. The focus is modern and experimental with a permanent exhibition by contemporary Icelandic artist, Erró.

Hallgrímskirkja

ⓘ *Skólavörðustígur, T510-1000. Daily 0900-1700. Suggested donation ISK 50, tower view ISK 350 adults.*

Dominating Reykjavik's skyline is this controversial 74-m church reminiscent

of a volcanic eruption. It was designed as part of a competition and took 49 years to build (it was completed in 1986). While the interior is quite bare, the views from the top out over the city are wonderful. In front of the church is a statue of **Leifur Eríksson**, the Viking who is believed to have discovered America around AD1000.

Perlan and the Saga Museum

ⓘ *Öskjuhlíð Hill, T562-0200, www.perlan.is. Observatory daily 1000-2330. Free. Bus 7 from Lækjatorg Sq.*

Sitting on top of Öskjuhlíð Hill, the Pearl is the nearest thing the city has to the Eiffel Tower, with viewpoints out over the city, a café and revolving gourmet restaurant inside. The iconic circular glass building sits atop the city's hot-water storage tanks and holds regular art exhibitions, expos and concerts and houses one of the city's best museums, the **Saga Museum** ⓘ *T511-1517, www.sagamuseum.is, daily 1000-1800, winter 1200-1700, ISK 800*, which charts the early history of the country through the medieval stories of the sagas.

Being so close to nature is a major appeal when visiting Reykjavík and it's easy to get out of the city for a half or full day. **Iceland Excursions**, www.icelandexcursions.is, or **The Activity Group**, www.activity.is, offer a variety of activities and tours, often in combination with a visit to the Blue Lagoon or Golden Circle. The numerous outdoor activities include **dog sledding**, **horse riding** across lava fields, and **river rafting** on thrilling white water rapids or through serene canyons. Thrill-seekers can try their hand at **snowmobiling**, an exhilarating way to see the breathtaking ice fields and glaciers, and **whale-watchers** can see Minke, humpback and orca in Iceland's waters, as well as dolphins and seals.

Down at the foot of the hill you'll find **Nauthólsvík Beach**, a quirky man-made beach with imported yellow sand and geothermal pools. A dip here is a must, come rain or shine.

Laugardalur Valley

ⓘ *Bus 14 from Lækjatorg Sq.*

The name Reykjavík literally translates as 'smoky bay', the first settlers having mistaken the steam from the hot springs in the Laugardalur Valley for smoke. The springs are now used to feed the the **Laugardalslaug Thermal Pool** ⓘ *Laugardalur, T553-4039, Mon-Fri 0650-2130, Sat-Sun 0800-2000, ISK 200*, the city's biggest swimming pool.

Across from the pool complex is the white-domed **Ásmunder Sveinsson Sculpture Museum** ⓘ *Sigtún, T553-2155, www.listasafnreykjavikur.is, May-Sep daily 1000-1600, Oct-Apr 1300-1600, ISK 500*. Ásmunder Sveinsson was one of the pioneers of Icelandic sculpture and many of his abstract sculptures draw on Icelandic literature, fairytales and nature.

Blue Lagoon

ⓘ *240 Grindavík, Reykjanes Peninsula, T420-8800, www.bluelagoon.is. 15 May-31 Aug daily 0900-2100,; 1 Sep-14 May daily 1000-2000. ISK 1400. 40 mins' drive.*

One of Iceland's most visited tourist attractions, the Blue Lagoon is best visited en route to the airport – it's the perfect way to relax at the end of your trip. The lagoon is a steaming pool of milky turquoise water that leaches minerals from the lava bed, filling it with healing properties. Lie back, put on a mud pack and try not to let that whiff of sulphur put you off.

Golden Circle

One of the most popular day trips, the Golden Circle takes in three of Iceland's finest natural and historic features within a day's journey of Reykjavík and is a good way to get a taste of the country's bizarre scenery. **Þingvellir National Park**, www.thingvellir.is, was the site of the ancient Viking parliament. In the centre of the park you can see a dramatic rift in the earth where the Eurasian and American continental plates are pulling part by 2cm a year. **Geysir**, is the site of the original spouting hot spring that gave its name to all such natural features. Although it's no longer very active, another hot spring, Strokkur, spurts up to around 30 m, every four minutes. **Gulfoss** is a huge two-step waterfall that partially freezes in winter. If possible, it's best to hire a car, but there are plenty of tours available.

Ásmunder Sveinsson Sculpture Museum

Blue Lagoon

🛏 Sleeping

Reykjavík has a great range of accommodation from extravagant hotels to quality guesthouses.

€€€ **Hotel 101**, Hverfisgata 10, T580-0101, www.101hotel.is. An ultra-fashionable boutique outfit with sculptures, murals, Icelandic art and an airy bar and restaurant. It's all very minimalist chic and the spa and gym downstairs will help you keep as glam as the surroundings. A futuristic luxury experience in the heart of the city.

€€€ **Hotel Borg**, Pósthússtræti 11, T551-1440, www.hotelborg.is. Reykjavik's finest, an art deco hotel in Austurvöllur Square with lovingly preserved rooms and modern art. It's a movie-star haunt: Catherine Deneuve shacked up here when she came to visit Björk and Marlene Dietrich stayed in 1944.

€€ **Hotel Klöpp**, Klapparstígur 26, T511-6060, www.centrehotels.is. Fashionable central 3-star hotel. Sleek modern design, neutral and beige colours and wooden floors. Klöpp means 'stone' or 'rock' and it has great views across the bay to Mt Esja.

€€ **Guesthouse 101**, Laugavegur 101, T562-6101, www.iceland101.is. Modern and spacious guest house with moderate-sized rooms in the centre of the city. Ideal location for shopping, drinking and dining in a large concrete building just off the main street.

€ **Salvation Army Guesthouse**, Kirkjustræti 2, T561-3203, www.guesthouse.is. The cheapest and best value place to stay in 101, with sleeping-bag accommodation, small shared rooms and a kitchen. Bathrooms are shared and it's a bit of a squeeze, but it's in a great location.

🍴 Eating

There is plenty of both Icelandic and international cuisine. Standards are high – and so are the prices.

🍴🍴 **Prir Frakkar**, Baldursgata 14, T552-3939, www.3frakkar.com. Meaning the 'three Frenchmen', this seafood restaurant specializes in Icelandic classics such as puffin and whale meat. Small, intimate and traditional. Free wine if you have to wait for a table.

🍴🍴 **Siggi Hall**, Thórsgata 1, T511-6677, www.siggihall.com. Reykjavik's finest restaurant. Siggi Hall is known to Icelanders all over for his regular weekly TV show and, now that he's opened up a city centre restaurant, for his shellfish soufflé and *bacalao* (salt cod). It's a stylish and relaxed place to dine, particularly good for its Icelandic fish, game and lamb.

🍴🍴 **Tveir Fiskar**, Geirsgata 9, T511-3473, www.restaurant.is. Refined Icelandic fish restaurant overlooking the harbour. Specialities include oyster soup, smoked puffin with pear marmalade and caviar. A high-quality gourmet affair with a feng-shui inspired interior.

🍴 **Sægreifinn**, Verbúð 8, T553 1500. Daily 0800-1800. Run by 3 local fishermen including the 'sea baron' himself, this is actually a fish shop with a couple of wooden benches outside. The charming harbour setting and truly rustic feel make it a good, cheap spot for lunch. Try the delicious lobster soup or a barbecued fish kebab.

🍴 **Baejarins Beztu**, corner of Tryggvagata and Pósthússtræti. Reykjavik's original hot dog kiosk has become something of an institution. The hot dogs (*pylsur*) come with mustard, ketchup and raw and fried onions and are very tasty.

🌙 Nightlife

Bars and clubs

For many people, Reykjavík's nightlife is the main reason for coming to this cold and windswept spot. It feels a bit odd compared to clubbing in other European destinations, particularly given the size of the city, but just as the country is geologically young and dynamic, so is nightlife. The long summer days and yawning winter nights give a whole new twist to the concept of partying till dawn. Friday and Saturday are the wildest nights with clubbing from 2400-0800. The bars and clubs don't really fill up until 2400 as the high prices force many of the locals to drink at home before heading into town. A pint of beer costs around ISK 600. You'll find plenty of bars on and around Laugavegur such as: funky **Sirkus**, Klapparstígur 30; bohemian **Kaffee Barinn**, Bergstadastræti 1; trendy **Oliver**, Laugavegur 20a; and lively **Vegamót**, Vegamótastígur 4. Later on **Pravda**, Austurstræti 22, is one of the larger clubs; **Sólon**, Bankastræti 7a, is also a popular spot to dance the night away. Many bars also have some very decent DJ sets at weekends. To round it all off when the bars and clubs have closed, head for Austurvöllur Sq where people tend to hang around before heading home.

Live music

Every other person in Reykjavík seems to be a musician and it's possible to find live music any night of the week here. The best places to try are: **Gaukur á Stong**, Tryggvagata 22; **Grand Rock**, Smiðjustígur 6; and **Nelly's Café**, Þinghóltstræti 2, for anything from jazz to rock.

Riga

Riga has long been the largest and most cosmopolitan city in the Baltic region, a trading port on the River Daugava which was once a member of the powerful Hanseatic League. Despite having spent almost all of its 800-year history under foreign rule – most recently by Nazi Germany and the Soviet Union – Riga has retained a strong sense of its own Latvian identity. Yet for all the historical riches of this UNESCO World Heritage Site, evident in buildings ranging from Gothic to art nouveau, this is a city looking to the future. While it may not yet have regained its1930s reputation as the 'Paris of the north', tourists are rapidly warming to Riga's attractive blend of bohemian charm and vibrant nightlife.

Arts & culture
★★★

Eating
★★

Nightlife
★★★

Outdoors
★★

Romance
★★★

Shopping
★★

Sightseeing
★★★

Value for money
★★★

Overall score
★★⁄

👁 Sights

The 350-m-tall **Freedom Monument** (Brivibas piemineklis or 'Milda'), built between the First and Second World Wars, just outside the old town, is a good place to start. Head across the canal past the **Laima clock** (Laimas pulkstenis) and linger in the bustling **Livs' Square** (Livu laukums) before climbing the steeple of **St Peter's Church** (Peterbaznica) ⓘ *Tue-Sun 1000-1800, Ls 2*, to get your bearings. From here it's a short distance to Town Hall Square and the recently rebuilt **House of the Blackheads** (Melngalvju nams) ⓘ *Tue-Sun 1000-1700, Ls 1.50*. Named after an organization of unmarried merchants, the Dutch Renaissance façade makes this one of Riga's most attractive buildings and it's worth squeezing in a visit to the museum to check out the interior. An ugly Soviet edifice nearby houses the

Town Hall Square

sobering **Museum of the Occupation of Latvia** (Latvijas okupacijas muzejs) ⓘ *Oct-Apr Tue-Sun 1100-1700; May-Sep daily 1100-1800, free,* detailing the horrors of the 20th century including a reconstruction of a gulag barracks. Head up Jauniela past *A&E* (No 17), the most upmarket of Riga's many amber shops, to visit the imposing mishmash

of architectural styles that is the **Dome Cathedral** (Doma baznica) ⓘ *Tue-Fri and Sun 1100-1600, Sat 1000-1400, Ls 0.50*. Don't miss the cathedral's impressive cross-vaulted gallery or the nearby **Three Brothers** (Tris brali), medieval buildings showcasing the styles of three different centuries. East of here, close to the canal, is the cylindrical **Powder Tower** (Pulvertornis) ⓘ *1000-1800, closed Mon- Tue, free,* once used to store gunpowder and now containing a war museum which is strong on 20th-century conflict. Head up Torna past the **Swedish Gate** (Zviedru varti) – all that remains of the old entrances to the city – to **Riga Castle** (Rigas pils). Originally built by crusaders and destroyed several times by townspeople, it now houses the Latvian president as well as two museums. One of these, the **History Museum of Latvia** (Latvijas vestures muzejs) ⓘ *Wed-Sun 1100-1700, Ls 0.70*, provides a good introduction to the

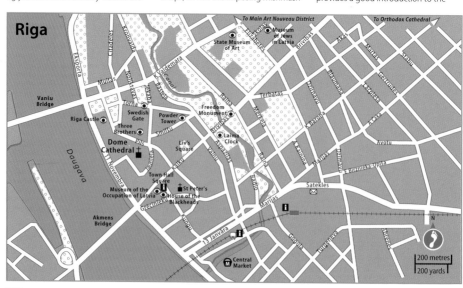
Riga

country. Crossing the canal on K Valdemara, a wander through the art nouveau district reveals numerous beautiful examples of the style: one of the best is at **Elizabetes 10b**. Return to the Freedom Monument via the small **Museum of Jews in Latvia** (Ebreji Latvija) ⓘ *Sun-Thu 1200-1700,* or the rather more grand **State Museum of Art** (Valsts makslas muzejs) ⓘ *Wed-Mon 1100- 1700, Ls 1, tour Ls 5,* with its comprehensive collection of Latvian art. The **Orthodox Cathedral** (Pareizticigo katedrale) is also worth visiting and was recently restored after being used as a planetarium in the Soviet period. Further south is the lively **Central Market** (Centraltirgus) ⓘ *daily 0800-1700,* housed in five huge Zeppelin hangars. Unless time is very short, visit the **Open Air Ethnographic Museum** (Etnografiskais brivdabas muzejs) ⓘ *daily 1000-1700; bus No 1 from corner of Merkela and Terbatas to Brivdabas, 30 mins,* which brings together rural buildings from all over Latvia. Craftspeople work on site, and traditional food and drink are available.

⏺ Sleeping

€€€ **Hotel Bergs**, Berga Bazars, Elizabetes iela 83/85, T777-0900, www.hotelbergs.lv. Formed from 2 19th-century buildings connected by a glass atrium, this boutique hotel in a fashionable district has been praised by *Condé Nast Traveller* and *Tatler* magazines.
€€ **Konventa Seta**, Kaleju 9/11, T708-7501, www.konventa.lv. A comfortable and central option housed in a 13th-century convent, with some rooms retaining oak beams alongside modern furnishings.

Central Market

APTIEKA

€ **Viktorija**, Caka 55, T701-4111, www.hotel-viktorija.lv. This restored art nouveau building is worth the short walk from the old town. Stay in the renovated wing unless on a very tight budget.

ⓐ Eating

ⓨ **Vincents**, Elizabetes 19, T733-2634. Celebrity chef Martiņš Ritiņš prepares innovative international cuisine, attracting stars and dignitaries to one of the best restaurants in the Baltics.
ⓨ **Lido Atputas Centrs**, Krasta 76, T750-4420. A hugely popular buffet housed in a giant log cabin, serving hearty Latvian standards – expect plenty of pork, potatoes, cabbage and bread – alongside many other dishes. There is also a restaurant and microbrewery, and an amusement park outside. Take tram 7 or 9 from the centre.
ⓨ **Sievasmates Piradzini**, Kalku 10. A great spot for a cheap meal of *piragi*, tasty Latvian pastries with a variety of fillings.
ⓨ **Traktieris**, Antonijas 8, T733-2455. Staff in traditional dress serve high quality Russian staples such as

⊖ Travel essentials

Getting there Riga International Airport is 8 km southwest of the city. There are regular buses to the centre, and taxis cost around Ls 6.

Getting around The best way to see the city centre is on foot, although there is an extensive network of buses, trolleybuses and trams with a flat fare of Ls 0.20 per journey. Minibuses ply fixed routes without a timetable and cost only a little more. When catching a taxi, look out for the yellow number plates of registered cabs.

Tourist information The main tourist office is at, Ratslaukums 6, T702-6072, www.rigatourism.com, daily 1000-1900. There are also tourist offices in the central train station and international bus station. The inexpensive publication *Riga In Your Pocket* is highly recommended. It lists upcoming events and includes a map showing public transport routes.

Exchange rate Latvian Lats (Ls). £1 = Ls 1.03. €1 = Ls 0.70.

borsch (beetroot soup) and bliny (pancakes), often accompanied by live folk music. A cheaper and quicker buffet is also available.

ⓞ Nightlife

In addition to world-class events at the **National Opera**, Aspazijas bulv 3, T707-3777, look out for organ recitals at the **Dome Cathedral**. Try **Cetri Balti Krekli**, Vecpilsetas 12, T721-3885, for live Latvian music, or enjoy a drink and the view from the 26th floor **Skyline** bar at the Reval Hotel Latvija, Elizabetes 55, T777-2222.

Clubbing options include the trendy **Spalvas Pa Gaisu**, Grecinieku 8, T722-0393.

Rome

All roads lead here, it wasn't built in a day and while in the city you should do as the locals do, which might at first glance appear to be a lot of suicidal driving, sitting in piazzas drinking *aperitivi* and shopping in expensive boutiques. The Eternal City is so layered with history, sights and legend that it's unwise to aim to do much more than scratch the surface. Much of Italy's best ancient Roman remains and Renaissance art and architecture is here, sometimes alongside (or even underneath) fascist-era monstrosities. The city's baroque fountains, despite being continually draped in camera-toting tourists, are spectacularly grand. And you should leave time for markets and museums, designer shops and *pizzerie* serving the thinnest, crispest pizzas. The Vatican – the world's smallest sovereign state, beloved of quiz masters everywhere – has more of interest than many large countries, from the gasp-inducing Sistine Chapel and Raphael masterpieces to St Peter's. Massively cleaned up and restored for the millennium, Rome is beginning to regain some of its patina but still has more monuments and churches open than was the case a decade ago. Its economy is bigger than New Zealand's and as the capital of a major European country and the centre of a world religion, it has a sense of being an intensely relevant, living city – a quality sometimes lacking in other Italian cities. Surrounded by over 2000 years of history, contemporary Rome continues to blithely go about its business.

Arts & culture
★★★★★

Eating
★★★★

Nightlife
★★★★

Outdoors
★

Romance
★★★★

Shopping
★★★★

Sightseeing
★★★★★

Value for money
★★

Overall score
★★★★✦

At a glance

Trains, and most of Rome's many visitors, arrive at **Termini** station, to the east of the city centre. Beyond the chaos in front of the station, via Nazionale heads from **piazza della Repubblica** southwest towards **piazza Venezia** and the main area of sights. The grandiose ugliness of the white marble **il Vittoriano** (Victor Emmanuel II monument), sits to the south of piazza Venezia, with the hill of the **Campidoglio** (one of Rome's famous seven hills, complete with great museums and a beautiful piazza) behind it. The biggest area of ancient ruins stretches east and south from the Campidoglio: the vast **Colosseum** (Colosseo) is beyond the **Foro Romano** and the hill of the

All things atrocious and shameless flock from all parts to Rome

Tacitus

Palatino – effectively a single archaeological zone of temples, arches, political and civic remains. The **River Tevere** (Tiber) winds through the city, with the central areas of Pantheon, Navona and campo

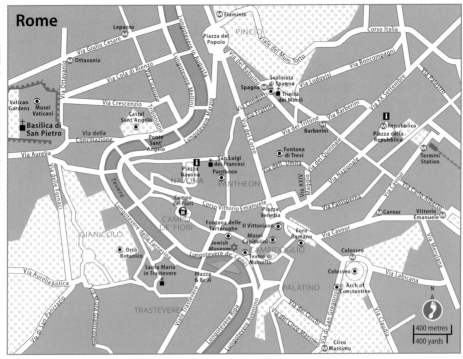

de' Fiori enclosed in the eastern side of a large bend. **Piazza Navona**, with grand fountains and buildings, is usually considered to be the central point of the city though the more earthy market piazza of **campo de' Fiori** just to the south has more reason to be thought of as Rome's heart. Also here are many of Rome's main sights – the **Pantheon** is the city's most complete Roman building and there are also many interesting churches and palazzi to visit. On the northeastern edge of this central area, **via del Corso** is a long straight road lined with many of the city's smartest shops, leading north to **piazza del Popolo** and the green hill of **Pincio**. On the eastern side of via del Corso are two of the prime stopping points on tour guides' itineraries: the **Fontana di Trevi** (Trevi Fountain) and the **Scalinata Trinità dei Monti** (Spanish Steps). On the other side of the river, **Trastevere** is leftfield and arty. Its laid-back streets are filled with bars and restaurants, though there's less in the way of conventional sights. To the north, also on the western side of the river, the **Castel Sant' Angelo** stands guard over a statue-lined bridge and from here, Mussolini's grand via della Conciliazione is the best approach to **San Pietro** (St Peter's) and the **Vatican**.

Piazza di Spagna

24 hours in the city

Get up early to wander around **piazza Navona** and the fruit and vegetable market in **campo de' Fiori**. Dedicate the rest of the morning to the **Forum** and the **Palatine**, ending up in the **Colosseum**. Then head northwest through the atmospheric streets near the river for lunch. In the afternoon hit **St Peter's**, leaving enough time to queue to get in and to climb up into the dome and onto the roof for spectacular views. (Even longer queues and visitor-unfriendly opening hours mean that trying to see the Sistine Chapel and the rest of the Vatican in one day is an inefficient use of your time. If you must see them, get here as early as possible and be prepared to wait.) In the evening return to the campo de' Fiori, by this time transformed into a chic *aperitivi* spot. After a *prosecco* here, head across the river for food in **Trastevere**, and, if you want to party, head further south to the increasingly fashionable area of **Testaccio**.

View from St Peter's dome

★ *Don't leave town without wandering through the bubbling streets of Trastevere late at night.*

👁 Sights

Musei Capitolini

ⓘ *piazza del Campidoglio, T06-6710 2475, www.museicapitolini.org. Tue-Sun 0900-2000. €6.20.*

Designed in the 16th century by Michelangelo, the handsome piazza del Campidoglio and museums on the Capitoline hill are a brilliantly conceived ensemble.

Michelangelo's regal Cordonata staircase leads up to the piazza from the via del Teatro di Marcello, just south of piazza Venezia. In placing the stairs on the western side of the piazza, Michelangelo changed its orientation: instead of facing the Forum it faces contemporary Rome.

The museums themselves are in the **Palazzo dei Conservatori** and **Palazzo Nuovo**: two buildings facing the piazza and connected by the **Galleria Congiunzione**, an underground passage opened as a part of the

Piazza del Campidoglio.

Millennium celebrations and also allowing access to the Roman **Tabularium**, the archive of ancient Rome. There are good views from here over the Roman Forum.

The **Capitoline Museum** in the Palazzo dei Conservatori contains statues, bronzes and other artefacts. In its courtyard are the remnants of the enormous statue of Constantine that once stood in the Forum, including his

gigantic foot. The rest of the statue was made of wood and has not survived. The second floor has works of art including a Caravaggio and a Titian.

The **Palazzo Nuovo** opposite has an extraordinary collection of ancient marble statuary.

Foro Romano and Palatine

ⓘ *piazza di Santa Maria Nova 53, T06-699 0110. Summer 0900-1930; winter 0900-1630. Forum free, Palatine €12, combined with the Colosseum.*

Rome was almost certainly first settled on the Palatine hill, overlooking a crossing of the river Tiber. According to legend, it was here that Romulus and Remus, the founders of the city, were brought up by a she-wolf. Roman emperors built their palaces on the hill, at the bottom of which (in the Forum) commerce, worship and justice took place.

Visitors are largely free to wander around among the broken columns and it's not hard to imagine the centre of

---

⊖ Travel essentials

Getting there **Fiumicino Airport**, T06-65953640, www.adr.it, 25 km southwest of the city centre, is the city's main airport. The **Leonardo Express** rail service connects the airport to Rome's main train station every half an hour from around 0630-2330. It's a 35-min journey and costs €9.50. A taxi to or from the centre of the city should cost around €40. **Ciampino Airport**, T06-794941, www.adr.it, 15 km southeast of the centre, is the smaller airport and serves budget airlines. There are various ways of getting to Ciampino, some of which are not quite as simple or cheap as they should be.

A Terravision bus service runs to coincide with Ryanair and EasyJet flights, €8 one-way, €13.50 return. Alternatively you can catch a bus (every 20 mins) the short hop to Ciampino station from where trains connect to Roma Termini every 10 mins or so.

Getting around The same ticket system covers bus, metro and tram systems. Standard tickets cost €1 and are valid for 75 mins from the time of being stamped on all forms of transport. Confusingly, however, they can only be used once on trains and metros. For €4 you can buy a *giornaliero* ticket which lasts all day. The bus system is relatively

efficient, though routes from the station to the Vatican have a reputation for pick-pockets. The metro is also efficient, though less useful to visitors since it mostly connects the suburbs to the city centre. Licensed taxis are white and have meters. Don't use anything else purporting to be a taxi.

Tourist information Azienda per il Turismo Roma, via Parigi 5, T06-36004399, www.romaturismo.com, near the train station. There are equally useful *Punti Informativi Turistici* around the city centre at locations such as at piazza delle Cinque Lune, T06-68809240, near piazza Navona.

In Roman mythology, Romulus and Remus were twins who founded the city of Rome. Their mother, Rhea Silvia, despite being a Vestal Virgin, was raped by Mars, the god of war and conceived the twins. Their uncle, Amulius, ordered a servant to kill the twins but instead they were cast adrift in a boat on the river Tiber. They were found by Tiberinus, the river god, and suckled by a she-wolf on the Palatine Hill, before being discovered by a shepherd who raised the children as his own. Once they became adults, Romulus and Remus returned home, killed their uncle and then built a settlement on the Palatine Hill, according to tradition in 753 BC. Remus killed Romulus but then, feeling remorse, named the city after his brother.

The extent to which Romulus and Remus were historical figures is unclear, and it seems that there was a settlement on the Palatine Hill which predates the traditional date of the founding of the city. However, such apparent facts haven't stopped the she-wolf becoming a symbol of the city – a bronze of her suckling the twins can be seen in the Capitoline Museums. A similar image was used on Second World War propaganda posters.

the Roman Empire as it would have been 2000 years ago. There's little or no information, however, and a map of the ruins is useful in order to make out what is what. Highlights include the **Temple of Castor and Pollux**, the **Arch of Septimus Severus** and the **Arch of**

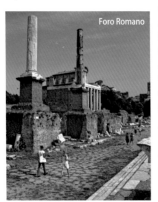

Foro Romano

Titus. **The Arch of Constantine**, next to the Colosseum, is the best preserved of all of Rome's ancient triumphal arches.

The Palatine hill has remains of grand palaces, as well as the 16th-century **Hortus Farnese**, Europe's oldest botanical gardens.

Colosseo

ⓘ *piazza del Colosseo, T06-3996 7700. Summer daily 0900-1930; winter daily 0900-1630. €10, €12 with Palatine. To avoid the queues, it's quicker to buy the joint ticket at the Palatine.*

Rome's most iconic building, sold in plaster miniature by souvenir-sellers all over the city, the Colosseum is an awesome structure. Built between AD 72 and AD 90, the city's ancient amphitheatre seated 50,000 people.

Used for gladiatorial combat, 9000 animals are reported to have been killed during its 100-day opening celebrations.

Built by Emperor Vespasian and his son Titus, it sits on the site of one of Nero's palaces, the Domus Aurea.

Colosseo

A floor has been constructed at the level where the original would have been but it is still possible to see down into the underground section where animals and combatants were kept.

The remaining marble with which it was once clad was removed during the Renaissance and baroque periods to build houses, and also in the construction of St Peter's.

Musei Vaticani
ⓘ *viale Vaticano 100, T06-6988 4947, www.vatican.va. Mar-Oct Mon-Fri 0845-1645 (last entry 1520), Sat and last Sun of month 0845-1345 (last entry 1220); Nov-Feb 0845-1545 (last entry 1220).*

The Vatican Museums have an extraordinary wealth of art, including the masterpieces of Michelangelo in the **Sistine Chapel** (Capella Sistina), and those of Raphael in the **Stanze di Raffaello**. Michelangelo famously lay on his back for four years, between 1508 and 1512, to create his astonishing *Creation* on the ceiling. (Goethe said of it: "Without having seen the Sistine Chapel one can form no appreciable idea of what one man is capable of achieving.") He returned 23 years later to spend

Sistine Chapel

Basilica di San Pietro

another six years painting the darker *Last Judgement* on the end wall above the altar. There is a self-portrait in it – Michelangelo paints himself as a flayed skin in the hand of St Bartholomew. Both paintings were subject to a controversial restoration in the 1980s and 1990s which some claim now makes the frescoes overly colourful.

The **Raphael Rooms** are only marginally less astounding – four rooms are frescoed with themes of Truth and Beauty as well as the achievements of popes. The most famous image includes depictions of Leonardo as Plato, Michelangelo as Heraclitus and Raphael as himself.

Start early and, especially in high season, be prepared for a long wait to get in. Once there, colour-coded routes help find a way through the Papal treasure troves. Most head straight for the Sistine Chapel but there is plenty else here to explore.

Basilica di San Pietro
ⓘ *piazza San Pietro, T06-6988 1662. Apr-Oct daily 0700-1900; Nov-Mar daily 0700-1800. Free. Cupola, Apr-Oct 0800-1800; Nov-Mar 0800-1700. €5. Those with bare shoulders or knees will not be allowed into the basilica.*

The biggest church in Christendom, **St Peter's** can hold 60,000 people. The basilica's current incarnation was started in 1506. The original plans were drawn up by Bramante but then changed by Raphael, who took over after the original architect's death. Michelangelo then took charge and changed the plans again and it was largely his Greek cross design and his enormous dome that was finally consecrated in 1626.

Inside, the enormity of the Vatican's church is emphasized by a line in the floor displaying the lengths of other big churches around the world. Of the many highlights Michelangelo's *Pieta* (a depiction of Mary holding the dead body of Jesus on her lap), sculpted from marble when he was only 24 years old, is the most affecting. Regrettably now behind glass, the sculpture loses some, but not all, of its disarmingly human qualities. Another highlight not to be missed is the climb up into the dome and out onto the terrace. From here there are great views down into the

Il Vittoriano

European City Breaks Rome

Vatican gardens in one direction and, in the other, over the 140 statues of saints on the colonnade to the piazza below. Note that there are 320 steps to climb even if you opt to take the lift up the first stage.

If you're here on Wednesday mornings you can get a glimpse of a distant Pope addressing enthusiastic crowds in piazza San Pietro.

Il Vittoriano

ⓘ *piazza Venezia. Monument and museum daily 0930-1830. Free.*

The Monumento a Vittorio Emanuele II, more often called simply il Vittoriano, or, with less deference, 'the wedding cake' or 'the typewriter', is one of Rome's most memorable monuments, if not its most beautiful. Always controversial, its construction involved the demolition of an old part of the city and many Romans consider it out of proportion and out of style with its surroundings.

Built at the turn of the 20th century in honour of King Victor Emmanuel, it now serves various purposes – the tomb of the unknown soldier is here, with an eternal flame, as are various exhibition spaces and the **Museo del**

Fontana di Trevi

Trinit   dei Monti

Risorgimento, with information about the unification of Italy.

Fontana di Trevi

ⓘ *piazza di Trevi.*

Made especially famous by Anita Ekberg, who took the plunge in *La Dolce Vita*, the Trevi Fountain sits at the end of the Aqua Virgo, one of the aqueducts that supplied ancient Rome with crucial pure water from outside the city. Rome's grandest, the baroque Trevi Fountain, follows a Roman tradition of building fountains at the ends of aqueducts. Designed by Nicola Salvi in 1730 using elements of an earlier design by Bernini, the fountain is these days purified with chlorine and semi- permanently surrounded by a sea of coin-throwing tourists.

Scalinata di Spagna

In some ways an unlikely candidate for tourist must-see status, the 18th-century **Spanish Steps** consist of 138 stairs originally built into the hill to connect the Spanish embassy with the Holy See. At the top of the monumental

stairs is the church of **Trinità dei Monti** from where the views across the city's rooftops are spectacular. Shoppers gather for a rest in the piazza di Spagna at the bottom. **John Keats** lived in a house at the bottom of the steps and died there in 1821. There is now a museum dedicated to the poet.

Pantheon

ⓘ *piazza della Rotunda, T06-6830 0230. Mon-Sat 0830-1930, Sun 0900-1800. Free.*

Built in AD 125 by Emperor Hadrian to replace an earlier building that had been destroyed by fire, the Pantheon is ancient Rome's most complete monument. A perfectly circular rotunda, the building is 43 m wide and 43 m high. A central oculus in the dome is open to the sky and lets through striking shafts of sunlight into the shadows. (The dome was also the largest in Western Europe until Brunelleschi's dome in Florence's Duomo was built in 1436.)

In AD 609 the building was consecrated as a Christian church and it was in part this that protected it from the damage inflicted upon other Roman structures. The reason for the

Pantheon

dome's survival may also have something to do with the composition of Roman concrete.

Since the Renaissance the building has been used for a tomb of the famous. Those buried here include Raphael and two Italian kings.

Piazza Navona

The central piazza of Rome, piazza Navona was built on top of the first century Stadium of Domitian, which explains its rectangular shape. Surrounded by baroque architecture, the main points of interest in the piazza are its fountains, notably Bernini's central **Fontana dei Quattro Fiume** (Fountain of the Four Rivers), representing the Danube, the Ganges, the Nile and the Río de la Plata. The **Fontana Nettuno** (Fountain of Neptune), to the northern end of the piazza is by Giacomo della Porta.

Campo de' Fiori

A more proletarian counterpoint to piazza Navona's aristocracy, the campo de' Fiori (commonly referred to simply as "Il Campo") has a lively and high-

Campo de' Fiori

quality market and plenty of equally lively bars and restaurants. In recent years il Campo has been increasingly gentrified but it retains some of its down-to-earth feel. It really comes into its own in the evenings, once the stalls are cleared away and locals descend to drink *aperitivi* at the outdoor tables and watch the world go by. The central statue is of Giordano Bruno, a philosopher burned at the stake here in 1600 for suggesting that philosophy was superior to religion. Julius Caesar also died nearby.

The Ghetto

ⓘ *Museo Ebraico di Roma, Lungotevere de' Cenci, T06-6840 0661. Apr-Sep Mon-Thu 0900-1930, Fri and Sun 0900-1330; Oct-Mar Mon-Thu 0900-1330, Fri 0900-1330, Sun 0900-1230. €6.*

Jews have lived in Rome for over 2,000 years, meaning that the Roman Jewish community is the oldest in Europe. The relative security of Roman Jews through the ages came at the cost of a tax imposed by the Catholic church from the 14th century onwards.

Shops offer kosher pizza and there

is an attractive synagogue in which the **Jewish Museum** details centuries of maltreatment by the Vatican as well as the rounding up of 2000 Jews in 1943.

Trastevere

The name Trastevere (the stress is on the first 'e') comes from the Latin *trans Tiberim*, meaning 'over the Tiber', and being on the 'other side' defines much of the area's left-bank, bohemian identity.

The area is at its best in the evenings, when many Romans descend on it for its lively bars and relatively cheap restaurants. It is also worth a wander during the day, however. The church of **Santa Maria in Trastevere** ⓘ *piazza Santa Maria in Trastevere, T06-5814802, daily 0730-2100,* is the area's most obvious sight and has glitteringly spectacular 13th-century mosaics in a cobbled piazza.

To the north is a green area of parks around the Gianicolo hill, including the **Orto Botanico** (Botanical Gardens) ⓘ *largo Cristina de Svezia 24.* Originally established in 1833, it hosts over 3500 species and includes a 'scent and touch' garden.

Piazza Navona

Santa Maria in Trastevere

● Sleeping

Many of Rome's cheaper sleeping options are grouped around the station, though few can be wholeheartedly recommended. The southern part of the *centro storico* offers many of the best mid-range options, while further north, around the Spanish Steps, prices and standards of service rise still further. In general the city's hotels are expensive compared to the rest of Mediterranean Europe.

€€€ **Hotel Art by the Spanish Steps**, via Margutta 56, T06-328711, www.hotelart.it. Sleekly modern and self-consciously hip, Hotel Art sometimes tries too hard, but in general its efforts pay off. Micro-lighting, wooden floors and colour schemes in place of floor numbers.

€€€ **Hotel Eden**, via Ludovisi 49, T06-478121, www.hotel-eden.it. If money is no object you may want to consider booking the penthouse here at a mere €3600 a night. It has refined old-fashioned elegance, a stylish bar and restaurant and great views from the terrace garden.

€€€-€€ **Astoria Garden**, via Bachelet 8, T06-446 9908, www.hotelastoria garden.it. One of the best options near the station, the Astoria Garden has smart if rather generic rooms and, as the name suggests, a garden. Good value out of season.

€€€-€€ **Campo de Fiori**, via del Biscione 6, T06-6880 6865, www.hotel campodefiori.com. A decent mid-range option with great views from the roof terrace, the hotel also have apartments for rent nearby.

€€€-€€ **Casa Howard**, via di Capo Le Case 18 and via Sistina 149, T06-6992 4555, www.casahoward.com.

The name is the Italian title of EM Forster's novel, *Howard's End*, from which you might imagine a staid attempt at Englishness – you'd be wrong. This excellent-value designer B&B is now in 2 houses where the design is bright and colourful and the attention to detail commendable, from the slippers and the fresh breakfasts to the carefully sourced soap.

€€€-€€ **Ripa**, via degli Orti di Trastevere 1, T06-58611, www.ripa hotel.com. A relatively early exponent of the design hotel, Ripa has the feel of an old-fashioned view of the future – a take on the sort of futuristic designs to be found in 1970s science fiction movies. Curvy minimalism and muted colours are used through the 170 rooms. The downside is that it's a little out of the way on the western side of Trastevere.

€€ **Hotel Navona**, via dei Sediari 8, T06-686 4203, www.hotelnavona.com. Very central and good value, Navona is plain, but you'd be hard pushed to find anything else as reasonable within a stone's throw of piazza Navona itself. The same owners also run the more upmarket *Residenza Zanardelli*.

€€ **Hotel Santa Maria**, vicolo del Piede 2, T06-589 4626, www.htlsanta maria.com. Near the Villa della Fonte hotel in Trastevere, Santa Maria has an attractive central courtyard with orange trees, where a good breakfast is served.

€€ **Villa della Fonte**, via della Fonte dell'Olio 8, T06-580 3797, www.villa fonte.com. With only 5 en suite rooms and a garden terrace, Villa della Fonte often fills up quickly. Not far from the piazza Santa Maria in Trastevere, simple rooms look out onto greenery-draped walls.

● Best of the rest

Fontana delle Tartarughe
ⓘ *piazza Mattei*. Giacomo della Porta's attractive fountain dates from the 1580s. The eponymous turtles were added a century later.
Teatro di Marcello ⓘ *via del Teatro Marcello*. Once a 15,000-seat theatre built by Julius Caesar, the ruins of the Teatro di Marcello were turned into Renaissance palazzi which fuse the two architectural styles, with ancient Roman arches making up the lower half of the construction.
Castel Sant'Angelo ⓘ *Lungotevere Castello 50*, T06-681 9111. Tue-Sun 0900-2000. €5. Hadrian's final resting place was built in AD 135 and has great views as well as a chapel designed by Michelangelo. Over the centuries it has served as both a refuge and a prison for popes and it was the setting for Puccini's opera *Tosca*.
San Luigi dei Francesi ⓘ *piazza San Luigi dei Francesi*, T06-68 8271. Fri-Wed 0830-1230, 1530-1900; Thu 0830-1230. Rome's French church has three Caravaggio paintings in its Contarelli Chapel.

● Eating

Many of the best restaurants in the centre are in the area around campo de Fiori or across the river in Trastevere, where eating out is traditionally a little cheaper. Rigatoni all'amatriciana (pasta with sausage and a spicy tomato sauce) is a traditional dish you'll find nearly everywhere.

Lunch

Il Forno di Campo de' Fiori, campo de' Fiori 22, T06-6880 6662. Simple but notoriously delicious white or red pizza by the slice attracts lots of local workers at lunchtimes. Closes for the afternoon at 1430, so don't leave it too late.

La Grotta, via delle Grotte 27, T06-686 4293. Just south of the campo de' Fiori, and much quieter, this is a great lunch spot. Traditional Roman food and generous portions.

Margutta Vegetariano, via Margutta 118, T06-3265 0577. A rare Italian vegetarian restaurant, the Margutta, near piazza del Popolo, has art, a busy, friendly atmosphere and good, though not ground-breaking, vegetarian food.

Òbikà, via dei Prefetti 26a, T06-683 2630. A restaurant based entirely around one ingredient – mozzarella. The real buffalo milk stuff arrives fresh daily from Naples, Salerno and Caserta. The design mixes steely minimalism with ancient Roman touches.

Cafés and gelaterias

Il Gelato di San Crispino, via della Panetteria 42, T06-679 3924. Some have suggested that the exceedingly good ice cream served here from under stainless steel lids might be the best in the world. Try trademark *gelato di San Crispino*, flavoured with honey and you may never be able to eat a Cornetto again.

Dinner

Magnolia, campo de' Fiori 4/5, T06-6830 9367. A more modern take on the traditional campo trattoria, Magnolia does great big bowls of salad and is also a good place to sit on the tables outside for a drink.

Supperclub, via de' Nari 14, T06-6880 7207. All the lighting and style of a chilled but colourfully lit club but serving modern international cuisine as well as trendy cocktails.

Al Bric, via del Pellegrino 51-52, T06-687 9533. A well-informed wine list is the centrepiece of this *enoteca* (wine bar), which also serves imaginative food, combining the traditional and the modern. Dishes include swordfish stroganoff and duck pappardelle.

Filetti di Baccalà, largo Librai 88, T06-686 4018. Closed Sun. A Roman institution, this battered cod joint has changed very little in a very long time. The menu consists of not much other than its trademark Roman dish but what it does it does very well.

Trattoria da Augusto, piazza de' Renzi 15, T06-580 3798. On communal tables outside in a less smart piazza than the nearby Santa Maria, Trattoria da Augusto can be chaotic but is never less than good-natured. The food is excellent, traditional fare. You'll do better with some Italian – menus are mostly of the spoken variety. Be prepared to hang around in the piazza for a table. Very Trasteveran.

Nightlife

Bars and clubs

Trastevere and the area around campo de' Fiori are usually considered the liveliest for nocturnal Roman activities but **Testaccio**, a previously working class area to the south is increasingly catching. Wine bars are becoming trendier but in general are places to eat as much as to drink. **Campo de' Fiori** is an especially good location for an early evening *aperitivi*.

Many of the city's nightclubs are smart and pricey and the live music scene is limited, though the number of alternative venues is increasing. Interesting events often happen at the city's *centri sociali*. During the summer months some clubs move out to the coast. Nights start (and finish) late – don't expect much action before midnight. Listings magazines like *Roma C'è* give up to date details of what's on.

Live music

Classical music and opera tends to fare better than other music, especially in summer, when festivals mean that events sometimes take place in great outdoor settings, from Testaccio's ex-slaughterhouse to the Baths of Caracalla and the Botanical Gardens. The Renzo Piano-designed **Parco della Musica**, via P de Coubertin 15, www.musicaperroma.it, which opened in 2002, has injected new life into Rome's music scene.

Shopping

Rome still has plenty of small shops run by local families rather than big chains – **Trastevere** and in the streets around **campo de' Fiori** are great areas for discovering bookshops, delicatessens, and shops selling antiques and garden tools. Rome's most famous products are shoes and other fashion accessories, such as bags and gloves. For fashion **via del Corso** and the roads that run off it make up Rome's main shopping area and you'll find the headquarters of brands such as Gucci and Bulgari here. Via Frattina, via Condotti and via del Babuino are especially good for burning holes in wallets.

"Here shall be a town", declared Peter the Great at the dawn of the 18th century and what a town it has turned out to be. St Petersburg is where East meets West. In its canals, squares, monuments, cathedrals and bridges you'll see an elaborate mix of European and Russian styles. The old capital of the Tsarist empire oozes history from its pores: it witnessed the opening shots of the Russian Revolution; the storming of the Winter Palace; Lenin's return from exile; and the enlightened days of Catherine the Great, who began the process of gathering the many treasures that can now be seen in its myriad museums. It is with good reason that St Petersburg is referred to by its residents as the *gorod muzei* or "the city of museums".

St Petersburg

Arts & culture
★★★★

Eating
★★

Nightlife
★★

Outdoors
★★

Romance
★★★★★

Shopping
★★

Sightseeing
★★★★★

Value for money
★★★★

Overall score
★★★☆

At a glance

St Petersburg forms a sort of bushy tree, looped by the River Neva, with the main thoroughfare **Nevsky Prospekt** forming the trunk and canals and streets branching off. The river separates the north part of St Petersburg from the main centre of the city and is lined with grand buildings from its golden days. The **Peter and Paul Fortress** is along the river on the **Petrograd Side**, one of the Neva delta's many islands. Cross back over the river to the south and the famous **Bronze Horseman statue**, a city icon, can be seen. **St Isaac's Cathedral** with its huge brassy dome dominates the skyline nearby. Go east of here and you'll find the **Winter Palace** and the **Hermitage Museum** beside the large, imposing **Dvortsovaya Ploshchad** (Tsar Alexander square). Further down Nevsky Prospekt on the right is the impressive bulk of

The Russians said that Peter made his city in the sky, then lowered it, like a giant model, to the ground.

Orlando Figes, 'Natasha's dance: A cultural history of Russia'

Kazan Cathedral and further down and off to the left is the stunning **Church of Our Saviour on Spilled Blood**, with its onion domes.

★ *Don't leave town without tasting* blini *and* ikra krasnaya *(pancakes and red caviar) – with vodka.*

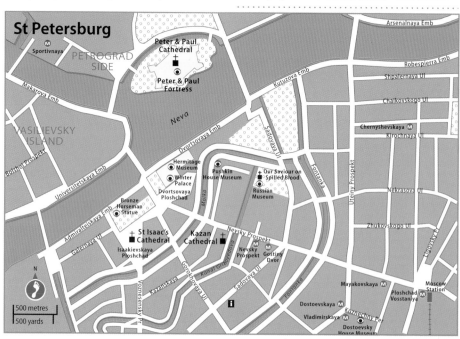

⊙ Sights

Winter Palace

Hermitage Museum

ⓘ *2 Dvortsovaya Ploshchad (Dvortsovaya Sq), T812-710 9625, www.hermitagemuseum.org. Tue-Sat 1030-1800, Sun and holidays 1030-1700. RUB 350 (combined ticket for Hermitage plus 3 other buildings in museum complex RUB 700). Metro Kanal Griboyedova, Nevsky Prospekt and Gostiny Dvor.*

St Petersburg's most famous attraction, the Hermitage Museum, consists of five connecting buildings: the Little Hermitage, the Old and New Hermitages, the Hermitage Theatre and the **Winter Palace**, the largest and main residence of the Russian tsars. The Palace rooms, decked out in marble and some in gold leaf, are well worth exploring in their own right, let alone for the stunning wealth of art that they contain.

The museum houses seven massive collections: Western European art and culture; Russian art and culture; antiquities of the former Soviet Union; antiquities of the Near and middle East; Classical antiquities; art and culture of the Middle and Far East; and a coin collection.

The collection of Western Art includes an impressive array of well-known artists such as Poussin, Renoir, Degas, Monet, Matisse, Gauguin, Van Gogh and Picasso. Renaissance artists include da Vinci, Michelangelo and Titian. Spanish painters are represented by El Greco, Velázquez, Murillo and Goya, and Flemish and Dutch art by Van Dyck, Rubens, Rembrandt and Hals. An excellent display of statuary from ancient Greece and Rome can also be seen.

Though undeniably dazzling, make sure you at least sample the six other collections. Highlights include the Golden Treasures Gallery, with jewellery from Scythian, Greek and Byzantine times, and ancient artefacts from Central Asia and Siberia, including Altai and Scythian relics.

European City Breaks St Petersburg

⊖ Travel essentials

Getting there Pulkovo Airport is 17 km south of the city centre. There are 2 terminals 5 miles from each other: Pulkovo 1, T812-104 3827, for domestic flights and Pulkovo 2, T812-104 3444, for international flights, with a free shuttle bus between them.

There are various options for getting to the centre from the airport. A taxi will cost about RUB 1000. The shuttle bus T-39 runs from both terminals to Moskovoskaya metro station and then into the centre. Bus No 13 runs to Moskovoskaya metro station (journey time about 30-40 mins), from where you can take the metro into the centre in about 25-30 mins (RUB 10). There are also *mashrutnoye* (minibuses that pick up paying passengers) to Moskovoskaya, costing little more than the bus fare (approximately RUB 5). If you are driving, head for Pulkovskoe Shosse (E95, M20), which becomes Moskovsky Prospekt and then Sadoyova St and Nevsky Prospekt.

Getting around The centre of St Petersburg is walkable but public transport around the city is cheap and efficient. Choose from metro, trolleybus, trams or buses. The metro is open from 0530 until 0030 and is a fast and convenient way to get about. Tokens can be bought at ticket offices and inserted into automatic barriers. 1 trip costs RUB 3; 7 days/15 trips pass costs RUB 24; 14 days/30 trips costs RUB 45). Trolleybuses, trams and buses are available from 0530-2400. There is 1 flat fare (RUB 2 per trip) and you can buy tickets from the conductor or driver. Hopping on the No 10 trolleybus will take you the length of Nevsky Prospekt, from Ploschad Aleksandra Nevskovo all the way over to Vasilievsky Island, allowing some good sightseeing opportunities. Taxis are plentiful and are typically yellow but private car drivers will also offer taxi rides (negotiate the fare before the journey). You can take a boat trip around the city for RUB 60 and it lasts 1 hr.

Tourist information Intourist, www.intourist.com, was formerly the state travel agency and, now privatized, it offers a wide range of information and travel services. A City Tourist Information centre can be found at Sadovaya ulitsa 14/52, T812-310 2231, www.ctic.spb.ru. 1000-1900, closed Sun.

Exchange rate Russian Ruble (RUB). £1 = RUB 50.22. €1 = RUB 33.99.

Russian Museum

ⓘ *Inzhenernaya str, 4, T812-595 4248, www.rusmuseum.ru. Wed-Sun 1000-1700, Mon 1000-1600. RUB 350 (combined ticket for 4 palaces RUB 600). Metro Gostiny Dvor and Nevsky Prospekt.*

Though overshadowed by the Hermitage, the Russian Museum (Russki Musei), off Nevsky Prospekt, is worth visiting and is the world's largest museum of Russian art. Housed in the former Mikhailovsky Palace it features the work of artists who would otherwise never or rarely be seen in the West, including the likes of Shishkin, Repin, Levitan, Fedotov, Kripensky, Bruni and Goncharova. Occasionally the museum stages a visiting exhibition, such as on Russian *skazka*, or fairy tales, and illustrations.

Peter and Paul Fortress

ⓘ *Thu-Mon 1100-1800, Tue 1100-1700, grounds open every night till 2200. Tickets (RUB 80) can be bought from the Ioannovsky Gate or Boat House.*

Standing on Petrograd Side, one of the islands in the Neva delta, Peter and Paul Fortress (Petropavlovskaya Krepost), is

Peter and Paul Fortress

the oldest building in St Petersburg. Built by Peter the Great to defend his new town, it served more as a prison for Russians than as a bulwark against invaders. Inside is **Peter and Paul Cathedral** (Petropavlovsky Sobor), constructed 1712-1732, with its golden needle spire and baroque interior. The cathedral is also the burial site for many Russian Tsars including Peter I and, in 1998, the last Tzar Nicholas II and the Romanov family were laid to rest here. The grounds outside the fortress are a major venue for several city festivals held throughout the year.

St Isaac's Cathedral

ⓘ *Isaakievskaya Ploschad 1, T812-315 9732. Thu-Tue 1100-1900, colonnade observation point Thu-Tue 1100-1800. RUB 250. Metro Nevsky Prospekt and Gvostiny Dvor.*

With its massive golden dome, St Isaac's Cathedral is one of the most familiar landmarks of the St Petersburg cityscape. Built in the first half of the 19th century, the church became a museum in 1931. The huge red granite columns, grey marble, bronze statues and domes clad

Russian Museum

in gold make it an imposing building to visit and the colonnade offers superb views of the city.

Church of Our Saviour on Spilled Blood

ⓘ *Nabetrezhnaya Kanala Griboyedova 2, T812-314 4053. Thu-Tue 1100-1800. RUB 100; buy ticket from inside church, not outside. Metro Nevsky Prospekt and Gvostiny Dvor.*

Near the Ekaterinsky Canal is the magnificent Church on the Spilled Blood (Khram Spasa-na-Krovi, also known as Cathedral of the Resurrection of Christ or Khram Voskreseniya Khristova). The cathedral was built on the place where the Tsar Alexander II was killed by terrorists in 1881. There's an exhibition about him inside. Make sure you take time to study the wonderful mosaics.

Pushkin House Museum

ⓘ *Naberezhnaya Reki Moika 12, T812-311 3131. Wed-Mon 1030-1730. RUB 100. Metro Nevsky Prospekt and Gvostiny Dvor.*

On the southern bank of the Moika is the Pushkin House Museum

St Isaac's Cathedral

St Petersburg's metro has been hostage to the fortunes of Russia's turbulent history. It was planned in 1899 but due to the outbreak of the First World War and the Russian Revolution, building was postponed. Spurred on by the construction of the Moscow metro in 1933, building began again just as Hitler's stormtroopers burst through the Russian frontier. After the Great Patriotic War the first metro line opened in 1955. While not as grand as Moscow's, St Petersburg's metro remains impressive as a feat of construction. It is the deepest subway in the world, has 61 stations and is 122 km long. Engineers also had to overcome stiff geological challenges such as the existence of several underground rivers and the proximity of the Finnish Gulf. The nature of these challenges are reflected in the collapse of the tunnel between Lesnaya and Ploschad Muzhestva. Despite this, the metro is a fast and efficient way of getting about St Petersburg: trains pass every 95 seconds during the rush hour and every four minutes for the rest of the day.

Pushkin metro station

There are four lines set out in a London Underground style format on the metro map: Line 1 - Kirovsko-Vyborgskaya - the red line; Line 2 - Moskovsko-Petrogradskaya - the blue line; Line 3 - Nevsko-Vasileostrovskaya - the green line; Line 4 - Pravobereznaya - the yellow line.

(Pushkinsky Dom), in the original apartment (built in the 18th century for a court dignitary) where the great poet wrote such pieces as *The Bronze Horseman* and *The Captain's Story*. It was here that he died in 1837,

after having been wounded in a duel over his beautiful wife, Natalia Goncharova. Apart from the poet's death-bed and death mask, you can see his desk, bookshelves and other personal items.

reconstructed from original plans and the writings of contemporaries, especially those of his wife and secretary, Anna Grigorievna. Here you'll find Dostoevsky's personal belongings and his books.

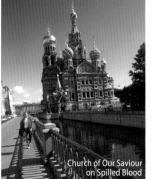
Church of Our Saviour on Spilled Blood

Dostoevsky House Museum

ⓘ *Kuznechny per 5/2, T812-117 4031, www.md.spd.ru. Tue-Sun 1100-1800. Metro Vladimirskaya and Dostoevskaya.*

Not far from Vladimirskaya metro station is the house where, in 1878, the writer Fyodor Mikhailovich Dostoevsky moved with his family and stayed till his death in 1881. It was here that he wrote *The Brothers Karamazov*. The house was later turned into communal apartments during Soviet times and had to be

Pushkin House Museum

◉ Sleeping

There are some good deals to be had in the top end luxury hotels but there are very few cheap or mid-range places in the city centre, and those few are generally modern and bland.

€€€ **Grand Hotel Europe**, Mikhailovskaya ul 1/7, T329-6000, www.grandhotel-europe.com. The city's oldest hotel with sumptuous art nouveau interiors, shopping arcades and several bars and restaurants.

€€ **Dostoevsky Hotel**, Vladimirsky Pr, 19, T812-331 3200. Modern 3-star hotel in the historic centre offering comfortable accommodation. The hotel occupies part of the building of one of the better shopping centres in the city (Vladimirsky Passage).

€€ **Matisov Domik Hotel**, Pryajka River Emb 3/1, T812-219 5441. Opened in 1993 and one of the first private hotels in the city, Matisov Domik is in a quiet district of town, close to the Mariinsky Theatre and 25 mins from Nevsky Prospekt; ideal for those who prefer peace and quiet to convenience. It has a intimate and bucolic feel and the staff strive to maintain a homely atmosphere.

€€ **Neva Hotel**, Tchaikovskovo St 17, T812-278 0504. In the fashionable Letney Sad (Gardens) districts, it's nothing fancy but good, solid, comfortable 3-star accommodation and reasonable value.

€€ **Oktyabrskaya Hotel**, Ligovsky Prospekt 10, T812-277 6330. Metro Ploshchad Vosstaniya. Just across the road from the Moscow Station is this huge 563-room 3-star hotel in a mid-19th century building. Ask for one of the upgraded rooms.

◐ Eating

St Petersburg now offers plenty of choice in terms of cafés and restaurants serving a wide range of cuisines, from Russian to French and Chinese, often all on the same menu. Cafés often serve the best food and most are open from morning well into the evening. Most restaurants are open from 1200-1430 and 1800-2330/2400.

††† **ME 100**, Lenin Ulitsa 18, T812-230 5359. A small restaurant offering Russian, Japanese and Italian dishes. Good food and good value eating.

††† **Shinok**, Zagorodny Prospekt 13, T812-311 8262. This restaurant is decked out like a Ukrainian village and offers typical dishes such as *borsht* (beetroot soup), *kyshka* (sausage) and *kutya* (special wheat). In the evenings musicians provide entertainment.

†† **Ketino**, 8th Line 23, Vailevsky Island, T812-326 0196. This place offers excellent Caucasian dishes such as Georgian cheese bread served with an egg in the middle and also has a display of Georgian art.

†† **Staroe Café**, Fontanka Embankment 108, T812-316 5111. Good Russian food (tasty soups and *blini*) in a cosy, intimate setting with 19th-century decor and a piano player in the evening. There's only a small number of tables available for dining, so make sure you book or come early.

† **Café Idiot**, Moika 82, T812-315 1675. Named after Dostoevsky's novel, this delightful café offers bags of atmosphere in the basement of a house on a canal, minutes from St Isaac's cathedral and Nevsky Prospekt. A cosy, 1950s-style interior with sofas and jazz music in 5 vaulted rooms, including an art gallery and a library with English

language books and magazines. The restaurant serves Russian and vegetarian food, coffee and speciality teas. Free vodka with every meal, which cost around RUB 300.

† **Troitsky Most**, Malaya Posadksaya Ul 4, Kronvergsky Prospekt 29, T812-232 6693. High quality vegetarian cuisine available at great value prices.

◑ Nightlife

There's plenty of varied nightlife on offer in St Petersburg. The famous **Mariinksy Opera and Ballet Theatre**, Teatralnaya Ploshchad 1, Bolshoi Concert Hall, Mikhailovskaya Ulitsa 2, box office T812-110 4257, is home to the St Petersburg Philharmonic Orchestra.

The **Maly Concert Hall**, Nevsky Prospekt 30, box office T812-312 4285, has performances by smaller ensembles, while the **Bolshoi Oktyabrsky Concert Hall**, Ligovsky Propsekt 6, box office T812-275 1175, concentrates on Russian classical music.

St Petersburg also offers a large range of clubs, divided into Dance, Music, Art and Erotic. Strict dress codes apply so dress up like young Russians do. Most clubs open between 2200 and 0600. Typical admission prices are RUB 165 before 2300 and RUB 275 before 2400. After 2400 at weekends, expect to pay around RUB 330. Most clubs are on or around Nevsky Prospekt and the embankment areas and include **Metro**, Ligovsky Pr, T812-166 0210; the stylish **Purga**, Neberezhnanya Reki Fontanki 13, T812- 313 4123; and **Plaza**, Neberezhnanya Makarov 2, T812-323 9090, which is popular with Russians and tourists.

Unusually for an inland city, Seville was once the most important port in the world. It directed the whole of Spain's trade with its New World colonies and the merchants and Crown salivated over the arrival of the gold- and silver-laden treasure convoys fresh from its mines. Today, the bristling ramparts of the Torre del Oro still dare invaders to do their worst, while many of the streets of Triana, the one-time sailors' barrio, still bear the names of the brave mariners who set forth into the unknown. You can find spots where Columbus prayed before his voyages or the ill-fated Magellan set forth to put a girth on the world. While the city's fortunes have waxed and waned, its allure has not; within Spain its name is spoken like a mantra, a word laden with sensuality and promise.

Seville

Arts & culture
★★

Eating
★★★

Nightlife
★★★

Outdoors
★★

Romance
★★★

Shopping
★★

Sightseeing
★★★

Value for money
★★★★

Overall score
★★★

At a glance

The historic hub of Seville is dominated by two awesome symbols of power and wealth, the **Alcázar**, and the **cathedral** with its emblematic **Giralda** – a sublime tower in beautiful brick. Nearby, Seville's Moorish and Jewish heritage is still elusively alive among the narrow streets of **Barrio Santa Cruz**, just east of the cathedral, and home to some fine tapas bars. South of the cathedral, the optimistic buildings erected for the 1929 Exhibition have been put to fine use; students bustle about and cityfolk stroll in the blessed shade of the **Parque María Luisa**, with its improbably-grand **Plaza de España** and two museums. **El Arenal**, west of the cathedral and once the sandy, seedy, flood plain of the Guadalquivir, was built up around Seville's bullring and is now a riverside area with a theatre, good tapas and the fine art of the Hospital de la Caridad. To the south, **Triana**'s trendified riverbank is a mass of bars and restaurants; its backstreets full of tradition and beautiful tiles.

A city that waylays rhythm, and coils it into labyrinths, like tendrils of the vine aflame

Federico García Lorca

A cluster of plazas and shopping streets fill the middle of Seville's old town (**Centro**), with baroque churches tucked away in its side streets. Quiet **San Vicente**, to its east has the Museo de Bellas Artes. **La Macarena**, to the north, has friendly local bars, lively markets and quiet lanes brimming with Gothic-Mudéjar convents and churches. The river island of **Isla de la Cartuja** was the site of World Expo 1992.

★ *Don't leave town without a long meandering evening route through the city's tapas bars.*

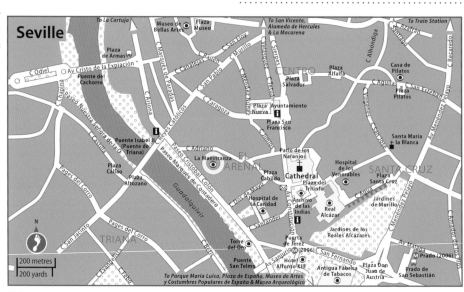

◉ Sights

Cathedral and La Giralda

ⓘ *Pl del Triunfo s/n, T954-214971.*
Mon-Sat 1100-1800 (last entry 1700);
Sun 1430-1900 (last entry at 1800);
Jul-Aug Mon-Sat 0930-1630, Sun
1430-1900. €7, free Sun.

At the beginning of the 15th century,
150 years after the fall of Seville to the
Christians, a cathedral was erected over a
mosque. **Santa María de la Sede** is the
result: a Gothic edifice of staggering
proportions and crammed full of artistic
treasures in nearly 50 chapels and its
massive five-naved central structure. The
mosque's minaret, the superb **Giralda**
tower (and the city's symbol), was
retained as the belltower, and can be
climbed via a series of ramps, while
pretty **Patio de los Naranjos**, the
Moorish ablutions area, has also survived.
The interior, combining grandeur, space
and solemnity, is magnificent; the
exterior arguably has more merit than all
the cathedrals of Andalucía put together.

La Giralda

Real Alcázar

ⓘ *Pl del Triunfo s/n, T954-502323, www.*
patronato-alcazarsevilla.es. Oct-Mar Tue-
Sat 0930-1800, Sun 0930-1430; Apr-Sep
Tue-Sat 0930-1900, Sun 0930-1700, last
entry 1 hr earlier. €5, students free.

The present Alcázar owes its Moorish
look (horseshoe arches, stucco, Arabic
calligraphy and coffered ceilings), not
to the Moorish rulers (little remains

from that period) but to the Castillian
kings Alfonso X and his son Pedro I.
As well as being a sumptuous palace
and a popular residence for visiting
Spanish royalty, the Alcázar was once
a considerable fortress, as you can see
as you pass through the chunky walls
of the red **Puerta del León**. From here
you emerge into a large courtyard
where the king's Hunt once
assembled. It's dominated by the
impressive façade of the main palace
of the Castillian kings (inscriptions
about the glory of Allah – Pedro I was
a pretty enlightened man – adjoin
more conventional Latin ones
proclaiming royal greatness). To the
left is the **Patio del Yeso**, one of the
few remaining Moorish structures.
Opposite, across the courtyard, are
chambers built by Fernando and Isabel
to control New World affairs. Magellan
planned his trip here and there's an
important *retablo* from this period of
the Virgen de los Navegantes. There's
also the vast and fantastic garden to
stroll and relax in; a peaceful break from
the sometimes frenetic city centre.

European City Breaks Seville

◉ Travel essentials

Getting there Seville Airport (SVQ),
T954-449 000, is 10 km northeast of the
centre. A bus runs to and from the airport
to central Seville (Puerta de Jerez) via the
train and bus stations every 30 mins
weekdays (less frequently at weekends)
and coincides with international flights.
It takes 30 mins to Puerta de Jerez (€2.30).
The last bus leaves the airport at 2330,
well after the last flight has got in. A taxi
to the city is around €21, slightly more at
night or on public holidays.

    Getting around Although Seville's
old town (where the main sights are) is a
fairly large area, walking is by far the best
way to get around. A stroll from the
cathedral to the Museo de Bellas Artes

takes 15-20 mins, from the Plaza de
España to the Alameda de Hércules
about 30 mins. The most useful **TUSSAM
bus** services are the circular routes;
C1 and C2 run a large circle via the train
station and Expo site (C1 goes clockwise,
C2 anti-clockwise), while C3 (clockwise)
and C4 (anti-clockwise) follow the
perimeter of the old walls, except for C3's
brief detour into Triana. A single fare is
€1 (drivers will give change up to a
point), but you can buy a *BonoBus* from
newspaper kiosks which costs €5 and is
valid for 10 journeys. A ride across town
in a **taxi** will cost around €6.

    The long awaited **metro** is finally
under construction, with the east-west

Line 1 due to open in late 2006. The
handiest station for the centre will be at
Puerta de Jerez.

    Tourist information Junta de
Andalucía, Av de la Constitución,
T954-221404, Mon-Fri 0900-1900,
Sat 1000-1400, 1500-1900, Sun
1000-1400. Near the cathedral,
this is the handiest tourist office, but it is
usually pretty busy. Other tourist offices
can be found by the Puente de Triana at
C Arjona 28, T902-194897, Mon-Fri
0800-2045, Sat-Sun 0900-1400; Plaza de
San Francisco 19, T954-595288, daily
0800-1800; at the airport and Santa Justa
train station, Mon-Fri 0900-2000, Sat-Sun
1000-1400.

Museo de Bellas Artes

Plaza del Museo 9, T954-221829, www.juntadeandalucia.es/cultura. Tue 1430-2000, Wed-Sat 0900-2030, Sun 0900-1430. Free for EU citizens.

Seville's major art gallery is a must-see, housed in a picturesque 17th-18th century convent. Thoughtfully laid out and thankfully uncluttered, it's a treasure trove of Spanish art from the 15th-20th centuries including El Greco, Velásquez, Murillo, Zurbarán – and a late portrait by Goya.

Barrio Santa Cruz

Once home to much of Seville's Jewish population, atmospheric Santa Cruz is the most charming of the city's *barrios*: a web of narrow, pedestrian lanes linking attractive small plazas with orange trees and shady terraces aplenty. There is a fairly standard tourist beat but you can easily get away from it. It's also a good place for hotels, restaurants and shopping. While there are a few sights of interest, such as the excellent baroque church of **Santa María la Blanca** and the **Hospital de**

Barrio Santa Cruz

Best of the rest

Archivo de las Indias *Pl del Triunfo s/n, T954-211234. Mon-Sat 1000-1600. Free.* In the 18th century this square and sober Renaissance building was converted into the state archive. It's a fascinating record of the discovery and administration of empire; from the excited scribblings of Columbus to mundane bookkeeping of remote jungle outposts. **Casa de Pilatos** *Plaza de Pilatos s/n, T954-225298. Daily 0900-1900. €5 lower floor, €8 both, free Tue from 1300.* A stunning 15th-century blend of Renaissance classicism and Mudéjar styles.

los Venerables *Daily 1000-1400, 1600-2000, €4.75,* the main enjoyment to be had is wandering around and trying to guess where you'll end up.

South of the cathedral

Much of the area south of the cathedral is taken up with the large green space of **Parque María Luisa**. It was used as the site for the grandiose 1929 Ibero-American Exhibition that the Primo de Rivera dictatorship hoped would return Seville and Spain to the world spotlight. The legacy is a public park and a beautiful series of buildings. The **Plaza de España** is an impressive colonnaded space and the **Hotel Alfonso XIII** to the northwest is one of the most sumptuous in Spain. Next door, the **Antigua Fábrica de Tabacos** *C San Fernando 4, T954-551000, Mon-Fri 0800-2030, free,* is the cigarette factory made famous in the late 19th century

by *Carmen*; it's now used by the university. In the park beyond, two of the pavilions have been converted into outstanding museums: the colourful **Museo de Artes y Costumbres Populares de Sevilla** *Pl de América 3, T954-232576, www.juntadeandalucía.es/cultura, Tue 1430-2030, Wed-Sat 0900-2030, Sun 0900-1430, free to EU residents, €1.50 for others;* and the rich **Museo Arqueológico** *Pabellón de Bellas Artes, Pl de América s/n, T954-232401, same website and opening details.* A walk through this part of town provides a fascinating view of an architectural ensemble built just years before the civil war that plunged the city and country into decades of poverty and monoculturalism.

El Arenal

Built up in the 19th century, El Arenal has some of Seville's major landmarks. The **Torre del Oro** *Paseo de Colón s/n, T954-222419, Tue-Fri 1000-1400, Sat-Sun 1100-1400, €1,* is a beautiful Moorish tower. The exhibition is mediocre but worth seeing for the prints of Seville in the late 16th century.

Torre del Oro

Semana Santa and Feria de Abril

Seville's Holy Week processions are an unforgettable sight. Mesmeric candlelit lines of hooded figures and cross-carrying penitents make their way through the streets accompanied by the mournful notes of a brass band and two large *pasos* (floats), one with a scene from the Passion, one with a statue of Mary. This isn't unique to Seville but what makes it so special is the Sevillians' extraordinary respect for, and interest in, the event. Members of nearly 60 *cofradías* (brotherhoods) practise intensively for the big moment, when they leave their home church and walk many hours through the streets to the cathedral and then home again. Some of the brotherhoods have well over a thousand in the parade; these consist of *nazarenos*, who wear pointed hoods (adopted by the KKK, but designed to hide the face of a man repentant before God), *penitentes*, who carry crosses, and *costaleros*, who carry the *pasos*. The first brotherhoods walk on Palm Sunday and the processions continue up until Easter Sunday, when a single *cofradía* celebrates the Resurrection.

Feria de Abril (usually in April, depending on Easter), originally a livestock market but now a major event in the Seville calendar, provides a lively antidote to the solemnity of Semana Santa. Line upon line of colourful marquees (*casetas*) reverberate to the slurping of manzanilla and the gyrations of pairs of dancing *sevillanas*.

La Maestranza ⓘ *Paseo de Colón 12, T954-224577, www.realmaestranza.com, Mon-Sun 0930-1400, 1500-1900 except fight days (spring and summer Sun and all week during Feria), when it's open 0930-1500, €4*, is one of Spain's most important temples to bullfighting.

Hospital de Caridad ⓘ *C Temprado 3, T954-223232, Mon-Sat 0900-1330, 1530-1930, Sun 0900-1300, €4*, is a nursing home with a remarkable collection of 17th-century Sevillan art including haunting masterpieces by Juan de Valdés Leal. The **Río Guadalquivir** itself is also a major attraction here; although there are no longer galleons bound for the Spanish Main, there are several outdoor bars, river cruises, and a place to hire canoes.

Triana

Triana is many people's favourite part of Seville. It has a picturesque riverfront lined with bars and restaurants, and

Price: £6.99
ISBN: 1 903471 86 9
www.footprintbooks.com

was for a long time the gypsy *barrio* and home of flamenco in Seville (its backstreet bars are still the best place to catch impromptu performances). Triana is also famous for ceramics; most of the *azulejo* tiles that so beautifully decorate Seville's houses come from here, and there are still many workshops in the area. It's got a different feel to the rest of the city, and *trianeros* are still a tight-knit social group. Many residents once lived in *corrales de vecinos*, houses centred around a common courtyard and there are still a few around to see. While the riverfront and surrounds are fairly trendy these days, venture into some of the smaller backstreets and you'll find that Triana preserves more of its history and associations than any other part of Seville.

◉ Sleeping

With dozens of hotels in renovated old Seville mansions, there's a wealth of attractive, intimate lodging to choose from.

€€ Las Casas de la Judería, Cjón Dos Hermanas 7, T954-415150, www.casasypalacios.com. Spread across several old *palacios*, this hotel has sparkling patios, pretty nooks and hanging foliage.

€€ Las Casas de los Mercaderes, C Alvarez Quintero 9, T954-225858, www.casasypalacios.com. A beautifully renovated hotel, sibling establishment to Las Casas de la Judería. Built around a beautiful arcaded patio.

€€ Las Casas del Rey de Baeza, Pl Jesús de la Redención 2, off C Santiago, T954-561496, www.hospes.es. An enchanting old *corral de vecinos* near Casa Pilatos, superbly restored. Rooftop pool and terrace as well as a beautifully decorated library and lounges.

€€-€ Hotel Amadeus, C Farnesio 6, T954-501443, www.hotelamadeus sevilla.com. A lovely small hotel. Some of the rooms are fabulous, some merely excellent. Roof terrace with views around the centre, including the Giralda. Highly recommended.

€ Hotel Simón, C García de Vinuesa 19, T954-226660, www.hotelsimon sevilla.com. Very attractive hotel built around a beautiful, airy courtyard with a fountain. There are plenty of *azulejos* and neo-Moorish features. Rooms are smallish but welcoming. Very well priced for the decor and ambience.

€ YH Giralda, C Abades 30, T954-228 324, www.yh-hoteles.com. Not to be confused with a youth hostel, this is a minimalist marble-decorated hotel in a great but quiet location. Good service and elegant and comfortable rooms.

◉ Eating

Your best moments in Seville are likely to be spent eating. Tapas was invented here and it's the place in Spain where it is done best. There's little distinction between tapas bars and restaurants, so we've listed them all together. A standard *tapa* will cost €1-2. The *menú del día*, a filling, set price three-course lunch (1330-1530 roughly) normally costs €6-12.

¶¶¶ Egaña Oriza, C San Fernando 41, south of Alcázar, T954-227211. 1330-1600, 2100-2400. A smart restaurant mixing Andalucían and Basque cuisine. Try the *salmorejo*, stewed wood pigeon, sole with saffron sauce and a great *ceviche* of monkfish and grouper.

¶¶ Kiosco de las Flores, C Betis s/n, T954-274576. Dining on the riverfront in Triana is a classic Sevilla experience. This is one of the best places to do it, with an enormous range of seafood and a lovely outlook.

¶¶ Taberna del Alabardero, C Zaragoza 20, T954-502721. Hospitality school and one of the city's best restaurants, with a delicious seasonal menu. House specials include *corvina* (sea bass). Downstairs is an atrium café/bar serving snacks and *raciones*.

¶ Bar Pepe Hillo, C Adriano 24, T954-215390. 1200-0100. A legend in its own tapas time, especially for stews such as the *caldereta de venao* venison. High-ceilinged, busy and buzzy.

¶ Bodega Santa Cruz, C Rodrigo Caro 2. 1200-2400. A busy and cheerful bar serving some of Seville's choicest tapas and *montaditos* (delicious little toasted sandwiches).

¶ Casa Morales, C García Vinuesa 11, T954-221242. Great old traditional place with big sherry jars, *montaditos*

served on wooden trays, and the tab chalked up on the bar in front of you.

¶ La Goleta, C Mateos Gago, Santa Cruz. Tue-Sun 0900-1500, 2000-2300. Tiny bar with loads of character. The tapas are limited but excellent, particularly the 'candid' tortilla.

◉ Nightlife

Seville's nightlife can't compete with Barcelona or Madrid but around Plaza Alfalfa and Calle Betis in Triana it's usually lively into the wee small hours. While much of the flamenco is geared to tourists, the quality of these performances is usually high, even if the atmosphere's a bit sterile. It's also possible to track down a more authentic experience; many bars have dedicated flamenco nights. The quality varies but the cost is minimal and occasionally you'll see something very special.

◉ Shopping

Seville's main shopping area is Centro around **Calles Sierpes**, **Tetuán**, **Velásquez**, **Cuna** and **Plaza del Duque**. This busy area is the place to come for clothes, be it modern Spanish or essential Seville Feria fashion; shawls, flamenco dresses, *mantillas*, ornamental combs, castanets and fans. Head to the **Alameda de Hércules** area for more offbeat stuff, either in the area's lively markets (Sun and Thu) or the smaller shops along Calles **Amor de Díos**, **Jesús del Gran Poder** or **Trajano**. If it's ceramics you're after, **Triana** is the place to go; there are dozens of attractively-decorated shops. Most can arrange reasonably-priced secure international delivery.

Elegantly built over several small islands, Stockholm can lay a fair claim to having one of the world's most beautiful city locations. In recent years it has shed its reputation as a provincial backwater and transformed itself into a far more cosmopolitan and dynamic place. No longer blond or bland, the city now pulsates with a creative energy which has helped form an urban culture with its sights firmly set on the world stage. Synonymous with both high-design and hi-tech it remains an eminently manageable and civilized place whose laid-back charm is reflected in its friendly, confident inhabitants, around a quarter of whom were born outside Sweden. Predominately young, these "new Swedes" are changing the way Stockholm thinks about itself.

Arts & culture
★★★

Eating
★★★

Nightlife
★★★

Outdoors
★★★★★

Romance
★★★

Shopping
★★★

Sightseeing
★★

Value for money
★★

Overall score
★★★

At a glance

The most important of Stockholm's 14 islands are the ones on which the city centre is built and they are all only a few metres from the mainland. At its heart, Stadsholmen, better known as **Gamla Stan**, is a mixture of narrow lanes and grand buildings while adjacent **Riddarholmen** is also rich in historical associations. **Skeppsholmen**, to the east, has the ultra-cool modern art museum while **Kungsholmen** to the west, houses the iconic City Hall. **Södermalm**, to the south, is the biggest island and one of the city's main entertainment districts. Here, around centrally placed **Medborgarplatsen**, you will find bars and restaurants that reflect the "New Sweden" with its cosmopolitan, design-led influences. It is also the centre of the city's relaxed gay scene. The modernist-inspired **city centre** is on the mainland 10 minutes from Södermalm. The streets around **Stureplan** offer exclusive clubbing and shopping, and **Vasastaden** is a busy commercial hub centred

I have never ceased to admire the genius who arranged that Stockholm be enclosed in a frame of wild nature.

Carl Jonas Love Almqvist (1793-1866)

round the train station T-Centralen. The walk from the centre east along the waterfront to the island of **Djurgården** is one of the most beautiful in any European city. With three of Sweden's biggest attractions (amusement park Gröna Lund, Skansen and the Vasa museums) it is also a great place to relax in rural tranquillity.

★ *Don't leave without stocking up on gravad sauce, elk ham and surströmming from Östermalmshallen.*

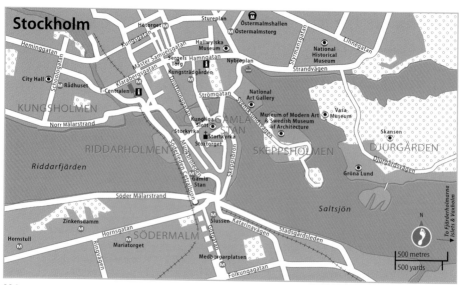

⊙ Sights

Gamla Stan

This island is the site of the majority of Stockholm's historic buildings and has been the stage on which much of Swedish history has been played out. Gamla Stan is still a partly residential area combined with a selection of government and royal buildings and plenty of cafés in its narrow streets with gabled roofs.

Just behind the main square, **Stortorget**, is Stockholm's impressive Cathedral and Royal Church, **Storkyrka** ① *Trångsund 1, daily 0900-1800, SEK 25.* It is ornately decorated and has a number of important Baroque artworks including the outstanding *St George and the Dragon* (Berndt Notke) from 1489.

Gamla Stan

Royal Palace (Kungliga Slott)

① *www.royalcourt.se. Times vary; some sections closed during state visits. SEK 120 for all parts of the palace or SEK 80 for individual sections.*

The massive bulk of Nicodemus Tessin's building dominates central Stockholm and is a powerful statement of the ambitions of the Swedish monarchy in the 18th century. Replacing an earlier palace which burnt down, it was completed in several stages and finally occupied in 1754. The austere façade is guarded by several stone lions. Its sumptuous interior is undeniably impressive – this is about as far as you can get from modern minimalist Swedish design.

During state visits the Royal Apartments are closed but the three museums within the palace stay open and have some interesting collections associated with the monarchy. The changing of the guard which takes place at 1215 every day (1315 on Sunday) is a well-drilled reminder that the Swedish monarchy is still solidly in place.

⊖ Travel essentials

Getting there Stockholm's main airport **Arlanda**, T08-797600, www.lfv.se, is 45 km from the city. **Arlanda Express** trains, www.arlandaexpress.com, cost SEK 360 return to T-Centralen and take just 20 mins. Trains leave from the station under the terminal. Buses with **Flyggbussarna**, www.flygbussarna.se, leave every 15 mins for the 40-min journey to the centre and cost SEK 89 single, SEK 170 return. A taxi will cost SEK 475 and take around 45 mins. **Stockholm Taxi**, T08-150000, www.taxistockholm.se.

Skavsta airport, T01-552804, www.skavsta-air.se, is the base for budget airlines including Ryanair. Buses are timed for the arrival and departure of flights. Fares are SEK 199 return, SEK130 single; it takes 80 mins to complete the 100 km trip. A taxi will cost around SEK 1250. **Nyköping Taxi**, T01-55217500.

From **Västerås airport**, T021-805600, www.vasterasflyggplats.se, **Flyggbussarna** take 75 mins to cover the 85 km to the city and charge SEK 199 return. A taxi will cost about SEK 1500 and take an hour. **Västerås Taxi**, T021-185000.

From **Bromma Airport**, T08-7976874, www.lfv.se, the 20-min journey with **Flyggbussarna** costs SEK 120 return. A taxi (**Stockholm Taxi**, T08-150000) will take 15 mins and cost about SEK 250.

Getting around Central Stockholm is compact and easily walkable. **Stockholm Transport**, www.sl.se, operate the efficient metro system as well as local buses, and commuter trains. The best value tickets are those valid for 24 or 72 hours (SEK 95 or SEK 180) and allow unlimited access to the whole network. Mainline services all depart from T-Centralen. Trains are operated by **Swedish Rail** (www.sj.se) or **Connex** (www.connex.se). Ferries to the

archipelago (see box overleaf) are run by **Waxholmsbolaget**, T08-6795830, www.waxholmsbolaget.se, and **Strömma Kanalbolaget**, T08-587140, www.strommakanalbolaget.com. They depart from Nybroplan on the mainland. For bike hire during the summer months **Rentabike**, T08-6607959, www.renta bike.se, is well established and reliable. Canoe hire is available from **Djurgårdsbrons Sjöcafé**, T08-6605757.

Tourist information The main tourist office, **Sverigehuset**, Hamngatan 27, T08-5082 8508, www.stockholm town.com, Mon-Fri 0900-1900, Sat 1000-1700, Sun 1000-1600, will deal with all inquiries. They also have a hotel booking service in T-Centralen T08-5082 8508.

Exchange rate Swedish Krona (SEK). £1 = SEK 14.21. €1 = SEK 9.62.

Vasa Museum

ⓘ *Galärvarvsvägen 14, Djurgården,
T08-5195 5810, www.vasamuseet.se.
Daily 1000-1700, longer hours in summer.
SEK 80.*

In 1628 at the height of Sweden's
military power the warship *Vasa*, which
was to be the flagship of the Swedish
navy, made its maiden voyage. It sank
barely one mile out to sea. The story of
the building of the *Vasa*, its demise and
ultimate rescue from the seabed is well
told in this purpose-built museum on
Djurgården. There is plenty of historical
background and multimedia
presentations but the main draw is
the ship itself. It is surprisingly large
and bulky and its stern has an
impressive number of warlike figures
and martial symbols.

Skansen

ⓘ *Djurgården, T08-4428000,
www.skansen.se. SEK 30-80 depending
on time of year. May 1000-2000; Jun-Aug
1000-2200; rest of year 1000-1600.*

Vasa Museum

Skansen

The prototype of all open-air
museums, Skansen holds a
sentimental place in every Swede's
heart. A kind of Noah's Ark for Swedish
rural buildings and industry, it first
opened its doors in 1892. All the
buildings were moved here from
other parts of Sweden in an attempt
to preserve a rural heritage that
was rapidly disappearing with
industrialization. There are displays
of traditional crafts and a collection
of Scandinavian animals including
bears and elks. The summer-only
open-air theatre hosts sing-a-long
concerts which are an unmissable
celebration of all things Swedish.

National Art Gallery

ⓘ *Södra Blasieholmshamnen, T08-
5195 4300, www.nationalmuseum.se.
Tue and Thu 1100-2000, Wed, Sat-Sun
1100-1700. Free.*

The paintings housed in this elegant
building reflect all periods of art
history. Highlights include Lucas
Cranach's portrait of Martin Luther
from 1526 and some fine Rembrandts.

◉ Best of the rest

Stockholm City Hall
ⓘ *Hantverkargartan 1, T08-5082
9058, www.stockholm.se/cityhall.
SEK 60 with tours everyday at 1000
and 1200. Metro T-Centralen.*
The Blue Room modelled on an
Italian Piazza and the Byzantine-
inspired mosaics are the highlights
of this iconic building which hosts
the Nobel Prize dinner.
National Historical Museum
ⓘ *Narvavägen 13-17, T08-5195
5600, www.historiska.se. Daily
1100-1700. Free.* Ancient gold,
art from the Romanesque and
Gothic periods plus the world's
oldest carpet and a unique Viking
collection out in Östermalm.
Hallwylska Museum
ⓘ *Hamngatan 4, T08-519555,
www.hallwylskamuseet.se. Tue-Sun
1200-1600. Free.* A remarkably
opulent house standing as a
monument to the various
collections built up over a
lifetime by its magpie-like owners.

National Art Gallery

With picturesque red houses, perfect beaches and beautiful scenery, the thousands of islands which make up Stockholm's archipelago make an excellent place for an excursion from the city. The islands vary in size and character. Some, like **Vaxholm**, are lived on all the time, while others have no permanent population. Geographically they are divided into the Northern, Middle or Southern archipelago depending on their position in the Baltic.

No matter how short your time in Stockholm a day trip should be a priority. Stockholmers are very proud of having them on their doorstep and the lucky ones try to commute by boat during the summer.

The closest are the **Fjärderholmarna islets**, about 25 minutes by boat. Vaxholm is a year-round option and a good introduction to the archipelago.

Some of the islands have ferry services throughout the year from Nybroplan on the mainland. The main companies operating ferries to the archipelago have detailed information on their websites. Waxholmsbolaget and Strömma Kanalbolaget are the biggest operators (see Travel essentials box, page 237).

The tourist office website (www.stockholmtown.com) has details of individual islands and accommodation options. For longer stays in wooden cottages **www.dess.se** (T08-5424 81 00) have an online booking service.

Swedish painters such as Larsson and Zorn are also well represented. The other permanent collection focuses on Swedish design and is a must-see for all those who have ever bought IKEA furniture or marvelled at a cleverly- designed household appliance.

Stockholm archipelago

Museum of Modern Art and Swedish Museum of Architecture

① *Exercisplan, Skeppsholmen, T08-5195 5200, www.arkitektur museet.se, www.modernamuseet.se. Tue-Wed 1000-2000 Thu-Sun 1000-1800. Free.*

Located on the city centre island of Skeppsholmen and housed in the same converted military building, these museums are rapidly becoming Swedish design icons. The strength of the Modern Art museum's permanent collection lies in its depth. Works include Magritte's *The Red Model* and paintings by Picasso, Dali and Matisse.

The outstanding Museum of Architecture has a permanent display illustrating the history of Swedish urbanism as well as temporary exhibitions. There is an excellent restaurant and café.

◉ Sleeping

Finding reasonably-priced accommodation in Stockholm can be a challenge and you are advised at all times to book well in advance. Most hotels in the centre have discounted weekend rates or other special

Museum of Modern Art

offers. Try the tourist office website, www.stockholmtown.com, for bed and breakfast accommodation.

€€€ Grand Hotel, Södra Blasieholmshamnen, T08-6793500, www.grandhotel.se. Stockholm's most famous hotel has an unrivalled position on the waterfront and is unsurpassed for class and service. Its exquisite bar is a good place to spot a famous face.

€€€ Rival Hotel, Mariatorget 3, T08-54578900, www.rival.se. Metro Mariatorget. Stylish and classy hotel in central Södermalm with individually designed rooms. The hotel is owned by Benny Andersson and if one of his musicals is in town there are good-value packages on offer.

€€ Nordic Sea Hotel, Vasaplan 7, T08-50563000, www.nordicsea hotel.se. Metro T-Centralen. One of a brace of hotels owned by Nordic Hotels, the Nordic Sea has a modern, efficient ambiance. The famous *Ice Bar* is on the ground floor.

€ Log Inn Hotel, Kajplats 16 Södermälarstrand, T08-4424420, www.loginn.se. Metro Slussen. A 10-min walk from Slussen, this is the best value of Stockholm's nautically themed hotels. Cabins are a little small but manage to squeeze in a bathroom. The view across to City Hall and the location make this an excellent option.

€ STF Hostel af Chapman, Flagmansvägen 8, Skeppsholmen, T08-4632266, www.stfturist.se. Metro Kungsträdgården. Deservedly famous central hostel. While most of the rooms are land-based some are aboard the old clipper moored permanently to Skeppsholmen. Book well in advance if you want one of these. There is also a bar.

🍴 Eating

Swedish food has undergone something of a revolution in the past few years with the opening up of a wave of restaurants specializing in international cuisine. Södermalm is the best place to find these while Gamla Stan has traditional Swedish food of a high quality and price.

¶¶¶ Den Gyldene Freden, Österlånggatan 51, T08-249760, www.gyldenefreden.se. Mon-Fri 1700-2400, Sat 1300-2400. Metro Gamla Stan. Sweden's oldest restaurant has been around for over 200 years. The fish-biased menu always has some Nordic influences. Romantic and classy.

¶¶¶ Gondolen på Södermalm, Katarinahissen, Stadsgården 6, T08-6417090. Mon-Fri 1130-0100, Sat 1600-0100. Metro Slussen. Sitting on top of the KF Huset at Slussen (take the lift from the waterfront) this is one of Stockholm's best restaurants. The modern menu competes with the decor for sophistication and the view from the restaurant is spectacular.

¶¶ Koh Phangan, Skånegatan 57, Södermalm, T08-6425040. Mon-Fri 1100-0100, Sat-Sun 1400-0100. Metro Medborgarplatsen. Wildly popular Thai-inspired place in Södermalm complete with beach hut decor. Booking essential at weekends.

¶ Jerusalem Kebab, Gåsgränd off Västerlånggatan, Gamla Stan. Tue-Thu 0900-0100, Fri-Sun 0900-0300. Metro Gamla Stan. Hidden away off Västerlånggatan this Palestinian-owned place serves up tasty and cheap Middle Eastern food with vegetarian options. There is a small courtyard terrace a few metres from the entrance.

¶ Stadshuskälleren, Stadshuset, T08-50632200. Metro Stadshuset. A good lunchtime option, this restaurant in a corner of City Hall has a competitively priced menu at SEK 125. However, its star offering is the menu from the Nobel Prize dinner which weighs in at a hefty SEK 1350.

🌙 Nightlife

Going out in central Stockholm is an expensive, flashy affair with a lot of queuing involved. The pubs around Medborgarplatsen and Frihemsplan are more relaxed. The best option is to pick a place with live music and spend the evening there. Note that smoking is now forbidden in all Swedish bars.

For clubs, **Berns**, Berzelii Park, T08-56632222, Metro Östermalmstorget, is an impressive complex tucked away at the back of Berzelii Park with a relaxed atmosphere and a young crowd. Book in advance to get to **The Ice Bar**, Nordic Sea Hotel, T08-50563124, www.nordicseahotel.se. SEK 140 entrance including drink. You are only likely to go here once but it is an unforgettable experience. After donning your silver Parka you will be served a drink in a bar where everything is made of ice.

Spy Bar, Birger Jarlsgatan 20, T08-54503701, Metro Östermalstorget, is the Armani-clad ruler of Stockholm designer nightclubs. For a friendly live music scene **Stampen**, Stora Nygatan 5, T08-205794, has a jazz club feel.

Tallinn, the medieval, upwardly mobile capital of Estonia, owes its fortunes and seemingly endless misfortunes to its strategic location on the eastern shore of the Baltic Sea. The city has been moulded by a combination of Teutonic efficiency and Russian extravagance, and has shaken off decades of Soviet occupation with astounding success. Although its architecture is often described as 'fairy-tale', there's nothing twee about it: the soaring spires and narrow Hanseatic merchants' houses leaning perilously into the streets and washed with watery limes, lemons and pinks, are unfussy, even austere. The Old Town, encircled by forest and rugged city walls, spirals down to the silvery Bay of Tallinn, and is especially alluring in snow when hotels slash rates and the cobbles seem coated with crushed diamonds.

Tallinn

Arts & culture
★★

Eating
★★

Nightlife
★★★★

Outdoors
★★

Romance
★★★★

Shopping
★★

Sightseeing
★★★

Value for money
★★★★

Overall score
★★★

At a glance

The heart of the city is the **Vanalinn** (Old Town), which is ringed by a rough limestone city wall. Traditionally the haunt of nobles, politicians and administrators, **Toompea** (Upper Town) sits in splendid isolation on the hill dominating the city, with spectacular views of the sea and the maze of medieval streets below. East of Toompea and down the hill, the kidney bean-shaped **All-Linn** (Lower Town) extends north from Harju Street along Pikk (Long) Street to the sea. Wedged between the wider streets is a higgledy-piggledy scrawl of cobbled lanes and medieval houses. Its focal point at all hours of the day and night is **Raekoja Plats** (Town Hall Square). Beyond the walls of the Old Town, bastions and a former moat have been transformed into lush parkland. The leafy seaside suburb of **Kadriorg**, with its baroque palace, is a 10-minute tram ride away. Further east, near the 1980 Olympics Centre, you can hit **Pirita** beach, take to the river and

Tallinn is probably the only foreign city in the world [outside Finland] where a poetry reading in Finnish can attract a crowd.

The Economist

admire The skeletal ruins of St Birgitta's convent. On the other side of town, a short bus ride away, is the cliffside Rocca Al Mare Open Air Museum, where you can get a unique insight into Estonian peasant life.

★ *Don't leave town without enjoying the views from Toompea in the early morning.*

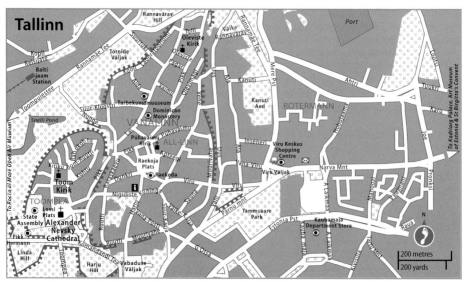

◉ Sights

Raekoja Plats (Town Hall Square)

Raekoja Plats is one of Europe's most appealing squares, especially on a summer evening, when the shade of the sky seems tailor-made for the gentle pinks, whites and blues of the façades. The Gothic **Raekoda** (Town Hall) ① *T645-7900, Jul-Aug Mon-Sat 1000-1600, EEK 35, guided visits by appointment Jun-Sep,* has been scrubbed clean to reveal the original creamy colour of the limestone, much to the surprise of the locals, who'd grown up with it being grey. The view from the **tower** ① *May-Aug 1100-1800, EEK 25,* is well worth the slightly perilous ascent.

Pühavaimu Kirik (Church of the Holy Ghost)

① *T644-1487, www.eelk.ee. EEK 10.*

Just north of Raekoja Plats, this modest yet prodigiously pretty church was

Raekiia Plats (Town Hall Square)

completed in 1360. The only hint of flamboyance on its façade is an alluring copper spire (added in 2002) and the city's oldest public clock, carved by Christian Ackermann in the 17th century. The interior has an intimate feel and contains one of the city's most prized medieval works of art, the 15th-century altar by Berndt Notke.

Katariina Käik (St Catherine's passageway)

East of Pühavaimu Kirik and next to the **Dominican Monastery ruins** ① *Vene 16, T644-4606, May-Sep daily 0930-1800, EEK 45,* is the city's most romantic alley. It's a narrow passageway with overhead vaulting, wrought-iron lamps and artisan workshops (where you can watch people at work). Look out for the medieval tombstones, too.

Tarbekunstimuuseum (Applied Arts Museum)

① *Lai 17, T627-4600. Wed-Sun 1100-1800. EEK 20.*

Towards the north of the Lower Town, in a former granary, storehouse and powder magazine, this is one of the city's best museums. Three floors are devoted to ceramics, glassware, leather, metalwork, textiles and jewellery.

Oleviste Kirik (St Olaf's Church)

① *Pikk 48, T641-2241. Spire Apr-Oct 100-1800. EEK 25.*

Two blocks northeast of Raekoja Plats is the dazzlingly white Oleviste Church,

---

⊖ Travel essentials

Getting there Ulemiste Airport, www.tallinn-airport.ee, is 4 km southeast of the city centre. Taxis charge about EEK 100 to central Tallinn. Bus 2 leaves every 20 mins, 0700-2400, and stops near the Kaubamaja department store; EEK 15, one-way. The journey takes 15 mins.

Getting around The Old Town is easily negotiable by foot; a gentle stroll around the historic centre takes about 4 hrs. Outside the city walls, there's a reliable network of buses, trolleybuses and trams (EEK 15 from the driver, EEK 10 from kiosks; day tickets EEK 40). The city bus terminal is under the Viru Keskus

shopping centre. Pick up a transport map from the tourist office, bookshops and kiosks. Taxis are much cheaper than in most western cities; there are ranks at road intersections and outside the bigger hotels. The Old Town is hilly and cobbled, but elsewhere there is a good system of cycle lanes. Further information is available at www.tallinn.ee.

Tourist information Tallinn's main tourist office is at Kullassepa 4/Niguliste 2, around the corner from Raekoja Plats, T645-7777, www.tourism.tallinn.ee. Jul-Aug Mon-Fri 0900-2000, Sat-Sun

1000-1700; Sep Mon-Fri 0900-1800, Sat-Sun 1000-1700; Oct-Apr Mon-Fri 0900-1900, Sat-Sun 1000-1700. They can put you in touch with specialist guides and provide a free map and information about sights and excursions around Estonia. White posters displayed around the city list cultural events. The **Tallinn Card**, available from the tourist office, offers free entry to museums, unlimited public transport and other activities; from EEK 130 for 6 hrs to EEK 400 for 72 hrs. Many museums are closed Mon-Tue.

Exchange rate Estonian Kroon (EEK). £1 = EEK 23.13. €1 = EEK 15.65.

once the tallest building in Europe. The dizzyingly high, needle-thin copper tower was used as a radio transmitter by the KGB. The viewing platform has breathtaking views.

Toompea (Upper Town)

Toompea's main square, **Lossi Plats** (Castle Square), has been the seat of power since ancient times. All that remains of its once imposing medieval castle, however, are the west and south walls and three grey towers, including the iconic **Pikk Hermann** ⓘ *to arrange a tour, T631-6357, Mon-Fri, 1000-1600.* The square is dominated by the fudge-coloured, onion-domed **Alexander Nevsky Cathedral**, erected in 1900 as a symbol of Russian authority. Much older and altogether more dignified is the austere but alluring **Toom Kirik** (St Mary's Cathedral) ⓘ *www.eelk.ee/ tallinna.toom.* The pink confection next to Nevsky Cathedral is the **State Assembly Building** ⓘ *T631-6357, www.riigikogu.ee, book in advance for tours, Wed-Fri, free,* home of Estonia's parliament, with an expressionist interior that belies the demure façade.

St Olaf's Church

Kadriorg Palace Park

Kadriorg Palace

ⓘ *Wezenbergi 37, T606-6400, www.ekm.ee/kadriorg. Tue-Sun 1000-1700, Oct-Apr Wed-Sun only. EEK 45.*

East of the Old Town, in a delightful park; the palace was designed in 1718 for Peter the Great by Italian architect Nicolo Michetti. Mulberry-coloured, with cream pillars and graceful oval windows, it is modest, sober baroque at its best, and a fine setting for the Estonian Art Museum's foreign section. Just north stands the new **Art Museum of Estonia** ⓘ *Weizenbergi 34/Valge 1, T644-9139, www.ekm.ee, Tue-Sun 1100-1800, winter Wed-Sun only, EEK 75 for all shows,* a superb glass and concrete structure dedicated to Estonian art from the 18th century to the present, as well as temporary international shows.

St Birgitta's Convent, Pirita

ⓘ *Kloostri 9, T605-5044. Jan-Apr, Nov-Dec daily 1200-1600, summer 1000-1800. EEK 20.*

The skeletal silhouette of this ruined convent, founded in 1407 by a trio of widowed merchants, is a spectacular sight. The gable was a useful orientation point for seamen. Damaged by Ivan the Terrible's troops, it was reduced to ruins during the Northern War. The remains have been sensitively restored and the nuns now live in an award-winning modern building with a guesthouse.

Rocca al Mare

ⓘ *Vabaõhumuuseumi tee 12, T654-9100. May-Aug 1000-2000, buildings until 1800; Sep 1000-1800, buildings until 1700; Oct 1000-1800, buildings until 1600; Nov-Apr 1000-1700, buildings closed. EEK 30 summer, EEK 15 winter.*

The "Rock by the Sea" is a collection of 18th-century farm buildings from Estonia, including thatched barn dwellings and windmills, assembled on a serene clifftop site overlooking Kopli Bay. On weekends between May and August, folk dance groups give humorous displays at 1100. The sometimes inelegant moves involve male dancers bumping each other's bottoms.

✻ Rampart rambles

Given the number of sieges, attacks and aerial bombardments Tallinn has endured, it's little short of miraculous that 80% of the city fortifications, including 29 towers, have survived. The bumpy limestone walls, splashed with orange-topped turrets, are the city's most distinctive feature – a reminder that this was once one of the most impregnable stongholds in northern Europe. Tallinn was further fortified in the 16th century, with earthen embankments and ramparts. In the 17th century, the Swedes planned to surround the city with 12 bastions; in the end, only a handful were built. For Peter the Great, Tallinn's strategic importance lay at sea and, following Russia's decision to strike Tallinn off the list of fortified towns in the mid-19th century, the bastions were handed over to the municipality, which had the good sense to transform them into parks and public gardens. The only surviving scraps of the Swedish bastions are Rannavärav, Harju and Linda hills. One of the best views of city towers is from Rannamäe, west of the city, while the loveliest stretch of reclaimed parkland runs from the manicured Tornide

Väljak (Square of Towers), between Rannamäe tee and the Old Town (reach it via Suurtuki Street, where cannon were once repaired), to the more romantic, rambling area around Šnelli Pond. Named after a local gardener, the pond is all that remains of the medieval moat. Watch out for pickpockets, who are sometimes a problem here.

◉ Sleeping

Prices are low by European standards. Early reservation is essential in summer, especially during the National Song Festival and around midsummer.
In winter, prices plummet with the temperature.

€€€ Three Sisters, Pikk 71, T630-6300, www.threesistershotel.com. A boutique hotel in a cream and yellow trio of medieval merchants' houses. Sleekly designed, with large glass windows that sit well with the old beams and vaulted ceilings. The soft cream furnishings are of superb quality, and the bathrobes and bed linen are to die for.

€€ Merchant's House Hotel, Dunkri 4/6, T697-7500, www.merchants househotel.com. The city's most central boutique hotel, with fresh, modern interiors and wooden floors in a medieval setting of painted and beamed ceilings, arranged around a pretty inner courtyard. Some rooms are on the small side. Cheaper summer rates Aug-Sep.

€€ Old Town Maestro's, Suur-Karja 10, T626-2000, www.maestro hotel.ee. This former merchant's dwelling, rebuilt in historicist style in 1928, has spacious, high-ceilinged rooms with large mirrors and dark wooden furniture. Unusually in Tallinn, most rooms have baths.

€ Eurohostel, Nunne 2, T644-7788, www.eurohostel.ee. One of Tallinn's newest and freshest-looking hostels. The rooms are sparse but reasonably stylish, and there's a guest kitchen.

€ Old House Guesthouse, Uus 22, T641-1464, www.oldhouse.ee. Simple rooms on a quirky street at the northeastern edge of the Vanalinn. Very quiet at night.

€ UniqueStay, Paldiski maantee 3, T660-0700, www.uniquestay.com. A fun, fresh hotel at the northwest foot of Toompea Hill, with bright colour schemes and crisp design throughout. Arty photos lend a touch of gravitas. The Zen rooms have NASA-designed chairs and whirlpool baths. Free parking, free 24-hr internet access.

🍴 Eating

Tallinn is packed with eateries serving everything from hearty German-influenced Estonian dishes to fine French cuisine with a local twist. The restaurant scene has developed pretty much from scratch in the past 15 years and establishments come and go at breakneck speed.

🍴🍴🍴 **Gloria**, Müürivahe 2, T644-6950, www.gloria.ee. Genuine pre-war nostalgia, with a resolutely retro interior and plush crimson furnishings. Serves French and Russian classics, with nods to local tradition and Italian cuisine: beluga caviar, borscht, fillets of sole, duck with mango and local lamb dishes. The best wine cellar in the Baltics, to boot.

🍴🍴🍴 **Vertigo**, Rävala puiestee 4, T5349-4222, www.vertigo.ee. Top Tallinn chef and TV personality Imre Kose's new chic but cosy restaurant, in a modern building south of the Old Town, has a seafood bar, lounge and fine dining section, as well as a rooftop terrace and stunning views. Expect inspired cuisine that makes the most of local produce as well as top-quality imports.

🍴🍴 **Olde Hansa**, Vanaturu kael 1, T627-9020, www.oldehansa.com. Themed medieval restaurant with a summer terrace popular with Tallinners and foreigners alike. Try authentic Hansa-era dishes such as slow-baked Wittenberg pork in beer or dried elk meat with juniper-ripened beef, all without a chip in sight. Huge portions, best washed down with a pot of honeyed beer.

🍴🍴 **Pegasus**, Harju 1, T631-4040, www.restoranpegasus.ee. For most locals, this is the place to see and be seen, but, though its sleek, white, 1970s-referencing decor is perfect for posing, Pegasus is utterly without pretension. The British chef makes splendid curries and is forever creating new dishes, among them scallops with asparagus and lime, sea bass with truffle sausage or beef tenderloin with morel sauce. Great views from the terrace and the upstairs dining area.

🍴 **Café Spirit**, Mere puiestee 6e, T661-6151, www.kohvikspirit.ee. Good sushi is one of the main attractions at this trendy but relaxed café that combines minimalism with comfy sofas. The salads are some of

❝❞ They say pre-war Tallinn never slept, not even in winter. After the blip of the Soviet era, that is pretty much the case again.

the best in town. Popular with fashionable locals and no doubt deliberately difficult for tourists to find (the entrance is round the back).

🍴 **Eesti Maja**, Lauteri 1, T645-5252, www.eestimaja.ee. An unpretentious institution south of the Old Town, serving traditional Estonian food: cabbage soup, chanterelles in cream, spiced sprats and pearl barley.

🍸 Nightlife

They say pre-war Tallinn never slept, not even in winter. After the blip of the Soviet era, that is pretty much the case again, and the city is a paradise for 24-hour party people. Admission and drinks are a bargain, with most venues attracting an up-for-it, unpretentious crowd. You'll find sophisticated sounds in the hippest places and more idiosyncratic music policies in the Old Town's cellar bars. Visit www.mutantdisco.com, www.vonkrahl.ee and www.stereo88.com for the best parties in town. For unfussy dancefloor fun, head to **Hollywood** (www.club-hollywood.ee), in an old Stalinist cinema. At the other extreme, **Võit**, www.lovesexmoney.ee, is a low-key underground venue with techno, drum'n'bass and rock nights.

Classical, contemporary and choral music concerts are absurdly inexpensive and of exceptional quality: don't miss performances by Hortus Musicus (early music), NYYD Ensemble (contemporary), the Estonian Philharmonic Chamber Choir or Ellerhein Girls' Choir.

🛍 Shopping

Visiting Tallinn today, it doesn't seem possible that only 14 years ago you had to queue for overpriced, over-ripe tomatoes or make do without toothpaste and toilet paper. Now the Old Town is awash with shops selling amber, Russian dolls, juniper-wood butter knives and impossibly thick winter socks. Viru Tänav, in All-Linn, is the main shopping street. There are regular handicraft markets on Raekoja Plats. For genuine Estonian handicrafts try the **Estonian Folk Art and Craft Union**, T660-4772, www.crafts.ee, which has several outlets. For cutting-edge Estonian design and clubwear, try **Nu Nordik**, Vabaduse Väljäk 8, T644-9392, www.nunordik.ee.

Turin

With its baroque castles and royal palaces, regal arcaded squares and stately tree-lined boulevards, all crowned by a breathtaking alpine backdrop, Turin displays all the grace of the Savoy family. It was in the aristocratic and artistic cafés of this sophisticated salon society that the idea of an Italian Republic was converted from a twinkle into a reality. Beneath Turin's classic exterior lurks the rebellious and possessed soul of an awkward child prodigy. It is the product of an incongruous collection of assets and eccentric character traits that combine to cast a peculiar sense of alchemy, like a shroud, over the city. These attractions, so long veiled in alpine mist and black magic mythology, are soon to be illuminated by the Winter Olympic flame.

Arts & culture
★★

Eating
★★★★

Nightlife
★★★

Outdoors
★★★★

Romance
★★

Shopping
★★★

Sightseeing
★★

Value for money
★★★

Overall score
★★★

● Sights

Turin is a long oblong of a city with north-south boulevards traversed by a grid of side streets. With a few exceptions, most of the city's sights, retail and nightlife lie within the boundary of corso Regina Margherita to the north and corso Vittorio Emanuele II to the south, piazza Statuto to the West and the River Po to the east.

Piazza Castello

In a city symmetrically balanced by many fine squares, **piazza Castello** is Turin's most majestic, a visual recorder of the city's history. Cloistered by a quadrangle of porticoes, three sides of it are flanked by the baroque and neoclassical façades of the former residences of the House of Savoy and Turin's main theatre. On the northern side is the **Palazzo and Giardini Reale**

Mole Antonelliana

ⓘ *T011- 4361455, www.ambienteto.arti. beniculturali.it, Tue-Sun 0900-1930, €6.50*, the Savoy royal palace and gardens. Annexed to the Palazzo Reale is **Duomo di San Giovanni Battista** ⓘ *T011-4361540, 0800-1200, 1500-1900*, the only remnant of Renaissance architecture in the city. The **Cappella della Santa Sindone** was once home

to the city's most famed asset: the **Shroud**. Since a fire in 1997 the chapel has been closed and the Shroud firmly guarded, only making the most occasional of appearances. At the centre of the piazza stands the **Palazzo Madama** ⓘ *T011- 4429931, www.comune.torino.it/palazzomadama, Tue-Fri and Sun 1000-2000, Sat 1000-2300, Mon closed*. The former Savoy castle, built on the original eastern Roman city gate, is a synthesis of the story of Turin.

East of piazza Castello

Between the atmospheric arches of via Po and corso Regina Margherita is the heart of Turin's university life, a tight network of lively and youthfully shabby streets. At the end of via Po the street opens out into **piazza Vittorio Veneto** which slopes down to the river and the **Murazzi**, scene of riverside cafés and subversive nocturnal activities. Rising

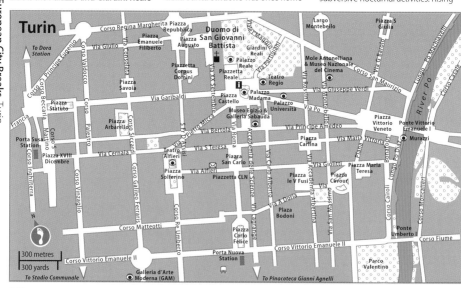
Turin map

Murazzi riverside cafés

above this quarter, a lone spire towering above the city, is the **Mole Antonelliana** ⓘ *via Montebello 20, T011-8125658, Tue-Sun 0900-2000, Sat until 2300, Mon closed,* Turin's equivalent of the Eiffel Tower. Inside, the acclaimed **Museo Nazionale del Cinema** ⓘ *www.museonazionale delcinema.org, Tue-Sun 0900-2000, Sat until 2300, Mon closed, €6.80,* is considered by many to be the most spectacular cinema museum in Europe.

Around the narrow streets south of via Po are some unexpected but world-class museums. The **Museo Egizio** ⓘ *via Accademia delle Scienze 6, T011-5617776, www.museoegizio.org, daily except Mon 0830-1930, €6.20,* has the largest collection of Egyptian artefacts outside Cairo; while **Galleria Sabauda** ⓘ *via Accademia delle Scienze 6, T011-547440, Tue-Sat, 0830-1930 (until 2330 on public holidays that fall on Sat), €4.13,* contains many classics by the old masters. Further south, across corso Vittorio Emanuele II and east of porta Nuova, is **Parco Valentino**, complete with botanical garden, a majestic baroque palace and a faux-medieval castle. Fiat (Fabbrica Italiana Automobili

Torino), the city's most famous company, was based around here. South along via Nizza is the former **Lingotto** factory, its roof-top testing track made famous by *The Italian Job.* It now houses a super-modern Renzo Piano museum, the **Pinacoteca Gianni Agnelli**, which is home to masterpieces from Canaletto to Picasso.

West of piazza Castello

Running south of piazza Castello, **via Roma** is a catwalk home for the flashiest boutiques, while west of here Turin is at its most Parisian – an area of art nouveau architecture appropriately found on **corso Francia**. At the heart of a more modern corner of Turin, south of corso Vittorio Emmanuele II, **Galleria d'Arte Moderna** ⓘ *via Magenta 31, T011- 5629911, www.gamtorino.it, Tue-Sun 0900-1900, €5.50,* is at the very cutting edge of modern art. South of the centre on corso IV Novembre is the **Stadio Comunale**, training ground of Juventus, Italy's pre-eminent football club and now Olympic theatre.

The alleyways north of **via Garibaldi**, the area of the original Roman

Price: £4.99
ISBN: 1 903471 84 2
www.footprintbooks.com

Design city

The dukes of Savoy may have given Turin its baroque splendour, but it was the city's industrial importance that shaped much of what it was to become. In promoting the car, Turin celebrated the values of the artists and architects of the early 20th-century avant-garde movements which were being theorized in Paris: the new, the fast and the marriage of design with function. The grand city of arcades and palazzi had to expand and adapt to its new vocation and many of the early industrial buildings, such as the Lingotto factory, were praised by Marinetti – founder of Futurism – for they were not merely simple industrial spaces but important pieces of a modernist architectural legacy. Due to its proximity to France and historic openness to French influence, Turin was the gateway through which many modernist inventions and movements such as art nouveau, pret-à-porter fashion and cinema first came to Italy.

settlement, see a weekly weekend **market**, while north of piazza Repubblica is Turin's monthly flea market, **Il Gran Balon**. Further north around the freight station are post-industrial warehouses, which have been turned into clubs and late lounges.

European City Breaks Turin

⊖ Travel essentials

Getting there Turin's **Sandro Pertini Airport (Caselle)**, T011-5676 6361/2, www.aeroportoditorino.it, is 16 km north of Turin. A taxi will cost around €40. The twice hourly train service (0500-2100) to Dora station, northwest of the centre, takes 20 mins. Tickets cost €2.58 one way. Buses to the centre run between 0515- 2300, every 30-45 mins depending on time of day. Tickets (purchased on board, in newstands or at the bus terminal) cost €5 each way for the 40-min journey. Stops in town include Turin's main railway stations, porta Susa and porta Nuova. The terminus at the corner of via Sacchi 8 and via Assietta.

Getting around Turin is quite a long city but most of the main sights are within an easy 20 mins' walk of each other. From 0500-2400 Turin is served by a very efficient network of **buses** and **trams**. A detailed map of line numbers and routes is available from the **Gruppo Trasporti Torino (GTT)**, www.gtt.to.it, with a sales office in porta Nuova station. Tickets are transferable between bus and tram and can be bought at bars or newsagents furnishing the 'T' (*Tabacchi*) sign outside, or from any public place displaying the GTT sticker. An *ordinario* costs €0.90 and lasts for 70 mins from the time you validate it on board the bus or tram.

The **TorinoCard**, available from any tourist office, offers either 48 hrs (€15) or 72 hrs (€17) unlimited transport and free entry to over 130 museums and sights.

Construction is still ongoing for Turin's **underground railway**, to be completed by 2006. There will be just one line initially connecting the centre and factory districts with the outlying countryside.

You can't hail **taxis** on the street so go to the nearest taxi rank or call one of the city's taxi co-operative numbers: T011-5737, T011-5730 or T011-3399.

Tourist information The main office is at the Atrium in piazza Solferino, T011-535181. There are other offices in piazza Castello inside the Palazzo Madama, T011-535901, at the airport, T011-5678124, and in the porta Nuova station, T011-531327. Useful websites include www.turismotorino.org and www.comune.torino.it.

⊕ Sleeping

€€€ Grand Hotel Sitea, via Carlo Alberto 35, T011-5170171, www.thi.it. A refined and elegant luxury hotel in an 18th-century palazzo with an understated decor that oozes charm. Also has fine restaurant.

€€€ Le Meridien Art & Tech, via Nizza 230, T011-6642000, www.lemeridien-lingotto.it. A little detached from the Turin of arcades, museums and shops, but nevertheless the number one choice for contemporary design.

€€ Dogana Vecchia, via Corte d'Appello 4, T011-4367272. A former 17th-century customs house, this is one of the most atmospheric of Turin's hotels. The wood-panelled rooms are full of baroque furniture.

€€ Liberty, via Pietro Micca 15, T011-5628801, www.hotelliberty-torino.it. On a road of fine art nouveau buildings, this palazzo (about to emerge from a refit) attracts an arty, film-world clientele.

€ Des Artistes, via Principe Amedeo 21/d, T011-8124416. An good value hotel in one of Turin's most evocative addresses. It's quiet and comfortable and the atmosphere both in and around the hotel does not disappoint.

⊘ Eating

♈♈♈ Neuv Caval 'd Brons, piazza San Carlo, T011-5627483. One of the city's gastronomic classics offering a menu that has kept up with the times.

♈♈♈ Ristorante del Cambio, piazza Carignano 2, T011-543760. Open since 1757 and one of Turin's most illustrious eateries. The decor is operatic, the food and service very much the same.

♈ Le Vitel Etonne, via San Francesco de Paola 4, T011-8124621. More of a winery than a restaurant but the food is delicious and servings substantial – it's just a question of priorities and the rustic atmosphere emphasizes this.

Caffe San Carlo, piazza San Carlo 156. With the air of a museum, this grand café's columns, sculptures and paintings could grace a royal court. Unmissable for its regal atmosphere.

⊙ Nightlife

When it comes to clubbing in Turin, don't expect the slightly dodgy techno of Milan or other Italian cities. Turin's edge is its grungy youth culture based around reggae, drum'n'bass and jazz. The late hour meccas are the Po-side **Murazzi**, where former boathouses have been transformed into riverside clubs (many only open in summer), and the jazz venues of the **Docks Dora** in the northwest. The revitalized *quadrilatero romano*, north of via Garibaldi, is virtually wall-to-wall with funky new bars, many sponsored by Martini (the original aperitif, born in Turin) who have invented the concept of the 'drinner' (a Martini or 2 with food and music). These bars become the city's late lounges with St Germain and their imitators turned up high on the speakers.

European City Breaks Turin

Valencia once languished in the shadow of flashy Madrid and trendy Barcelona but its days as a wallflower are long over. The word is out: Valencia, with its vibrant medieval core, fantastic nightlife, shopping and restaurants, sandy beaches, and some of the most spectacular new architecture in Europe, is the hottest destination on the Mediterranean. But Valencia has only just begun: the decision to host the 2007 America's Cup will mean a new marina and several slick new amenities all cementing its position as one of the most forward-looking cities in Spain. But its traditional charms – the palm-lined boulevards, baroque belltowers, Modernista markets and golden beaches – still assert their pull. It's a city in which old and new, shabby and sleek, co-exist peacefully.

Valencia

Arts & culture
★★★

Eating
★★★

Nightlife
★★★★

Outdoors
★★★

Romance
★★

Shopping
★★

Sightseeing
★★★

Value for money
★★★

Overall score
★★★

At a glance

Valencia divides neatly into three general areas, each with a distinctive atmosphere. The **Old City**, 4 km inland, is still the heart of Valencia, home to most of the sights and the best selection of nightlife and shopping. It's the perfect neighbourhood for a wander – you won't need public transport. Spreading out from the Old City eastwards to the sea is the **New City**, a largely anonymous area of bland offices and apartments, but also the site of the glittering new **Ciutat de les Arts i les Ciències** (City of Arts and Sciences). It's quite a walk (around 3 km) from the Old City, but a pleasant stroll along the gardens which line the former riverbed of the Riu Túria. The New City connects the Old City with Valencia's vast working **port** and the main city beach of **Malvarrosa**. This long, golden stretch is lined with a modern promenade, behind which are the scruffy, cheerful neighbourhoods of Malvarrosa and Cabanyal which once belonged to the dock workers and fishermen.

I have tried to get close to the frontier between architecture and sculpture and to understand architecture as an art.

Santiago Calatrava,
architect of the City of Arts and Sciences

★ *Don't leave town without checking out the obscene sculpture on the doorway to La Llotja.*

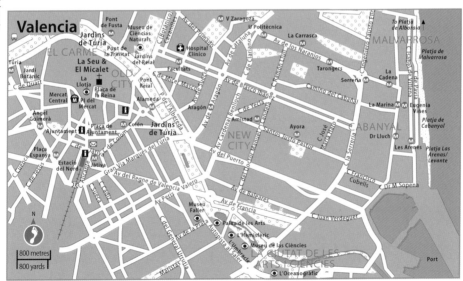

⊙ Sights

La Seu and El Micalet (Catedral and El Miguelete)

ⓘ Pl de la Reina 1, T963-918127,
www.archivalencia.org. Cathedral: Mon-
Sat 1000-1730, Sun 1400-1730. €3
includes admission to museum. Museu de
La Seu: Mon-Sat 1000-1300, 1630-1900.
Micalet 1000-1230, 1630-1830, Sun
1000-1300, 1700-1930. €1.20/ 0.80.

Plaça de la Reina, a long, elegant square
surrounded by cafés and palm trees, is
one of the most important squares in
Valencia. (It's also the most touristy: you
can't miss the horse-drawn carriages
clattering around the narrow streets for
a fat fee.) It's dominated by Valencia's
vast, imposing **cathedral**, topped with
the city's much-loved symbol, the
octagonal bell tower known as the
Micalet. Largely completed by the end
of the 15th century, baroque craftsmen
decided to tinker with the cathedral in
the late 1700s and added the florid
façade with thickly encrusted sculptural
decoration and swooping lines.

Plaça de la Reina

The cathedral's greatest treasure is
kept in the **Capilla del Santo Cáliz**,
where a jewel-encrusted chalice carved
from agate is set into a pale alabaster
altarpiece that fills an entire wall. (Drop
a euro in the machine to light up the
altarpiece for full operatic effect.)

The chapel sits next to the Sala
Capitular, which houses the cathedral
museum with a fascinating collection
of religious art, statuary and sculpture.

A separate entrance leads to the
Micalet, the slim belltower with lacy,

Gothic tracery. Huff and puff up the 207
steps for staggering views across the
blue-tiled cupolas, baroque towers and
higgledy-piggledy maze of the Old City.

Mercat Central (Mercado Central)

ⓘ Pl del Mercat, T963-829101. Mon-Thu
0800-1430, Fri 0800-2030, Sat 0800-1500.
There's no fish market on Mon.

Southwest of the cathedral in the other
main square of the old city, Valencia's
central market is one of the most
beautiful in the country; a vast,
Modernista concoction of wrought iron
and stained glass surmounted with
cupolas and whimsical weathervanes.
The Comunitat Valenciana isn't known
as 'Spain's orchard' for nothing and
inside you'll find a breathtaking array
of colourful, fresh produce with almost
1,000 stalls to choose from. Ceramic
mosaics twist around the walls in a
hymn to Valencia's abundance, spilling
over with fruit and flowers, and light
pours in through huge stained-glass
windows. A massive cupola, encrusted
with more elaborate mosaics, drenches

European City Breaks Valencia

⊖ Travel essentials

Getting there Valencia's International
Airport, T961-598500, www.aena.es,
is in Manises, 8 km west of the centre
of town. There is an airport bus into
the centre every 20 mins, daily from
0630-2345 (€1). Taxis from outside
the departures hall cost €15-18 to the
city centre.

Getting around The Old City is
best explored on foot, most of the main
sights are within walking distance of
each other. An excellent **bus** network will
take you to places further afield like
La Ciutat de les Arts i les Ciències, the
port and beaches, and the Llac Albufera.
The N1 nightbus connects the seaside

neighbourhoods with the centre.
A single ticket (available on the bus)
costs €1. The **metro** system is aimed
at commuters, but Line 4 (a tram-line
above ground) is handy for the beach
at Malvarrosa. Single metro or tram
tickets (€1.10) are available from
machines in stations. Useful **ticket
passes** include: BonoBus (10 single rides
for €5.05), B10 (10 single rides on buses
or metro for €5.65, and a free transfer
within 50 mins of beginning your
journey), T1 (1-day ticket for unlimited
transport on bus, tram and metro (€3).
The Valencia Card is valid for 1, 2 or 3
days (€6/10/12) and offers unlimited

public transport, plus discounts
in museums, shops and restaurants.
Available from tourist offices, metro
stations, some tobacconists and hotels.

Tourist information Offices at:
Pl de l'Ajuntament, T963-510417,
Mon-Fri 0830-1415 and 1630-1815,
Sat 0915-1245. C de la Paz 48,
T963-986422, Mon-Fri 1000-1830,
Sat 1000-1400; and Estació del Nord,
C Jàtiva 24, T963-528573, Mon-Fri
0900-1830, www.turisvalencia.com,
www.valencia.es. They have a transport
map and a callejero street map, which
is more detailed than the usual one.

the stalls in the main hall with sunlight. But perhaps the prettiest section of all is the fish market, a semi-enclosed hall, with a spectacular array of fresh seafood glistening on slabs beneath another cupola, this one adorned with playful, ceramic fish. The market is always busy, but get there early to catch it in full swing – breakfast at one of the dozens of stalls inside the market or tucked around the edges is an institution.

La Llotja (La Lonja)
ⓘ *Pl del Mercat, T963-525478. Tue-Fri 0915-1400, 1730-2100, Sun 0900-1330.*

The Silk Exchange is quite simply the most beautiful building in Valencia. Sitting squarely opposite the main entrance to the central market, it is one of the finest examples of civic, Gothic architecture in Europe and was declared a World Heritage Monument by UNESCO in 1996. Construction on the new commodity exchange began in 1483 under the direction of the brilliant Pere Compte, a master stone-mason, engineer and architect. The project was completed in just 15 years. The splendid

La Llotja

main hall, the Sala de Contratación, is vast with a lofty, vaulted ceiling which reaches almost 18 m at its highest point. To feel an echo of the buzz which would have animated the Llotja 500 years ago, visit it on a Sunday morning when a popular stamp and coin market is held in the Sala de Contratación.

La Ciutat de les Arts i les Ciències (La Ciudad de las Artes y las Ciencias)
ⓘ*Av Autopista al Saler 1-7, T902-100031, www.cac.es. Museu de les Ciències: mid Jun-mid Sep daily 1000-2000, mid Sep-mid Jun Sun-Fri 1000-1800, Sat 1000-2000, €7.20. L'Hemisfèric: Mon-Thu 1000-2100, €7.20. L'Oceanogràfic: mid Sep-mid Jun Sun-Fri 1000-1800, Sat 1000-2000; mid Jun-end Jul and first two weeks of Sep daily 1000-2000, Aug daily 1000-2400, €21.20. Combined tickets also available.*

Valencia couldn't fail to see how new architecture had revitalized the fortunes of Barcelona up the coast and the glossy, new La Ciutat de les Arts i les Ciències was commissioned in order to raise the city's international profile. The gamble

has paid off: the futuristic complex designed by local celebrity architect Santiago Calatrava is an overwhelming success and you may need to book in advance to get in to some of its attractions in the high season. There are five main sections: **Museu de les Ciències** (an inventive science museum that looks more like a 23rd-century airport), **l'Hemisfèric** (laser shows, IMAX and planetarium), **L'Umbracle** (a palm-lined walkway), **L'Oceanogràfic** (an aquarium in a series of beautifully sculpted pale pavilions, the biggest in Europe), and the **Palau de les Arts** (a venue for the performing arts). The buildings – although that seems too tame a term for these bold, graphic shapes – seem to emerge from the cool, blue pools which surround them.

Platjas (Playas/Beaches)
ⓘ *North: bus 1, 2, 19, 31 and summer only services 20, 21, 22. South: to El Palmar with Autocares Herca Mon-Fri 0700, 1200, 1400, 1500, 1800, 2000, 2100. Sat-Sun 0700, 0900, 1300, 1600, 2000. Bus is marked Valencia-El Saler-El Perelló. €1.70, 30 mins.*

Mercat Central

La Ciutat de les Arts i les Ciències

Valencia's fiery fiesta

Las Fallas is one of the most important fiestas in Spain. It dates back to the Middle Ages, when carpenters used to light a bonfire in honour of Sant Josep, their patron saint. Gradually, effigies were thrown into the fire, often depicting rival organizations. Now, the vast creations take all year to build and are paraded through the streets from 13-19 March. They can be of anything – cartoon characters, politicians, buxom ladies, animals – and each neighbourhood vies to create the best. They are accompanied by mini-versions (*Ninots*), the winning *Ninot* being the only one to escape the flames. Each day, firecrackers blast out over Plaça de l'Ajuntament, bullfights are held and the evenings culminate with a massive firework display. The fiesta finishes with a bang on 19 March when the Fallas are thrown into an enormous pyre, the *Cremá*. You can find out more about the event at **Museu Faller/Museo Fallero** (Fallas Museum) ⓘ *Pl Monte-olivete 4, T963-525478, Tue-Sat 1000-1400 and 1630-2030, Sun and holidays 1000-1500. €2. Bus 13 from Pl de l'Ajuntament.*

Heading north of the port is a long, long sandy beach which stretches for several miles. Valencianos usually just call the whole thing the Platja de Malvarrosa, but in fact it is divided into sections: nearest the port is **Platja de Levante** or **Platja Las Arenas**, where you'll find a string of restaurants, hotels and bars squeezed

Platja Las Arenas

next to each other on the Passeig Neptuno. It quickly becomes the **Platja de Cabanyal** then **Platja de Malvarrosa**, and finally the **Platja de Alboraia**. The water is a tad murky, owing to the proximity of the port (the beaches south of the city are cleaner), but it is still fine for swimming. There are rows of stripy beach huts, sun-loungers for rent, snack bars and showers along the whole length of the beach. A long, modern promenade lined with palms and an outdoor market in summer backs the whole length of the beach. The further north you trek, the fewer people you'll find, but this is still a city beach and you won't find a quiet corner in the height of summer.

The beaches south of the port are quieter, cleaner and wilder than the main city beach of Malvarrosa. They are also harder to get to, unless you have your own transport, and have fewer amenities – bring a packed lunch and lots of water. The beach of **El Saler** becomes the

beach of **La Devesa**, with a small nudist section at its most southerly end. These beaches are backed by beautiful sand dunes and a dense, gnarled pine forest. There are walks through the forest, and plenty of opportunities to see some of the sea birds which have made their home around the Llac Albufera.

● Sleeping

€€€ Palau de la Mar, C Navarro Reverter 14-16, T963-162884, www.hospes.es. A handsomely converted 19th-century mansion and one of the city's most stylish hotels. Chic cream and black decor, a pool, gym, sauna and excellent restaurant. It's near the City of Arts and Sciences.

€€ Ad Hoc, C Boix 4, T963-919140, www.adhochoteles.com. An utterly charming, chic little hotel in a converted 19th-century mansion. The restaurant (expensive) has become a very fashionable haunt.

€€ Cónsul del Mar, Av del Puerto 39, T963-625432, www.hotelconsuldelmar.com. The whitewashed Modernista former consulate's residence has beautifully decorated rooms some with the original plasterwork and fittings. It overlooks a busy street, but is not too far from the beaches or the City of Arts and Sciences.

€€ Parador El Saler, Platja del Saler, T961-611186, www.parador.es. Yellow metrobus services 190a, 190b, 191, 290 to El Perelló. Ask to be dropped off at the 'parador'. A modern hotel overlooking sand dunes and surrounded by pine forest. There's an 18-hole golf course, swimming pool and good restaurant and the beaches are empty (well, sometimes) and golden. Paradors often have special deals, so check the website before you go.

€ Antigua Morellana, C/En Bou 2, T963-915773, www.hostalam.com. Excellent *hostal* in an 18th-century mansion just a step from the Llotja and the Mercat Central with charming owners and clean, well-equipped rooms all with bathrooms.

● Eating

Restaurants

ψψψ Ca Sento, C Méndez Núñez 17, T963-301775. Tue-Sat 1330-1530, 2100-2330, Sun-Mon 2100-2330. Closed Aug. One of the most talked-about restaurants in the city. Tuck into classic, regional recipes given a creative new twist

ψψψ Joaquín Schmidt, C Visitació 7, T963-401710. Tue-Sat 1330-1530, 2100-2330, Sun-Mon 2100-2330. Quirky and highly original, both in decor and cuisine. Offers distinctive variations on Mediterranean and international food.

ψψ Casa Mario, C Roters 3, T963-924452. Tue-Sat 1200-1600, 2000-0100. Simple, relaxed restaurant and tapas bar tucked behind the cathedral, specializing in fresh and tasty seafood. The *revueltos* (scrambled egg dishes) are also good.

ψ Casa Roberto, C Maestro Gozalbo, T963-951361. Tue-Sat 1300-1600 and 2100-2300, Sun 1300-1600. Closed Aug. Pictures of famous bullfighters set the scene in this traditional stalwart on the Valenciano restaurant scene. All kinds of rice dishes (*arroces*) are on offer; a great place to try an authentic paella.

ψ Corretgeria 33, C Corretgeria 33, T963-924161. Tue-Sun 1330-1700 and 2100-2400. A stylish and cosy choice in the Barri del Carme serving innovative Mediterranean specialities.

Tapas bars and cafés

ψ Bar Pilar, C Moro Zeit 13, T963-910497. 1200-2400. A timeless, old bar just off the Plaça del Tossal, where the thing to do is order up a portion of mussels and toss the shells in the orange buckets ranked underneath the bar. Give your name to the waiter if you want to get a seat.

Bodega Montaña, C Josep Benlliure 69, T963-672314. Tue-Sun 1200-1500, 1930-2300. Traditional, buzzy tavern still going strong thanks to its excellent range of quality wines and tapas.

Café Lisboa, Pl Dr Collado 9, T963-919484. 0900-0230. A big favourite, this arty café looks out over a pretty square with an ancient olive tree and serves great sandwiches and salads as well as cocktails in the evenings.

Café Sant Jaume, C Cavallers 51, T963-912401. Daily 1200-0200. Beautiful little café set in a former pharmacy, with swirling Modernista woodwork. In the centre of the city's main street for nightlife so perfect for people-watching.

La Edad de Oro, C Don Generoso Hernández 1, T963-924724. Tue-Sat 0900-0100, Sun-Mon 1900-0100. Laid-back café in the Barri del Carme, with changing art exhibitions and special events, serving snacks.

● Nightlife

Valencia's nightlife is concentrated in different places, but the best place to start is the hip **Barri del Carme** in the Old City, where stylish restaurants, clubs, and bars are nudged up against each other. There are more bars and clubs near the **university** in the new part of town. Check out the streets around the Pl Honduras, near Avinguda Blasco Ibáñez. In summer, everyone piles down to Malvarrosa beach. Look out for the following favourites: **Radio City** (Old City), **La Indiana, Jam Disclub, Akuarela, Jimmy Glass, Roxy Club** (New City). Valencia has a buzzy gay scene mainly on **C Quart** in the Old Town).

Venice

Photogenically wet, Venice can seem like a beautiful relic – a vulnerable novelty without much of a contemporary purpose. A one-time global sea-power, Venice may or may not actually be sinking but its precarious hold on dry land is increasingly at risk from rising sea levels – high tides in winter regularly flood its piazzas and streets. At the very least, however, it is an extraordinary and gorgeously unlikely city, built on shifting sands, filled with great art, churches and palaces and with a wonderfully peaceful absence of road traffic. And if you can get away from the massed tourists in piazza San Marco to one of the city's less popular corners, you'll find that despite the *acque alte* there is life in Venice, and no small amount of pride.

Arts & culture
★★★★★

Eating
★★★

Nightlife
★

Outdoors
★★★

Romance
★★★★★

Shopping
★★★

Sightseeing
★★★★★

Value for money
★★

Overall score
★★★✦

At a glance

Most visitors to Venice arrive in the city's far west, from where, once you leave the train or car, all transport is by water or on foot. From here the **Canal Grande** snakes in a reverse 'S' through the city, crossed only by the **Ponte degli Scalzi**, by the station, the arcaded **Ponte Rialto** and the **Ponte Accademia**. (A new bridge, designed by Santiago Calatrava, is being built between the station and piazza Roma, the road terminus.) To the north of the canal are the generally quieter districts of **Cannaregio** in the west and **Castello** to the east. In the second bend of the Canal, the busy central area of **San Marco** is where many of the main sights are. On the southern side, **Santa Croce** and **San Polo** are nestled into the first bend of the Grand Canal with another more residential area, the **Dorsoduro**, on Venice's southern edge. Orientation in the narrow winding streets is notoriously hard, though you can get an excellent overview of the city from the top of

Venice is like eating an entire box of chocolate liqueurs in one go.

Truman Capote

the Campanile in **piazza San Marco**. Many visitors start here and follow the signposts which dot a circuitous route to and from the station via the Rialto. Around the Venetian lagoon and a ferry ride away are the islands of **Guidecca**, **Murano**, with its glass-blowing industry, colourful **Burano** and the packed but fashionable beaches of **Lido**.

★ *Don't leave town without getting hopelessly lost along the winding canals.*

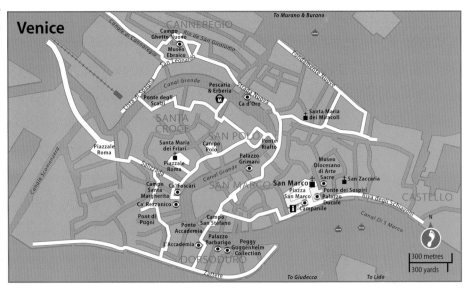

24 hours in the city

Venice is at its best early in the morning, so get up with the sun, when only locals and workers will be around. Have a *caffè* and a cornetto in a café (the touristy ones won't open until the trains start arriving a bit later) and check out the fruit and vegetable markets and, especially, the *pescaria* (fish market) in the **Rialto**. Starting early will also enable you to get to **San Marco** before the tour groups and hordes of pigeon-feeders arrive. Have a look in the basilica and perhaps the **Palazzo Ducale** and go to the top of the **Campanile** before the crowds get too big. For lunch pick one of the cafés and restaurants on or around the busy **campo Santa Margherita** in the Dorsoduro, such as *Il Caffe*. From here you are well placed for a wander along the waterside **Zattere** and to take in some visual art at either the **Accademia** or **Peggy Gugenheim Collection**. Next, head slowly across the city to reach atmospheric **Cannaregio** by supper time, perhaps looking in on a

Vaporetto on the Grand Canal

church such as Santa Maria dei Frari in **San Polo** and having an ice cream or an *aperitivo* along the way. A boat ride is probably best left until the evening; avoid the twee temptations of gondolas and opt instead for a *vaporetto* up the **Grand Canal**.

⊖ Travel essentials

Getting there Venice Marco Polo, www.veniceairport.it, T041-2609240, is the city's main airport, to the north of the lagoon. It is connected by boat to San Marco and the Zattere every hour (journey time around 1 hr, €10, www.alilaguna.it). Water taxis are much more expensive (as much as €100) but will take you right to your hotel. It's also possible to travel on dry land to piazzale Roma. Buses leave at least every half hour (journey around 40 mins, €1).

About 32 km from Venice, **Venice Treviso**, T0422-315131, is a small airport used by Ryanair. Buses run to and from piazzale Roma to the airport to coincide with flights (€4.50 single, €8 return). Alternatively, bus 6 runs from outside

Treviso train station (frequently connected to Venice by train) to the airport every half hour.

Getting around Despite the canals, the best way to get around is on foot. *Vaporetti* are fairly large passenger boats which ply several routes around and through the city, primarily up and down the Canal Grande and the Canale di Cannaregio and to other islands. *Traghetti* are gondolas without the silly hats, which cross the Canal Grande at places where there are no bridges. *Vaporetti* tickets cost €3.50 single, €10.50 for 24 hrs or €22 for 72 hrs. *Vaporetti* tickets are available from booths at the stops. *Traghetti* cost €0.40 per crossing – pay the boatman and stay standing, if you can. Gondolas cost

€73 for 50 mins, maximum 6 people per gondola. The price rises to €91 after 2000.

Tourist information Azienda di Promozione Turistica, www.turismovenezia.it/eng, has 2 central offices: in piazza San Marco, S Marco 71/f, T041-5298711, 0900-1530; and in the Ex Giardini Reali, T041-5298711, 1000-1800.

Venice Discovery Tours, www.venice.city-discovery.com, combine a walking tour in the morning with a boat tour (limited to 8 people) in the afternoon, €60 per person. You can also hire a private boat and a driver to take you around the canals or out into the lagoon, although this is significantly more expensive.

👁 Sights

San Marco

ⓘ *May-Sep Mon-Sat 0945-1730, Sun 1400-1600; Oct-Apr Mon-Sat 0945-1630, Sun 1400-1600. Main basilica free, tickets can be booked in advance at www.alata.it. Treasury, Loggia and Museo, Pala d'Oro all €1.50 each.*

Originally built in the ninth century to house the body of St Mark (stolen from Alexandria), the ornate and spectacular basilica of San Marco is the city's cathedral and its piazza is a magnetic gathering point for Venice's pigeons and tourists. John Ruskin called San Marco a "treasure-heap" and it is indeed a bewildering collection of styles and ornamentation, from the Gothic spires of its façade and 19th-century mosaics, to a group of porphyry figures (the Tetrarchs), probably from fourth-century Egypt.

The centrepiece of the city, it has a large dome surrounded by four marginally smaller ones. Despite having been rebuilt and redecorated over the years, its form has changed little, though much of it dates from the 11th century.

Basilica of San Marco

Palazzo Ducale

The **Pala d'Oro** – the extravagantly rich golden altarpiece – is the highlight of the interior. The **Loggia**, complete with life-size horses (the original bronzes, probably second-century Roman, are now in the Museo) is well worth the climb for the view over the piazza below.

Palazzo Ducale

ⓘ *T041-2715911. Apr-Oct 0900-1900, Nov- Mar 0900-1700. Musei di Piazza San Marco ticket (€11) also allows entrance to other museums around the city: Museo Correr, Museo Archeologico and the Sale Monumentali della Biblioteca Marciana.*

Adjacent to the basilica, the Doge's Palace – largely a result of 14th- and 15th-century construction – combines Verona pink marble with ornate Gothic porticos to great effect. Doges were crowned at the top of the so-called Giants' Staircase. Inside, Domenico and Jacopo Tintoretto's *Paradiso* covers the end wall of the Great Council Hall.

The **Ponte dei Sospiri** (Bridge of Sighs) is an enclosed passageway through which prisoners once walked between their cells and the interrogation rooms in the palace. The best view of it is from Ponte della Paglia, at the palace's southeastern corner.

Campanile di San Marco

ⓘ *T041-5224064. Jul-Aug 0900-2100; Apr-Jun and Sep-Oct 0930-1615; Nov-Mar 0930-1615. €6.*

Until the smaller but more ornate **Torre dell'Orologio** ⓘ *T041-5224951,* reopens, the 99-m Campanile is unquestionably Venice's top tower. Originally ninth-century, the present incarnation of San Marco's belltower dates from 1514. Views from its summit are fantastic – it's rare enough to get big vistas in the city and here is nearly the whole island laid out in one enormous sweep. The Campanile collapsed in 1902 and was subsequently rebuilt.

L'Accademia

ⓘ *Dorsoduro 1050, T041-5222247, www.gallerieaccademia.org. Mon 0815-1400, Tue-Sun 0815-1915. €6.50.*

Across the wooden Ponte dell' Accademia, Venice's "art school" occupies an ex-convent on the

Campanile di San Marco

✳ That Venice is sinking is a fact that has been repeated so often as to be accepted by almost all visitors to the city. However, most recent studies have suggested that the subsidence of the city from 1920 to 1970 has all but stopped. Venice is probably sinking by only 0.5 mm a year – roughly in line with the rest of the Adriatic coast.

That may not be much consolation to local residents as they wade through their city or move their valuables upstairs. The *acque alte* (high waters) are an increasingly frequent problem in winter – high tides combined with wind from the wrong direction brings the sea sweeping across Venice's *campos* and streets and into its buildings. Sirens and a network of raised walkways mean that life goes on but it's far from a happy situation in which to live.

In part the flooding can be blamed on rising sea levels. The loss of 10 cm of height during the 20th century also contributed. (Most now accept that this was due to the industrial extraction of water from rocks below the surface – a practice that was outlawed in the 1960s.) There is much less agreement about the solution, however. In 2003 the Italian government under Silvio Berlusconi gave their approval to MOSE (nominally the Modulo Sperimentale Elettromeccanico, but with a biblical nod to the holding back of the Red Sea), a grand plan to block the high water with a series of pontoons at the entrances to the lagoon. Costing around €4 billion and due to be completed around 2011, environmentalists think the pontoons will destroy the important ecosystem of the Venetian lagoon. Others point out that a project originally designed in the 1980s may be ineffective to cope with sea levels which are now predicted to rise with global warming.

southern side of the Canal Grande and houses one of Italy's great art collections, including works by Giovanni Bellini, Canaletto, Andrea Mantegna, Tintoretto, Titian and Paolo Veronese.

Canal Grande

Canal Grande

Venice's most famous canal is its biggest: a watery highway cutting the city in two. Crossed only by three bridges, a trip on the canal is a must. Apart from being the quickest way to travel, it's also the best way to see some of Venice's greatest buildings: baroque **Ca' Rezzonico**, decorative **Ca d'Oro**, Michele Sanmicheli's frescoed **Palazzo Grimani**, Gothic **Ca' Foscari**, and **Palazzo Barbarigo** with its Murano glass mosaics. Also on the canal is the **Peggy Guggenheim Collection** ⓘ *Palazzo Venier dei Leoni, 701 Dorsoduro, www.guggenheim-venice.it, Mon and Wed-Sun, 1000-1800, €10.* Once the collector's home, there's now Picasso, Kandinsky, Pollock and a notoriously erect horse rider on view.

Pescaria

For a glimpse of Venice as it might be without tourists, head to the fish market near the Ponte Rialto early in the morning. Next door in the **Erberia**

Rialto market

market the abundant fruit and vegetables of the Veneto are sold with equal panache. Venice's market moved here to the Rialto area in 1097.

Ponte Rialto

The city's oldest bridge, originally made of wood, collapsed in 1444 and again in 1524. Antonio da Ponte's stone design was completed in 1591 and has stood ever since, becoming one of Venice's icons. The jewellery shops which line the arcades of the bridge are expensive and best avoided.

Museo Diocesano di Arte Sacra
ⓘ *Castello 3412, T041-5226581. 0900-1700. €4.*

The beautiful Romanesque Chiostro di Sant' Apollonia, inside the Museum of Sacred Art, is one of Venice's less well known architectural beauties and dates from the early 14th century. The museum itself is less impressive, but it does contain some remnants of an earlier version of the Basilica of San Marco which are nearly 1000 years old.

Ponte Rialto

Cannaregio

Cannaregio

With fewer sights than most other Venetian *sestieri*, Cannaregio is perhaps the least touristy of the city's quarters, except along its southern edge. Long parallel canals retain some of their working class feel and it can be one of the most rewarding parts of the city in which to wander. It also has some of the best restaurants. The **Canale di Cannaregio** itself was once the main way into the city and has some suitably grand buildings to mark the fact. East of here three parallel canals have less ostentatious charms. Just south off the Rio di San Girolamo, the **Ghetto Nuovo** was the original Jewish ghetto and the origin of the name. A museum, the **Museo Ebraico** ⓘ *Sun-Fri 1000-1800*, tells the story of Venetian Jews. In the far east of the district, **Santa Maria dei Miracoli** is an exquisite early Renaissance church built in the 1480s.

Le Zattere and the Dorsoduro

The Zattere, the 2 km of quayside at Venice's southern extremity, is one of the city's best spots for the evening

◉ Best of the rest

Lido ⓘ *vaporetti from San Zaccaria.* Venice's famously fashionable beach sits on the far side of an island dedicated almost entirely to it. Just about every grain of sand is occupied in summer and you have to pay (or be staying at smart hotels) for access to many parts.
Frari ⓘ *campo dei Frari, T041-5222637.* An enormous church filled with art by Titian, Giovani Bellini and others, Santa Maria Gloriosa dei Frari is almost always referred to by its shorter name.
Ca' Rezzonico ⓘ *Fondamenta Rezzonico 3136, T041-2410100.* Perhaps the best opportunity to experience the interior of one of Venice's baroque palaces. Giorgio Massari's enormously grand ballroom and paintings by Canaletto and Tiepolo are some of the highlights.
Murano ⓘ *vaporetti from Fondamente Nuove.* On this island, a near neighbour of Venice, there is a museum dedicated to Venetian glass and you can visit glass-blowing factories. There are also some interesting churches.

passegiata, with great views across to the island of the Guidecca.

North of here, the Dorsoduro is Venice's youngest, hippest quarter, centring on buzzing **Campo di Santa Margherita**, which has some great bars and is especially lively in the evenings.

The **Ponte di Pugni** ("Bridge of the Boxers") still has engraved footprints where those taking part in east (*castellani*) versus west (*nicolotti*) punch-ups were supposed to stand.

Excursion: Burano

Exactly why Burano's houses are painted such bright colours may be lost in myth – the most often told story is that it was once so that fishermen could recognize their houses from the sea. What is clear is that the island's colour scheme is now its biggest selling point and permission to paint one's house is closely controlled. But there are attractions other than the colourful houses: the ferry journey across the northern lagoon gives a good perspective to Venice's seafaring roots and its lagoon position. The island's lace industry, which began in the 16th century, means there is a school, a museum and lace shops, though genuine hand-woven Burano lace is hard to find. The Church of San Martino has a tall campanile and a Tiepolo painting of the crucifixion. The whole place has a slow, quiet charm. Neighbouring Mazzorbo is connected by a wooden bridge and has orchards and a 14th-century church with its original 1318 bell. ① *Vaporetto No 12 from Fondamente Nuove, 40-50 mins, sometimes via Torcello.*

● Sleeping

Venice's accommodation is, by reputation, expensive and over-booked. It's certainly worth reserving ahead at busy times, and during the Biennale or the Film Festival rooms may be hard to find but at other times a little ringing around should suffice. Most of Venice's visitors are day-trippers and the advantages of being able to wander around the relatively unfrequented city in the evenings or early mornings far outweigh the price of a room.

€€€ Bellini, Canareggio 116/a, T041-5242488, www.boscolo hotels.com. Right on the Grand Canal and near the station, the Bellini has plenty of sophisticated antique Venetian elegance, but it all comes at a price.

€€€ Ca' Pisani, Dorsoduro 979/a, T041-2401411, www.capisanihotel.it. A Venetian rarity, Ca' Pisani is a chic modern hotel in a 16th-century building. Sharp lines and hip colour schemes contrast effectively with the Dorsoduro surroundings.

€€€-€€ Hotel Flora, San Marco 2283/a, T041-5205844, www.hotelflora.it. Venetian opulence abounds – lots of antiques and a vine-covered courtyard in a building where Titian may have painted.

€€€-€€ Locanda ai Santi Apostoli, Cannaregio 4391/a, campo Santi Apostoli, T041-5212612, www.locandasantiapostoli.com. Some of the city's most reasonably priced views over the Grand Canal, from wooden-beamed rooms.

€€ Ca' delle Acque, San Marco 4991, T041-2411277, www.locanda delleacque.it. About as central as you can get, halfway between piazza San Marco and the Rialto, Ca' delle Acque is a pretty place with apartments sleeping up to 8 as well as rooms.

€€-€ Pensione Seguso, Zattere 779, T041-5286858. On the corner of a canal and the Zattere waterfront in the Dorsoduro, the smart Seguso has an English colonial air, very proper service and some excellent views.

€€-€ Villa Rosa, C della Misericordia 389, T041-718976, www.villarosahotel.com. Very convenient for the station yet far enough back from the tourist traps of Rio Terrá Lista di Spagna to be quiet, the flower-clad Villa Rosa is an attractive option on the edge of Cannaregio.

● Eating

Venice's culinary reputation is not great but find a table outside in a piazza on a warm summer's evening or beside a canal watching the boats go by and the food will almost certainly taste pretty good. It's worth bearing in mind that most places close much earlier in the evening (around 2100) than in the rest of Italy. Eating out is also expensive here. The Dorsoduro and the northwest parts of Cannaregio are the best places to get away from the trilingual menus and experience something cheaper and nearer Venetian tradition. Risotto is a Venice staple, as is seafood, but there are plenty of restaurants specializing in other Italian delights.

ⵉⵉⵉ **Harry's Bar**, San Marco 1323, T041-5285777. Closed Mon. Famous (and wealthy) enough to threaten legal action against places around the world who copy the name, Harry's is a Venetian institution on the Canal Grande. Frequented by film and opera stars, those who can afford the high prices for both food and drink, and those who come just to gawp.

ⵉⵉ **All'Arco**, San Polo 436, T041-5205666. Closed evenings and Sun. One of Venice's *ombre* (dialect for a glass of wine) places which also serve *cicheti* (snacks and light dishes). Near the Rialto, you could accompany your Prosecco with crostini, ham and gorgonzola.

ⵉⵉ **Aqua Pazza**, campo Sant'Angelo, San Marco 3808/10, T041-2770688. Open late, Aqua Pazza serves truly excellent southern Italian pizzas out in the campo for extortionate prices and with an authentic air of slightly surly chaos. There are also other good southern Italian options such as deep fried vegetables and a mixed fish grill which make putting up with the poor service worthwhile.

ⵉⵉ **Osteria Alla Zucca**, Santa Croce 1762, Ponte del Megio, T041-5241570. Near San Giacomo dell'Orio, this friendly little trattoria is good for vegetarians. The 4 or 5 tables outside on the street fill up quickly.

ⵉⵉ **Osteria Anice Stellato**, Fondamenta de la Senza, Cannaregio T041-720744. Closed Mon. A reminder of Venice's one-time status as an important port linking east and west, Anice Stellato uses more spices than are usual in Italian cooking, combining them with Venetian cuisine to good effect. Out of the way on one of Cannaregio's long quiet canals, this colourful little place usually has more

locals than visitors. If it's full, **Ai 40 Ladroni**, T041-715736, next door is also a good option.

ⵉⵉ **Osteria Bea Vita**, 3082 Fondamenta degli Ormesini. A rarity in that you can sit outside beside a canal and be as likely to share tables with locals as with tourists. The good value €10.50 lunch menu is pasta- and risotto-based.

ⵉⵉ **Osteria Vecio Forner**, Dorsoduro 672, campo San Vio, T041-5280424. Closed Sun. A fashionably smart little bar on the corner of a campo near the Guggenheim museum with good food options, especially for a light lunch. Dishes of the day €8-15.

❝ ❞ ...find a table outside in a piazza on a warm summer's evening or beside a canal... and the food will almost certainly taste good.

ⵉ **Osteria da Toni**, Fondamenta di San Basilio 1642, T041-5286899. Closed Mon. A long hike from San Marco, da Toni is a traditional no-nonsense trattoria of a kind rarely found in Venice. Popular with students and locals it's an excellent place for Venetian seafood and simple pasta and wine lunches. Not far from the western end of the Zattere, there are a few tables outside beside the canal.

ⵉ **Taverna Da Baffo**, San Polo 2346, Campo Sant'Agostin, T041-5208862. Closed Sun. A popular café which opens early and stays open until late with good coffee early, live music late and decent food in between. Free buffet on Tue evenings.

◑ Nightlife

Bars

Venice's nightlife is infamously somnolent – wander around the city at an hour when most Mediterranean cities would be sparking into life and you will probably find dark empty streets. The **Dorsoduro** is the area which bucks this trend somewhat: campo Santa Margherita is the best for a *giro de ombre*. When performed by Venetians these bar-crawls of local nightspots usually involve the over-consumption of glasses of "spritz", a misleadingly cheap and quaffable combination of wine, soda water and a bitter, usually Campari, Aperol or Cynar.

Live music

Nightclubs are practically non-existent though some bars have live music (**Il Caffe**, campo Santa Margherita) and the jazz scene is perhaps the least moribund of the Venetian performing arts. **Paradiso Perduto**, Fondamenta della Misericordia in Cannaregio, has jazz and blues. **La Fenice**, www.teatro lafenice.it, is one of the country's top opera venues.

◉ Festivals

Venice comes into its own during festivals. There's the profusion of contemporary art in the **Biennale** (www.labiennale.org), the cinematic buffs of the **Film Festival** (late Aug, early Sep) or the masks and thicker-than-ever throngs of tourists during **Carnevale** (Feb). Look out too for lesser known festivals such as **Venezia Suona** (www.veneziasuona.it, Jul), a music festival, and **Festa di Liberazione**, the Communist Party's annual knees up in late summer.

Red-roofed and pastel-shaded, on the edge of the mountains and the cusp of the plain, Verona likes to think of itself as both the beginning and the distillation of the real Italy. At the crossroads of the north-south route from the Brenner Pass to Rome and the east-west Milan-Venice road, the city has long been of strategic importance. Apart from Rome itself, Verona is Italy's best-preserved Roman city (with a Roman amphitheatre, a bridge, gates and theatre) and also has richly decorated Romanesque, Gothic and Renaissance aspects, with spectacular frescoed churches and houses. And all this antiquity is given an opulent sheen by a well-dressed 21st-century population who have, in the main, done very nicely out of wine, opera, European integration and a select brand of tourism.

Verona

Arts & culture
★★★

Eating
★★★★

Nightlife
★★

Outdoors
★★

Romance
★★★★

Shopping
★★

Sightseeing
★★★

Value for money
★★★

Overall score
★★★

◉ Sights

Centro storico

Bordered on three sides by the River Adige, the streets of Verona's ancient centre follow the Roman layout. As well as the city's main shopping streets, including the shiny **via Mazzini**, most of the well-known sights are here between **Ponte Pietra**, the bridge which predates the city, in the north, along narrow winding streets to the original Roman gates of **Porta Leoni** in the south and **Porta Borsari** in the west. The site of the old Roman forum is now expansive **piazza Erbe**, the heart of the city and filled with Renaissance and Gothic buildings dating from the 14th to the 18th centuries. On the eastern side of the piazza, **Casa Mazzanti** has a cycle of allegorical frescoes by Cavalli from around 1530. The portico, filled with

Ponte Pietra

cafés selling various ice-cream concoctions, was built in 1480. In the cellars, 3.5 m below the present-day surface, the original paving of the Roman forum has been found. **Fontana Madonna Verona** in the piazza's centre and one of the beloved symbols of the city, is a mishmash of Roman remains.

The basin was taken from the thermal baths of Sant'Anastasia, the statue from the Capitol. It was erected in the fourth century in honour of the emperor's lifting of the city's debts, and the fountain was added by Cansignorio della Scala in 1368.

Piazza dei Signori, leading off piazza Erbe, is more refined; a celebration not of commerce and the market, but of power and of poets, and in particular of the Scaligeri family, rulers of the city in the 13th and 14th centuries. While the foundations are also Roman, much of what sits on top is Gothic, Romanesque and Renaissance and narrow streets of ancient palazzi, many still frescoed, stretch up to the Adige. The piazza's most attractive building, and the best place from where to sit and watch the daily comings and goings, is the Renaissance **Loggia del Consiglio** (built between 1476 and 1492 by Fra' Giocondo) on the northwest side.

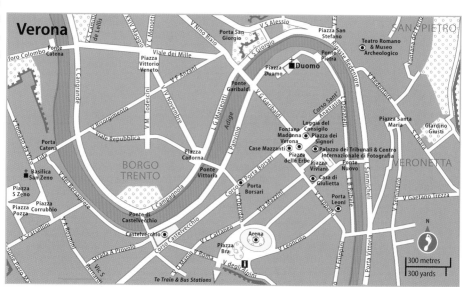

The **Duomo** ⓘ *piazza Duomo, T045-592813, Mon-Sat 0930-1800, Sun 1300-1800, €2.50, €5 for combined ticket for 5 main churches,* is just one of many spectacular churches in Verona. It has a beautiful façade, a stunning Titian (*Assumption* in the Cappella Cartolari-Nichesola, the first on the left), a Sanmicheli-designed belltower, griffins and plenty of historical interest. The stamp of the medieval rulers, the della Scala family, is visible most ostentatiously in their elaborate **Gothic tombs**.

The collection of ancient excavated remains under **piazza Viviani** and the cortile del Tribunale in the very centre of old Verona is the spectacular, if slightly damp, setting for excellent large-scale photography exhibitions at the **Centro Internazionale di Fotografia** ⓘ *T045-8007490, www.comune. verona.it/scaviscaligeri, opening times and prices change according to exhibitions.* Recent exhibitions have included Giuliana Traverso and Willy Ronis.

Also within the walls of the old city is **Casa di Giulietta (Juliet's House)** ⓘ *23 via Cappello, T045-8034303, Mon 1330-1930, Tue-Sun 0830-1930, entrance to the house €3.10, courtyard free,* an

extraordinary indictment of modern tourism but also strangely magnetic. A heaving mass of day-trippers throng in and out of the courtyard to take photos of the famous fictional balcony (added to the building in the 1930s).

Arena

ⓘ *piazza Bra, T045-8003204, www.arena.it. Mon 1330-1930, Tue-Sun 0830-1930, 0900-1530 during opera season. €4, €1 first Sun of the month.*

At the other end of via Mazzini from the enormous spread of piazza Erbe, **piazza Bra** forms an alternative centrepiece to the city, with the giant elliptical Roman Arena dominating it. Verona's most famous sight is the third largest Roman amphitheatre still in existence after the Colosseum and the little-visited amphitheatre in Capua. Still dominating much of the city, it is used as a 20,000-seater stadium and a theatre for the summer opera season. To the west, **Castelvecchio** ⓘ *corso Castelvecchio 2, T045-592985, www.comune.verona.it/ castelvecchio/cvsito, Mon 1330-1930, Tue-Sun 0830- 1930, ticket office closes at 1845, €4, free first Sun of the month,* has all the attributes you'd wish for in a

castle, plus a great bridge, and is now the Civic Museum of Art. Further west, the ornate 12th-century **Basilica San Zeno** ⓘ *piazza San Zeno, T045-592813, Mon-Sat 0830-1800, Sun 1300-1800, €2,* is justifiably the city's favourite church.

North and east of the Adige

The steep hill of San Pietro was the original site of settlement in the city. At its base, looking out across the river, sits the **Teatro Romano and the Museo Archeologico** ⓘ *Rigaste Redentore 2, T045-8000360, Mon 1345-1930, Tue-Sun 0830-1930, ticket office closes at 1845, €2.60, free first Sun of the month, information on summer events T045-8077201, www.estateteatral everonese.it.* From its top are fantastic panoramic views over the city. To either side of the hill are residential areas of the old city. There are some atmospheric little districts of winding streets, especially in Veronetta to the south, home to many of the city's best bars and restaurants. Beyond rise hills of olives and vineyards, with the first signs of the Alps to the north.

Duomo

Arena

⊖ Travel essentials

Getting there Verona Villafranca Airport (Valerio Catullo), T045-8095666, www.aeroportoverona.it, is served by APTV bus which run every 20 mins to and from the train station, 0700-2335. There is also one at 0005 (journey time around 15 mins, €4.20 each way). Taxis cost around €20 to the centre. Tiny **Brescia Montichiari Airport** (Gabriele D'Annunzio) T030-9656511, www.aeroportobrescia.it, used by Ryanair, is about an hour away from Verona by bus. Ryanair runs a service between the airport and Verona train station which co-ordinates with their flights and costs €11 single, €16 return. Tickets are available from an office inside the arrivals/departures hall (or, on the return journey from Verona, on the bus).

Getting around The compact size of Verona's centre means that walking is by far the best way to get around and see the sights. Orange **AMT**, T045-8871111, www.amt.it, buses serve the city. All services centre on the sprawling bus station, opposite the train station, south of piazza Bra. Tickets must be bought (either from tobacconists, marked with a large 'T' outside or from AMT machines at the station) before boarding and stamped on board, after which they are valid on any bus for one hour. An ordinary ticket costs €1. A 10-journey ticket ('*una tessera*') is also available for €9, and a day-ticket ('*giornaliero*') for €3.50. The most useful city services are likely to be 11, 12, 13, and 14 between the station (from beside the AMT booth) and piazza Bra, continuing over the river to via XX Settembre. At weekends and on holidays these are replaced by services 91, 92 and 98.

Tourist information The main Verona information office is at via degli Alpini 9 (just behind the Arena), T045-8068680, iatbra@tiscalinet.it. Mon-Sat 0900-1900, Sun 0900- 1500. As long as you know what you want, they'll probably be more than willing to help. There's an 'office' at the railway station, Porta Nuova FS, T045-8000861, iatfs@tiscalinet.it, Mon-Sat 0900-1800, Sun 0900-1500, which is no more than a man at a desk, but can nevertheless be useful for those arriving at the station.

⊖ Sleeping

€€€ Gabbia D'Oro, corso Porta Borsari 4a, T045-8003060, www.hotel gabbiadoro.it. A stone's throw from piazza Erbe Gabbia D'Oro, this hotel has the luxury of medieval features such as areas of bare wall and wooden beams. Rooms are similarly plush.

€€ Aurora, piazza Erbe, T045-594717, www.hotelaurora.biz. Overlooking piazza Erbe, the friendly Hotel Aurora has a great sunny terrace and unfussy air-conditioned rooms.

€€ Torcolo, vicolo Listone 3, T045-8007512, www.hoteltorcolo.it. On a quiet road behind piazza Bra, Torcolo has charm and style. Attic rooms on the third floor, with sloping ceilings, are particularly attractive.

€ Armando, via Dietro Pallone 1, T045-8000206. In an attractive, quiet area between piazza Bra and Ponte Aleardi, Hotel Armando is plain but comfortable, and much better value than all the hotels further south.

⊖ Eating

The line between bars and restaurants is a fine one in Verona. Osterie serve food of varying complexity and trattorie often have good, and enormously long, wine lists. There is little tradition of drinking without eating but, having said that, Verona's student population adds a lively edge and some of the city's drinking spots stay open well into the early hours. (Via Sottoriva, around San Zeno and Veronetta are the best areas.) Wine predominates, though most places also have beer on tap.

¶¶ Al Bersagliere, via Dietro Pallone 1, T045-8004824. Mon-Sat 1200-1430, 1930-2200, also open as a bar from 0800. Traditional Veronese and Lessinian food, plenty of polenta-based dishes as well as smoked goose breast, trout with Soave wine and lots of wine and home-made desserts.

¶¶ Hostaria la Vecchia Fontanina, piazzetta Chiavica 5, T045-591159. Mon-Sat 1200-1430, 1930-2230. An attractive little restaurant serving a mixed crowd of mainly Italians. A varied and interesting menu includes pasta with nettles and even the bread and house wine are a cut above average.

¶ Carro Armato, vicolo Gatto 2a, T045-8030175. Mon, Tue, Thu-Sat 1100-0200, Sun 1100-0000. Generally considered a night-spot, Carro Armato buzzes in the evenings, has an excellent wine list and also does extremely good local dishes.

¶ Osteria Trattoria Al Duomo, via Duomo 7a, T045-8004505. Mon-Sat 1100-1500, 1800-0000, kitchen 1200-1430, 1930-2230. One of the city's best trattorie. The service and the 1980s pop blasting out of the stereo might put you off but the excellent food makes up for this.

Caffè Tubino, 15d corso Porta Borsari, T045-8032296. Daily 0700-2300. Excellent coffee and *cornetti* in a distinctive little café.

Vienna

For centuries the most powerful city in continental Europe, Vienna oozes with the memories, riches, traditions and ambitions of Europe's most calculatingly expansionist dynasty: the Hapsburgs. Imposing yet florid palatial architecture defines the city, whether lining grand boulevards or set among landscaped parks. The opera house, myriad concert halls and art collections bear testimony to a taste for high culture in a city that harboured Beethoven, Mozart, Brahms, Klimt and Schiele. Traditionally straight-laced and uptight, this one-time outpost of Cold War Europe now finds itself at the heart of a territory it once ruled. Blowing off its cobwebs and newly alive with the influences that come from standing at a cultural crossroads, it is impossible not to have a good night in Vienna.

Arts & culture
★★★★

Eating
★★★★

Nightlife
★★★

Outdoors
★★

Romance
★★★★★

Shopping
★★★

Sightseeing
★★★

Value for money
★★

Overall score
★★★☆

At a glance

The cultural core of Vienna lies within the city's old town (Altstadt), defined by the **Ringstrasse**, formerly the medieval walls. A tram ride will cast you back to fin de siècle Hapsburg times and past the famous **Opera** that echoes with Mozart, Brahms and Beethoven. The **Museums Quarter** (MQ) lies in the southwest of the Ring and consists of the Imperial Palace (now the Kunsthistoriches Museum – one of the most important fine arts museums in the world), the former Imperial Stables with their unique balletic Lippizaner white stallions, and also the MUMOK and Leopold museums of contemporary and modern art. Between your Brueghels and Klimts, you'll be able to enjoy a host of atmospheric, relaxed and even hip bars, restaurants and shops in the ultimate meeting of high art and high life. For film aficionados (and kids) the **Prater funfair** and ferris wheel of *Third Man* fame lie to the northeast across the Danube. If you'd rather just recline and be Austrian for the weekend, the

The best coffee in Europe is Vienna coffee, compared to which all other coffee is fluid poverty.

Mark Twain

elegant, tightly-packed streets of the Altstadt are the home of Vienna's unsurpassable cafés. By day you can follow in the footsteps of Trotsky and Freud with some cake and a whipped-cream coffee, and by night enjoy the studied melange of new-imperial and ultra-modern. Vienna is a long way from the waltzes of Johann Strauss and that famous 1980s pop video by Ultravox.

★ *Don't leave town without a slice of your own delicious Sachertorte.*

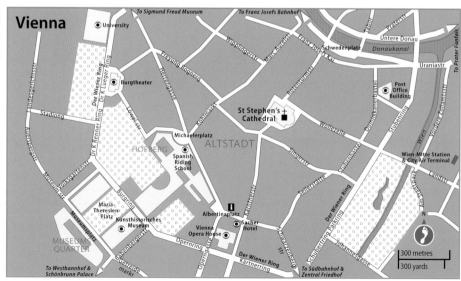

◉ Sights

Der Wiener Ring

In 1857 the Hapsburgs razed the city's medieval wall to create a monument to their vanity. This took the form of a grand boulevard circling the centre, lined with extravagant and imposing royal buildings, private residences, vast squares and parks, puffed up monuments and elegant cafés. Nearly 150 years on it acts as a walk-by window on the Hapsburg dynasty and is best viewed by hopping on either the number 1 or number 2 tram. In doing so you will be able to take in, at least from the outside, Otto Wagner's Post Office building, Vienna Opera House, the Imperial Palace, Museum of Fine Arts, the Burgtheater and the University.

St Stephen's Cathedral

St Stephen's Cathedral

ⓘ T01-51552 3256, www.stephans dom.at. Mon-Sat 1030-1500. €1.

Austria's most important Gothic building, Vienna's cathedral was begun in the 12th century although the oldest remaining parts are the Romanesque Great Gate and the Towers of the Heathens, which date from the 13th century. If you have a head for heights you can climb the 343 steps to the top of the 448-ft high South Tower (*Steffl* to the locals). Gothic was out of vogue by 1579 when the North Tower was capped by a cobbled-together Renaissance spire. Inside are a number of treasures, notably the red-marble sepulchre of Emperor Frederick III, sculpted from 1467 to 1513 by Niclas Gerhaert van Leyden.

Imperial Palace and Museums Quarter (MQ)

ⓘ MQ, T01-523 5881 (ext 1731), www.mqw.at. Daily 1000-1900.

Until the end of the First World War the Imperial Palace was the centre of the

⊖ Travel essentials

Getting there Schwechat Airport, T01-70070, www.viennaairport.com, is 19 km southeast of the city centre. The **City Airport Train** (CAT), www.cityair porttrain.com, takes you non-stop to the City Air Terminal at Wien-Mitte junction near Vienna Hilton and St Stephen's Cathedral. Journey time is around 15 mins, daily 0538-2335 (€9, €16 return). On the way back you can check in at the City Air Terminal. **Vienna Airport Lines** buses link the city to the airport from Schwedenplatz, Suedtiroler Platz, the City Air Terminal at Hotel Hilton and Westbahnhof (€6, €11 return). Journey time is around 20 mins, daily 0500-2400. The S-bahn is the cheapest option. Take line S7 (about 35 mins). Get an "Aussenzonen" (outer zone) ticket for €4 (€2 if you have a Vienna Card, see below) and have it punched before entering the train. A taxi will cost around €15. Bratislava's **MR Štefánika Airport** in Slovakia is only 60 km east of Vienna and close enough to be an alternative to Schwechat. There are various options for shuttling to and from the airport as well as car rental desks.

As Central Europe's main rail hub Vienna has good connections to most other major European destinations. **Eurostar**'s London-Vienna service via Paris takes around 14 hrs. Vienna has several train stations; check whether you're arriving at Westbahnhof, Südbahnhof or Franz Josefs Bahnhof.

Getting around Vienna is very pleasant for exploring on foot. The city's network of efficient and picturesque trams (especially Nos 1 and 2 which go clockwise and anti-clockwise around the famous Ring), buses or the art nouveau underground system, is easy to use. A single trip costs €1.50, a 24 hr card costs €4 and a 72-hr card costs €11.

Tourist information Over 200 discounts are available in the city with the **Vienna Card** (€16.90) available at hotels, the Tourist Information Centre, 1 Albertinaplatz, T01-211 14222, www.info.wien.at, daily 0900-1900. The card is also available at all sales offices or information booths of the Vienna transport system. It allows unlimited travel by underground, bus and tram, discounts on airport transfer services, reductions (see prices in brackets in Sights section) at museums, theatres, concerts, shops, restaurants, cafés and bars. There's another tourist office in the Arrivals hall at the airport, 0700-2300. **Wien-Hotels & Info**, T01-24 555, 0900-1900, has a hotel booking service.

Austro-Hungarian empire. Since then it has been transformed into a veritable empire of the arts. The Museums Quarter ranks as one of the 10 largest cultural complexes in the world, complete with bars and restaurants in which to digest it all. The following are just some of the highlights the area encompasses.

Spanish Riding School (Spanische Hofreitschule)
ⓘ 1 Michaelerplatz, T01-533 9031, www.srs.at. Daily 0900-1700. Free to visit; 15-min guided tours Tue-Sat 1230-1700. Performances cost up to €22; check website for details.

Even if you are not of an equine inclination it is impossible not to be moved by the beauty of the famous Yugoslavian Lippizaner white stallions on display. The art of classical riding taught by the school dates back to the Renaissance. (The stables are some of the few Renaissance buildings in Vienna.) Here you can live the history of these horses and admire gala balletic exhibitions of incredible precision. The impressive riding hall was furnished in baroque style by Joseph Emanuel

MUMOK

Fischer von Erlach between 1729-1735 and was originally intended to provide children of the aristocracy with the opportunity to take riding instruction. You can watch the morning training sessions and visit the stables. The nearby Lipizzan Museum provides further information.

Kunsthistorisches Museum
ⓘ 1 Maria-Theresien-Platz, T01-525 240. Daily 1000-1800, Thu until 2100. Closed Mon. €10 (€9).

Vienna's Museum of Fine Arts was built in 1891 next to the Imperial Palace in order to house the extensive collections of the Hapsburgs. During their reign they managed to amass the largest collection of Brueghel paintings in the world, including his *Farm Wedding*. Also among their collection are Raphael's *Madonna in the Meadow*, Vermeer's *Allegory of Painting*, Velazquez's Infanta paintings and masterpieces by Rubens, Rembrandt, Duerer, van Dyk, Holbein, Titian and Tintoretto. As such, it must surely rank among the most important fine art museums in the world.

Leopold Museum
ⓘ 7 Museums platz, T01-525 70, www.leopoldmuseum.org. Wed-Mon 1000-1900, Thu until 2100. €9 (€8.10).

The passionate art lover Dr Rudolf Leopold amassed hundreds of masterpieces and has his own museum to showcase, among other things, the world's largest collection of works by Egon Schiele. Other major artists featured are Gustav Klimt and Oskar Kokoschka as well as furniture and other pieces by Otto Wagner. They combine to give an insight into the Vienna of the early 19th century.

MUMOK
ⓘ www.mumok.at. Tue-Sun 1000-1800, until 2100 on Thu. €8 (€6.50).

The Museum of Modern Art traces the path of the Vienna's avant-garde through Pop Art, Nouveau Réalisme and Vienna Actionism. Warhol, Jasper Johns, Marcel Duchamp, George Brecht and Otto Muehl are all here. MUMOK also presents art history from classic modern works up to the present, ranging from Kupka to Kandinsky.

Schönbrunn Palace

Spanish Riding School

Vienna and *The Third Man*

In his 1949 story of drug-racketeering in war-torn Vienna, film director Carol Reed masterfully turned the city into as towering and brooding a character as the film's central figure – Orson Welles' Harry Lime. With his sense of Impressionism coupled with stark chiaroscuro he produced some of the most iconic and memorable scenes in world cinema, the locations of which are easily visited to this day. Harry Lime first appears, or rather a white cat appears at his shiny feet, in the doorway of **number 8 Schreyvogelgasse** before the two set off in a nocturnal chase around the city. The famous ferris wheel scene which closes with Lime's immortal put-down about the Swiss and cuckoo-clocks, takes places on the Riesenrad in the **Prater funfair park**. The 65-m wheel with its wood cabins is still in use. The windblown cemetery where Lime is twice buried (alongside Beethoven and Brahms) is the **Zentral Friedhof** on Simmerigen Hauptstrasse. Joseph Cotton stays at the **Sacher Hotel**, famous for its eponymous cake. If you can stomach it, parts of the sewers, where the film reaches its climax, can be visited by joining a guided **Third Man tour of the city**, www.viennawalks.tix.at.

Schönbrunn Palace

ⓘ *Schönbrunner Schlossstrasse, T01-81113, www.schoenbrunn.at. Apr-Jun and Sep-Oct daily 0830-1700; Jul-Aug till 1800; Nov-Mar 0830-1630. €11.50 (€10.20).*

This mouthwatering baroque palace was built around 1700 and is now a UNESCO World Heritage Site. It includes 2,000 rooms of wall-to-wall imperial splendour (only 40 can be visited), all set in a symmetrical classically- landscaped garden complete with maze and the world's oldest zoo. Emperor Franz Joseph (1848-1916) was born here in 1830, later marrying the Empress Sisi and keeping her in unsustainable style, and spending the the last two years of his reign here.

Sigmund Freud Museum

ⓘ *Berggasse 19, www.freud-museum.at. Daily 0900-1700. €6 (€4.50).*

Psychology students or anyone who rails against the therapy culture should

Sigmund Freud Museum

make a conscious effort to visit the apartments where it arguably all started. Freud lived and worked here from 1891 to 1938 and all his furniture, possessions, letters, documents, photographs and even an oedipal home movie by his daughter are here.

Riesenrad

ⓘ *Prater 90, T01-729 5430, www.wienerriesenrad.com. Oct-Apr 1000-2000; May-Sep 1000-2200. €7.50 (€6.50).*

Vienna's 19th-century ferris wheel, damaged during the Second World War, was restored in 1948, just in time for the filming of *The Third Man*. The wheel sits within the city's **Prater funfair park** where there are still many original and traditional carousel rides.

Sleeping

Vienna is rich in stylish, sometimes overblown, hotels recalling its imperial past, as well as a new breed of design hotels more conscious of the city's contribution to modernism. However, there is not much choice at the bottom end.

€€€ **Hotel Imperial**, Karntner Ring 16, T01-501 10, www.luxurycollection.com/imperial. An extravagant converted palace famed for the visits of its politicians from Hitler to Blair.

€€€ **Hotel Sacher**, Philharmonikerstrasse 4, T01-514560, www.sacher.com. Deliberately and eccentrically old fashioned, this family-run hotel likes to live in a 19th-century time warp. Romantic, at times camp, but never dull, this is the best address for those wanting a taste of Hapsburg decadence.

€€€ **Style Hotel**, Herrengasse 12, T01-227 800, www.stylehotel.at. Housed in an art nouveau building opposite the city's famous *Café Central* the interiors are more art deco. The 78 well-appointed rooms offer every luxury while delicious Italian cuisine is served in the *Sapor* restaurant and the bar is increasingly attracting a stylish post-prandial clientele.

€€ **Hotel Das Triest**, Wiedner Hauptstrasse 12, T01-589 180 www.designhotels.com. 17th-century on the outside but Conran on the inside. Not for those wanting a slice of Old Vienna but bright, clean and comfortably modern.

€€ **Hotel Riviera**, Schönlaterngasse 13, T01-907 6149. A very laid-back, Mediterranean atmosphere with a lovely garden and an attractive and welcoming bar make this is a good mid-market choice.

€ **Alstadt Vienna Hotel**, Kirchengasse 41, T01-522 66 66, www.altstadt.at. Old-world pretentions at half the price. A historic patrician's house in the centre of the old city comfortably furnished with Italian furniture and a striking decor. Family-run, 25 rooms, some with lovely views and plenty of atmosphere.

66 99 A visit to at least one of Vienna's famous cafés should not be missed...

Eating

The line between food and fun has been blurred in Vienna, as in many cutting-edge European cities. There are classic Viennese restaurants but as an alternative, or even after your Wienerschnitzel, the main focus is on a wide variety of hybrid bar-restaurants and restaurant-clubs. A visit to at least one of Vienna's famous cafés should not be missed.

Steirereck im Stadtpark, Am Heumarkt 2A, Landstrasse,1030, T01-713 3168, www.steirereck.at. Mon-Fri 1130-1500 and 1900-2300. An old gourmet favourite of Vienna foodies. Choose your room for a formal or relaxed ambience. Always grand but refreshingly laid-back.

Café Central, Herrengasse 14. 0900-2300. With its gaudy Gothic vaulted ceiling this was a favourite of Trotsky and also supposedly where Hitler sat down and thought up *Mein Kampf*. A piece of the city's heritage as much as any museum.

Café Landtmann, Karl Lueger Ring 4, T01-24100, www.landtmann.at. Daily 0730-2400. One of Vienna's many historic cafés set in an enormous, high-ceilinged theatrical space with great views of the Burgtheater.

Lutz/A1 lounge, 6-7, Mariahilfer Strasse, T01-585 3646/526 0026, www.lutz-bar.at, www.a1lo. 1000-0400 (Lutz), Mon-Wed 0930-2200, Thu-Fri 0930-2400 (A1). Two bar-restaurants in one. Lutz is elegant and classic, themed with wood panelling and a great cocktail and wine list. A1 is futuristic with glass, metal and dry ice, and packed with technical gimmicks.

Palmenhaus, Burggarten, T01-533 1033, www.palmenhaus.at. Daily 1000-0200. A beautifully renovated palmhouse in the heart of the museum district. Summer seating outside and good quality nibbles year round. The air of sophistication is replaced by a groovy clubbing scene on Fri nights.

Santo Spirito, Kumpfgasse 7, T01-512 9998. Mon-Thu 1800-0200, Fri -0300, Sat 1100-0300, Sun 1100-0200. A modern take on Vienna's contribution to classical music, the volume rising through the evening, sets a great backdrop for a cultured if lively evening.

Café Alt Wien, Bäckerstrasse 9, T01-512 5222. Daily 1000-0200. A studenty vibe ensures the intellectual traditions of this café continue over illuminating drinks and a renowned goulash.

Point of Sale, Corner Schleifmühl-gasse 12, Operngasse, T01-966 98 91. Sun-Thu 1000-0100, Fri-Sat 1000-0200. Late breakfast is the principal attraction here, served into the afternoon as you watch life go by on the lively Schleifmuehlgasse.

Zagreb

Now firmly on track for EU membership, possibly as early as 2009, Croatia has emerged from the break-up of Yugoslavia with a new sense of pride and optimism. One in four Croats reside in Zagreb, the country's cultural, economic and administrative centre. In contrast to the Mediterranean attitude of the coast, the mood here is Central European: think late-19th century Secessionist architecture, Viennese-style cafés, and an efficient tram system. The oldest and most lovely part of the city is medieval, developed from two separate fortified hillside settlements: the religious Kaptol (centring on the cathedral) and the secular Gradec. After centuries of squabbling, the two were finally unified in 1850, and took the name Zagreb, meaning "behind the hill". Go and find out what this city is hiding.

Arts & culture
★★

Eating
★★★

Nightlife
★★

Outdoors
★★★

Romance
★★★

Shopping
★★

Sightseeing
★★

Value for money
★★★★★

Overall score
★★★

Sights

The loveliest part of Zagreb is **Gornji Grad** (Upper Town). A two-hour stroll through peaceful cobbled streets will take you to the cathedral and several other notable churches, the Sabor (Croatian Parliament) and a handful of good museums.

Trg Bana Jelačića

Trg Bana Jelačića, the main square, is a vast paved space and an important public meeting point. Buildings date from 1827 onwards, and include several fine examples of Vienna Secessionist architecture. In the centre stands a bronze equestrian statue of **Ban Jelačić**, a 19th-century Croatian viceroy, first erected in 1866. Tito, who regarded Jelačić as a symbol of Croatian nationalism, had the statue dismantled but in 1991, following independence, a

Trg Bana Jelačića

campaign was launched for the statue's return. Several months later, with a spectacular firework display, the new president, Franjo Tudjman, performed a triumphant re-inauguration ceremony.

On the northern edge of the square lies **Dolac** ⓘ *Mon-Fri 0700-1600, Sat-Sun 0700-1200*, the city's main market since 1930. Arranged on two levels, it's a colourful and entertaining affair.

Katedrala (Cathedral)

ⓘ *Kaptol 31. Daily 0800-2000.*

Much of the original structure of this cathedral, dating from the 12th century, was destroyed by the Tartars in 1242. While more work took place between the 13th and 16th centuries, this in turn was badly damaged by the 1880 earthquake. The neo-Gothic façade and twin steeples were designed by Austrian architect, Herman Bolle during the 1880s. Inside is an inscription of the Ten Commandments in 12th-century Glagolitic script, and a relief by Ivan Meštrović (see Meštrović Atelier below). In front of the cathedral, a gilded statue of the Virgin, protected by four angels, stands on a high column.

Kamenita Vrata (Stone Gate)

Kamenita Vrata was formerly one of four entrances into the walled town of Gradec. In 1731, after a devastating fire

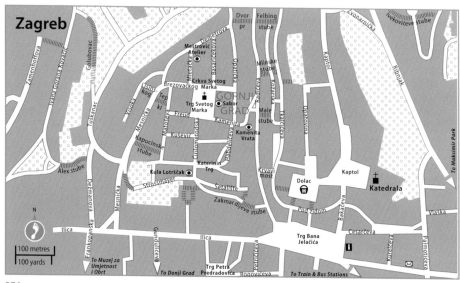

had consumed the surrounding wooden buildings, a painting of the Virgin Mary was found in the ashes, remarkably undamaged. Kamenita Vrata was reconstructed and became regarded as a place of miracles. Today locals come here to pray and pay tribute to the Virgin. Close by, at Kamenita 9, stands a pharmacy dating back to the mid-14th century and still functioning today. On the wall, a memorial stone records that the grandson of the Italian poet Dante Alighieri worked here in 1399.

Trg Svetog Marka

Kamenita Ulica leads to Trg Svetog Marka, for centuries the centre of Zagrebian political, cultural and commercial life. A daily market used to be held here until Trg Bana Jelačića took over during the 19th century. The centrepiece is **Crkva Svetog Marka** (St Mark's Church) ⓘ *Markov Trg, 0800-2000*, erected in the 13th century as the parish church of Gradec. Its steeply pitched roof, added during reconstruction in 1880 and decorated in red, white and blue tiles, depicts the coats of arms for Zagreb (on the right)

Katedrala

Crkva Svetog Marka

and the Kingdom of Croatia, Dalmatia and Slavonia (on the left).

Facing the main entrance to the church stands the **Sabor** (Croatian Parliament), housed within a neoclassical building completed in 1910. On 25 June 1991, this was the very place where members of the Sabor voted in favour of independence, thus marking the beginning of the end of the Socialist Federal Republic of Yugoslavia.

Meštrovič Atelier

ⓘ *Mletačka 8, T01-4851123, www.mdc.hr/mestrovic. Tue-Fri 1000-1800, Sat-Sun 1000-1400. HRK 20.*

A short walk north of the square will bring you to the charming Meštrović Atelier. During the 1920s, the Dalmatian sculptor Ivan Meštrović refurbished this 17th-century building to serve as a home and studio. He lived and worked here on and off until fleeing the country during the Second World War. When he died in 1962 it was turned into a memorial museum with a beautifully presented exhibition of his sculptures and drawings.

Strossmayer Šetalište

Strossmayer Promenade follows the line of Gradec's former south-facing wall, offering stunning views over the city's rooftops. Pride of place is taken by **Kula Lotrščak** (Lotrščak Tower) ⓘ *Tue-Sun 1100-1900, HRK 10*, part of the 13th-century fortifications which now houses a gallery. Each day at noon, a small (but extremely loud) cannon is fired from the top in memory of the times when it was used to warn off the possibility of an Ottoman attack.

Muzej za Umjetnost i Obrt (Arts and Crafts Museum)

ⓘ *Trg Maršala Tita 10, T01-4826922, www.muo.hr. Tue-Fri 1000-1800, Sat-Sun 1000-1300, closed Mon. HRK 15.*

On the western side of the vast, green Trg Maršala Tita (Marshall Tito Square) stands probably the best museum in Zagreb, after the Meštrović Atelier. An extraordinary collection of furniture is laid out in chronological order, illustrating how Croatian design has been influenced by Austrian and Italian tastes, from the baroque period up to the Modern Movement.

> ### ⊛ Outside Zagreb
>
> If you have a day to spare, a trip to the **Plitvice Lakes National Park**, www.np-plitvicka-jezera.hr, south 128 km south of Zagreb is recommended. The stunning emerald-green lakes, connected by a series of waterfalls, can be explored by boat or on foot.
> ⓘ *Tickets cost HRK 95 (Jul-Aug), HRK 80 May-Jun and Sep-Oct, HRK 50 Nov-Apr and the park is open daily 0800-1900.*

Travel essentials

Getting there Zazreb Airport, www.zagreb-airport.hr, is at Pleso, 17 km from the city centre. Shuttle buses run to the city centre every 30 mins from 0700-2000 (journey time 25 mins, cost for a one way ticket HRK 25) and at other times to coincide with arriving flights. A taxi to the centre should cost around HRK 150.

Getting around The city centre is compact and reasonably manageable on foot. An amusing (though rather unnecessary) funicular links Donji Grad to Gornji Grad, operating 0630-2100, tickets HRK 3. To reach more outlying sights you may need to rely on public transport. Regular tram and bus services operate through the day 0400-2345, with slightly less frequent services at night 2335-0345. Tickets cost HRK 8 and can be bought either from a kiosk or from the driver. You can find taxis in front of the bus and train stations, near the main square and in front of the larger hotels.

Tourist information The main tourist information centre is on the main square, at Trg Bana Jelačića 11, T01-4814051, www.zagreb-touristinfo.hr. Mon-Fri 0830-2000, Sat 0900-1700, Sun 1000-1400. There's a smaller office at Trg Nikole Šubića Zrinskog 14, T01-4921645, close to the train station. Mon-Fri 0900-1700. The centres are helpful and all the staff speak English. They can provide information about accommodation, events, public transport etc plus maps and promotional material. The TIC by the train station deals specifically with organizing guided tours of the city.

Exchange rate Croatian Kuna (HRK). £1 = HRK 10.87. €1 = HRK 7.39.

Sleeping

€€€ Hotel Regent Esplanade, Mihanovićeva 1, opposite train station, T01-4566666, www.regenthotels.com. Built in 1925 for travellers on the *Orient Express*, old-fashioned grandiosity and luxury is mixed with mod-cons.

€€ Hotel Palace, Strossmayerov Trg 10, between train station and main square, T01-4814611, www.palace.hr. A Secessionist building and the city's first hotel. There are 126 modern rooms, and a Viennese-style café.

€ Ilica, Ilica 102, a 15-min walk west of the main square, T01-3777622, www.hotel-ilica.hr. A friendly modern hotel, decorated with an eclectic array of furniture and artwork.

€ Jadran, Vlaška 50, T01-4553777, www.hup-zagreb.hr. A 5-min walk from the main square, is this tastefully-furnished 48-room hotel with basic amenities but no extras.

€ Vila Tina, Bukovačka Cesta 213, close to Maksimir Park, T01-2445204, www.vilatina.com. A small family-run hotel. Rooms are adorned with fresh fruit and flowers. Also has an excellent restaurant, solarium and sauna.

Eating

††† Dubravkin Put, Tuškanac Park, 10 mins from the main square, T01-4834975. Considered by many to be the best fish restaurant in town. It has a light and airy dining room and the house speciality, *brodet* (fish stew), is prepared with fresh herbs.

†† Baltazar, Nova Ves 4, T01-4666824. Closed on Sun. North of the cathedral, Baltazar specializes in classic Balkan dishes such as *raznijici* (mixed grilled meat), *ñevapčići* (kebabs) and *zapečeni grah* (oven-baked beans). There are tables outside in a pretty courtyard.

†† Pod Gričkim Topom, Za kmardijeve stube 5, T01-4833607. A small, homely restaurant, lying just below Strossmayer Šetalište, serving mainly Dalmatian fish dishes. Try the *lignje na žaru* (barbecued squid).

† Stari Fijaker, Mesnička 6, T01-4833829. 5-mins along Ilica from the main square. Traditional Zagrebian fare such as roast meats and *zagorski štrukli* (baked cheese dumplings) served in an old-fashioned dining room with wooden panelled walls.

† Vinodol, Nikole Tesle 10, T01-4811341. The specialities here are lamb and veal prepared under a *peka*. There's outdoor seating on a large summer terrace, with a whole lamb turning on a spit.

For informal café-bars, head for the pretty street of Tklačićeva, where you'll find a wide choice of laid-back haunts. Try **Sunčani Sat**, at number 27, otherwise head for **Gradska Kavana** or **Mala Kavana** on Trg Bana Jelačića.

Nightlife

Zagreb nightlife is rather tame, and although Croatians like drinking, this is hardly a place to party the night away. Interesting newcomers to the scene include 2 chic lounge-bars: **Škola**, Bogovićeva 7, close to the main square, and **Hemingway**, Trg Maršal Tita 1, opposite the National Theatre. An alternative scene centres around **Tvornica**, Šubićeva 2, www.tvornica-kulture.hr, and **Močvara**, Trnjanski Nasip bb, www.urk.hr, both of which occupy disused factories and stage concerts, film and theatre, attracting grungy intellectual types.

Essentials

Airline information

Listed below are the major airlines for each country covered in this guide, with their main hubs and connections to or from UK or Irish cities. The table on page 282 shows further details of where each airline flies to in Europe. Useful websites for cheap flights include www.you fly4less.com, www.ebookers.com, www.cheapflights.co.uk, www.flightline.co.uk and www.lastminute.com.

Airlines

Adria Airways, www.adria-airways.com. Main hub is Ljubljana. Flights to London Gatwick.

Aer Lingus, www.aerlingus.com. Main hub is Dublin. Flights to Birmingham, Bristol, Edinburgh, Glasgow, London Heathrow and Manchester.

Aeroflot Russian International Airlines (SU), www.aeroflot.com. Main hub is Moscow. Flights to London Heathrow.

Air Baltic, www.airbaltic.com. Main hub is Riga. Flights to Dublin, London Gatwick and London Heathrow.

Air Europa, www.aireuropa.com. Main hub is Madrid. Flights to many European cities and New York. No flights to or from the UK.

Air France, www.airfrance.com. Main hub is Paris. Flights to Aberdeen, Birmingham, Dublin, London City, London Gatwick, London Heathrow, Manchester, Newcastle and Southampton.

Alitalia, www.alitalia.co.uk. Main hubs are Milan and Rome. Flights to Aberdeen, Birmingham, Bristol,

Edinburgh, London Gatwick, London Heathrow and Manchester.

Austrian Airlines Group, www.aua.com, consisting of Austrian Airlines (OS), Lauda Air (NG) and Tyrolean Airways (VO). Main hub is Vienna. Flights to London Heathrow.

BMI Baby, www.bmibaby.com. Main hub is London Heathrow. Also flies from Aberdeen, Belfast City, Belfast International, Birmingham, Cardiff, Dublin, Durham Tees Valley, Edinburgh, Glasgow, Leeds, London Heathrow, Manchester and Nottingham to many European destinations.

British Airways, www.ba.com. Main hubs are London Heathrow and London Gatwick. Also flies from Aberdeen, Birmingham, Bristol, Edinburgh, Glasgow, Manchester and Newcastle to many European destinations and New York.

British Midland, www.flybmi.com. Main hub is London Heathrow. Also flies from Aberdeen, Belfast, Birmingham, Edinburgh, Glasgow, London City, London Gatwick, Luton, Manchester, Norwich and Newcastle to many European destinations and New York.

Continental, www.continental.com. Main hubs are Houston and Newark. Flights to Belfast, Birmingham, Bristol, Dublin, Edinburgh, Glasgow, London Gatwick and Manchester.

Croatia Airlines, www.croatia airlines.hr. Main hub is Zagreb. Flights to London Heathrow.

Czech Airlines, www.csa.cz. Main hub is Prague. Flights to London Heathrow, London Stansted and Manchester, Birmingham, Edinburgh and Glasgow.

Easyjet, www.easyjet.com. Main hubs are Belfast, Bristol, London Stansted, London Gatwick, Liverpool, Luton and

Newcastle; also useful are Bournemouth, Doncaster, East Midlands and Inverness. Flights to many European destinations.

Estonian Air, www.estonian-air.ee. Main hub is Tallinn. Flights to Dublin, London Gatwick and Manchester.

German Wings, www.german wings.com. Main hubs are Cologne, Stuttgart, Berlin and Hamburg. Flights to Birmingham, Dublin, Edinburgh, London Gatwick and London Stansted.

Iberia, www.iberia.com. Main hubs are Madrid and Barcelona. Flights to Aberdeen, Birmingham, Dublin, Edinburgh, Glasgow, London Gatwick, Manchester and Newcastle.

Iceland Air, www.icelandair.net. Main hub is Reykjavik. Flights to Glasgow and London Heathrow.

Iceland Express, www.iceland express.com. Main hub is Reykjavík. Flights to London Stansted.

Jet2.com, www.jet2.com. Main hub is Leeds, with other hubs at Manchester and Belfast. Also flies from Blackpool, Edinburgh, London Gatwick and Newcastle to a number of European destinations.

KLM, www.klm.com. Main hub is Amsterdam. Flights to Aberdeen, Birmingham, Bristol, Cardiff, Durham, Edinburgh, Glasgow, Humberside, Leeds, London City, London Gatwick, London Heathrow, Manchester, Newcastle, Norwich and Southampton.

Lufthansa, www.lufthansa.com. Main hubs are Frankfurt and Munich. Flights to Birmingham, Edinburgh, London City, London Heathrow, Manchester and Newcastle.

Malev Hungarian Airlines, www.malev.com. Main hub is Budapest. Flights to Dublin and London Heathrow.

Olympic Airways, www.olympic
airlines.com. Main hub is Athens.
Flights to London Heathrow and
Manchester.

Portugalia Airlines, www.flypga.com.
Main hub is Lisbon. Flights to
Manchester.

Ryanair, www.ryanair.com. Main hubs
are Dublin and London Stansted. Also
flies from Aberdeen, Birmingham,
Blackpool, Bournemouth, Bristol,
Cardiff, Doncaster, Durham, East
Midlands, Edinburgh, Glasgow, Leeds,
Liverpool, London Gatwick, Luton,
Manchester and Newcastle to a
number of European destinations.

SAS (Scandinavian Airlines System),
www.scandinavian.net. Main hubs are
Stockholm and Copenhagen. Flights to
Aberdeen, Belfast, Birmingham,
Edinburgh, Glasgow, Leeds, London
City, London Heathrow, Manchester,
Newcastle and Teeside.

SN Brussels, www.flysn.com. Main
hub is Brussels. Flights to Birmingham,
Bristol, Glasgow, London Gatwick,
Manchester and Newcastle.

Swiss International Air Lines,
www.swiss.com. Main hub is Zurich.
Flights to Birmingham, Dublin, London
City, London Heathrow and
Manchester.

TAP Air Portugal, www.tap.pt. Main
hub is Lisbon. Flights to Aberdeen,
Belfast, Birmingham, Edinburgh,
Glasgow, Leeds, London Gatwick,
London Heathrow and Manchester.

Turkish Airlines, www.turkish
airlines.com. Main hub is Istanbul.
Flights to London Heathrow, London
Stansted and Manchester.

Virgin Express, www.virgin
express.com. Main hub is Brussels.
Flights between various European
destinations, no connections in UK.

Rail information

From the UK to Europe

Eurostar, T08705-186186, www.euro
star.com. From London to Paris, Lille
and Brussels, with onward
connections to all over Europe.

Dutch Flyer, www.amsterdam
express.co.uk. Rail and boat tickets to
any station in the Netherlands.

Venice Simplon Orient Express,
www.orient-expresstrains.com.
Weekly sleeper services from London
and Paris to Venice and Budapest in
restored British Pullmans.

Inter-European connections

Artesia, book through www.rail
europe.com. Sleeper trains from Paris
to Rome, Florence, Milan and Venice.

Cisalpino Trains,
www.cisalpino.com. Connects
Stuttgart with Zurich and Milan.

City Night Line,
www.citynightline.ch. 'Hotel trains'
between Cologne and Vienna, Berlin
and Zurich.

Elipsos International, www.elip
sos.com. 'Trenhotel' services from Paris
to Madrid, Paris to Barcelona, Milan to
Barcelona and Zurich to Barcelona.

Nachtzugreise, www.nachtzug.de
Sleeper trains from Germany to Paris,
Italy, Austria, Denmark, Poland,
Switzerland.

TGV, www.tgv.com. French train
network connecting Paris with Lyon,
Turin, Milan and Brussels.

Thalys, www.thalys.com. High-speed
trains between Paris, Brussels,
Amsterdam and Cologne.

X2000, www.sj.se. Connects
Copenhagen and Stockholm.

European country networks

The major network for each country
covered in the guide is listed below.

Austria ÖBB (Österreichische
Bundesbahnen), www.oebb.at.

Belgium SNCB (Société Nationale
des Chemins de Fer Belges),
www.b-rail.be.

Croatia HZ (Hrvatske Zeljeznice),
www.hznet.hr.

Czech Republic CD (Ceské Dráhy),
www.cdrail.cz.

Denmark DSB, www.dsb.dk.

Estonia Edelarautee, www.edel.ee
and www.elektriraudtee.ee. **EVR
Ekspress**, www.evrekspress.ee. Sleeper
trains from Tallinn to St Petersburg
and Moscow.

France SNCF (Société Nationale des
Chemins de Fer, www.voyages-
sncf.com.

Germany DB (Deutsche Bahn),
www.bahn.de. **ICE** (Intercity Express)
connects Berlin and Munich with
Brussels and Vienna.

Greece OSE (Organismos
Sidirodromon Ellados), www.ose.gr.

Hungary MAV (Magyar
Allamvasutak), www.mav.hu.

Ireland IR (Iarnrod Eireann),
www.irishrail.ie.

Italy Trenitalia (Ferrovie dello Stato),
www.trenitalia.it. Italy. Trains to
France, Austria, Germany and Spain.

Netherlands NS (Nederlandse
Spoorwegen), www.ns.nl.

Portugal CP (Caminhos de Ferro
Portugueses), www.cp.pt.

Russian Federation RZD (Russkiye
Zheleznye Dorogi), www.rzd.ru.

Spain RENFE (Red Nacionale de los
Ferrocarriles Españoles), www.renfe.es.
Spain. Sleeper trains from Paris to
Madrid, Paris to Barcelona, Milan to
Barcelona, Zurich to Barcelona and
Madrid to Lisbon.

Airlines	Adria Airways	Aer Lingus	Aeroflot Russia	Air Baltic	Air Europa	Air France	Alitalia	Austrian Airlines Group	BMI Baby	British Airways	British Midland	Continental	Croatia Airlines	Czech Airlines	Easyjet
Amsterdam	●	●	●	●		●	●	●	●	●	●	●	●	●	●
Antwerp															
Athens			●			●	●	●		●				●	●
Barcelona			●	●	●	●				●				●	●
Belfast										●	●	●			●
Berlin			●	●		●	●	●		●					●
Bilbao		●			●	●	●	●		●				●	●
Bologna		●				●	●			●				●	
Brussels		●	●	●		●	●	●	●	●	●	●	●	●	●
Budapest		●	●		●	●	●	●		●				●	●
Copenhagen		●	●	●		●	●	●	●	●	●	●		●	●
Dublin		●		●						●		●		●	
Edinburgh						●	●	●		●	●	●		●	●
Florence						●	●			●					
Glasgow						●				●	●	●	●	●	●
Istanbul	●		●	●									●	●	
Lisbon		●				●	●	●		●		●		●	●
Ljubljana	●		●			●								●	
London	●		●	●		●	●	●	●	●	●	●	●	●	●
Lyon		●				●				●					
Madrid		●	●		●	●	●	●	●	●	●		●	●	●
Milan		●	●	●	●	●	●	●	●	●	●	●	●	●	●
Munich	●	●		●		●	●	●		●			●	●	●
Naples		●				●	●			●		●			
New York					●	●	●			●		●		●	
Paris	●	●	●	●	●	●	●	●	●	●	●	●	●	●	●
Prague		●	●			●	●	●	●	●	●		●	●	●
Reykjavík															
Riga		●	●	●				●		●				●	●
Rome		●	●		●	●	●	●		●		●	●	●	●
St Petersburg			●	●		●	●			●				●	
Seville		●			●	●	●			●					
Stockholm			●	●		●	●	●		●	●	●		●	●
Tallinn			●	●										●	●
Turin						●	●	●		●					●
Valencia		●			●	●	●			●					●
Venice		●	●			●	●	●	●	●	●			●	●
Verona						●	●			●					
Vienna	●	●	●	●		●	●	●		●	●		●	●	
Zagreb			●			●	●						●	●	

Estonian Air	German Wings	Iberia	Iceland Air	Iceland Express	Jet2.com	KLM	Lufthansa	Malev Airlines	Olympic Airways	Portugalia Airlines	Ryanair	SAS	SN Brussels	Swiss International	TAP Air Portugal	Turkish Airlines	Virgin Express
●		●	●			●	●	●	●	●		●		●	●	●	●
	●	●				●	●	●	●					●	●	●	●
	●	●	●		●					●			●				
					●												
●	●	●				●	●				●	●				●	
			●			●				●	●		●				
	●	●				●					●						
●		●				●	●	●				●		●	●	●	●
●		●	●	●		●	●	●				●		●		●	●
●		●				●	●	●								●	
	●	●			●	●										●	
												●	●				
		●	●			●					●		●				
	●						●	●					●		●		
	●	●				●	●						●	●	●		●
						●					●						
●	●	●	●			●	●	●		●	●	●	●	●	●	●	●
	●	●				●	●		●				●				
	●	●	●			●	●	●			●	●		●	●	●	●
●		●	●			●						●				●	●
	●	●	●			●	●	●			●	●		●	●	●	
	●																
●		●			●	●	●					●		●		●	●
			●	●													
●		●				●	●					●	●	●		●	
	●	●			●								●				●
						●					●		●				
●	●	●				●					●		●	●			
●						●							●				
		●				●					●	●					●
		●			●	●					●	●	●	●	●		
	●													●			
	●	●				●	●		●	●		●	●	●	●	●	
	●					●	●	●							●		●

Slovenia SZ (Slovenske Zeleznice), www.slo-zeleznice.si.

Sweden SJ, www.sj.se.

Turkey TCDD (Türkiye Cumhuryeti Devlet Demiryollan), www.tcdd.gov.tr.

UK National Rail, www.nationalrail.co.uk. **Scotrail**, www.firstscotrail.com.

Ticket agencies in the UK

Deutsche Bahn, T08702-435363, www.deutsche-bahn.co.uk. German railways booking office in the UK. For journeys from London to Germany. Also useful for travel to Scandinavia, Austria (via Brussels/Germany), eastern Europe and Russia.

Railchoice, T08701-657300, www.rail choice.co.uk. For tickets across Europe, railpasses and flexipasses.

Rail Europe, T08705-848848, www.raileurope.co.uk. The biggest European rail agency, owned by SNCF. For journeys from London to France, Italy and Spain.

TrainsEurope, T08717-007722, www.trainseurope.co.uk. European rail agency offering Eurostar, rail-and-sea tickets and railpasses.

Voyages SNCF, www.voyages-sncf.com. From London or Paris to anywhere in France and to major cities in Italy, Germany, Austria and Spain. Other useful agencies include:

European Rail, T020-7387 0444, www.europeanrail.com.

International Rail, T01962-773646, www.international-rail.com.

Rail Traveller, T01902-326662, www.thetravelbureau.co.uk.

Useful websites

www.seat61.com Comprehensive travel information for train journeys all over Europe and the world.

www.bahn.hafas.de Up-to-date timetables for most trains in Europe.

www.europerail.net/maps/maps. html Train routes across Europe.

Recommended reading

Thompson Publishing issue the extremely useful monthly *European Rail Timetable*. Available from www.thomascooktimetables.com.

Visa information

The information provided below is subject to change. Check the embassy of the relevant country before travelling. British citizens can also contact www.fco.gov.uk.

Turkey

Tourist visas are valid for 3 months. Citizens of Britain, the US, Canada, Australia and most Western European countries can obtain tourist visas either at the port of entry in Turkey or in advance from a consulate. For British passport holders the cost is £10 on arrival or £36 in advance. Note that on arrival visa fees must be paid in cash; travellers cheques or Turkish lira are not accepted. See www.turkish consulate.org.uk or www.turkish embassy.org for further details.

Russian Federation

Nearly all visitors to Russia require a visa. 30 day tourist visas are available for £75, but supporting documents must be provided, including a letter of invitation or tourist voucher from an authorized Russian travel agency or hotel. Plenty of agencies can help to organize this for a fee of around £20,

including: www.myrussianvisa.com, www.visatorussia.com, www.gotorussia.co.uk, www.russiadirect.net.

United States

Visitors to the US do not need a visa if they are covered under the Visa Waiver Program (WVP), which includes the UK, Australia, New Zealand, Japan and a number of European countries. Check www.usembassy.org.uk for further details. Travellers must have a valid, individual, machine readable passport, an onward ticket and must be staying for less than 90 days.

International dialling codes

Austria	+43
Belgium	+32
Croatia	+385
Czech Republic	+420
Denmark	+45
Estonia	+372
France	+33
Germany	+49
Greece	+30
Hungary	+36
Iceland	+354
Ireland	+353
Italy	+39
Latvia	+371
The Netherlands	+31
Portugal	+351
Russia	+7
Slovenia	+386
Spain	+34
Sweden	+46
Turkey	+90
UK	+44
US	+1

Currencies

Country	Currency	£ 1 =	€1 =
Croatia	Croatian Kuna (HRK)	HRK 10.87	HRK 7.39
Czech Republic	Koruna (CZK)	CZK 43.78	CZK 29.70
Denmark	Krone (Kr)	Kr 11.03	Kr 7.47
Estonia	Kroon (EEK)	EEK 23.13	EEK 15.65
Euro Zone	Euro (€)	€1.49	
Hungary	Forint (HUF)	HUF 370.34	HUF 253.35
Iceland	Kronur (ISK)	ISK 106.12	ISK 71.65
Latvia	LAT (Ls)	Ls 1.03	Ls 0.70
Russia	Roubles (RUB)	RUB 50.22	RUB 33.99
Slovenia	Tolar (SIT)	SIT 354.11	SIT 240.99
Sweden	Krona (SEK)	SEK 14.21	SEK 9.62
Turkey	Turkish Lira (TRY)	TRY 2.4	TRY 1.6
UK	Pound Sterling (£)		£0.67
US	Dollar (US$)	US$ 1.76	US$ 1.19

ICELAND

NORWAY

FINLAND

RUSSIAN FEDERATION

SWEDEN

ESTONIA

REPUBLIC OF IRELAND

To New York

UNITED KINGDOM

DENMARK

LATVIA

BELORUSSIA

Atlantic Ocean

NETHERLANDS

BELGIUM   GERMANY

POLAND

UKRAINE

CZECH REPUBLIC

FRANCE

AUSTRIA

HUNGARY

SLOVENIA

ROMANIA

PORTUGAL

SPAIN

CROATIA

ITALY

BULGARIA

Mediterranean Sea

TURKEY

GREECE

N

200 km
200 miles

Euro Zone

Credits

Editor: Sarah Thorowgood
Assistant editors: Nicola Jones and Emma Bryers
Picture editor: Robert Lunn
Publisher: Patrick Dawson
Editorial: Alan Murphy, Sophie Blacksell, Felicity Laughton, Claire Boobbyer
Cartography: Sarah Sorensen, Claire Benison, Kevin Feeney
Design: Mytton Williams
Sales and marketing: Andy Riddle
Advertising: Debbie Wylde
Finance and administration: Sharon Hughes, Elizabeth Taylor,

Contributors

Amsterdam	Francisca Kellett
Antwerp	Clare Thomson
Athens	Jane Foster
Barcelona	Mary-Ann Gallagher
Belfast	Sean Sheehan and Pat Levy
Berlin	Nina Hamilton
Bilbao	Andy Symington
Bologna	Ben Donald
Brussels	Clare Thomson
Budapest	Annie Dare
Copenhagen	Sean Sheehan and Pat Levy
Dublin	Sean Sheehan and Pat Levy
Edinburgh	Alan Murphy
Florence	Julius Honnor
Glasgow	Alan Murphy
Istanbul	Dominic Whiting
Lisbon	Caroline Lascom and Alix McAlister
Ljubljana	Francisca Kellett
London	Charlie Godfrey-Faussett and Sarah Thorowgood
Lyon	Francisca Kellett
Madrid	Mary-Ann Gallagher
Milan	Julius Honnor
Munich	Francisca Kellett
Naples	Julius Honnor
New York	Katie Anderson
Paris	Sophie Warne and Stephanie Smith
Prague	Francisca Kellett
Reykjavík	Laura Dixon and Nicola Jones
Riga	John Oates
Rome	Julius Honnor
St Petersburg	Patrick McConnell
Seville	Andy Symington
Stockholm	David Jackson
Tallinn	Clare Thomson
Turin	Ben Donald
Valencia	Mary-Ann Gallagher
Venice	Julius Honnor
Verona	Julius Honnor
Vienna	Ben Donald
Zagreb	Jane Foster

Print

Manufactured in India by Nutech Photolithographers, Delhi. Pulp from sustainable forests

This product includes mapping data licensed from Ordnance Survey® and the Ordnance Survey Complete Atlas of Ireland, with permission of the Controller of Her Majesty's Stationery Office © Crown Copyright 2005. All rights reserved. Licence number 100027877.

Footprint feedback

We try very hard to make each Footprint guide as up to date as possible but, of course, things always change. To let us know about your experiences – good, bad or ugly – go to www.footprintbooks.com and send in your comments.

Publishing information

Footprint European City Breaks
© Footprint Handbooks Ltd
January 2006
ISBN 1 904777 55 4
CIP DATA: A catalogue record for this book is available from the British Library

® Footprint Handbooks and the Footprint mark are a registered trademark of Footprint Handbooks Ltd

Published by Footprint
6 Riverside Court
Lower Bristol Road
Bath BA2 3DZ, UK
T +44 (0)1225 469141
F +44 (0)1225 469461
discover@footprintbooks.com
www.footprintbooks.com

Distributed in the USA by Publishers Group West

Photography

Prelims & Essentials: Alamy (allOver photography), Superstock (Aguililla & Marin), TIPS (Chad Ehler). **Amsterdam:** Alamy (nagelestock.com, Travel-Shots), Netherlands Board of Tourism & Conventions (Anton Nijboer, Anne Frank Huis, Ben Deiman Fotografie, Eduard Bergman, Het Museum Rembrandthuis, Joods Historisch Museum, Van Gogh Museum). **Antwerp:** Tourism Flanders-Brussels. **Athens:** Alamy (Manos Kilouris, Robert Harding Picture Library Ltd), Hemisphere (Bertrand Gardel/Monde), Superstock (Alvaro Leivs, Chmura, Kevin O'Hara), Tips Images (Guido Alberto Rossi). **Barcelona:** Alamy (AA World Travel Library, Kevin Foy, Vincent Lowe), Claire Benison, Julius Honnor, Spanish Tourist Office. **Belfast:** Alamy (David Robertson), GoToBelfast.com. **Berlin:** www.berlin-tourist-information.de, Susannah Sayler. **Bilbao:** Hemisphere (Franck Guiziou/Monde), TIPS (Andrea Pistolesi). Bologna: Julius Honnor, Fototeca ENIT (Vito Arcomano). **Brussels:** Alamy (Art Kowalsky, eye35.com), SuperStock (Steve Vidler), Tourism Flanders-Brussels. **Budapest:** Alamy (Sergio Pitamitz), Superstock (Walter Bibikow), TIPS (Charles Mahaux, Guido Alberto Rossi), www.budapestinfo.hu. **Copenhagen:** Alamy (Robert Harding Picture Library Ltd), Superstock (Nils-Johan Norenlind, P. Narayan, Sergio Pitamitz), TIPS (Marvin Newman). **Dublin:** Alamy (Andre Jenny, Danita Delimont, FAN travelstock, Ian M Butterfield, ImageState, PCL), Superstock (Marco Cristofari), Susannah Sayler, visitdublin.com. **Edinburgh:** Alamy (Arch White, Iain Masterton), Hemisphere (Philippe Renault/Monde), Kevin Feeney, Photolibrary (Index Stock Imagery), Superstock (Bruno Perousse), TIPS (Alberto Nardi). **Florence:** Alamy (Ken

Welsh), Fototeca ENIT (Paola Ghirotti, Vito Arcomano), Hemisphere (Franck Guiziou/Monde, Pawel Wysocki/Monde), Julius Honnor, Superstock (Javier Larrea, Etienne), TIPS (Marvin Newman). **Glasgow:** Alamy (Stephen Saks Photography, Yadid Levy), Hemisphere (Pawel Wysocki/ Monde), Superstock (Brian Lawrence). **Istanbul:** Alamy (f1 online), Superstock (Bruno Morandi, J.D. Dallet, Renaud Visage, Targa), TIPS (Charles Mahaux), Hemisphere (Patrick Frilet/ Monde, Pawel Wysocki/Monde). **Lisbon:** Hemisphere (Bertrand Gardel/Monde, John Frumm/Monde, Pawel Wysocki/Monde, Patrick Frilet/Monde), Superstock. **Ljubljana:** Alamy (Diomedia), Hemisphere (Patrice Thomas/Monde), Superstock (M&M Valledor). **London:** Alamy (Ace Stock Limited, Alan Copson City Pictures, Andrew Holt, Christopher Baines, Curzon Studio, David Hoffman Photo Library, Eye Ubiquitous, Geogphotos, Image Group Ltd, IML, Mike Booth, Simon Hall, The Steve Bicknell Style Library, Tim Gartside, Topix). **Lyon:** Alamy (Art Kowalsky, images-of-france, Nick Hanna), Hemisphere (Franck Guiziou/France, Laurent Giraudou/France), Superstock (Walter Bibikow). **Madrid:** Alamy (Guy Moberly, Ian Dagnall, John Stark, Kevin George), José Resino, Spanish Tourist Office, Superstock (Javier Larrea, Mattes), TIPS (Luis Castaneda). **Milan:** Fototeca ENIT (Vito Arcomano), Hemisphere (Philippe Renault/Monde), Superstock (Alan Copson). **Munich:** Alamy (Art Kowalsky), Hemisphere (Maurizio Borgese/Monde, Patrick Frilet/Monde), Superstock (Alan Copson, Doug Scott, P. Narayan, Thomas Lauterback), TIPS (Chad Ehlers). **Naples:** Julius Honnor, Superstock (Atlantide S.N.C, Bruno Morandi, Doug Scott). **New York:** Alamy (Kevin Foy), Julius Honnor, Susannah

Sayler. **Paris:** Alamy (BL Images Ltd, David L. Moore, Ian Dagnall, ImageGap, Network Photographers), TIPS (Chuck Pefley, Guido Alberto Rossi, Luis Castaneda), Susannah Sayler. **Prague:** Alamy (David Sanger photography, Humberto Olarte Cupas), CzechTourism. **Reykjavík:** Alamy (Arctic Images, Bill Bachmann, Nordicphotos), Hemisphere (Romain Cintract/Monde), Superstock (Jose Fuste Raga), www.visitreykjavik.is. **Riga:** Alamy (Dennis Cox, Travelog Picture Library), Superstock (Yoshio Tomii). **Rome:** Alamy (Adam Eastland, Frank Chmura, Hideo Kurihara, ImageState, PCL, Stock Italia, Travelog Picture Library), Fototeca ENIT (Vito Arcomano), Superstock (G.V.P, Javier Larrea, Jon Ivern, Silvio Fiore), TIPS (Sandra Baker). **St Petersburg:** Alamy (Imagebroker, Jon Bower, Maurice Joseph, Robert Harding Picture Library Ltd), Superstock (Doug Scott, Wojtek Bliss), TIPS (Andrea Pistolesi). **Seville:** Superstock (Witold Skrypczak), Susannah Sayler. **Stockholm:** Alamy (John Lens), Hemisphere (Rabouan-Fiori/Monde), Superstock (Doug Scott), TIPS (Chad Ehlers, David W. Hamilton). **Tallinn:** Tallinn City Tourist Office (Jaak Nilson, Tavi Grepp, Toomas Volmer). **Turin:** CAPE' TABAC (Adriano Bachella), Città di Torino (Michele d'Ottavio), Fototeca ENIT (Vito Arcomano). **Valencia:** Spanish Tourist Office, SuperStock (Bjorn Svensson, Jordi Puig), Susannah Sayler. **Venice:** Alamy (Chuck Pefley, Worldwide Picture Library), Fototeca ENIT (Vito Arcomano), Julius Honnor, TIPS (Luca Invernizzi Tettoni). **Verona:** Fototeca ENIT (Vito Arcomano), Julius Honnor, Superstock (Stefano Cellai). Vienna: Hemisphere (John Frumm/Monde, Maurizio Borgese/Monde), Superstock (Mattes, San Rostro), TIPS (Marvin Newman, Riccardo Sala). **Zagreb:** Alamy (Diomedia, Neil Setchfield, Robert Harding Picture Library Ltd).

There is a passion for travel and discovery at **Footprint** that has been reflected in our publishing since the *South American Handbook* was first published back in 1924. More than 80 years on, our aim is still simple: to give travellers a refreshingly different view that helps them to follow their own route and have a unique, memorable experience.

 Don't just take our word for it!

If 'the essence of real travel' is what you have been secretly yearning for all these years, then Footprint are the guides for you. Under 26 magazine

Who should pack Footprint–readers who want to escape the crowd. The Observer

Footprint can be depended on for accurate travel information and for imparting a deep sense of respect for the lands and people they cover. World News

I carried the South American Handbook from Cape Horn to Cartagena and consulted it every night for two and a half months. I wouldn't do that for anything else except my hip flask. Michael Palin, BBC Full Circle

The Publishers of the best travel guide in the world. Grahame Greene

The guides for intelligent, independently-minded souls of any age or budget. Indie Traveller

Footprint
Travel guides

www.footprintbooks.com